Editors
Dona Herweck Rice
Gisela Lee

Editorial Manager
Karen J. Goldfluss, M.S. Ed.

Editor-in-Chief
Sharon Coan, M.S. Ed.

Illustrator
Larry Bauer

Cover Artist
Denice Bauer

Art Coordinator
Denice Adorno

Imaging
Alfred Lau
Ralph Olmedo, Jr.

Product Manager
Phil Garcia

Publishers
Rachelle Cracchiolo, M.S. Ed.
Mary Dupuy Smith, M.S. Ed.

Practice and Learn

Ages 9–11

Part 1 Compiled and Written by
Dona Herweck Rice

Part 2 Compiled and Written by
Char-lee L. Hill

Practice and Learn

Part 1

Table of Contents

Introduction 6

Grammar 7

Parts of Speech

Nouns 7
By the Book 8
Common and Proper Nouns. 9
Collective Nouns. 10
Puzzle Change-O. 11
On the Go with Plurals 12
School of Fish 13
"Stepping Up" with Plurals 14
Predicting Plurals 15
Possessives 16
Action Verbs 17
Take Action! 18
We're Here to Help! 19
Verb Tenses 20
Past and Present 21
Changing Irregular Verbs. 22
Was and Were 23
Is, Am, and Are 24
Just One or More? 25
Adjectives 26
Enchanted Enhancements 27
More Enhancements 28
Articles: A and An. 29
Comparison Suffixes 30
Adverbs. 31
Ly Endings 32
Descriptive Occupations 33
Pronouns 34
Write About It 35

Antonyms/Homophones/Synonyms

Synonyms 36
More Synonyms 37
Synonyms and the Thesaurus. 38
Antonyms 39
Find the Antonyms 40
Draw the Antonyms. 41
I Spy Homophones 42
Which Word? 43
Turn In to Homophones. 44
Synonym and Antonym Review. 45
Antonyms, Synonyms, and Homophones. 46

Capitalization

Days, Months, and Holidays 47
Capital Places 48
Capitalizing Sentences. 49
It's All Relative 50

Contractions

Con"trap"tions 51
Blooming with Contractions 52
Now You See Me; Now You Don't. 53
Contractions 54

Punctuation

End Marks. 55
Commas in a Series 56

Names and Commas 57
Set Off an Appositive 58
Separate Day and Year. 59
Separate Cities and States 60
Comma Review 61
Set It Off! 62
That's Mine 63
Using Quotation Marks 64
May I Quote You? 65
Punctuation Challenge 66

Subjects and Predicates

What Is a Subject?. 67
Subject Practice 68
What Is a Predicate? 69
Complete Sentences 70
Take Your Pick 71
Word Muncher 72

Complements

My Complements to This Sentence! 73
More Complements. 74

Sentences

Sentence Emergencies. 75
More Sentence Emergencies 76
Whoa! 77
Bits and Pieces 78
Fragment Search 79
What's That You Say? 80
Can You Handle This? 82

Spelling and Phonics 83

Consonants and Vowels

Consonants and Vowels 83
Consonant Blends 84
Digraphs 85
Long Vowel Quilt Square. 86
Short Vowel Quilt 87
Long and Short 88

Silent Letters

Silent E 89
Silent Letters 90

Irregular Letter Sounds

The Phunny Elefant? 91
Gh. 92
The K Sound. 93

End Sounds and Rhymes

Rhyme Zoo 94
Rhymes 95

Compounds

Compound Words 96
More Compound Words. 97
Hidden Compounds 98

Syllabication

Stressed Out Syllables 99

Root Words

Getting to the Root of It 103
Root It Out 104

Table of Contents *(cont.)*

Prefixes and Suffixes
Break It Up 105
Prepare for Prefixes 106
Painting with Prefixes 107
Prefix Party 108
Surfing with Suffixes 109
Prepare for Suffixes 110
A Bucketful of Suffixes 111
Sounds Greek to Me 112

General Spelling
Double Anyone 113
Two of a Kind 114
Begin and End 115
Anagrams 116
Four-Letter Words 117
Education 118
Summertime 119
Clipped Words 120
Shawn's Homework 121

Abbreviations
Abbreviations 122
More Abbreviations 123

Pronunciation
Alike Yet Different 124
Pronunciation Keys 125
What's the Word? 126

Reading 127
Alphabetizing
Alphabetizing 127
Alphabetical Order 128

Multiple Meanings
What Does It Mean? 129
Define It 130

Following Directions
Making Face Paint 131
Color This Design 132
Derek's Day 133

Sequence
Sequencing Pictures 134
Reading Adventures 135
Put Them in Order 136
Kelly's Week 137
What Happened Next? 138

Main Idea
What's the Point? 139
Writing Text for Pictures 140
What's It About? 141
Practice on Main Idea 142
Main Idea of a Paragraph 143
Main Idea Story Parts 144

Comprehension and Recall
Max 145
George Washington 146
My Dream 147
The Big Game 148

Making Inferences

Inferences 149
Making Inferences 150
Marta and Janis 151
Drawing Conclusions 152
What Next? 153

Cause and Effect
Cause and Effect 154
What's the Effect? 155

Recognizing Fact and Opinion
Facts and Opinions 156
Evaluating Bias 157

Tone
Tone 158
Identifying Tone 159

Recognizing Voice
Identifying the Speakers 160
First-Person Voice 161
Third-Person Voice 162
Pronoun Referents 163

Idioms
Idioms 164
More Idioms 165

Analogies
Analogies 166
More Analogies 167
Still More Analogies 168

Classifying
All Together Now 169
Categories 170

Summarizing
Get Rid of the Details 171
Summarize 172
Practice Summarizing 173
Your Day 174

Evaluating Information
Pick a Part 175
Read All About It 176
Character Web 177

Writing 178
Sentences
Complete the Sentences 178
Write a Sentence 179
Start with a Noun and a Verb 180
Sentence Expansions 181
What Do You Think? 182
Word Muncher 183
Combining Sentences 184

Paragraphs
Get to the Point 185
How About a Little Help? 186
Missing Parts 187
And Then... 188
This Is the Story 189
Start Explaining 190
Give Us a Description 191

Table of Contents *(cont.)*

I Will Convince You 192
In My Opinion. 193
Define This! 194
When I Grow Up. 195
Sticky Glue 196
Paragraph Starters 197

Outlining
Getting Your Paragraph Organized 198

Descriptive Writing
Writing by Sense. 199
Similes 200
More Similes. 201
Metaphors 202

Creative Writing
Writing Stories in Parts 203
Story Time! 205
Circus Balloon. 206
Dreams 207
What a Success! 208

Cursive Writing
Letter Review 209

Math 218

Addition
Add It Up 218
Mouse in the House. 219
How Much?. 220
Word Problems 221
Sum It Up 222
Add Three 223
Addition Challenge 224

Subtraction
Cup o' Tea. 225
Word Problems 226
Subtraction Solutions. 227
What's the Difference? 228
Find the Difference 229

Addition and Subtraction
What's the Scoop?. 230
Sign In 231

Multiplication
Times Tables 232
Multiplication 234
Column Multiplication. 235
By Three 236
Double Time 237

Division
Division Facts 238
Divide and Conquer. 240

All Functions
Which Is It?. 241

Fractions
Picture Fractions 242
Slice It Up! 243
Circle Graph 244
Slices. 245

Measurement
At the Playground 246
Measurement Choices 247
How to Measure 248
From Here to There 249

Money
How Much Is It Worth?. 250
Change, Please 251
Change for Fifty Cents 252
Change for a Dollar. 253

Time
A.M. and P.M.. 254
Timely Chore 255

Logic
Exam Time 256
Theodore. 257
Favorite Teams 258
A Visit to the Amusement Park 259
Softball Lineup 260

Social Studies 261

Maps, Charts, and Graphs
Intermediate Points 261
Can You Find Home? 262
I've Got the Key! 263
Grids 264
Where in This City? 265
Where Is It?. 266
How Many Degrees? 267
Road Maps 268
How Many Miles to Go? 269
Political Maps 270
Historical Maps 271
Product Maps 272
Population Maps 273
Weather Maps 274
It All Adds Up! 275
How Far to New York? 276
Tables 277
Chart the Read-a-Thon! 278
Time Line 279
Events in My Life 280
Pictographs 281
Diagrams. 282
Ant City! 283
Graph Game 284
Movie Schedule. 285

Geography
Go East! 286
Go West! 287
Country and City Match 288
Where Am I?. 289
"State" My Name 290
What Country Am I? 291
A Mystery Country 292

Answer Key 293

Introduction

To Parents and Teachers

The wealth of knowledge a person gains throughout his or her lifetime is impossible to measure, and it will certainly vary from person to person. However, regardless of the scope of knowledge, the foundation for all learning remains a constant. All that we know and think throughout our lifetime is based upon fundamentals, and these fundamentals are the basic skills upon which all learning develops.

Within this book are hundreds of pages designed to teach and reinforce the skills that are mandatory for a successful completion of fourth-grade curricular standards. The table of contents (page 2) clearly delineates the skills. To use this resource effectively, simply refer to the contents list to find the work sheets that correspond to the desired skills.

Skills are reinforced in these areas:

- Grammar
- Handwriting
- Reading
- Writing
- Spelling and Phonics
- Math

The work sheets within this book are ideal for use both at home and in the classroom. Research shows us that skill mastery comes with exposure and drill. To be internalized, concepts must be reviewed until they become second nature. Parents may certainly foster the classroom experience through exposing their children to the necessary skills whenever possible, and teachers will find that these pages perfectly complement their classroom needs.

In addition to this resource, there are a variety of hands-on materials that will prove vital when reinforcing basic skills. These include math flash cards; measuring spoons, cups, and weights; Celsius and Fahrenheit thermometers; a clock with hour, minute, and second hands; play money in various denominations; and a globe, maps, charts, and graphs. Kinesthetic learners will also benefit from plastic letters or numbers they can manipulate and use for figuring and writing, and every child will enjoy hands-on science experiences of all kinds.

Keep in mind that skills can be reinforced in nearly every situation, and such reinforcement need not be forced. As parents, consider your use of basic skills throughout your daily business, and include your children in the process. For example, while grocery shopping, let your child manage the coupons, finding the correct products and totaling the savings. Also, allow your child to measure detergent for the washing machine or help prepare a meal by measuring the necessary ingredients. You might even consider as a family the time you spend viewing television and calculate how much of the allotted time goes to advertisements. Likewise, there are countless ways that teachers can reinforce skills throughout a school day. For example, assign each child a number and when taking roll, call out math problems with those numbers as the answers. The children will answer "present" when they calculate the problems and realize that their numbers are the answers. You might also play the game of bingo with parts of speech, matching problems, or vocabulary words.

Since basic skills are utilized every day in untold ways, make the practice of them part of your children's or students' routines. Such work done now will benefit them in countless ways throughout their lives.

Nouns

A **noun** names a person, place, thing, or idea. Underline the words used as nouns in the following sentences.

1. The dog chased the cat up the tree.

2. Leaves fell from the trees as the wind blew.

3. My brother loves to play baseball.

4. I like to paint pictures with my new paints.

5. Freedom is something we celebrate in this country.

6. Love is very important in a family.

7. The electricity failed so we had no light.

8. The student wrote a story about a rabbit and a fox.

9. The soldiers came home from the foreign land.

10. The girl has been saving her money in her bank.

11. The boys will clean the desk when they finish the project.

12. Three monkeys swung from the vines in the jungle.

13. Her braid was tied with a pink ribbon.

14. Your soccer team has a better record than that team.

15. The museum was so crowded that we could not get near the exhibit.

By the Book

Choose a book. While reading, be aware of the nouns. Skim through your book to find the kinds of words described below. Look for a word that names . . .

1. a number _____

2. a color _____

3. a place _____

4. a girl's name _____

5. a boy's name _____

6. an animal _____

7. a sport or game _____

8. a flower or tree _____

9. a thing to eat _____

10. a thing to wear _____

Try some bonus questions! Look for a word naming something made of the following:

glass _____   metal _____

cloth _____   wood _____

Common and Proper Nouns

Proper nouns begin with capital letters, and **common nouns** are just regular nouns. The word *cat* is a common noun, but *Boots,* the cat's name, is a proper noun. Circle each word used as a common noun you find in the sentences below. Underline the proper nouns.

1. I live in the last house on Elm Street.

2. My dog, Max, and I went for a walk.

3. There are several Ryans in my class.

4. My family is planning a trip to the Grand Canyon.

5. "Mom, where is my shirt?" Jenny asked her mother.

6. Where is Primrose Park?

7. The only vegetable I like is broccoli.

8. Our cat is named Sylvester.

9. My teacher is Mrs. Simms.

10. Ricky, Sam, and Tim played football in the park.

11. Katie and Emily live in Jasper City, but their cousins live in Walton.

12. My brother and his friend liked the rollercoaster at the Maple County Fair.

13. March was too windy this year, but April was a beautiful month.

14. Brent and Kenneth played basketball last Saturday.

15. Have the children ever seen *Star Wars?*

Collective Nouns

Collective nouns are words used to describe a group of things. Below are some collective nouns used to group animals. Use the list below to complete the sentences. Notice that the word *of* plus a plural noun always follow the collective noun.

> **Example:** People gather every year in March to watch the first *flight of swallows* return to San Juan Capistrano.

crash of rhinoceroses	tribe of monkeys
gang of elk	clowder of cats
pod of whales	school of fish
flight of swallows	murder of crows

1. A _____ snuggled under our porch during the storm.

2. A _____ were spotted in the meadow.

3. The fishermen were surprised to find a _____ close to the boat.

4. When we visited the zoo we observed a _____ .

5. A _____ were found near the corn in the farmer's meadow.

6. We saw a _____ when we visited Yellowstone National Park last summer.

7. We took the cruise from San Diego, hoping that we would see a

   _____ .

8. We saw a nature show on TV about a _____ .

Action Verbs

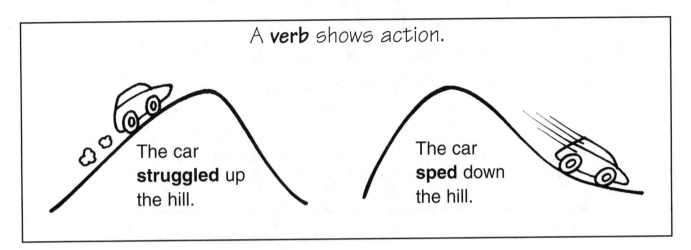

A **verb** shows action.

The car **struggled** up the hill.

The car **sped** down the hill.

Write the words used as verbs on the lines.

1. Barbara plays basketball well. _____

2. The bird flies over my head. _____

3. The bicycle makes Frank happy. _____

4. The children ran to the playground. _____

5. The balloon popped in front of me. _____

6. The pen ran out of ink. _____

7. I fell on the sidewalk. _____

8. I eat a piece of fruit each day. _____

9. The old horse stood quietly in the field. _____

10. Our teacher reads a story to us each day. _____

Take Action!

An **action verb** tells what the subject does. It shows action.

Examples: run, swing, jump, laugh, see, hit, leap

What are some of your favorite action verbs? Write them here:_____

_____

In the following paragraph, there are 50 action verbs. Can you find at least 40 of them?
When you find one, underline it in the paragraph and then write it on another sheet of paper.

In the morning, Benjamin woke up and jumped out of bed. He landed on his brother, Timothy, who was asleep in the bottom bunk. Timothy sat up and rubbed his eyes. He grumbled at Benjamin and then fell back on his bed. Benjamin looked at Timothy for a long time. He wanted to see if Timothy was asleep. Then Benjamin ran to the corner and grabbed his horn. Benjamin blew into his horn and played some musical notes. He liked the way his horn sounded. But he heard another sound. He stopped and listened. A moaning sound came from Timothy. Benjamin didn't like that sound. He grabbed his horn and ran out the door. He sat on the front lawn and played some more music. The notes floated in the air. He felt happy until he heard another sound. He stopped and listened. A groaning sound came from his next door neighbor. Benjamin ran into the backyard. He played his horn some more. He liked the notes. Then he heard another sound. It was his mother. She called his name again. He went inside. His mother took his horn and put it away. Then she put Benjamin back in his bed. She told him it was too early to get up. Benjamin's mother went back to bed, too. Benjamin tried to imagine the sounds of his horn. Suddenly, he heard another sound. He stopped and listened. Timothy snored again and again. Benjamin moaned. He stuck his fingers in his ears, but he still heard Timothy. So he covered his ears with his pillow. Soon he fell fast asleep.

We're Here to Help!

Some **non-action verbs** help action verbs do their work. They work together in a sentence, like a team. These non-action verbs are called **helping verbs**.

Example: People **can travel** in many ways.   The non-action helping verb is *can*.

The action verb is *travel*.

The complete verb is *can travel*.

Find the helping and action verbs in sentences shown below. Use the following list of verbs to help you. Then fill in the chart at the bottom of the page by writing the helping and action verbs from the sentences.

Helping Verbs:	am	is	should	are	were	has	have	had	can	will
Action Verbs:	drink	ridden	pushed	driven	move	pulled	going	ride	seen	go

1. Jimmy should ride his bicycle.
2. An elephant is ridden in India.
3. The scooters were pushed by the children.
4. An airplane can move quickly.
5. Amy has driven a bus.

6. Sled dogs have pulled the children across the snow.
7. I have seen a bear.
8. You will go to a birthday party.
9. Henry is going to eat all the cake.
10. We will drink all the punch.

Helping Verbs

1. _____
2. _____
3. _____
4. _____
5. _____
6. _____
7. _____
8. _____
9. _____
10. _____

Action Verbs

1. _____
2. _____
3. _____
4. _____
5. _____
6. _____
7. _____
8. _____
9. _____
10. _____

Verb Tenses

The words below are written in the **present tense** (today). On the blank after each word, write its form in the **past tense** (before today). The first one has been done for you.

present tense	past tense
paint	painted

1. paint   __painted__
2. climb   _____
3. play   _____
4. laugh   _____
5. shout   _____
6. jump   _____
7. run   _____
8. see   _____
9. eat   _____
10. come   _____

11. make   _____
12. build   _____
13. sleep   _____
14. give   _____
15. take   _____
16. bring   _____
17. sing   _____
18. hold   _____
19. go   _____
20. write   _____

Past and Present

Verbs in the **present tense** show action that is happening now. In the **past tense**, verbs show action that already happened.

Change each of these present tense verbs to the past tense by adding *d* or *ed*.	Change each of the past tense verbs to the present tense by removing the *d* or *ed*.
1. turn _____	11. smiled _____
2. cook _____	12. folded _____
3. roll _____	13. closed _____
4. watch _____	14. painted _____
5. park _____	15. climbed _____
6. fill _____	16. shared _____
7. color _____	17. joked _____
8. fold _____	18. matched _____
9. close _____	19. laughed _____
10. look _____	20. played _____

Changing Irregular Verbs

Change the following irregular verbs from present to past tense.	Change the irregular verbs from past to present tense.
1. blow _____	11. caught _____
2. come _____	12. read _____
3. sing _____	13. rode _____
4. wear _____	14. drank _____
5. take _____	15. swung _____
6. cry _____	16. shone _____
7. make _____	17. paid _____
8. give _____	18. wrote _____
9. fall _____	19. swept _____
10. fly _____	20. tore _____

Was and Were

Write **was** or **were** in each sentence.

Four little birds **were** chirping a song.

1. What _____ that?

2. Where _____ you going?

3. I _____ at the movies.

4. We _____ cleaning the room.

5. She _____ very helpful today.

6. They _____ afraid of the big dog.

7. Jan and Laura _____ playing in the sand.

8. Tim _____ in the kitchen.

9. My friend and I _____ just about to leave.

10. Who _____ in charge of the show?

Is, Am, and Are

Write **is**, **am**, or **are** in each sentence.

Today **is** Marc's birthday.
How old **is** he?

1. Who _____ you waiting for?

2. Where _____ we going tomorrow?

3. I _____ very hungry.

4. The boy _____ a good reader.

5. The children _____ playing in the park.

6. We _____ having a good time.

7. They _____ having some trouble with their car.

8. Terry _____ a good friend.

9. How _____ I going to get there?

10. I _____ feeling very tired.

Just One or More?

Subjects and verbs are very important parts of a sentence. They need to get along well. If they do not agree with each other, your sentence will not sound right. It is important that they agree in number. A **singular subject** tells about one person, place, or thing. It needs a singular verb. A **plural subject** tells about more than one person, place, or thing. It needs a plural verb.

Examples

Singular Subjects		Plural Subjects	
dress	rabbit	dresses	rabbits
car	Michael	cars	Michael and Jason
boy	house	boys	houses
Singular Verbs		**Plural Verbs**	
has	jumps	have	jump
is	hops	are	hop
runs	sings	run	sing

In the following sentences, circle the correct verb. On the line before each number, write an **S** if you circled a singular verb or a **P** if you circled a plural verb.

_____ 1. The dress (has, have) a big bow in back.

_____ 2. These cars (runs, run) funny.

_____ 3. The boys (jumps, jump) from the tree.

_____ 4. The rabbit (hops, hop) around the yard.

_____ 5. Michael and Jason (sing, sings) this morning.

_____ 6. My house (are, is) yellow and white.

_____ 7. All the houses on our street (are, is) one story.

_____ 8. Michael (hop, hops) on one foot.

_____ 9. My old toy car (are, is) rusty.

_____ 10. Our rabbit (has, have) a large cage.

Now write your own sentences on the lines below. Write one sentence with a singular subject and verb and another sentence with a plural subject and verb. Make your sentences as interesting as you can.

1. Singular: _____

2. Plural: _____

Adjectives

Adjectives are words that describe people, places, and things. Circle the adjectives in the following sentences that are descriptive words.

1. The unusual man came to our front door.

2. A playful puppy ran through our yard.

3. I like the green bike with the long seat.

4. We can play with this funny, old toy.

5. I am wearing a new pair of gray shoes.

6. My mother is tall and pretty.

7. My teacher is smart and funny.

8. I saw a silly show on television.

9. The happy pig rolled in the mud in the large barnyard.

10. There was a small, black spider hanging from the shiny web.

11. The choir members wore colorful robes during their lively performance.

12. My grandfather is kind and generous.

13. Should I wear my orange shirt or my yellow one?

14. The little girls pretended to have tea at their imaginary party.

15. The night was quiet when the barn owl began to hoot.

Enchanted Enhancements

Sometimes a simple, complete sentence is all that is needed. However, at other times it is a good idea to give more details.

Descriptive language and additional information about the subject are very useful and make the sentence more interesting.

A word that helps describe something is an **adjective**. There are three types of adjectives.

- **Demonstrative Adjectives:** These point things out. They answer the question, "Which one(s)?"

   Examples: *this, that, these, those*
   I like this dress. Those cookies look delicious.

- **Common Adjectives:** These describe the subject in a general way. They answer the question, "What kind of?" or "How many?"

   Examples: *soft, warm, six, blue, sunny, tired, tall*
   The building is tall. The kitten is soft.

- **Proper Adjectives:** These are made from proper nouns and are always capitalized. They answer the question, "What kind of?"

   Examples: *Irish, Martian, African American, Native American*
   I love French cheese! There are many Japanese cars.

In the following sentences, circle the adjectives. Then, on the lines, write the questions (*What kind of? How many? Which one?*) that the adjectives answer.

1. I don't like this sandwich. _____

2. The old man came to the door. _____

3. Most French students speak English. _____

4. We're learning a Scottish dance tomorrow. _____

5. The yellow flowers are wilting. _____

6. I have three brothers. _____

7. For dinner tonight, they're serving a delicious, spinach casserole. _____

8. Give me your dollar, and I'll give you my comic book._____

9. Tim doesn't want that soft pear. _____

10. Watch out for the mean dog down the street. _____

11. My clueless brother threw away my homework._____

12. Those black shoes are too small._____

More Enhancements

Now it is your turn to enhance the sentences in the following story. Fill in the blanks with descriptive words or phrases. You may use demonstrative adjectives (such as *this, that, these,* and *those*), common adjectives (such as *birthday, large, frozen, lovely, three),* and proper adjectives (such as *British, German,* and *Jurassic*). You may also wish to use descriptive phrases (such as *weather-beaten* or *pocket-sized*). Have fun with this activity but remember to try for interesting images with descriptive language rather than choosing words or phrases that will make the sentences sound silly.

It was my _____ birthday so I ran home from school. When I got to my _____ house it looked like no one was home. "Hello!" I shouted. "Where is my _____ family? Your _____ son and brother is home now!" No one answered. I went to our _____ kitchen to see if there was a note. No note. Not even a _____ note. I went into the _____ room and turned on the _____ television. There was a _____ show on. I turned the television off. I went back into the kitchen to get something to eat. "I want something that's _____ to eat," I said to myself. I saw yogurt, but it was pineapple flavored. "I don't want _____ yogurt. I want _____ yogurt," I said, grabbing a _____ yogurt. I sat down to eat the _____ yogurt. Then I looked for something else. I found _____ candy. I was just about to eat it when the _____ telephone rang. "Hello?" It was my _____ mom. She told me she would be home soon but needed me to go into the _____ basement to get a _____ chicken from the _____ freezer. "Okay," I said. Then I ate some _____ candy.

The telephone rang again. "Honey," my mom said, "please get the _____ chicken from the basement now!"

"Okay!" I said again. As I walked toward the _____ basement stairs, I started wondering how she knew I hadn't gone down to the basement yet. I opened the _____ door. I slowly crept down the _____ steps into the _____ basement. I was getting the creeps. How did she know? Why was it so dark? The _____ stairs made creaking noises. Finally, I got to the bottom and waved my hand around to try to find the _____ light switch. I felt some _____ cobwebs and shrieked just a little. Just then, the _____ lights came on, and I heard _____ voices screaming, "Happy birthday!" I nearly ran all the way back up the _____ steps. My heart was pounding so hard I thought it would break right through my _____ chest! I saw the _____ basement was full of _____ people. They were holding _____ balloons and _____ gifts. Everyone I knew was there—my _____ mom, my _____ Aunt Amelia, my _____ sister Lindsay, all our _____ neighbors, and all of my _____ friends.

So _____ is where everyone was, and _____ was how my _____ mom knew I hadn't come downstairs yet. The _____ chicken, I just remembered! I went to the _____ freezer and opened the door to grab a _____ chicken. Everyone stared at me. Then they all started to laugh. "No, honey," my mom said, "we don't need a chicken after all. Tonight we're having _____ pizza and _____ birthday cake with _____ candles!" We went upstairs and had a party!

Articles: A and An

Articles are a kind of adjective. The three most common articles are *the, a,* and *an. A* is used before words that begin with a consonant sound while *an* is used before words that begin with a vowel sound. Write **a** or **an** in the blanks below.

1. _____crayon

2. _____ape

3. _____saucer

4. _____egg

5. _____monkey

6. _____pill

7. _____itch

8. _____orange

9. _____house

10. _____leaf

11. _____ ant crawled across the leaf.

12. Have you seen _____ purple butterfly?

13. I would like to eat _____ sandwich for lunch.

14. _____ apple a day keeps the doctor away.

15. _____ goat chewed on my pant leg!

Comparison Suffixes

Some adjectives end in *er* or *est*. These endings are used to show how people, places, or things compare to each other. The suffix **er** compares two nouns or pronouns and the ending **est** compares more than two nouns.

Examples: December is *cold.*   Mary is *young.*

January is *colder* than December.   Jane is *younger* than Mary.

February is the *coldest* month of the year.   Micheal is the *youngest* of the family.

Use adjectives that end in *er* or *est* to complete the following sentences.

1. Chris is tall, but Marcos is _____ than Chris. Carey is the

   _____ of the three boys.

2. Cookies are sweet, but cakes are _____ than cookies. Candy is the

   _____ of all three desserts.

3. An orange is small. A plum is _____ than an orange. A grape is the

   _____ fruit of them all.

4. Joe's room is messy, but Tom's room is _____. Of all the rooms in

   the house, the kitchen is the _____.

5. A rock is big. A hill is _____ than a rock. A mountain is

   the _____ of all.

6. A flower is pretty. A bouquet is _____. A garden is the

   _____ of them all.

7. Pearls are hard. Rubies are _____, but a diamond is the

   _____ gem of all.

8. This magazine is thick. That book is _____. The dictionary is the

   _____.

Adverbs

Adverbs are describing words that tell **when** (a time), **where** (a place), or **how** (how something is done).

The monkey eats his banana **quietly**.
(**How**)

Underline the adverbs. On the lines, write **how, where,** or **when** to show the way in which the adverb is used.

_____   1. I walked quietly.

_____   2. We will go tomorrow.

_____   3. We can play later.

_____   4. My cousins will come here.

_____   5. The cheetah growled fiercely.

_____   6. The mother sang softly.

_____   7. The ballerina dances gracefully.

_____   8. Yesterday I played baseball.

_____   9. The orchestra played well.

_____   10. He completed his homework quickly.

Ly Endings

Adverbs are words that describe verbs. Remember, **verbs** are words that show action. Many adverbs that describe an action end in *ly*. Make a list of 10 verbs. Then list an adverb with an *ly* ending that describes how the verb can be performed.

Example: The rabbit *runs* **quickly**.   *Runs* is a verb.

Quickly is an adverb that describes how someone might run.

Verb	Adverb
1.	
2.	
3.	
4.	
5.	
6.	
7.	
8.	
9.	
10.	

Descriptive Occupations

Many adverbs end in *ly.* Look at the occupation statements below. Choose an adverb that fits each statement.

Example: "I work *painlessly*," said the dentist.

1.   "I work _____ ," said the banker.

2.   "I work _____ ," said the sea captain.

3.   "I work _____ ," said the butcher.

4.   "I work _____ ," said the hairdresser.

5.   "I work _____ ," said the lawyer.

6.   "I work _____ ," said the doctor.

7.   "I work _____ ," said the teacher.

8.   "I work _____ ," said the firefighter.

9.   "I work _____ ," said the librarian.

10.   "I work _____ ," said the astronaut.

Pronouns

Pronouns are words that are used in place of nouns. Some pronouns are *I*, *we*, *you*, *it*, *he*, *she*, and *them*. There are other pronouns as well. Read the sentences below. Rewrite the sentences using the correct pronoun to replace the noun in bold print.

1. **The boy** played baseball. _____

2. **The girl** swam across the pool. _____

3. **The children** climbed the trees. _____

4. **Mary and Frank** rode their bikes to school. _____

5. The team surprised **Lily** with a trophy. _____

6. Kim saw **the dog** run across the street. _____

7. **Mom** read the new best seller. _____

8. **Gary** saw a strange shadow. _____

9. The girls walked to **Mary's** house. _____

10. The family found **kittens** in a basket on their porch. _____

11. Where should I put **the presents**? _____

12. **My dad** put gas in the car. _____

13. **The players** won the championship! _____

14. Where is **the key**? _____

15. Please, give that to **Rick**. _____

Write About It

Use each of the pronouns below in a sentence.

1. it _____

2. he _____

3. she _____

4. you _____

5. me _____

6. I _____

7. we _____

8. they _____

9. them _____

10. her _____

11. him _____

12. us _____

Synonyms

When comparing and contrasting objects and ideas, it is helpful to use special words called synonyms. **Synonyms** are words that mean nearly the same thing. See the examples in the box below.

good, helpful	**strong, powerful**	**gentle, mild**
fast, quick	**sour, tart**	**bad, evil**
little, small	**big, large**	**tired, sleepy**

Circle the synonyms in each row.

1.	busy	tired	active	bad
2.	nibble	chew	hit	play
3.	cook	flavorful	tasty	show
4.	joyful	happy	sad	angry
5.	walk	fall	stand	trip
6.	pretty	huge	anxious	enormous
7.	worried	anxious	smart	angry
8.	mad	angry	funny	disappointed
9.	talk	kick	chat	sing
10.	laugh	sneeze	cry	weep

More Synonyms

Draw a line to connect synonym pairs.

1.	neat	see
2.	sad	calm
3.	thin	chilly
4.	look	skinny
5.	plain	powerful
6.	strong	stingy
7.	cold	large
8.	big	small
9.	cheap	wealthy
10.	quiet	pointed
11.	poor	simple
12.	little	unhappy
13.	sharp	spotless
14.	loud	needy
15.	rich	noisy

Synonyms and the Thesaurus

A **thesaurus** is a book that provides a list of words with the same, or nearly the same, meaning. Locate each word in a thesaurus. Draw a line to connect the synonyms.

1.	like		true
2.	snip		fat
3.	plump		infant
4.	fly		soar
5.	bark		similar
6.	clown		whole
7.	huge		cut
8.	real		gigantic
9.	entire		yelp
10.	baby		jester

Antonyms

When comparing and contrasting objects and ideas, another kind of word that is helpful to use is called an antonym. **Antonyms** are words that have opposite meanings. See the examples in the box below.

night, day	up, down	bad, good
sad, happy	fresh, spoiled	clean, dirty
dark, bright	cool, warm	large, small

Circle the antonyms in each row.

1.	laugh	smile	cry	run
2.	even	fast	slow	easy
3.	hurt	heal	harmful	sad
4.	shiny	sea	dull	air
5.	wake	sleep	rest	cat
6.	girl	bird	boy	enormous
7.	coffee	fire	water	tea
8.	truth	confess	fly	lie
9.	smart	lively	ugly	pretty
10.	furry	hard	light	soft

Find the Antonyms

Complete each sentence with an antonym. You may choose to use a dictionary or a thesaurus to help you find the best antonym. There are many correct answers.

1. A flower is soft, but a rock is _____.

2. Sugar is sweet, but a lemon is _____.

3. Fire is hot, but ice is _____.

4. Let's do the work now and not wait until _____.

5. Tell the truth. Don't _____.

6. Try to be kind and not _____.

7. The water is clear and not at all _____.

8. The sun rises in the east and sets in the _____.

Which Word?

Words that sound or sometimes look similar often have meanings that are not alike at all. Decide which of the two word choices on the right is the correct one to correspond with the word or phrase on the left and then circle it.

1. strength	*mite/might*
2. in no way	*not/knot*
3. well liked	*popular/poplar*
4. fruit	*plumb/plum*
5. without covering	*bare/bear*
6. cry	*ball/bawl*
7. forbidden	*band/banned*
8. French money	*frank/franc*
9. musical instrument	*symbol/cymbal*
10. cold	*chilly/chili*
11. odor	*scent/sent*
12. religious song	*hymn/him*
13. market	*bazaar/bizarre*
14. color	*blew/blue*
15. breakfast food	*cereal/serial*

Tune In to Homophones

Written on each television screen is a message. The messages are full of misused homophones. Rewrite the messages and correct the homophones.

1.

Whether Flash...heavy reigns dew inn an our.

4.

Watch Mussel Man weakly lift waits on Channel too.

2.

Next on The Whirled Turns...Elizabeth is never scene again.

5.

Special Announcement! Ice skating pear wins gold metals!

3.

News Extra! A wild hoarse and dear escape from zoo.

6.

Try a knew serial just for kids! Awesome Oats!

Synonym and Antonym Review

Synonyms are words that have the same or almost the same meanings.

Antonyms are words that have the opposite meanings.

Read the words below. Write **S** next to the synonyms and **A** next to the antonyms.

1. heat, warmth		11. quiet, loud	
2. litter, trash		12. buy, sell	
3. happy, sad		13. angry, mad	
4. speak, talk		14. bright, shiny	
5. hot, cold		15. long, short	
6. hard, soft		16. dark, light	
7. fast, slow		17. mild, gentle	
8. wet, damp		18. loss, gain	
9. loud, noisy		19. remember, forget	
10. hungry, starving		20. ignore, disregard	

Antonyms, Synonyms, and Homophones

List whether each pair of words is made of antonyms, synonyms, or homophones.

1. complex/simple _____

2. independence/liberty _____

3. dawn/sunset _____

4. colonel/kernel _____

5. empty/vacant _____

6. chute/shoot _____

7. board/bored _____

8. write/record _____

9. mix/separate _____

10. furnish/supply _____

11. fare/fair _____

12. plump/thin _____

13. over/under _____

14. job/work _____

15. air/heir _____

16. near/far _____

17. plain/fancy _____

18. beat/beet _____

19. move/transport _____

20. individual/group _____

Days, Months, and Holidays

What day of the week is today? _____

Did you use a capital letter to begin your answer? If you did, you used a capitalization rule.

What month of the year is today? _____

Did you use a capital letter to begin your answer? If you did, you used a capitalization rule again!

What is your favorite holiday? _____

Did you use a capital to start? If you did, you know the rules for capitalizing days, months, and holidays!

- Always capitalize the **days of the week.**
- Always capitalize the **months of the year.**
- Always capitalize the **names of holidays**.

That should be easy to remember. Now for some practice.

Put these words in order on the circle and capitalize them (start with Sunday).

- friday
- saturday
- thursday
- monday
- sunday
- tuesday
- wednesday

List the months of the year in order on the the lines. Don't forget to capitalize!

- january
- february
- march
- october
- may
- june
- august
- september
- april
- november
- december
- july

1. _____

2. _____

3. _____

4. _____

5. _____

6. _____

7. _____

8. _____

9. _____

10. _____

11. _____

12. _____

Capital Places

It's vacation time! Do you like to go to museums, zoos, or parks? Do you like to travel to lakes, oceans, rivers, or mountains? Proper names of places need capital letters because they are proper nouns.

Here is a list of places that need capital letters. Write the capital letters that are needed above the names of the places. Then choose three of the places you would like to visit.

pacific ocean	sahara desert	rocky Mountains
Grand canyon	North pole	hyde park
Mt. rushmore	san diego zoo	disneyland
amazon River	lake Louise	niagara falls

I would like to go to . . .

1. _____

2. _____

3. _____

In the space below, draw one of the places you chose.

Capitalizing Sentences

One of the most important capitalization rules is also one of the easiest to remember. **Always capitalize the first word of every sentence**. It doesn't matter whether the word is *I, you, me, Africa, a, the,* or *people,* the first word of every sentence is always capitalized. It doesn't matter whether it is a word that is normally capitalized or not.

Let's see how you do. In the story below, there are some words that need to be capitalized. Use a colored pencil or pen to write the capital letter above the letter that is there.

one day, Mike and Chris were riding their skateboards at the park. when they stopped to rest, they noticed something in the bushes. "what is that?" Chris asked. mike looked more closely. "it's furry!" Mike said. both boys stood and stared, and then they saw it move just a little bit.

"ohhh," Chris said, "that scared me!"

"it's a little bunny!" Mike exclaimed. sure enough, it was a scared little brown bunny hiding in the bushes. mike and chris cornered it, and then Mike scooped it up. he could feel its heart beating very rapidly.

the boys walked around the park asking people if they had lost a bunny. nobody claimed it, so Mike and Chris took it home.

mike sat in a chair watching TV and holding the bunny close to his chest. chris made telephone calls to try to find out who had lost the bunny. next, they made signs and put them up around the park and in the neighborhood. the signs said, "Lost Bunny" and gave their telephone number. no one claimed the bunny.

"you can't keep it," Chris and Mike's dad said.

"why not?" Chris asked.

"we already have a bunny cage," Mike added.

"well, okay," Dad said, "but you'll have to give it food and water every day."

the boys were happy. they named the rabbit "George," even though it was a girl rabbit. they fed her all the vegetable scraps from the kitchen, rabbit food, cabbage, dandelions, and water. george grew to be a big fat rabbit who would sometimes visit the neighbors' yards to eat weeds and dandelions which are, to this day, her favorite foods.

It's All Relative

In the following sentences, circle the letters that need to be changed to capitals and write the capital letters above. If there is a capitalized word that should not be capitalized, draw a line through the appropriate letter.

1. uncle Jorge sat on the front porch.

2. I said, "mom, what I really want to do is stay home!"

3. My mom and my dad won't be home until 7 P.M.

4. His grandma made a quilt for his birthday.

5. My Cousin and my Grandma will be coming with my mom.

6. Our Grandparents have a surprise for Aunt Aimee.

7. I wrote "Dear grandma," at the top of my stationery.

8. I wish my aunt lived closer to us; she looks just like mom.

9. Then dad stopped and looked behind him.

10. I like to go to grandmother Norton's house in the summer.

11. My favorite Cousin is Jimmy because he makes me laugh.

12. At the wedding we saw aunt Marsha and cousin Brad.

13. My Mom and Dad are taking me to dinner after the awards assembly.

14. At the reunion I saw Aunt Edith and uncle Jacques, and Cousins Kathy, Meredith, Hector, and Samantha.

15. For my birthday I'm inviting cousin Sarah, Cousin Leigh, aunt Susie, and my uncle, whose name is Mike.

Extension: Make a family chart on a large piece of butcher paper. Put your name and a picture of yourself (a photograph or a self-drawn portrait) in the proper position. If you have brothers and/or sisters, put their names (and pictures if you wish) next to yours. Your parents' names should appear above yours. Make as many lines as you need to represent your grandparents, aunts, uncles, and cousins. Be sure the lines appear in logical positions. A sample diagram appears below.

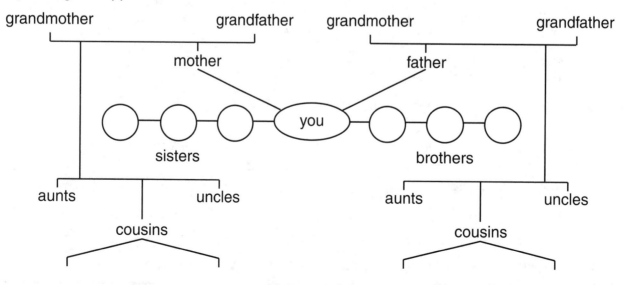

Now You See Me; Now You Don't

Take out the apostrophe in the contractions and write the two words next to them that mean the same thing.

1. don't   _____   _____

2. wouldn't   _____   _____

3. won't   _____   _____

4. aren't   _____   _____

5. shouldn't   _____   _____

6. he's   _____   _____

7. I've   _____   _____

8. they've   _____   _____

9. we're   _____   _____

10. she's   _____   _____

11. you'll   _____   _____

12. didn't   _____   _____

13. isn't   _____   _____

14. wasn't   _____   _____

15. we'll   _____   _____

16. I'd   _____   _____

Contractions

Here is your opportunity to make contractions. In the story below, underline any words that may be combined into a contraction. On another paper list the contractions. There are 52.

I cannot believe it. I wrote 25 invitations that said: "You are invited to a surprise party for Serena. Do not tell her or she will not come." We could not have the party on any day but the 18th because it is close to Serena's birthday, and it is the only day in the entire month of April that is free. I stamped them and said to my dog, Sugar, "Let us mail these before it is too late." You will not believe what happened next.

It must have taken Sugar and me three hours just to mail the invitations after I had spent six hours making them because Sugar must have stopped at every tree. And then she barked at every bird; she would lie down if I tried to hurry her. Then she chased a cat up a tree, and she did not want to leave. There have been some new families who have moved in down the street, so Sugar wanted to sniff each of their new driveways. There must have been a dozen. A huge dog came running out at us. I should not have run, but I could not help it. It is instinctive to run when a snarling dog appears. It would have eaten us both alive, or at least that is what I was thinking when I decided that I had better run. I ran, dragging Sugar at the same time because she had decided that she would save the universe from the world's meanest dog. I will make a long story short by telling you that while I was trying to avoid death and while Sugar was trying to save the universe, the mean dog would have had us both for breakfast, but all three of us ended up tangled together in a whimpering, snarling knot of fur and tasty human skin. I was not doing a very good job of getting out of the mess, but at least the dogs were also stuck so we were not going anywhere. Then I heard a voice, "Who is this, Fluffy? It looks like we are meeting our neighbors." Fluffy? I was thinking it would have been better to name this dog Terminator. There I was. I was covered with dog slobber and fur, and I was not a pretty sight. Instead of meeting a new neighbor while standing, I could not believe that I was saying hello on my back while one dog, which should not be allowed on the street, was sitting on my stomach and drooling on my face, and another dog, which would not ever be allowed out of the house again, was licking my leg. What is wrong with this picture? My very good-looking neighbor must not have a very interesting life because he was laughing and enjoying the whole thing.

And if that were not enough, when I got home my mother told me that she would have stopped me if she had known that I was mailing the invitations. I had not been gone for three minutes when my sister called and told my mom that she had decided when to have her wedding and that she would like me to be a bridesmaid. Here is the part that convinces me that it is not a good idea to get out of bed on some days. She has decided to have her wedding on the 18th—you know, the day of Serena's surprise party? She has already reserved the church. I am so embarrassed. Now I will need to cancel the party. And my neighbor still laughs at me every time he sees me.

End Marks

Every sentence must end with a punctuation mark. A sentence may end with a period, a question mark, or an exclamation point.

- A period comes at the end of a sentence that tells something.

    Examples: I have a purple bicycle. Turn left at the corner.

- A question mark comes at the end of a sentence that asks a question.

    Examples: What color is your bicycle? Is that your house?

- An exclamation point comes at the end of a sentence that contains a strong feeling.

    Examples: Watch out for that car! What a wonderful surprise!

The following sentences need end marks. Think about which kind of end mark each sentence needs. Then write the correct punctuation mark at the end of each sentence.

1. I love my purple bicycle
2. I saved enough money to buy it last year
3. Would you like to try it
4. My brother has a blue bicycle
5. One time he crashed into me, and I fell off my bike
6. Have you ever fallen off your bike
7. Did you skin your knee
8. I was so mad at my brother
9. He told me he was sorry
10. I'm so glad that my bike did not break
11. Watch out for the glass in the road
12. Don't ride your bike in the street
13. Can you park a bike right here
14. I have to go inside now
15. Will I see you tomorrow

Commas in a Series

Always use commas to separate words in a series. Place commas in the sentenes below to separate words in a series.

Example: James, Ralph, and Sara went to the park.

1. Tommy's three sisters are Amy Katy and Melissa.

2. Manual likes to play basketball baseball and volleyball.

3. Katy Melissa and Tommy do not play volleyball.

4. Amy wants to be a geologist an astronaut or a chemist.

5. Tommy, the youngest, has three dogs whose names are Skip Tiger and Rags.

6. Casey's favorite classes in school are math science and art.

7. Tommy Amy Katy and Melissa live in Dallas with their parents.

8. Tommy loves his parents his sisters and his dogs.

9. Manuel has three birds two cats and one dog.

10. Casey knows Tommy Amy and Manuel.

56

Names and Commas

Use a comma to set off a person's name when that person is being spoken to.

Example: Bobby, when is your book report due?

1. Mrs. Burnett may we go out to recess now?

2. Yes, we are going out to recess now Jason.

3. Mary will you swing with Tommy and me?

4. Sure Jason I love to swing.

5. Mary is going to swing with us Tommy.

6. No Jason I'm sliding with Matt.

7. Matt can swing with us Tommy.

8. Jason we can all swing first and then we can all slide.

9. Jason do you want to go on the slide first?

10. Tommy what time is recess over?

Set Off an Appositive

Always use commas to set off an appositive from the rest of the sentence.

Example: James, my best friend, lives a mile away.

Place the commas in the sentences below.

1. Amy Jones my best friend has a very large family.

2. Joe her oldest brother works for an airline company.

3. The youngest in the family Tony is only three years old.

4. The oldest daughters Karen and Sue often help with the younger children.

5. My other good friend Nicole and I spend a great deal of time at Amy's house.

6. Mrs. Jones Amy's mother says that two more children are coming tomorrow.

7. Amy's dad Mr. Jones works hard to take care of seven children.

8. Rags and Slick the Jones' pets get a great deal of attention.

Separate Day and Year

Use a comma to separate the day and the year from the rest of the sentence. Place a comma after the year when it comes in the middle of a sentence.

1. Jerry was born on October 5 1986.

2. My favorite Christmas was December 25 1992.

3. Susan's mom came home from the hospital on April 6 1994.

4. We took our summer vacation on July 21 1993.

5. My grandfather was born on August 11 1941.

6. On April 6 1994 Susan's mom brought a new baby girl home from the hospital.

7. My grandfather remembers July 20 1969 as an important date in history.

8. On July 21 1993 my family went to Hawaii for our summer vacation.

Separate Cities and States

Use a comma to separate a city from a state.

Example: Eric was born in Eugene, Oregon.

Place the commas in the sentences that follow.

1. The state capital is in Austin Texas.

2. My home is in Denver Colorado.

3. Her grandparents live in Bangor Maine.

4. Our tournament is in Ardmore Oklahoma.

5. Disney World is in Orlando Florida.

6. Her father is stationed in Fairbanks Alaska.

7. Queen Elizabeth lives in London England.

8. We rode the ferry in Seattle Washington.

Comma Review

Rewrite these dates and addresses using a comma correctly.

1. April 15 1972 _____

2. July 27 1640 _____

3. September 13 1910 _____

4. Monday January 31 _____

5. Sunday November 16 _____

6. Anaheim California _____

7. Albuquerque New Mexico _____

8. Quebec Canada _____

9. Bangor Maine _____

10. Little Rock Arkansas _____

Use a comma correctly in these letter parts.

11. Dear Joe _____

12. Your friend _____

13. Sincerely yours _____

14. Love _____

15. Yours truly _____

Add commas where they are needed in these sentences.

16. All birds have feathers wings and beaks.

17. The Shetland pony is small friendly and gentle.

18. A friendly playful dog makes a good pet.

19. I have three cats named Boots Muffin and Tiger.

20. I like to color with pencils markers and crayons.

Set It Off!

In the sentences below, add the missing commas to "set it off."

1. No Marlene does not like being squirted in the face.

2. Christopher how long have you been on the telephone?

3. Well just what did you have in mind?

4. Sure Laura I'd love another jelly donut.

5. My brother the world's scariest boy likes escargots.

6. The plane we are taking a 747 will have plenty of room.

7. You realize of course that you will not be allowed out of the house in that outfit.

8. My orthodontist Dr. Baugh decorated his office for Halloween.

9. All right if that's what you think, let's just eat all of the chocolate.

10. In the future we will be able to speak to our computers.

11. No kidding you went rock climbing?

12. We went to Bouquet Canyon a canyon near Valencia to attend a harvest festival.

13. You could read for example some books about the historical period in which your novel takes place.

14. For Valentine's Day my dad gave me two pounds of my favorite treat candy corn.

15. I don't care what you think I'm going to go back there and help that little boy.

That's Mine

When a word shows that something belongs to it, it shows ownership. *Possession* is another word for ownership. An apostrophe is used to show possession.

Example: *Friskie's leash* (To whom does the leash belong? The leash belongs to the dog, Friskie.) You usually add *'s* to a noun to show possession.

Show possession in the following examples. Don't forget the apostrophe. The first two have been completed for you.

1. food belonging to a cat   cat's food
2. a nest belonging to a bird   bird's nest
3. a bike belonging to Miguel   _____
4. a store that is owned by Kim   _____
5. a CD player belonging to David   _____
6. a book belonging to my sister   _____
7. a skateboard owned by my brother   _____
8. some toys that belong to a baby   _____
9. a desk that belongs to the teacher   _____
10. a brush that belongs to a painter   _____

Rewrite each sentence below, adding an apostrophe where one is needed to show possession.

11. Nicky ran screaming into Manuels house.

_____

12. My dad knocked down a hornets nest.

_____

13. I wish I could drive my brothers car.

_____

14. An alien ate Marielas homework.

_____

15. Grandpas spaghetti is the best in the world.

_____

Using Quotation Marks

Quotation marks and commas are used to set off quotations.

Example: She said, "I don't like bananas." (The comma after "she said" tells us to pause before speaking the quote. The quotation marks show exactly what was said.)

Place quotation marks and commas where they are needed in the sentences below.

1. Ryan asked What do you want to play, Martha?

2. Martha answered Let's play baseball.

3. Okay, we'll play baseball first said Ryan but let's play basketball after that.

4. Mom called The cookies are ready.

5. Oh, boy the boys yelled at the same time let's eat!

Write four sentences below. Make them a conversation between you and your best friend. Be sure to place the quotation marks and commas where they belong.

_____

_____

_____

_____

_____

_____

_____

_____

May I Quote You?

In the sentences below, place a check mark in front of those that need quotation marks added. On the line below each sentence, write the sentence again with the correct punctuation. If the sentence is correct, do nothing. The first one has been completed for you.

1. What is that bizarre thing upon your head? It looks like an octopus, said Mr. Grimmy.

   "What is that bizarre thing upon your head? It looks like an octopus," said Mr. Grimmy.

2. The teacher told the students to read the poem, "The Raven" by Friday.

   _____

3. I call my sister Idget, but I have no idea why.

   _____

4. "Hey!" Jacques shouted, "Didn't you hear the coach? He said, 'Stop when you get to the fence!' "

   _____

5. And then I will cover you with fragrant rose petals, Mama said, and sing a lullaby.

   _____

6. I found a book that said, Dinosaurs may be more closely related to birds than to lizards.

   _____

7. We have family nicknames, and my brother's is "Greasy Bear."

   _____

8. Did you hear what Nicole said? Amy asked us. She said, You guys are just too chicken to try it. She doesn't know what she is talking about!

   _____

9. I thought you would be too cool to go on the merry-go-round with me.

   _____

10. She watched *Somewhere in Time* so many times she wore out the tape.

    _____

11. My brother always talks in his sleep. Last night he said, "Hurry and purple it before the snails get it!"

    _____

12. After we watched *Twister*, we couldn't stop watching the clouds.

    _____

13. Come with us, Dad said, and we can stop for ice cream on the way.

    _____

14. I need to find the root word for transient.

    _____

15. Mom says we shouldn't say "Where's he at?" because it is not proper English.

    _____

Punctuation Challenge

Read the letter. There are 21 punctuation errors. Circle the punctuation that is wrong and correct it. Add any missing punctuation.

Dear Pen Pal

I love to go to the circus! On May 6 1999, the circus came to my hometown of Jackson Wyoming. A parade marched through our streets and soon the big top could be seen. Ken my brother, and I went to watch the performers prepare for opening night. We saw clowns, acrobats, and even the ringmaster. What a sight? Have you ever seen anything like it. You should go if you ever get the chance.

I also really enjoy playing baseball. My favorite team is the New York Yankees but I also like the St. Louis Cardinals. When I grow up I want to be a baseball pitcher, first baseman, or shortstop. Do you like baseball? What do you want to do when you grow up. I wish you could see my cool baseball card collection, but Kens collection is even better.

Oh, I almost forgot to tell you about my family! There are four people in my family. They are my mom my dad my brother and me. Scruffy my cat is also a family member. In August 2000 my grandpa will probably move in with us. I cant wait for that! Didn't you say your grandma lives with you. Ill bet you really like that.

Well thats all for now. Please write back to me soon. See you!

Your pal,

Brent

What Is a Subject?

All sentences have subjects. A **subject** tells who or what a sentence is about.

Example: Blake loves to paint. (Who loves to paint? **Blake** loves to paint.)
Blake is the subject of the sentence.

First, ask yourself who or what the sentence is about. Then, underline the subject of the sentence. Finally, write the subject of the sentence on the line. The first one is done for you.

1. <u>Blake</u> has a paintbox.

   Who has a paintbox? _____ Blake _____

2. The paintbox has three colors.

   What has three colors? _____

3. The colors are red, yellow, and blue.

   What are red, yellow, and blue? _____

4. Blake can make more colors.

   Who can make more colors? _____

5. Green is made by mixing together blue and yellow paints.

   What is made by mixing together blue and yellow paints? _____

6. Orange is made by mixing together yellow and red paints.

   What is made by mixing together yellow and red paints? _____

7. Blake loves to paint.

   Who loves to paint? _____

8. Blake's favorite color is blue.

   What is blue? _____

9. Mom hung up Blake's painting.

   Who hung up Blake's painting? _____

10. The painting is of a sailboat on the ocean.

    What is of a sailboat on the ocean? _____

Subject Practice

The **subject** is who or what the sentence is about. When an artist creates a painting of a vase full of colorful flowers set upon a white cloth in front of a blue background, the subject of the painting is the vase of colorful flowers. The rest of the painting just gives more information about the vase of flowers, such as where they are and what kind of light is shining on them.

Example: Swimming is fun. (What is fun? **Swimming** is fun.)
Swimming is the subject of the sentence.

First, ask yourself who or what the sentence is about. Then, underline the subject of the sentence. Finally, write the subject of the sentence on the line. The first one is done for you.

1. <u>Kids</u> love to swim at the pool and the beach.

   Who loves to swim at the pool and the beach? _____ **Kids** _____

2. Baseball is a fun sport to play or watch.

   What is a fun sport to play or watch?_____

3. Swimming is a good way to cool off when it is hot.

   What is a good way to cool off when it is hot?_____

4. I like to eat ice cream in the summer.

   Who likes to eat ice cream in the summer?_____

5. Summertime is my favorite time of the year.

   What is your favorite time of the year?_____

6. In the summer, Jeremy likes to take a vacation.

   Who likes to take a vacation in the summer? ___Jeremy___

7. Mosquitoes are numerous in the summer.

   What are numerous in the summer? _____

8. My skin itches when I get a sunburn.

   What itches when you get a sunburn?_____

9. Every summer seashells wash up on the shore.

   What washes up on the shore every summer? _____

10. The summer is over, but it will be back next year.

    What is over but will be back next year? _____

What Is a Predicate?

Just as all sentences have subjects, they also have predicates. The **predicate** tells us important things about the subject. It tells us what the subject does, has, or is.

Examples

- Tommy had a cold.

  What did Tommy have? Tommy **had a cold.**
  The predicate of the sentence is *had a cold.*

- Felicia jumps into the lake.

  What does Felicia do? Felicia **jumps into the lake.**
  The predicate of the sentence is *jumps into the lake.*

- The inner tube is leaking air.

  What is the inner tube doing? The inner tube **is leaking air.**
  The predicate of the sentence is *is leaking air.*

First, ask yourself what the subject does, has, or is. Then write the predicate of each sentence. The first one is done for you.

1. The water is very cold. _____ **is very cold** _____

2. We jump into the water. _____

3. Luke splashes us. _____

4. Tonia is cold. _____

5. She gets out of the water. _____

6. Nick does a handstand underwater. _____

7. Everyone claps for him _____

8. The inner tube has a leak in it. _____

9. Luke throws the inner tube onto the shore. _____

10. Tonia sits on the inner tube. _____

11. The inner tube deflates with Tonia on it. _____

12. Everyone laughs with Tonia. _____

13. Tonia jumps into the water. _____

14. Luke swims as fast as he can. _____

15. Tonia races Luke. _____

Complete Sentences

Before you can write a good story, you must be able to write good sentences. Remember, a sentence has a subject and a predicate. When the two parts are written together, all the words make sense. In each sentence found below, circle the complete subject and underline the complete predicate.

Example: (Mom and dad) took us to the beach.

1. Uncle Tony invited us to the baseball game.

2. His truck carried us to the field.

3. The parking lot was crowded.

4. We finally found our seats.

5. Uncle Tony bought popcorn and peanuts.

6. Two batters hit home runs.

7. Our team won the game.

8. People pushed to get out of the stadium.

9. We drove home late at night.

10. My sister was very tired.

Take Your Pick

Look at the lists of subjects and predicates. Choose any five subjects and predicates and write five sentences. Remember to use a capital letter at the beginning of each sentence and punctuation at the end.

Subjects	Predicates
the oak tree	swayed in the breeze
a horse	jumped on a lily pad
a bullfrog	baked a birthday cake
I	walked down my street
my mother	wrote a letter
my friend	crashed the car
a giant	danced a jig
that snake	sang a song
my sister	jumped off the bridge
the clown	landed on my head
the parrot	skipped backwards
the monkey	played the piano
the teacher	blindfolded me
an organ grinder	skipped and whistled

1. _____

2. _____

3. _____

4. _____

5. _____

Word Muncher

A word muncher is a kind of monster that only eats parts of sentences. You can tell that a word muncher has been here because these sentences are full of holes. See if you can save these sentences by filling in the missing subjects or predicates.

1. The word muncher _____

   _____

2. _____ (was, were) very hungry.

3. _____ jumped up and down on my bed.

4. Twelve gorillas _____

   _____

5. _____ fell into the trunk of my neighbor's car.

6. A tiny little dancer_____

   _____

7. _____ sat on a mushroom.

8. A large box of soap _____

   _____

9. My Aunt Gertrude _____

   _____

10. _____ (is, are) sloshing around in my pocket.

11. _____(is, are) tumbling down the front steps.

12. My friend, Tiffany, _____

   _____

13. _____ bit my ear!

14. _____escaped from (his, her, their, its) cage.

15. Your elbow _____

   _____

My Complements to This Sentence!

When you eat at a nice restaurant, the food tastes good because the chef does not cook just plain food. The chef makes the food with lots of extras, such as herbs and spices. If you tasted the plain food, you would say, "This is good." If you tasted the food with herbs and spices added, you would say, "This is delicious!"

The same is true with sentences. You can add information to a plain sentence to make it more interesting. As you have learned, every predicate has a verb. Sometimes a predicate has extra words that are called complements. A **complement** is a word or group of words that completes the predicate. It adds more information to a sentence.

Examples

- Jimmy jumps.

  Jimmy jumps on me. The complement is *on me.*
- I walked.

  I walked into the post. The complement is *into the post.*

Now it is your turn. Use your imagination to add some complements to the following phrases and sentences. Remember that a **complement** is a word or group of words that adds extra information to the predicate.

1. The race car driver sped _____

2. My sister screamed _____

3. The monster climbed _____

4. I saw a fat giraffe _____

5. An alien spacecraft landed _____

6. I want to run _____

7. Don't tell _____

8. My baby brother threw _____

9. A ton of broccoli fell _____

10. A big, purple bird flew _____

11. An ugly spider is crawling _____

12. Shameka and Patty ran _____

13. I don't want to see _____

14. The shooting star burst _____

15. Hector closed _____

More Complements

Sentence complements complete the predicate of a sentence. The complement can drastically change the meaning of a sentence. For each sentence below, write two different complements. An example has been done for you.

The car sped . . .
The car sped **around the racetrack.**
The car sped **through a red light.**

1. The parrot talked . . .

_____

_____

2. The girl wrote . . .

_____

_____

3. The people laughed . . .

_____

_____

4. The skaters raced . . .

_____

_____

5. The children danced . . .

_____

_____

6. My cat ran . . .

_____

_____

7. Their artwork hung . . .

_____

_____

8. The team of gymnasts demonstrated . . .

_____

Sentence Emergencies

These sentences need your help. Be a sentence doctor and make these sentences better.
Rewrite the sentences correctly. Put a capital letter at the beginning of each sentence. Use a
period, question mark, or exclamation point at the end of each sentence.

1. tuesday is the day we go to the library

    _____

2. who is your teacher

    _____

3. the students in my class were reading

    _____

4. what a wonderful day it is

    _____

5. jordan, come play with us

    _____

6. watch out, Michelle

    _____

7. do you like math

    _____

8. i will paint today

    _____

9. what time is lunch

    _____

10. i got a sticker

    _____

More Sentence Emergencies

Unscramble these words to make a sentence. Remember to capitalize the first word in each sentence and to add punctuation at the end of each sentence.

1. bananas eat gorillas ripe

   _____

2. the door opened magician secret the

   _____

3. sense this makes sentence

   _____

4. broke the on egg my head

   _____

5. the nap a took dog tired

   _____

6. zookeeper bit the snake the

   _____

7. his pencil sharpened the boy

   _____

8. for computer the girl a her program made

   _____

9. mother called I phone my the on

   _____

10. the television watched Susie

    _____

Whoa!

You have learned that each sentence is a complete thought. What about sentences that do not stop when they should? A sentence that runs on to the next thought is called a **run-on sentence.**

> **Example:** Cake is the best dessert chocolate is my favorite flavor. (*run-on*)
> Cake is the best dessert. Chocolate is my favorite flavor.

Each of the following sentences is a run-on sentence. Write each run-on sentence as two separate sentences. The first one has been done for you.

1. My books are on the table my math book is on top.
   <u>My books are on the table. My math book is on top.</u>

2. They were closing the store it was time to go home.

3. Watch out for the slippery ice you could fall and hurt yourself.

4. I got a new blue dress the blue shoes match perfectly.

5. My brother made the team will I be able to play baseball some day?

6. I like to go camping the last time we went, we saw a bear.

7. My teacher was not at school we had a substitute.

8. I don't like lima beans I only want mashed potatoes.

9. Can you spend the night at my house we can have pizza for dinner.

10. My dog has fleas we had to get her some special medicine.

Bits and Pieces

You have learned that a sentence needs to be a complete thought to make sense. When a sentence is an incomplete thought, it is called a **sentence fragment**. Usually, a sentence fragment is missing a piece of information. You might not know the subject. The subject tells who or what the sentence is about. You might not know the predicate. The predicate tells what the subject has, does, or is.

Read the sentence fragments shown below. They are missing important pieces of information. Use your imagination to change these fragments into complete sentences. Rewrite the fragments as complete sentences, adding whatever information you wish. The first is done for you. Remember to capitalize and punctuate every sentence.

1. The big bad wolf
   <u>The big bad wolf blew down the little pig's house.</u>

2. went flying in the air
   _____

3. my best friend
   _____

4. Alan's birthday party
   _____

5. fell off the fence
   _____

6. was blowing big bubbles
   _____

7. a giant spider
   _____

8. ran into the street
   _____

9. her hamster
   _____

10. ate a bug
    _____

Fragment Search

On this page you will find five complete sentences and five sentence fragments. Write the five complete sentences using correct capitalization and punctuation. Use your own words to change the five sentence fragments into complete sentences. Be sure to write these new sentences using correct capitalization and punctuation. You should have written 10 complete sentences when you are finished.

1. bruce has many things in his room

_____

2. books on shelves

_____

3. is there a box of toys under the bed

_____

4. a rug is in front of the closet

_____

5. two stuffed animals

_____

6. i can see trees from my window

_____

7. the bedspread and curtains

_____

8. my favorite game

_____

9. look out for

_____

10. latoya cleans her room every day

_____

What's That You Say?

You already know about ending sentences with periods, question marks, and exclamation points. Sentences with these different endings have different names. Use the information below and on page 79 to learn about the four kinds of sentences.

- Sentences that make statements end with periods. They are called **declarative sentences.**

    Examples: Sunday is my grandma's birthday. It will rain tomorrow.

- Sentences that ask questions end with question marks. They are called **interrogative sentences.**

    Examples: Is this seat taken? Can I play? Do you want this? Where are you going?

- Sentences that express strong emotion end with exclamation points. These are called **exclamatory sentences**.

    Examples: We're going to Disney World! Tommy's cat won first prize at the fair!

- Sentences that make requests end with periods. Sentences that give commands or make strong or urgent requests end with exclamation points. All of these types of sentences are called **imperative sentences.**

    Examples: Put the book on the shelf. Watch out! Don't put those peas on your head!

- It might seem like an imperative sentence does not have a subject. You cannot see it in the sentence, but it is there. The subject is *you*. Test it for yourself. When someone says to you, "Please put the book on the shelf," the subject *you* is not in the sentence. However, you know that the person is speaking to you. The person could say, "You please put the book on the shelf." You can add the subject *you* to the beginning of any imperative sentence.

    Examples: (*You*) Wash the dishes. (*You*) Return the books.

Decide whether the following sentences are imperatives or declaratives. On the line before each number, write an **I** if it is an imperative sentence or a **D** if it is a declarative sentence.

_____ 1. The top fell off my new toy soldier.   _____ 6. I can't find my shoes.

_____ 2. Put me down, please.   _____ 7. Give me my hat.

_____ 3. Open your science books.   _____ 8. Marie, I will tickle you.

_____ 4. My dog ate my homework.   _____ 9. Stop!

_____ 5. Take out the trash now!   _____ 10. I warned you not to do that.

What's That You Say? (cont.)

Sentences that end with question marks are always interrogatives. **Interrogative sentences** ask questions. Another way to tell if a sentence is an interrogative is to ask yourself, "Does the main verb come before the subject?" If the main verb comes before the subject, it is an interrogative sentence.

Write five questions that you would like to ask your teacher.

1. _____

   _____

2. _____

   _____

3. _____

   _____

4. _____

   _____

5. _____

   _____

Great job! You have written five interrogative sentences.

Put a period at the end of each declarative sentence or imperative sentence that makes a request. Put an exclamation point at the end of each exclamatory sentence or imperative sentence that gives a command or makes a strong or urgent request.

1. I am very tired ☐

2. Let's sit down here ☐

3. What a wonderful idea ☐

4. Ouch ☐

5. Watch where you throw that ball ☐

6. Well, then, let's have some lunch ☐

7. The sandwich is for you ☐

8. That lasagna is very hot ☐

9. I didn't think you wanted lasagna ☐

10. Sue would like a hamburger, please ☐

11. Bob, you don't have to get so upset ☐

12. This sandwich tastes good ☐

13. I love roast beef ☐

14. Take your brother to the park ☐

Can You Handle This?

You have probably noticed that some sentences could be either exclamatory or declarative. The more writing you do, the more you will notice that you are in control. You, as the writer, determine whether or not sentences will express strong feelings. The way you punctuate affects the meaning as shown in the following examples.

Examples: 1. I got a B on the test!   2. I got a B on the test.

In the first sentence, the student is very happy and excited about earning a B. In the second sentence, the student is just telling someone that he or she earned a B.

Correct the paragraph shown below. You will need to remember everything that you have learned about complete sentences, capitalization, and punctuation. When you have finished correcting the paragraph, proofread it to avoid any careless errors. You may wish to change some of your answers. Revise the paragraph and read it one more time. After you have rechecked your answers, use another paper to write a new paragraph that includes as many declarative, interrogative, imperative, and exclamatory sentences as you can. This is your chance to be creative and use your imagination.

---

i went to the store because i needed to get something for lunch my stomach was growling so much that a little boy sitting in a shopping cart could hear it Mom, he said, he has a rumbly tumbly Shush said his mother i turned to the little boy and asked i have a what A rumbly tumbly he said and smiled shyly. A rumbly tumbly, a rumbly tumbly i said over and over again the little boy started to giggle and i was even hungrier than before yikes i said to the little boy. i have to get something to eat before my rumbly tumbly tumbles the little boy stopped giggling, pointed his finger at me, and said, go get something to eat right now before your rumbly tumbly tumbles okay i said as i rushed down the aisle toward the apples and bananas.

Consonants and Vowels

Most letters of the alphabet are consonants, but five of them are vowels. The vowels are *A*, *E*, *I*, *O*, and *U*. Every word must have at least one vowel. Sometimes, *Y* acts as the vowel in the word.

Look at the pictures. Do the items begin with a vowel or consonant sound? Write **V** for vowel and **C** for consonant and write what the picture is in each box.

1. _____

2. _____

3. _____

4. _____

5. _____

6. _____

7. _____

8. _____

Consonant Blends

List all the words you can think of that begin with the following consonant blends.

bl   br   cl   cr

_____ _____ _____ _____

_____ _____ _____ _____

_____ _____ _____ _____

_____ _____ _____ _____

dr   fl   fr   gl

_____ _____ _____ _____

_____ _____ _____ _____

_____ _____ _____ _____

gr   pl   pr   sl

_____ _____ _____ _____

_____ _____ _____ _____

_____ _____ _____ _____

sp   st   str   tr

_____ _____ _____ _____

_____ _____ _____ _____

_____ _____ _____ _____

_____ _____ _____ _____

Digraphs

When two consonants are placed together and form one consonant sound, they are called a **digraph**. *Ch, sh, th,* and *wh* are the most common digraphs. When you say them together, you only hear one sound. Digraphs can come at the beginning, middle, or end of a word.

Add one of the four digraphs to each letter group. Then say the words you have formed.

| ch | sh | th | wh |

1. _____ick

2. _____oose

3. _____op

4. _____ape

5. ma_____

6. _____ank

7. _____eese

8. _____eck

9. _____irst

10. _____istle

11. ba_____

12. wi_____

13. _____ip

14. ben_____

15. wa_____ing

16. tra_____

Long Vowel Quilt Square

Listen for the long vowel sound in each word. Color the spaces this way:

long a = red **long e = purple** **long i = yellow**

long o = green **long u = blue**

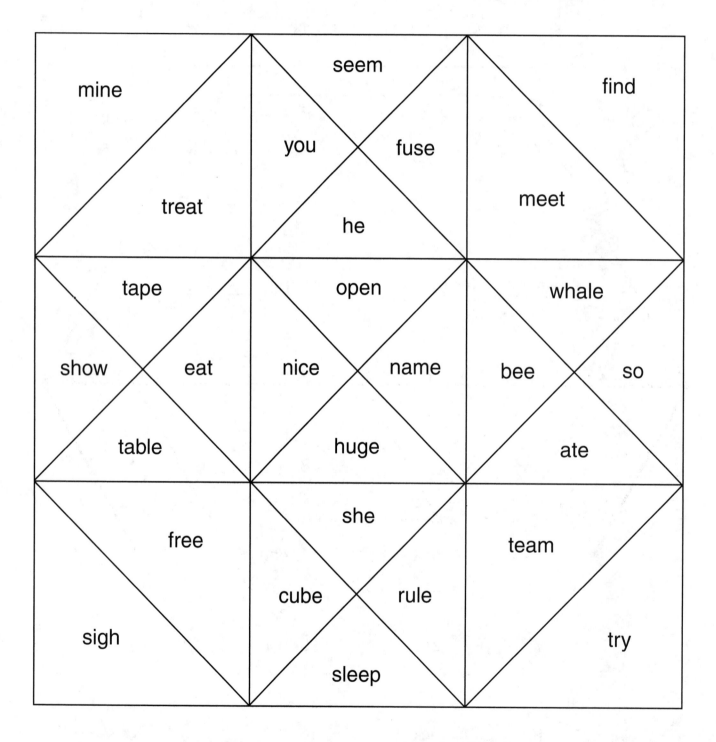

Short Vowel Quilt

Listen for the short vowel sound in each word. Color the spaces this way:

short a = purple　　　　　　short e = blue

short i = red　　　　　　　　short o = yellow

short u = green

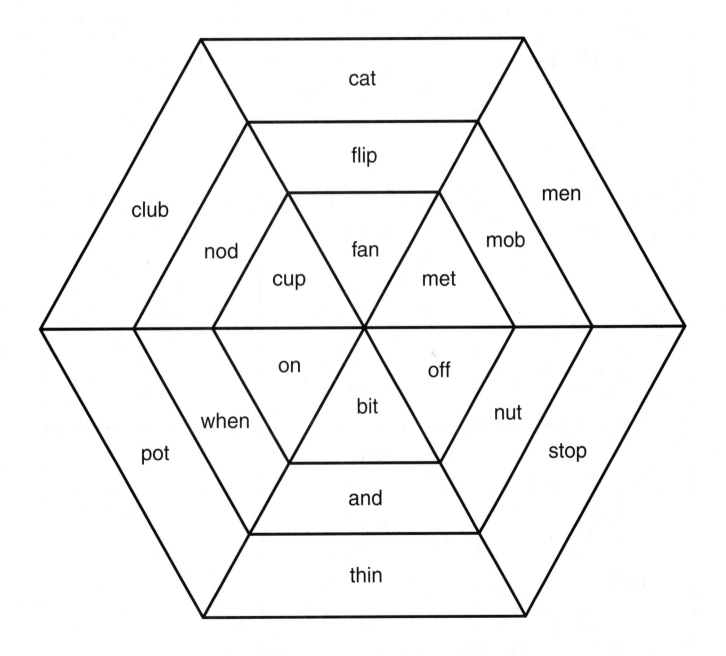

Long and Short

Read the words in the word box. If the vowel sound is long, write the word in column A. If the vowel sound is short, write the word in column B.

bat	bun	hot	maid	note
beach	cake	jack	moth	pump
beg	eat	let	mule	tin
boat	fish	light	muse	write

A (long vowels)   B (short vowels)

_____   _____

_____   _____

_____   _____

_____   _____

_____   _____

_____   _____

_____   _____

_____   _____

Silent E

Sometimes the letter *e* in a word has no sound, but its job is still important. It changes a short vowel sound to a long one. Read the words below. Then write the word on the blank and add an **e** to the end of each word. Read the new words.

1. can   2. sit   3. cap

4. tub

5. dot

6. not

7. rat

8. lob   9. bit

10. cub

11. grim

12. fin

13. bath   14. van   15. plan

1. _____

2. _____

3. _____

4. _____

5. _____

6. _____

7. _____

8. _____

9. _____

10. _____

11. _____

12. _____

13. _____

14. _____

15. _____

Silent Letters

Letters other than *e* may be silent in a word. Sometimes they change the sound of the other letters, and sometimes they do not. There are no easy rules for these silent letters. You must practice them to learn them.

Each word below is missing a silent letter. Choose a letter from the letter bank to complete the words. (Be sure to use a letter that will remain silent in the word.) Then say the words aloud.

b	h	k	t	w

1. _____rite

2. wi_____ch

3. _____hole

4. dum_____

5. _____not

6. no_____ch

7. _____new

8. com_____

9. _____onest

10. lam_____

11. g_____ost

12. w_____ale

13. _____rench

14. ba_____ch

15. w_____ip

16. _____our

17. ca_____ch

18. _____rong

19. _____rinkle

20. ma_____ch

21. _____night

22. _____nee

23. crum_____

24. _____nife

25. thum_____

26. _____nit

The Phunny Elefant?

The *f* sound is created in different ways. Sometimes the sound is made by the letter *f.* Other times it is made by *ff*, *ph*, or *gh*. Choose an **ff**, **ph**, **f**, or **gh** to complete each of the words below.

1. al_____abet

2. aw_____ul

3. cou_____

4. dol_____in

5. ele_____ant

6. el_____

7. enou_____

8. _____antastic

9. _____ish

10. _____un

11. gira_____e

12. lau_____

13. mu_____

14. _____onics

15. rou_____

16. ta_____y

17. tele_____one

18. tou_____

Gh

The letters *gh* are pronounced two ways. Sometimes they make the *f* sound as in *cough.*
Other times, they are silent as in *sigh.*

Read the words. Write each word in the correct column.

cough	naughty	slough
daughter	night	taught
dough	right	though
enough	rough	tough
knight	sigh	trough
light	sight	

F Sound	Silent

The K Sound

The *k* sound can be made in four different ways: *c, k, ck,* and *ch.* Fill in the blanks with the correct letters to make the *k* sound. Read the words.

k	c	ck	ch

1. a_____e

2. ba_____

3. ban_____

4. bea_____

5. _____ane

6. _____ut

7. _____rumb

8. do_____

9. ja_____

10. _____eep

11. _____ey

12. _____ind

13. loo_____

14. ma_____e

15. ne_____

16. ni_____el

17. pa_____

18. po_____et

19. s_____are

20. s_____ool

21. s_____in

22. so_____

23. spo_____e

24. stoma_____

25. wal_____

26. ra_____e

　　　　　　　　93　　　　　　　　#3646 *Practice and Learn*

Rhyme Zoo

Think of an animal that rhymes with each word. Write the rhyming animal on the lines.
Remember, rhyming words do not always end in the same letters.

Example: *Chair* and *hare* rhyme but do not end the same way.

1. big _____

2. sea _____

3. lake_____

4. drama_____

5. herd _____

6. habit _____

7. course _____

8. hear _____

9. box _____

10. log _____

Can you think of 4 pairs of rhyming animals? **Example:** *sow, cow*

1. _____   _____   2. _____   _____

3_____   _____   4. _____   _____

Rhymes

Rhyming words have the same end sounds, but those end sounds are not always spelled in the same way. Match the rhyming pairs by coloring each matching pair the same color.

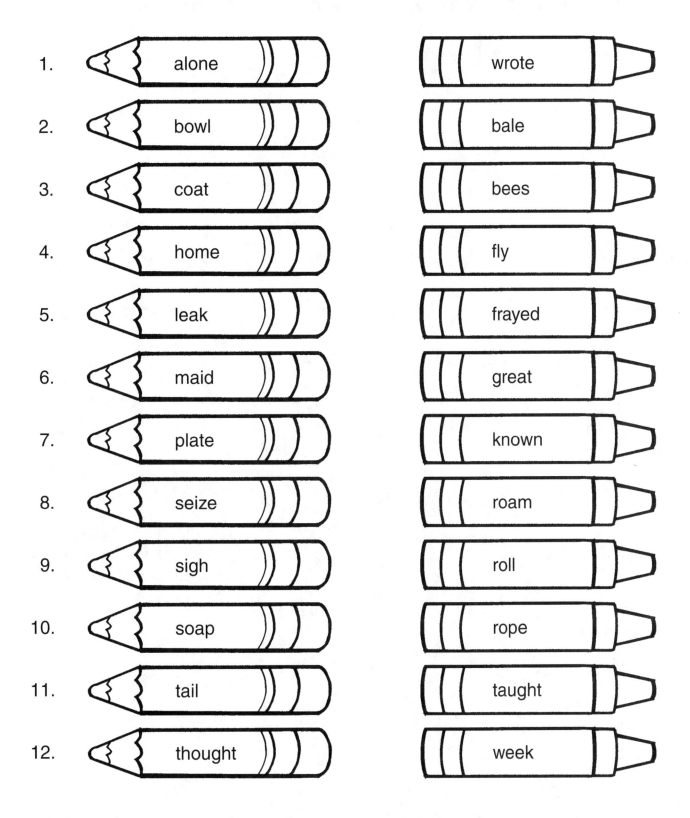

1. alone
2. bowl
3. coat
4. home
5. leak
6. maid
7. plate
8. seize
9. sigh
10. soap
11. tail
12. thought

wrote
bale
bees
fly
frayed
great
known
roam
roll
rope
taught
week

Compound Words

A **compound** is combination of two or more words to create a new word. Write a word in the blank between each set of words. The trick is that the new word must complete a compound word both to the left and to the right of it. The first one has been done for you.

1. news   <u>**paper**</u>   boy

2. drop   _____   side

3. frog   _____   hood

4. foot   _____   room

5. honey   _____   light

6. water   _____   out

7. head   _____   house

8. look   _____   side

9. time   _____   spoon

10. text   _____   case

11. left   _____   board

12. birth   _____   dream

13. dark   _____   mate

14. round   _____   keep

15. butter   _____   cake

More Compound Words

Choose a word from column **A** or **B** and combine it with a word from column **C** or **D** to make a compound word. Some words will go together in more than one combination, but there is only one combination that will use all of the words.

A	B
cup	handle
foot	jelly
gold	over
high	pony
pepper	rain
rail	silver
shoe	suit
spot	tip
sun	wind
sweat	wrist

C	D
ball	case
bar	fish
bow	fish
cake	light
lace	mill
look	mint
set	shirt
tail	toe
watch	ware
way	way

_____

_____

_____

_____

_____

_____

_____

_____

Hidden Compounds

A **compound word** is a single word that is made by joining two smaller words.

Examples: starlight, treetop, doorbell

How many compound words can you find in the picture? See if you can find 12.

Stressed Out Syllables

Words are divided into sounds called **syllables**. Two-syllable words have a stressed and unstressed syllable. A stressed syllable is the sound spoken loudest in a word. The unstressed syllable is the sound which is spoken more softly.

Rule #1

When a word has a double consonant, the word is divided between the two consonants.

Example: bub´-ble

Divide each word below into syllables and place a stressed syllable mark (´) on the syllable you think is stressed. Use a dictionary to check your answers.

1. pillow   _____

2. fellow   _____

3. pizza   _____

4. suppose   _____

5. surround   _____

6. scissors   _____

7. collect   _____

8. hurrah   _____

9. address   _____

10. silly   _____

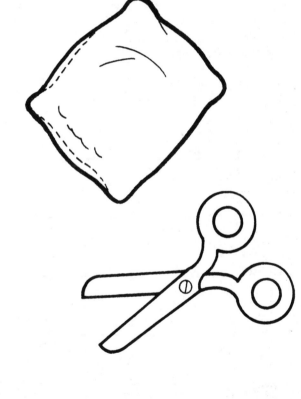

Stressed Out Syllables (cont.)

Rule #2

When a word ends in a consonant plus *le*, the word is divided before the consonant.

Example: pur´-ple

Divide each word below into syllables and place a stressed syllable mark (´) on the syllable you think is stressed. Use a dictionary to check your answers.

1. turtle _____

2. beetle _____

3. bubble _____

4. candle _____

5. juggle _____

6. hustle _____

7. baffle _____

8. cradle _____

9. bottle _____

10. trouble _____

Stressed Out Syllables (cont.)

Rule #3

When the first vowel in a word has the short vowel sound, the word is divided after the next consonant.

Example: shad´-ow

Divide each word below into syllables, and place a stressed syllable mark (´) on the syllable you think is stressed. Use a dictionary to check your answers.

1. cartoon _____

2. cinder _____

3. droplet _____

4. extra _____

5. express _____

6. imprint _____

7. jungle _____

8. salad _____

9. magic _____

10. picture _____

Stressed Out Syllables (cont.)

Rule #4

When the first vowel in a word has the long vowel sound, the word is divided after that vowel.

Example: ba´-by

Divide each word below into syllables, and place a stressed syllable mark (´) on the syllable you think is stressed. Use a dictionary to check your answers.

1. humor   _____

2. able   _____

3. begin   _____

4. kiwi   _____

5. paper   _____

6. locate   _____

7. open   _____

8. profile   _____

9. rosette   _____

10. erupt   _____

Getting to the Root of It

Sometimes a word has letters added to the beginning or end of it that change the meaning of the word. The main word is called the **root word**, and the added letters are **prefixes** and **suffixes**. For example, in the word *soundless* the root word is *sound,* and in the word *unusual* the root word is *usual.* Notice how the meanings of these two words change with the added letters.

Read the words below. Write the root words in the spaces provided.

1. irresponsible _____

2. misunderstand _____

3. meaningful _____

4. worthless _____

5. immaterial _____

6. disengage _____

7. unaware _____

8. prearrange _____

9. semicircle _____

10. biweekly _____

11. mountainous _____

12. unicycle _____

13. triangle _____

14. nonsense _____

15. admiralty _____

Root It Out

On each flower is the name of a person who does an action. Find the root word in each name and write it below the flower. (**Note:** Sometimes letters from the root word are left off or changed to form the new word. Be sure to spell the root word correctly.)

1.
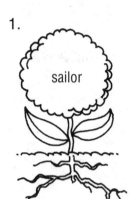
sailor

_____

2.

runner

_____

3.
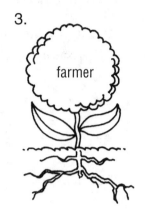
farmer

_____

4.

buyer

_____

5.

pharmacist

_____

6.
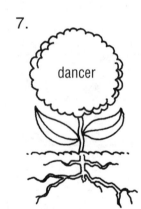
director

_____

7.
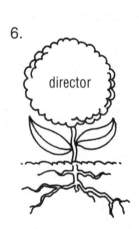
dancer

_____

8.
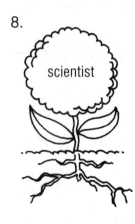
scientist

_____

9.

photographer

_____

10.
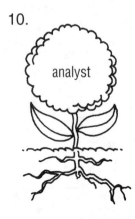
analyst

_____

11.
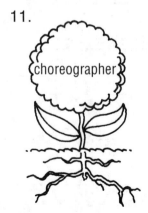
choreographer

_____

12.

biographer

_____

Break It Up

A **prefix** is one or more syllables at the beginning of a root word. When a word has a prefix, the syllable division is between the prefix and the root word. Circle the prefixes in the following cards. Write the word on the cards using hyphens to divide it into syllables.

unknown	**rephrase**
disrespect	**remake**
precook	**misalign**

Prepare for Prefixes

Here are nine common prefixes. How many words can you find that begin with these prefixes? Write them in the columns. One word in each column has been done for you.

un	dis	pre
unusual	discover	preorder

under	re	mis
understand	remake	mistake

ir	over	im
irresponsible	overwrought	immaterial

Painting with Prefixes

The prefix **un** can mean *not* or *opposite of*.

The prefix **re** can mean *again* or *back*.

Write the word on the paint can that tells the meaning of the clue.

Color the paint cans with the prefix *un* green.

Color the paint cans with the prefix *re* yellow.

1.

heat again

2.

playback

3.

not safe

4.

opposite of lucky

5.

do again

6.

not fair

7.

read again

8.

write again

9.

opposite of cover

Prefix Party

The prefix **over** can mean *too much*. The prefix **under** can mean *not enough*. Circle the words in the paragraph containing the prefixes *over* and *under*. Then write each word and its meaning on the lines below.

Kate was excited! She was going to have her birthday party with all her friends. That morning she overslept! She was behind on all her chores. She quickly overstuffed her toy box and underwatered the plants. She even forgot Shadow, her cat, and left her underfed. When she was washing the dishes, the water accidentally overflowed onto the floor. She was in such a rush! She took her birthday cake out of the oven too soon and then it was undercooked. She thought to herself, "I'm glad my birthday only comes once a year."

Word	**Meaning**
_____	_____
_____	_____
_____	_____
_____	_____
_____	_____

Surfing with Suffixes

A **suffix** is one or more syllables at the end of a root word. When a word has a suffix, the syllable division is between the suffix and the root word. Circle the suffix in each word and then rewrite each word on the waves with a hyphen to divide each word into syllables.

1. kindness

2. careful

3. helpful

4. seedless

5. clearly

6. healthful

Prepare for Suffixes

Here are nine common suffixes. How many words can you find that end with these suffixes? Write them in the columns. One word in each column has been done for you.

ful	less	ty
beautiful	worthless	royalty

ness	ly	ic
goodness	lonely	majestic

ist	er	ism
scientist	farmer	patriotism

Double Anyone

Use the following clues to find words that contain consecutive double letters.

1. an animal _____

2. one of the four seasons _____

3. sport played in the fall _____

4. high level of understanding _____

5. to draw aimlessly _____

6. pirate _____

7. winged insect _____

8. animal with a long neck _____

9. person who asks for handouts _____

10. Earth's natural satellite _____

11. seasoning _____

12. flock of geese _____

13. move from side to side _____

14. to take for a period of time _____

15. grief, sadness _____

16. poem of fourteen lines _____

17. paper used in secret voting _____

18. great work of literature _____

Two of a Kind

Make a list of words that contain two of one letter of the alphabet. Examples include _aardvark_, _baby_, _cartoon_, and _dawdle_.

_____   _____

_____   _____

_____   _____

_____   _____

_____   _____

_____   _____

_____   _____

_____   _____

_____   _____

_____   _____

_____   _____

_____   _____

_____   _____

_____   _____

_____   _____

_____   _____

Begin and End

Each phrase below is a clue for an answer that begins and ends with the same letter.

1. antonym of low   h _ _ h

2. a type of boat   k _ _ _ k

3. the most abundant gas in

   the atmosphere   n _ _ _ _ _ _ n

4. children's sidewalk game   h _ _ _ _ _ _ _ h

5. the loss of memory   a _ _ _ _ _ a

6. opposite of minimum   m _ _ _ _ _ m

7. payment to stockholders   d _ _ _ _ _ _ d

8. a gas used in lighted signs   n _ _ n

9. one TV show in a series   e _ _ _ _ _ e

10. the fireplace floor   h _ _ _ _ h

11. blue-green   a _ _ a

12. a small infant   n _ _ _ _ _ n

13. a ray of moonlight   m _ _ _ _ _ _ m

14. a place for performances   a _ _ _ a

15. one who forms opinions and

    gives judgments   c _ _ _ _ c

16. a continent   A _ _ _ _ _ _ _ _ a

17. another continent   A _ _ _ _ _ _ _ a

18. another continent   A _ _ _ _ _ a

19. another continent   A _ _ a

20. another continent   E _ _ _ _ e

Anagrams

An **anagram** is a word formed by rearranging the letters of another word. Reorder the letters of each word below to make new words.

1. ocean _____

2. snap _____

3. Brian _____

4. owl _____

5. melon _____

6. pots _____

7. flea _____

8. ring _____

9. art _____

10. gum _____

11. heart _____

12. bat _____

13. paws _____

14. ape _____

15. tone _____

16. tap _____

17. stop _____

18. not _____

19. pore _____

20. wee _____

Four-Letter Words

Below are listed the middle letters of some four-letter words. Fill in the blanks to make four-letter words.

____ a n ____	____ i d ____
____ e a ____	____ o v ____
____ a r ____	____ a i ____
____ e l ____	____ a m ____
____ o a ____	____ f a ____
____ i k ____	____ a v ____
____ o l ____	____ o r ____
____ a r ____	____ v e ____
____ o u ____	____ y p ____
____ o o ____	____ a s ____

Here are the initial and final letters of some four-letter words. Fill in the blanks to make four-letter words.

c ____ ____ t	b ____ ____ d
s ____ ____ t	m ____ ____ t
d ____ ____ e	t ____ ____ e
r ____ ____ n	p ____ ____ t
l ____ ____ d	b ____ ____ t
f ____ ____ d	h ____ ____ e
s ____ ____ d	d ____ ____ r
s ____ ____ r	e ____ ____ n
a ____ ____ e	g ____ ____ e
h ____ ____ t	m ____ ____ t

Education

List all the words you can make from the letters in *education*. (**Note:** All of the words in your list must have at least 3 letters and each letter can be used only once in each word.)

_____	_____
_____	_____
_____	_____
_____	_____
_____	_____
_____	_____
_____	_____
_____	_____
_____	_____
_____	_____
_____	_____
_____	_____
_____	_____
_____	_____
_____	_____
_____	_____
_____	_____

Summertime

List words related to summertime that begin with each letter of the alphabet.

A _____

B _____

C _____

D _____

E _____

F _____

G _____

H _____

I _____

J _____

K _____

L _____

M _____

N _____

O _____

P _____

Q _____

R _____

S _____

T _____

U _____

V _____

W _____

X _____

Y _____

Z _____

Clipped Words

The following words are written in their shortened forms. Write the long forms of these words in the blanks to their right.

1. vet _____

2. tie _____

3. movie _____

4. champ _____

5. photo _____

6. copter _____

7. ref _____

8. mart _____

9. dorm _____

10. exam _____

11. ad _____

12. doc _____

13. lab _____

14. prom _____

15. flu _____

16. teen _____

17. gas _____

18. stat _____

19. lunch _____

20. mum _____

Shawn's Homework

Shawn wrote a report about a class trip to the zoo, but he had some trouble spelling. Help him to correct his paper before he gives it to his teacher. First, read his homework. Then circle the misspelled words and then write the correct spellings below each word on the lines provided.

> One day the forth-graid class went on a tripp
>
> too the zoo. They took a bus to get their. Then
>
> evryone joyned in groops to ture the zoo. The blew
>
> group went to sea the bares, the read group went to
>
> the seels, and the yelow grupe wawked to the monkie
>
> area. At nune, all the grupes meet for luncth. The
>
> children eight sandwitches and drank alot of watir.
>
> Aftar lunch, they saw a burd show in the zoo theeter.
>
> When the show wus ovur, it was thime to go home.
>
> The childern pilled into the buss and away thay went.
>
> They had a grate daye!

Abbreviations

An **abbreviation** is a shortened form of a word and is usually followed by a period. An abbreviation is never used by itself as a word. It is always used with other words or names.

- You **wouldn't** write . . .

  I live on the St. next to the park.

- You **would** write . . .

  I live at 4342 Pumpkin St. next to the park.

- And you **wouldn't** write . . .

  That's a Mt. I would like to climb.

- But you **would** write . . .

  Someday I want to climb Mt. Whitney.

List of some common abbreviations.

apt.	apartment	cont.	continued	Jr.	Junior
Aug.	August	Corp.	Corporation	kg	kilogram
Ave.	Avenue	Dec.	December	lb.	pound
Bldg.	Building	Dept.	Department	Oct.	October
Blvd.	Boulevard	ft.	feet	oz.	ounces
Capt.	Captain	in.	inches	Rd.	Road
cm	centimeters	Jan.	January	yr.	year

Match the abbreviations with the words they stand for. Then copy the abbreviation correctly. Don't forget periods!

Letter

_____ 1. Wed.

_____ 2. Mr.

_____ 3. St.

_____ 4. Dec.

_____ 5. U.S.

_____ 6. Capt.

_____ 7. tbs.

_____ 8. Blvd.

_____ 9. Aug.

_____ 10. Gov.

_____ 11. Jr.

_____ 12. gal.

_____ 13. Dr.

_____ 14. Tues.

_____ 15. yr.

Abbreviation

a. Boulevard _____

b. Mister _____

c. year_____

d. Governor_____

e. December _____

f. tablespoon _____

g. Tuesday_____

h. Street _____

i. gallon _____

j. Captain _____

k. Doctor _____

l. United States _____

m. Junior _____

n. Wednesday_____

o. August_____

More Abbreviations

Write the meaning of each abbreviation.

1. pres. _____

2. ASAP _____

3. adj. _____

4. lbs. _____

5. max. _____

6. etc. _____

7. Sept. _____

8. M.A. _____

9. I.O.U. _____

10. B.A. _____

11. c.o.d. _____

12. R.S.V.P. _____

13. S.A.S.E. _____

14. S.A. _____

15. bldg. _____

16. RR _____

17. prep. _____

18. hdqrs. _____

19. D.A. _____

20. D.S.T. _____

Alike Yet Different

Some words are spelled the same but are pronounced differently and have different meanings.

Examples

re′cord	record′	con′test	contest′
re′fuse	refuse′	close (clos)	close (cloz)
con′duct	conduct′	desert′	de′sert
con′tent	content′	read (rēd)	read (red)
sub′ject	subject′	ad′dress	address′

Choose the correct way of pronouncing the word in italics in each sentence below. Write the word at the end of the sentence and put the accent mark or vowel marks where they belong.

1. Our teacher will *record* us as we sing the national anthem. _____

2. We are studying about *desert* plants and animals. _____

3. Our little kitten was very *content* after we fed her. _____

4. Kim and I entered the art *contest*. _____

5. How can anyone *refuse* to do an act of kindness? _____

6. My mother *read* the directions for the recipe. _____

7. Please *close* the door gently. _____

8. Our *conduct* should be appropriate at all times. _____

9. What is your favorite *subject*? _____

10. My *address* is 221 Main Street. _____

Pronunciation Keys

When you use the dictionary, you will find guides to each word's pronunciation in parentheses. The dictionary will also give you a guide about how to read the pronunciations. However, if you know some basics, it will help. Use these tips.

A vowel written by itself makes the **short vowel** sound.

Examples: a, e, i, o, u

A vowel written with a straight line above it makes the **long vowel** sound.

Examples: ā, ē, ī, ō, ū

Read the pronunciation guides below. Using the two vowel tips above, write the words on the blanks.

1. mat _____

2. māt _____

3. tīn _____

4. tin _____

5. fed _____

6. fēd _____

7. us _____

8. ūs _____

9. mēt _____

10. met _____

Now it is your turn. Write two word pairs with pronunciation guides that change only by the long or short vowel sound.

_____   _____

_____   _____

What's the Word?

Read the pronunciation guides. Write the words.

1.	tāl	
2.	mōst	
3.	trās	
4.	hā′-zē	
5.	dō	
6.	dū′-əl	
7.	frā	
8.	trāl	
9.	re-plā′	
10.	whēl	
11.	mē′tər	
12.	mō′tər	
13.	gēs	
14.	chī′nə	
15.	luv	

Alphabetizing

Circle the words that are not in alphabetical order. Rewrite the words in their correct places.

ape	_____	put	_____
banana	_____	putt	_____
apple	_____	otter	_____
bear	_____	other	_____
cornhusk	_____	over	_____
carrot	_____	quitter	_____
cheese	_____	quit	_____
dandelion	_____	quilt	_____
dandy	_____	raise	_____
eggplant	_____	roast	_____
egg	_____	season	_____
grapes	_____	satisfy	_____
grass	_____	salt	_____
friend	_____	state	_____
frond	_____	town	_____
heaven	_____	tune	_____
hover	_____	tuna	_____
house	_____	umbrella	_____
ice	_____	under	_____
icicle	_____	underneath	_____
jump	_____	very	_____
juice	_____	voice	_____
kick	_____	violin	_____
kiss	_____	wisdom	_____
list	_____	wig	_____
laugh	_____	wonder	_____
limb	_____	xylophone	_____
mote	_____	yeast	_____
mother	_____	yesterday	_____
many	_____	yes	_____
neck	_____	zebra	_____
noise	_____	zoology	_____
pout	_____	zoo	_____

Alphabetical Order

Place these words in alphabetical order.

rover	jump	launch	scientist
river	light	cane	cell
moon	umbrella	candy	cello
cart	dog	same	dear
friend	sort	simple	deer
house	loop	grass	join
ghost	lope	grassy	tune
vest	game	lion	salt
silent	gamble	line	ghastly
tunnel	lunch	science	moan

_____   _____   _____   _____

_____   _____   _____   _____

_____   _____   _____   _____

_____   _____   _____   _____

_____   _____   _____   _____

_____   _____   _____   _____

_____   _____   _____   _____

_____   _____   _____   _____

_____   _____   _____   _____

What Does It Mean?

Many words have more than one meaning. When reading, you can use context clues to determine the meaning of a word in a sentence. Read the sentences below and then write the letter of the definition that shows how the underlined word is used in each sentence.

_____ 1. Tell me your <u>address</u> so I can find where you live.

      a. speak or write to

      b. manner of speech

      c. place where a person lives

_____ 2. Why do you <u>refuse</u> to come to the fair?

      a. decline to accept

      b. garbage

      c. decline to do

_____ 3. Lost in the <u>desert</u> for hours, the people were hot, hungry, and thirsty.

      a. dry, sandy wasteland

      b. abandon

      c. something deserved

_____ 4. The children at <u>play</u> were running and laughing with joy.

      a. put in motion

      b. taking part in a game or recreation

      c. a dramatic work

_____ 5. Are any cookies <u>left</u> for me?

      a. to the westward direction when one is facing north

      b. remaining

      c. departed

Define It

Each of these words has more than one meaning. Use a dictionary to write at least two meanings for each word.

1. **wind**
   a. _____
   b. _____

2. **close**
   a. _____
   b. _____

3. **record**
   a. _____
   b. _____

4. **part**
   a. _____
   b. _____

5. **conduct**
   a. _____
   b. _____

Choose one meaning for each word. Write the letter of the definition in the blank before each word. Then use the word in a sentence that shows the meaning.

_____ 1. **wind** _____

_____

_____ 2. **close** _____

_____

_____ 3. **record** _____

_____

_____ 4. **part** _____

_____

_____ 5. **conduct** _____

_____

Challenge: How many other words can you think of that have multiple meanings? Make a list and keep adding to it to see how many you can find.

Making Face Paint

Look at the directions for creating face paint found in the box below and then follow these directions:

A. Underline the important or key words in each sentence.

B. Number each step in the directions.

C. Draw a circle around each word that is a form of measurement.

D. Read the directions to a partner before you begin.

E. On another sheet of paper, make a list of the ingredients that you will need to do this project.

After creating a batch of face paint, work with a partner and paint your faces to look like zoo creatures.

In each container, mix 1 teaspoon of cold cream and 2 teaspoons of cornstarch.

Wash five small, empty food containers such as yogurt cartons or margarine tubs.

Add 1 teaspoon of water and a few drops of food coloring to each container. Blend carefully.

Be sure to use a different color for each container: blue, green, red, yellow, and brown.

Note: 1 teaspoon = 5 mL

Color This Design

Color this design so that no shapes of the same color touch one another. You may use only three colors. (*Hint:* Think out the design before you begin to color.)

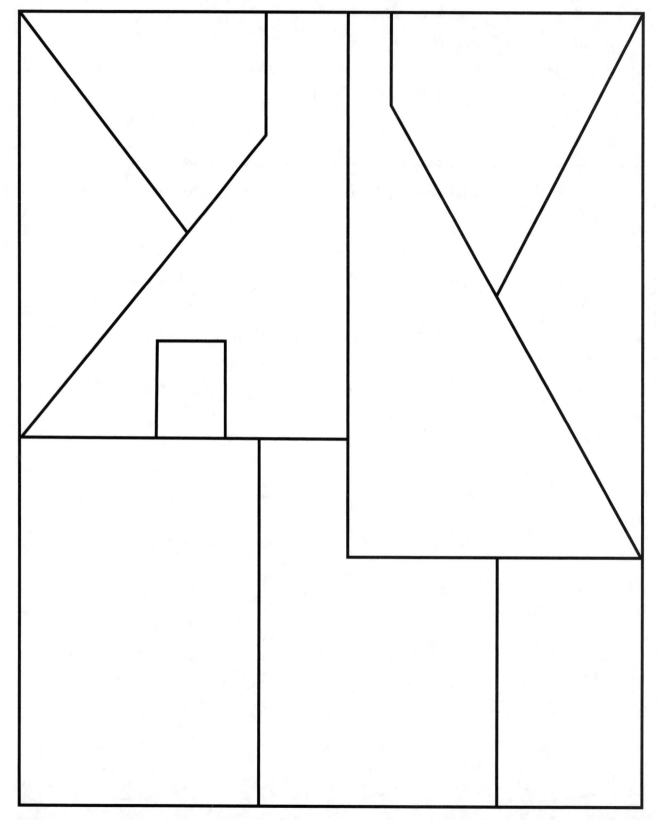

Derek's Day

One type of graph that gives us information is called a circle graph. In a circle graph, you can show how things are divided into the parts of a whole.

Derek's 24-Hour Day

at the
ball field
2 hours

asleep in bed
9 hours

at home
(but not in bed)
7 hours

at school
6 hours

- Color the place Derek spends 6 hours a day red.

- Color Derek's sleeping time blue.

- Color the time Derek spends on the ball field green.

- Color Derek's non-sleeping time at home yellow.

- On a separate paper, write some of the things you think Derek might do at home in seven hours.

Sequencing Pictures

Indicate the correct order of the pictures in each row by putting a 1, 2, or 3 in each box.

Reading Adventures

Read each story and then answer the questions.

Miles and Robin wanted to go to the zoo. Their mother said they could go after they finished their chores. First, they cleaned their rooms. Next, they mopped the kitchen floor. After that, they washed the family's car. Finally, they got ready to go to the zoo.

1. What did Miles and Robin do first? _____

_____

2. What did the boys do after they mopped the floor?_____

_____

3. What was the final thing the boys did? _____

_____

Miles and Robin were on an imaginary safari. First, their mother gave them a map of the zoo. Then, the boys went to the shark pool. Next, they found their way to the tiger cage. After that, they visited the wolf den. Finally, they met their mother at the alligator exhibit. Miles and Robin had a busy afternoon!

4. What animal did the boys visit first? _____

_____

5. Where did the boys go after they saw the tiger? _____

_____

6. What did the boys do last? _____

_____

Put Them in Order

Read the sentences. Rewrite them in a paragraph in the correct sequence.

I got out of bed and looked in the mirror.
I ran to my mother to show her what had happened.
She said, "Those seeds you swallowed yesterday have planted inside you."
I woke up one morning feeling strange.
Then she looked in the phone book for a good gardener to come over to trim me.
What a shock I got when I saw a plant growing out of my ears!
I am feeling better now, but I still have to water myself every day.

_____

_____

_____

_____

_____

_____

_____

_____

_____

_____

Kelly's Week

Kelly was having a busy week. She wrote down a list of things to do each day, but her little brother accidentally ripped it up. Put the scraps back in order by writing Kelly's list below.

Write my book report on Thursday.

Call Janet on Saturday.

Bake cookies for school on Tuesday.

Practice the violin on Friday.

Go to baseball practice on Wednesday.

1. _____

_____

2. _____

_____

3. _____

_____

4. _____

_____

5. _____

_____

What Happened Next?

When you write about something that happened to you or something that you do, it must be in the right time order. Another name for this is **chronology**. The things you write about in a paragraph should usually be in *chronological* (time) *order* to make sense.

Here are some lists of events that are out of order. Put them into time (chronological) order by marking them from first (1) to last (5). The first one has been done for you.

A.

2	eat breakfast
1	get up
5	go to school
4	go out the door
3	brush teeth

B.

_____	bait a hook
_____	clean a fish
_____	eat a fish
_____	catch a fish
_____	cook a fish

C.

_____	mail the letter
_____	put the letter in envelope
_____	write the letter
_____	wait for an answer
_____	seal the letter

D.

_____	write a book report
_____	click on word processing
_____	turn on printer
_____	turn on computer
_____	print book report

E.

_____	slap your arm
_____	see a mosquito
_____	feel a bite
_____	hear a buzz
_____	scratch a bump

F.

_____	buy popcorn
_____	leave the theater
_____	stand in line
_____	buy a ticket
_____	watch a movie

G.

_____	find an old Halloween mask
_____	clean up your room
_____	sneak up on your brother
_____	put it on
_____	jump out at him

H.

_____	snap on the leash
_____	pull your dog back home
_____	get the leash
_____	whistle for your dog
_____	walk your dog

What's the Point?

Each paragraph has a series of sentences in a special order. The sentences work together to develop a single idea. Each of the sentences in a paragraph must relate to the main idea.

Cross out the idea in each list that does not relate to the main idea. The main idea is in boldface type.

1. **inside my house**

kitchen	football field
bedroom	bathroom
living room	attic

2. **colors**

red	yellow
blue	bird
green	purple

3. **countries**

Canada	Mexico
United States	Beverly Hills
France	Australia

4. **homework**

erasers	paper
fortune cookies	pencils
books	crayons

5. **tools**

screwdriver	diving board
hammer	saw
wrench	pliers

6. **food**

beans	spinach
towels	tomatoes
corn	bread

7. **sports**

soccer	tennis
baseball	basketball
scissors	golf

8. **animals**

dogs	cats
flowers	horses
cows	mice

9. **musical instruments**

piano	harmonica
tomato soup	guitar
drums	trumpet

10. **clothes**

jackets	spaghetti
pants	socks
sweaters	shirts

Extension: Choose one of the topics above and write an outline for a paragraph using four subtopics. For example . . .

Clothes

A. jackets
   1. sports jackets
   2. dressy jackets
B. pants
   1. leggings
   2. jeans
   3. dress pants

C. socks
   1. sweatsocks
   2. wool socks
D. sweaters
   1. _____
   2. _____

Writing Text for Pictures

Write a sentence under each picture that gives the main idea of the picture.

What's It About?

Draw a picture that shows the main idea of each paragraph.

The baby chicks began to hatch very slowly. We could see their tiny beaks poking through the cracked shells, and we could hear their tiny peeping. We held our breaths and watched with excitement with every crack they made. It would be so wonderful to see the chicks when they are fully hatched!

The three friends went camping and had a great time. Danny pitched the tent, and Carl hunted for firewood. Larry laid out all the supplies and made sure they were not disturbing any animal's home. Everyone helped, and that made the trip even better.

Practice on Main Idea

Read the paragraph below. Circle the details that help you find the main idea. Then color the magnifying glass that has the main idea that makes sense.

Clues At the Zoo

Juan and Julie want to work at the city zoo when they grow up. They read books about animals from all around the world so that they can learn about animals. Every Saturday, Julie and Juan visit the zoo around feeding time. It is interesting to see what the animals eat and how they feed their young. Many of the animals eat vegetables and fruits. Julie and Juan know that they must be good at science if they want to work at the zoo. Zoology is the science that deals with animals and animal life. A person who studies zoology is called a zoologist. A zoologist must be smart and hardworking.

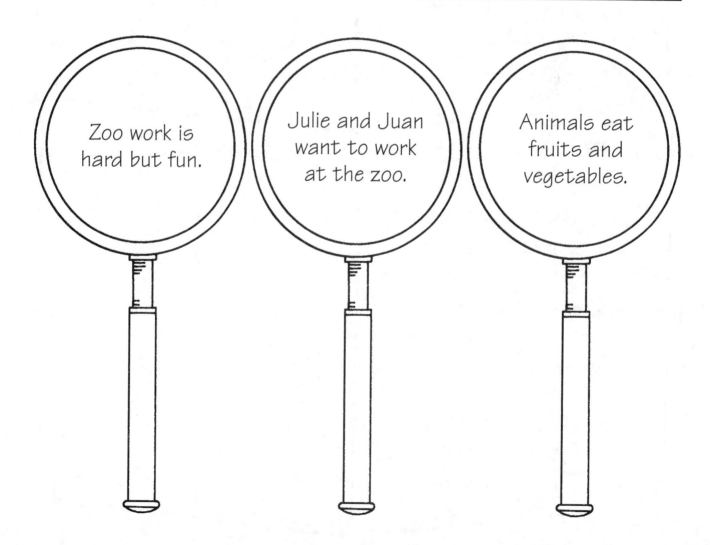

Zoo work is hard but fun.

Julie and Juan want to work at the zoo.

Animals eat fruits and vegetables.

Main Idea of a Paragraph

It is easy to write the main idea of a paragraph. Read the paragraph carefully and answer the three Ws. You do not need to use complete sentences here. Then make a good sentence out of your answers. Read your new sentence carefully to make sure it makes sense. Practice with the paragraph found below.

> Lola loved to watch the big, beautiful birds from South America. She stared at the parrots' bright green wings as the birds flew gracefully in their giant bird cage. Lola laughed when they called to each other with loud, squeaky voices. The parrots were Lola's favorite animals at the zoo.

1. Who? _____

2. What? _____

3 Why? _____

4. Write a sentence using your answers.

_____

_____

Check to make sure your sentence is complete.

1. Does your sentence make sense? ☐

2. Does it start with a capital letter? ☐

3. Does it end with a period? ☐

Main Idea Story Parts

Read each story and then write a sentence that best tells the main idea.

The students in Mrs. Lee's class were having a great time at the Riverside Zoo. As they were walking to visit the chimpanzees again, Mrs. Lee suddenly stopped. "Is anyone wearing a watch?" she asked. "I'm afraid that mine has stopped."

Amanda looked at her watch. "It's 1:40," she said.

Mrs. Lee's eyes opened wide. "Oh, no! We were supposed to meet Mrs. Miles' class at 1:30. We're late!"

Mrs. Lee and her students began running for the bus.

Main idea: _____

One of the penguins was ready to play. He waddled up the icy hill as fast as he could. Then he flopped onto his stomach and slid down. Some of the penguins were eating lunch. They swallowed the fish as quickly as the zookeeper could empty the big buckets of food. A few of the penguins were sleeping quietly.

The children watched the penguins for a long time. When it was time to leave the exhibit, all of the children were sad to go. Many of the children liked the penguins exhibit best.

Main idea: _____

Max

Read the story and then answer the questions.

A very young boy named Max visited the nature center last Monday. While he was there, several penguin eggs hatched. Max was one of the first people to see the baby penguins because he happened to be nearby when the babies were born. Max was very happy to be a part of this exciting event.

1. Who is the story about?

   _____

2. What does he do?

   _____

   _____

3. Why does he do this?

   _____

   _____

4. Use your answers to write a main idea sentence.

   _____

   _____

5. Draw a picture of the main idea.

George Washington

Read the story and then answer the questions.

One of the greatest leaders in American history is George Washington. He was a general in the Revolutionary War against the British. The people of the new nation were proud of the work he did during the war, and many people thought he would be the best person to lead the country as its first president. General Washington became president for eight years in all, and he is still remembered as an excellent leader.

1. Who is the paragraph about?

   _____

2. What is this person known as?

   _____

   _____

3. Why is this person known in this way?

   _____

   _____

4. Use your answers to write a main idea sentence.

   _____

   _____

5. Write a short paragraph with additional information that you have discovered about George Washington.

   _____

   _____

   _____

   _____

   _____

   _____

My Dream

Read the story and then answer the questions.

I had a dream last night that I was five inches tall. In my dream, I climbed down my bedpost and onto the floor. I walked right under my bed and across the room. It was a good thing my mom wasn't in the dream, because if she had seen everything stuffed under my bed, she would have made me clean my room! Instead, I walked over to my dollhouse and through the front door. Everything was just my size! I arranged all the furniture for a party, and I invited all my dolls to come over. We danced around the dollhouse, told jokes, and ate the cookies on my nightstand, left over from my bedtime snack. We had such a great time, I decided to live in the dollhouse forever. I went upstairs to the doll bedroom, and stretching out on the tiny bed, I fell asleep.

When I woke up from my dream, I smiled as I remembered it. Then I looked inside my dollhouse and wondered. How did those cookie crumbs get in there?

1. How does the girl get down from her bed? _____

_____

2. What is the girl glad her mother does not see? _____

_____

3. What does the girl do to get ready for the party? _____

_____

4. What do the partygoers eat? _____

_____

5. What surprises the girl when she wakes from her dream? _____

_____

The Big Game

Read the story and then answer the questions.

> Kenny couldn't wait. Today was the day, his big chance. For weeks he had been practicing every day, throwing to anyone who was willing. Now he would get to do what he had been preparing for since the season began. Today he would pitch in the big game!
>
> Kenny dressed excitedly and raced on his bicycle to the ballpark. His coach was already there, ready for warmups. The coach sent Kenny to the bullpen, and he began to throw. He could feel the excitement building with every pitch. Before he knew it, it was game time!
>
> While his teammates covered the bases and outfield, Kenny went to the mound. As the batter stepped into the box, Kenny knew he was ready. He threw his first pitch, a fastball that hit just inside the strike zone. "Strike!" the umpire called, and Kenny knew this would be his game.
>
> Nine innings later, Kenny found he was right! His team won, 12 to 8, and Kenny was named Most Valuable Player. It was a game to remember!

1. Why couldn't Kenny wait? _____

_____

2. What had Kenny been practicing? _____

_____

3. How did Kenny get to the ballpark? _____

_____

4. What did Kenny do first thing at the ballpark? _____

_____

5. What was Kenny named? _____

_____

Inferences

When you use clues to draw conclusions about things, you are making inferences. Read the short paragraph below and make an inference.

> "What a mess! It's raining cats and dogs out there! I could barely get through the flood in front of the walkway," Karly complained as she walked into the classroom, soaking wet.

Is Karly (1) happy about the rain, (2) annoyed about the rain, or (3) worried about the rain?

If you said annoyed, you are right. List three clues in the paragraph that tell you that Karly is annoyed.

1. _____

2. _____

3. _____

Now it is your turn. Write a short paragraph that shows Karly is either happy or worried about the rain.

_____

_____

_____

_____

_____

_____

_____

_____

_____

_____

_____

Making Inferences

Read the examples and answer the questions that follow each example.
(Remember, when you use clues to draw conclusions about things, you are inferring.)

"It sure is dark in here. Could we turn on some lights?" asked Wendy and Jack.

"The Fun House is too spooky!" said Jack as he walked through it.

"I'm ready to go on the Ferris wheel," said Wendy.

1. What can you infer? _____

_____

2. What clues did you find to prove you inferred correctly?

_____

_____

"I am not jealous of your new dress," said Mary. "I don't like that color on me anyway. My mother buys me more expensive things than that. I think the material looks like it would rip easily and not wash well. Where did you buy it? Was that the only one they had left?" asked Mary.

1. What can you infer? _____

_____

2. What clues did you find to prove you inferred correctly?

_____

_____

Marta and Janis

Read the story. Then use the lines under the story to write how the two friends are the same and how they are different from each other.

Marta and Janis are both eight years old. They have been best friends for two years, even though Marta does not speak much English. Marta is from Mexico. She speaks Spanish very well, a language that Janis does not understand. Marta is teaching Janis to speak Spanish, and Janis is helping Marta to speak better English.

Every afternoon, the girls do their homework together. They munch on their favorite snack, popcorn. Sometimes Janis has to bring her little brother along. He colors in his coloring book while the girls study. Marta loves little Pete, and she wishes she had a baby brother or sister.

After they finish their homework, Marta and Janis go to the city park. Marta takes her skates. She is a wonderful skater. Janis brings her scooter. She loves to ride. When Pete comes along, all the children swing and slide. They all enjoy that! It is good to have a best friend!

---

1. How are Marta and Janis alike?

_____

_____

_____

_____

_____

2. How are Marta and Janis different?

_____

_____

_____

_____

_____

Drawing Conclusions

Read the sentences below and then answer the questions.

Answer

1. I live on a farm. I have feathers and wings. I wake up the farm in the morning. What am I?	
2. You watch me in a large building. There are a screen and a projector. People eat popcorn and drink soda while I am playing. What am I?	
3. Some people use me to write, other people use me to play games, and many people use me to find information and to send messages to each other. I can be found in many homes and most businesses. What am I?	
4. I grow from the ground. I smell sweet. My stem has thorns, but I am beautiful. What am I?	
5. I make beautiful sounds. I have a long neck and strings. Some people use a pick to play me. They strum my strings, and the sound vibrates. What am I?	

What Next?

Finish the story below by drawing a cartoon and writing a conclusion.

"What's that?" Cindy asked as a bright light shone overhead.

"I don't know for sure, but I know it's not a helicopter or an airplane," Liz answered.

"Do you think it's dangerous?" Cindy wondered out loud.

"I don't want to stay around to find out!" Liz yelled as the bright light began to land.

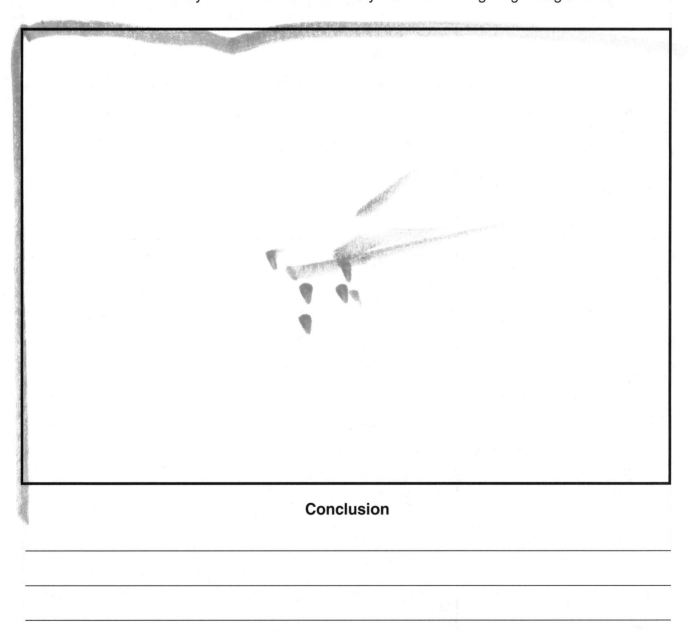

Conclusion

_____

_____

_____

_____

Cause and Effect

Everything that happens (**effect**) is caused by something else (**cause**). Read the effects in the first column. Write a cause in the second column.

Effect	Cause
1. spilled milk	
2. torn jeans	
3. trampled flowers	
4. flat tire	
7. happy children	
8. frustration	
9. coldness	
10. tiredness	
11. wealth	
12. peace	
13. tears	
14. illness	
15. friendship	

What's the Effect?

Whatever makes something happen is called the **cause**. Read the causes in the first column. Write a reasonable effect of each in the second column.

Cause	Effect
1. dog running through house	
2. children playing	
3. woman pruning flowers	
4. driving fast	
5. forgetting an appointment	
6. eating poorly	
7. watching eight hours of television	
8. wearing sandals and shorts on a cold day	
9. spending too much money	
10. oversleeping	
11. forgetting to return a book to the library	
12. losing your wallet	

Facts and Opinions

When you write a research paper, you must be very careful to stick to the facts. A research paper is written to give people information that is true or that can be proven true.
Is this a fact? **"France is the best place in the world to live."** Whether you agree or not, it is just someone's opinion. It is not a fact.

In the blanks before each sentence below, write **F** for fact or **O** for opinion.

Fact

Many plants have thorns.

_____ 1. The moon orbits the earth.

_____ 2. The moon is inspirational to all who see it.

_____ 3. A banana tastes disgusting.

_____ 4. A banana is a fruit.

_____ 5. Abraham Lincoln was killed.

_____ 6. Abraham Lincoln was the best president.

Opinion

Thorny plants are not good in gardens.

_____ 7. Canada has the most beautiful lakes in the world.

_____ 8. Canada has many lakes.

_____ 9. Red and yellow mixed together make orange.

_____ 10. Orange is the prettiest color.

Now write one fact and one opinion about your school.

1. Fact: _____

2. Opinion: _____

Evaluating Bias

Facts tell only what can be proven. Biased statements tell a person's **opinion**. Underline the biased statements below.

1. Lions roar loudly.

2. Pigs are the laziest of all animals.

3. Horses must be brushed often to keep them clean.

4. Dogs are better pets than cats.

5. The Riverside Zoo was built three years ago.

6. More than 400 animals live in the Riverside Zoo.

7. The Riverside Zoo is the best zoo in the world.

8. The emperor penguin is the most interesting animal to watch.

9. Snakes should not be allowed at the zoo because they frighten visitors.

10. Polar bears are large, white animals.

Tone

> The **tone** of a story is the feeling it has and the feeling it makes the reader have. A tone can be happy, sad, excited, fearful, or many others.

Word Bank

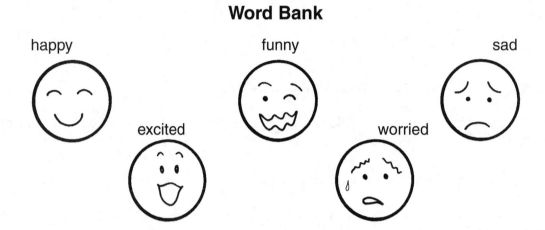

Read each group of sentences below. Then write the tone each group of sentences sets. Choose from the words in the word bank.

1. Wow! Today is my birthday. I know it will be a great day. We are having a chocolate cake and are playing lots of games. I can hardly wait until my friends arrive.

   Tone: _____

2. I can't believe my best friend is moving away. I want to cry. Even the sky looks gray and rainy today. Nothing will ever be the same without my friend.

   Tone: _____

3. Can a pig learn tricks? My pet pig, Sally, can roll over and shake hands. Or should I say shake snouts? She is a funny pig who really likes to "hog the show."

   Tone: _____

4. I can't believe our arithmetic test is today. I forgot to study, and I don't understand multiplication. I just know I will fail this test. This could ruin my math grade. Oh, why didn't I study last night?

   Tone: _____

5. It is a beautiful day today! The sun is shining, the birds are singing, and the air smells sweet and fresh. It feels good to be alive!

   Tone: _____

Identifying Tone

Read the sentences. Each one suggests a mood or feeling. This is called the **tone**. On the blanks, write the tone of each.

1. The sunset fell in beautiful shades of orange, pink, and yellow.

   _____

2. The children ran through the yard like puppies at play.

   _____

3. Rain ran down the windowsill while the twins watched, sighing and cupping their chins in their hands.

   _____

4. The fans went wild, shouting and stomping their feet while he rounded the bases for another home run.

   _____

5. The two bighorn sheep clashed their horns together angrily.

   _____

6. The tiny baby screamed and cried until she fell asleep.

   _____

7. The fingernails screeched loudly across the chalkboard.

   _____

8. Slam! The basketball swished through the hoop to make the winning point!

   _____

9. The roar of the engines drowned their voices as they tried to shout to each other at the racetrack.

   _____

10. Oh, I wish I had a million dollars!

   _____

Identifying the Speakers

Read the story and answer the questions below.

Tracy had a big surprise when he took the trash out one night. He saw a small, furry animal hanging upside down in the trash can. "Get out of there!" yelled Tracy.

"What is going on?" called his father.

"Raccoons are hunting in our garbage," said the boy. He went back into the house and got a broom to chase the raccoons away. But when he came back, the furry raccoons were already gone. "I guess I'd better make sure that the lid is on tightly," he said.

1. How many speakers are in the story? _____

2. Who are the speakers? _____

3. Who said that he should make sure that the lid was on tightly?

_____

4. How do you know Tracy is a boy? _____

_____

First-Person Voice

Read the entry in the diary below. The author, Ashley, recorded her thoughts and feelings. She used the words *I* and *me* often. When she reads her diary again, she will know that she means herself when she reads those pronouns. When you read something with the words *I* or *me*, meaning the author, that is written in what is called the **voice of the first person**. The diary entry below is written in the voice of the first person.

Dear Diary,

I wonder how the animals in the zoo feel when the weather is this cold? I worry that their fur and feathers will not keep them warm enough. It bothers me to think that the animals may be cold. Tomorrow I will ask my teacher about how animals keep warm.

Ashley

Put a check after the sentences below that are written in the first person.

1. I am happy about our trip to the zoo. _____

2. The three girls watched the polar bear dance. _____

3. The zookeeper let me hold the owl. _____

4. I could feel the smooth skin of the snake. _____

5. The old monkey fussed at the younger ones. _____

Third-Person Voice

Read the story below.

> Two kangaroos shared a cage at the zoo. Matilda kept her side of the cage as neat a pin. Elsie never picked up her belongings. Matilda often thought that Elsie was lazy about housekeeping, but she never fussed at Elsie about it. The two kangaroos lived peacefully together.

The author wrote about the kangaroos as if she were an invisible person in their cage. They did not know she was there, but she pretended to see and hear them all of the time. She could even pretend to know what they were thinking. When an author writes about someone else and pretends to know what he says, does, and thinks, the author is writing in the **voice of the third person**. Remember, when the author is the person speaking in the story, that is the **voice of the first person**. Write a **1** by the sentences written in the first person. Write a **3** by the sentences written in the third in person.

1. _____ The boys were excited about the new movie.

2. _____ I am anxious to go to the zoo.

3. _____ Please walk with me to the hippopotamus exhibit.

4. _____ Seven seals swam happily back and forth in the pool.

Pronoun Referents

Read each set of sentences. Notice the words in bold. They are pronouns.
Then answer the questions.

1. Alicia would like a new doll. **She** hopes to get one for her birthday.
   Who is she?

   _____

2. Luke and Chris are playing baseball. **They** want to become
   professional ball players one day. Who are they?

   _____

3. The movers came to take our furniture away. **They** will deliver it to
   our new house. Who are they?

   _____

4. I played with my dog, Sam, yesterday. **He** loves to play catch.
   Who is he?

   _____

5. **You and I** should go to the movies. There is a new movie we
   would really like to see. Who are we?

   _____

6. My computer is broken. **It** will not turn on when I push the power
   button. What is it?

   _____

7. Tom and his sisters went next door to play. **He** was told to keep
   an eye on **them**. Who is he? Who does them refer to?

   _____

   _____

Idioms

Idioms are expressions whose meanings are different from the literal ones. Explain what the idioms below actually mean.

1. When Angelica said, "That movie **took my breath away**," she meant _____
   _____

2. "When Dad finally **put his foot down**, my brother started to do better in school," said
   Boris. What Boris meant was _____
   _____

3. Dana stood and said, "I guess I'll **hit the road** now." What Dana meant was
   _____

4. When Mario said that he was a bit **under the weather** last weekend, he meant that
   _____

5. When Nicholas said that he **slept like a log** last night, he meant _____
   _____

6. "I'll be **in the doghouse** for sure," exclaimed Roberto. What Roberto really meant was
   _____

7. "**Hold your horses**," remarked the police officer. The police officer meant _____
   _____

8. When Ryan asked Patricia, "Are you **getting cold feet**?" he was actually asking
   _____

9. If Grandpa loves **to spin a yarn**, he _____
   _____

10. When Leslie says that she is **in the dark** about what's going on, she means
    _____

More Idioms

Idioms are expressions with meanings which are different from the literal ones. Explain what the idioms below actually mean.

1. Dinner's on the house. _____

    _____

2. John got up on the wrong side of the bed. _____

    _____

3. My cousin has a green thumb. _____

    _____

4. Money burns a hole in my pocket. _____

    _____

5. He should mend fences before leaving. _____

    _____

6. Cathy didn't have the hang of it yet. _____

    _____

7. Mother told us to straighten up the house. _____

    _____

8. Dad always gets up with the chickens. _____

    _____

9. The sick child wasn't out of the woods yet. _____

    _____

10. Crystal was down in the dumps all day. _____

    _____

Analogies

Analogies are comparisons. Complete each analogy below.

Example: <u>Ear</u> is to <u>hearing</u> as <u>eye</u> is to <u>seeing</u>.

1. Cardinals is to St. Louis as Dodgers is to _____

2. A.M. is to before noon as P.M. is to _____

3. Three is to triangle as eight is to _____

4. Tear is to tore as see is to _____

5. Springfield is to Illinois as Austin is to _____

6. Carpet is to floor as bedspread is to _____

7. Go is to green as stop is to _____

8. Purple is to grapes as red is to _____

9. Ghost is to Halloween as bunny is to _____

10. Son is to dad as daughter is to _____

11. Jelly is to toast as syrup is to _____

12. Ear is to hear as eye is to _____

13. Oink is to pig as cluck is to _____

14. Mississippi River is to U.S. as Nile River is to _____

15. Clock is to time as thermometer is to _____

16. V is to 5 as C is to _____

17. Up is to down as ceiling is to _____

18. Car is to driver as plane is to _____

19. Sleep is to tired as eat is to _____

20. Bird is to nest as bee is to _____

More Analogies

Analogies are comparisons. Complete each analogy below. An example has been done for you.

Example: <u>Kangaroo</u> is to <u>joey</u> as <u>bear</u> is to <u>cub</u>.

1. See is to eye as _____ is to nose.

2. Ping-Pong® is to paddle as _____ is to racquet.

3. Bob is to Robert as Liz is to _____.

4. Writer is to story as poet is to _____ .

5. Car is to _____ as plane is to pilot.

6. Kennedy is to John as _____ is to Theodore.

7. Glove is to hand as boot is to _____ .

8. Hammer is to _____ as pen is to writer.

9. Bear is to _____ as bee is to hive.

10. _____ is to picture as curtain is to window.

11. Sing is to song as _____ is to book.

12. _____ are to teeth as contact lenses are to eyes.

13. Left is to _____ as top is to bottom.

14. _____ is to pool as jog is to road.

15. Wrist is to hand as _____ is to foot.

16. Hammer is to nail as _____ is to screw.

17. Paw is to dog as _____ is to fish.

18. Meat is to beef as _____ is to apple.

19. _____ is to pig as neigh is to horse.

20. Princess is to _____ as prince is to king.

                                                           #3646 Practice and Learn

Still More Analogies

Analogies are comparisons. Complete each analogy below. An example has been done for you.

Example: <u>Wide</u> is to <u>narrow</u> as <u>tall</u> is to <u>short</u>.

1. Big is to _____ as large is to small.

2. Hat is to head as shoe is to _____ .

3. Bird is to nest as _____ is to hive.

4. Rug is to _____ as curtain is to window.

5. _____ is to road as boat is to lake.

6. Boy is to man as _____ is to woman.

7. _____ is to room as gate is to yard.

8. Sleep is to tired as _____ is to hungry.

9. Zoo is to animals as library is to _____ .

10. Floor is to _____ as ceiling is to top.

11. _____ is to grass as blue is to sky.

12. Belt is to _____ as bracelet is to wrist.

13. Car is to driver as airplane is to _____ .

14. Book is to _____ as television is to watch.

15. Grape is to vine as peach is to _____ .

16. Ear is to hearing as _____ is to seeing.

17. _____ is to day as dusk is to dawn.

18. Thanksgiving is to November as Christmas is to _____ .

19. Calf is to cow as _____ is to lion.

20. _____ is to uncle as niece is to aunt.

All Together Now

Each set of words belongs to a different group. Classify the group by writing its name on the blank.

1. Easter, Yom Kippur, and Thanksgiving are _____.

2. Shawna, Kate, and Mariella are _____.

3. Denmark, Greece, and Cuba are _____.

4. Bananas, apples, and strawberries are_____.

5. Cows, chickens, and sheep are _____.

6. Violet, plum, and lavender are _____.

7. Pencils, pens, and markers are_____.

8. Goofy, Mickey, and Donald are _____.

9. Clowns, trapeze artists, and the ringmaster are _____.

10. Stanford, Princeton, and Yale are _____.

11. Nile, Colorado, and Thames are _____.

12. East, south, and northwest are _____.

13. "Little Boy Blue," "Mary Had a Little Lamb," and "Little Miss Muffet" are _____.

14. Van Gogh, Michaelangelo, and Da Vinci are_____.

15. Lincoln, Kennedy, and Reagan are _____.

16. Three, fourteen, and twenty-nine _____.

17. A, Q, and Z are _____.

18 Donut, cookie, and pie are _____.

19. Jones, Lopez, and Chang are _____.

20. Hammer, saw, and wrench are _____.

Categories

Place the following words in each of the categories below. There are seven for each.

bassoon	harp	peccary	sloth
carnation	impatiens	meerkat	snipe
strawberry	iris	phoebe	sweet William
cello	kayaking	pineapple	triathlon
crocus	lacrosse	Ping-Pong	toucan
cummerbund	loganberry	poncho	trousers
flute	mandolin	primrose	trumpet
football	mango	quetzal	tux
gardenia	moccasin	quince	violin
gown	papaya	rugby	
guava	parka	soccer	

Animals

_____
_____
_____
_____
_____
_____
_____

Fruits

_____
_____
_____
_____
_____
_____
_____

Flowers

_____
_____
_____
_____
_____
_____
_____

Sports

_____
_____
_____
_____
_____
_____
_____

Instruments

_____
_____
_____
_____
_____
_____
_____

Clothing

_____
_____
_____
_____
_____
_____
_____

Get Rid of the Details

Read the paragraph below. It has too many details to be a summary. You must decide which words or phrases are not important enough to be in a short summary. Cross out the words or phrases that are not important details. To create a summarizing paragraph, copy the sentences and words you did not cross out.

Every animal has babies. Sometimes the mother takes care of the baby until it can take care of itself. Baby animals are cute. Sometimes the whole group of animals care for the babies. Baby bears are called cubs. The cubs like to eat honey. Baby animals must eat. Mothers and fathers protect their babies. Some baby animals, like kangaroos, live in pouches. Other baby animals travel on their mothers' backs. Possums and monkeys carry babies on their backs. Baby animals are fun to watch.

Summary

_____

_____

_____

_____

_____

_____

_____

_____

Summarize

Read the paragraph and then follow the directions below.

Butterflies are beautiful insects. They flutter around in the spring air. They rest upon the tulips and daisies. Butterflies can be dark brown, bright yellow, orange, blue, or any number of colors. They begin life as caterpillars. Then, they spin silky covers called cocoons. Inside the cocoon, the caterpillar turns into a butterfly. Butterflies help to spread pollen from one flower to another, so butterflies are helpful as well as beautiful.

You can shorten a paragraph through summarizing. When you summarize, you include the main idea and the most important details, leaving out everything else. Summarize the paragraph above.

_____

_____

_____

_____

_____

_____

_____

_____

_____

Practice Summarizing

Write a paragraph about your favorite animal. You can use the facts from your science book or an encyclopedia. Be sure to begin each sentence with a capital letter and end each sentence with a period.

_____

_____

_____

_____

_____

_____

_____

Write two sentences that summarize your paragraph. Give the main idea and the most important details.

_____

_____

_____

Your Day

On the blanks, write everything you can remember doing today in chronological order (beginning with waking up).

_____   _____

_____   _____

_____   _____

_____   _____

_____   _____

_____   _____

Now, take what you wrote above, and group the ideas together under three or four headings (such as "getting ready" or "being at school"). Write your group headings here.

_____   _____

_____   _____

_____   _____

Finally, write a summary of your day, using your group names. Write the summary in no more than three sentences.

_____

_____

_____

_____

_____

_____

Pick a Part

Read a book and describe your favorite parts.

The part that was the funniest was _____

_____

_____

_____

The part that was the saddest was _____

_____

_____

_____

The part that was the most unbelievable was _____

_____

_____

_____

The part I liked best was _____

_____

because _____

_____

_____

Read All About It

Find an article that you think is interesting in a newspaper or magazine. Read the article and then answer these questions.

What is the topic of the article?

_____

_____

_____

_____

What new things did you learn about the topic?

_____

_____

_____

_____

What else would you like to learn about the topic?

_____

_____

_____

_____

Why is this article interesting?

_____

_____

_____

_____

Character Web

You can see this is a special kind of web. It is a **character web.**

Read a book. Draw a picture of the main character in the center circle. In each of the spaces, answer the question about the character.

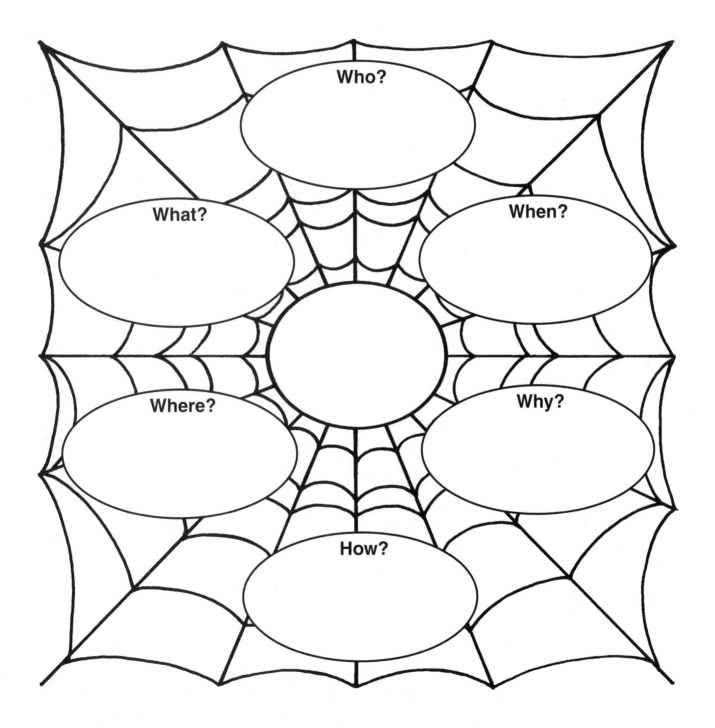

Complete the Sentences

Sentences begin with capital letters and end with a period, exclamation point, or question mark. Every sentence must also have a subject and a predicate. Here are some incomplete sentences. Complete them, being sure to add punctuation at the end.

1. Sandy cried when she _____

_____

2. The best place in the world to _____

_____

3. Who can _____

_____

4. I wish I had _____

_____

5. There aren't many _____

_____

6. This is the best _____

_____

7. It's times like this that _____

_____

8. When are you going to _____

_____

9. I can't believe _____

_____

10. It was the _____

_____

Write a Sentence

Write a sentence for each picture.

1. _____

   _____

2. _____

   _____

   _____

3. _____

   _____

4. _____

   _____

5. _____

   _____

6. _____

   _____

7. _____

   _____

8. _____

   _____

Start with a Noun and a Verb

Draw a line to match each noun to a verb. (**Note:** Change the tense of each verb to best fit each sentence.)

Nouns	Verbs
children	climb
squirrel	sleep
sun	blare
orchestra	run
wind	crumble
television	shout
father	shine
teenager	color
horse	play
paint	blow

Write a sentence for each noun-verb pair.

1. _____

2. _____

3. _____

4. _____

5. _____

6. _____

7. _____

8. _____

9. _____

10. _____

Sentence Expansions

The sentences below are complete because they each have a subject and a predicate. However, they are the simplest sentences possible. Add words to each sentence to make it more interesting.

1. Vine climbed. _____

_____

2. Cat leapt. _____

_____

3. Cake burned. _____

_____

4. Donkey brayed._____

_____

5. Toddler fell. _____

_____

6. Lightning struck. _____

_____

7. Mother called._____

_____

8. Truck stopped. _____

_____

What Do You Think?

You have learned that every sentence must begin with a capital letter and end with a period, question mark, or exclamation point. You have also learned that a sentence must be a complete thought. A sentence needs to have enough information to make sense. It needs to ask you a complete question or tell you a complete idea. There are 10 incomplete sentences on this page. Rewrite the sentences to make them complete.

1. Jennifer wants to

   _____

2. Yesterday, while it was raining, I

   _____

3. Do you

   _____

4. all the way down the hill

   _____

5. is very annoying

   _____

6. I wish I had

   _____

7. Did they try

   _____

8. Watch out for the

   _____

9. is a big, scary monster

   _____

10. jumped into the spaghetti

   _____

Word Muncher

Here are some sentences that are missing subjects or predicates. Choose a subject or predicate from the box to complete each sentence. Then, on the line before each number, write a **P** if you added a predicate or an **S** if you added a subject to the sentence. The first one is done for you.

The following subjects and predicates may be used more than once.

My teacher	An ugly grasshopper	fell on my toe.
The mail carrier	The tree	is growling.
My kitten	has an attitude.	is singing in an opera.
has a cute little hat.	is crying.	is really an alien.
A ladybug	climbs on the furniture.	is covered in stripes.
Uncle Gerald	is lost in space.	was under the house.
My sister	Dinner	is as big as Australia.
A cute little baby	My bed	is a spy.
A suitcase	drove over the hills	The doctor
is very gross.	ran on the playground.	floats away.
is drooling.	snores.	is purple with polka dots.

___S___ 1. _____My Kitten_____ sat on the birthday cake.

_____ 2. _____ ate worms for breakfast.

_____ 3. Laurie _____ .

_____ 4. _____ slipped on a banana peel.

_____ 5. Mrs. Crabapple _____ .

_____ 6. _____ is a big, hairy beast.

_____ 7. A giant elephant _____ .

_____ 8. My little brother _____ .

_____ 9. The grizzly bear _____ .

_____ 10. _____ is very heavy.

_____ 11. _____ has the measles.

_____ 12. A jet plane _____ .

_____ 13. _____ is green.

_____ 14. My science book _____ .

_____ 15. _____ is growing blue fur.

Combining Sentences

Combine these simple sentences into compound sentences. **Compound sentences** will combine two or more complete sentences by using commas and conjunctions.

1. Liz and Tanya are best friends. They do everything together. They want to be sisters.

   _____

   _____

2. Michael has three favorite sports. He likes to play baseball. He likes to play basketball. He likes to bowl.

   _____

   _____

   _____

3. You can do many things with a computer. You can use it to write. You can use a computer to play games. You can use a computer to create art.

   _____

   _____

   _____

4. The tiger walked through the savanna. She was looking for food. She wanted to feed her young.

   _____

   _____

5. The children were out of school for the day. They played a game together. They had fun.

   _____

   _____

6. Two fish live in the fishbowl. There are colorful rocks and a small castle in the fishbowl. The fish swim through the castle.

   _____

   _____

   _____

Get to the Point

In the paragraph below, cross out the sentences that are not related to the main idea.

I love food, but I do not like to cook. First of all, I am not very good at cooking. I cut myself, I burn food, and I spill things that stain all my clothes. My clothes are nice things that cost most of my money, even though I usually get them on sale. The other day I stained a nice, corduroy shirt which made me really mad. It was robin's egg blue. Then there is something about the ingredients that is a great mystery to me. I usually like mysteries—in fact, I check out mysteries each week at the library. I can follow a recipe very closely, but it never comes out right. The food might be too salty, too sweet, or just too weird. And then there's the mess. I need to clean up my room, too. It is such a big mess right now. The food sticks to pots and pans and stains the sink. There is a really strange stain on the ceiling in the hallway; it looks like an octopus. The floor, the dog, and I get covered in flour or onion juice. When I get finished with all that labor, I'm anxious to taste my masterpiece, but it is always a disappointment, and there are so many dishes that I don't have time to go out and get something really good to eat! I should just give up cooking altogether!

Rewrite the corrected paragraph on the lines below.

_____

_____

_____

_____

_____

_____

_____

_____

_____

_____

How About a Little Help?

A topic sentence does not work alone to explain the main idea of a paragraph. **Helping sentences**, also known as **body sentences** or **supporting sentences**, work to help the topic sentence. They help make the main idea clear.

There are four main ideas listed on this page. In the word bank below, find the helping or supporting ideas for each main idea. The main idea would be included in your topic sentence. The helping ideas would be included in your body sentences.

Word Bank		
lemons	ovens	frying pans
tires	dandelions	bumpers
ears	knees	thumbs
refrigerators	steering wheels	bananas

1. Main Idea: **car parts**

   Supporting Ideas: _____

   _____

   _____

2. Main Idea: **kitchen things**

   Supporting Ideas: _____

   _____

   _____

3. Main Idea: **body parts**

   Supporting Ideas: _____

   _____

   _____

4. Main Idea: **yellow things**

   Supporting Ideas: _____

   _____

   _____

Extension: Take the four categories above and write four paragraphs, each with a topic sentence and three supporting sentences.

Missing Parts

Here is a paragraph that is missing some parts. The three reasons that support the topic sentence are missing. Can you fill them in? Be sure to use complete sentences.

I would not like to lose my favorite toy for three reasons. The first reason is_____

_____

_____

Another reason is _____

_____

_____

Finally, if I lost my favorite toy, _____

_____

I want to keep my favorite toy!

     ✦   ✦   ✦   ✦   ✦   ✦   ✦

Try writing another paragraph.

I should receive an "A" on this assignment for three reasons. _____

_____

_____

_____

_____

_____

_____

Extension: Try some more on a separate piece of paper:

- I would like to build a fort in my backyard for three reasons.
- My (sister/brother/cousin/friend) is from another planet, and there are four items of evidence to prove this.
- I (do, do not) like cats for four reasons.
- There are three reasons I (would, would not) eat a snail—even for one hundred dollars.

And Then . . .

Sentences in paragraphs need to make sense with each other. They need to be connected. The words that help connect ideas between sentences are called **transitions**. These transitions help make your writing easier to understand.

Using the transitions in the parentheses, connect the sentences below. Write the new sentences in paragraph form. Be sure to indent and make sense.

1. I'll eat a salad.

   I feel like eating a hot, cheesy pizza.

   I've been eating too many pizzas lately.

   (**however**, **so**, **today**)

   Today, I feel like eating a hot, cheesy pizza.

   However,_____

   so _____

   _____

2. She made me do my homework.

   My mother rushed in and unplugged my stereo.

   I was enjoying music in my room.

   (**suddenly**, **after that**)

   _____

   _____

   _____

   _____

3. I sprinkle everything with nuts.

   I pour fudge or strawberry sauce over the scoops.

   I love to make ice-cream sundaes.

   I scoop ice cream into bowls.

   (**first**, **then**, **finally**)

   _____

   _____

   _____

   _____

Extension: Using old newspapers or magazines, look at paragraphs and see what kinds of transitions are used to make the writing smoother. Use a highlighter to mark the transitions. Listen to the radio or television news. In these programs they call transitions segues ("segways"). Listen for segues and write down your favorites.

This Is the Story

One kind of paragraph is called *narrative*. A **narrative paragraph** gives the details of an experience or event in story form. It explains what happens in a natural time order. You have probably written a narrative paragraph before, but you just didn't know what to call it. You have definitely spoken a narrative paragraph. On the first day of school, you probably went home and told someone all about it in chronological order. In each of the paragraphs below, choose one of the main ideas in parentheses or use one of your own. Use another piece of paper if you need more room.

The first time I ever (*rode a bike, cooked, babysat)* was a total disaster.

First, _____

_____

Next, _____

_____

Then, _____

_____

Finally,_____

_____

◆   ◆   ◆   ◆   ◆   ◆   ◆

I had never been (*more embarrassed, more angry, more excited*) in my life!

_____

_____

_____

_____

_____

_____

◆   ◆   ◆   ◆   ◆   ◆   ◆

On (*my first day at school, my last birthday, my last vacation*), I_____

_____

_____

_____

_____

_____

_____

_____

Start Explaining

One type of paragraph is the *expository paragraph*. **Expository writing** gives facts, explains ideas, or gives directions. Below are some expository paragraph topics. Choose one and on the lines below, write one paragraph for the topic that you choose.

❑ Explain how you wash your hair.

❑ Give the facts about your favorite baseball team.

❑ Explain how you make a peanut butter sandwich.

❑ Explain how to ride a bike.

❑ Tell what abilities are needed to participate in your favorite sport.

❑ Explain how to write a poem.

❑ Tell why you like hamburgers.

_____

_____

_____

_____

_____

_____

_____

_____

_____

_____

_____

Give Us a Description

Another kind of paragraph is the *descriptive paragraph*. A **descriptive paragraph** gives a clear picture of a person, place, idea, or thing. Think of the word picture whenever you are writing a descriptive paragraph. Your writing needs to make a word picture. A good way to make a word picture is to use as many of the five senses as you can in your description.

Imagine that you have gone to a strange new mall with your family. You turn to look at something, and when you look back your family is no longer in view. Everywhere you look there are strangers in an unfamiliar mall. You feel anxious and a little bit afraid. Fill in the lines below with descriptions.

❑ What do you see?

_____

_____

❑ What do you hear?

_____

_____

❑ What do you smell?

_____

_____

❑ What do you touch?

_____

_____

❑ What do you taste?

_____

_____

❑ How do you feel?

_____

_____

On another piece of paper, write a descriptive paragraph about what you are experiencing and how you are feeling. Use details to describe your main idea. Be sure to use the things you described above to write your paragraph.

I Will Convince You

A **persuasive paragraph** is what you write when you express an opinion and try to convince the reader that your opinion is correct. Think of how you try to persuade a parent to buy your favorite cereal or a new pair of shoes that you are convinced you must have. You may be convinced, but you will need to work hard to persuade others. To persuade, you will need lots of *examples, details*, and *evidence to prove your point.*

Here is an example of a persuasive paragraph.

> Everybody needs to have a pet. Have you ever noticed that people who do not have pets are grouchier than those who do? If they were greeted whenever they came home by a furry creature thrilled to see them, they would be a lot less grouchy. A pet is affectionate and a good companion. Pets like to snuggle and be with people. Also, pets are always positive. If you give them a special treat, they act as if you've given them the world's largest diamond or the fastest car. They shudder with joy, leap, and prance. If you've had a hard day, they still greet you with enthusiasm. They don't care what you do. You can be a complete failure, and they still treat you as if you are a king or queen. Pets love you unconditionally. If you forget to feed them, they forgive you the moment you remember. Pets are also good safety devices. They can scare away strangers. They can warn you if there is a fire or something wrong inside or outside the house. All they ask in return is a bag of food, some water, and some TLC (tender, loving care). If everybody had a pet, everybody would go around smiling.

Choose a topic below or create your own topic and, on a separate piece of paper, write a persuasive paragraph. Remember to be as convincing as you can.

- ❏ Pets are a waste of time and money.
- ❏ We should continue to explore space.
- ❏ Space exploration is not a good use of our money.
- ❏ Libraries are invaluable.
- ❏ Bookstores are better than libraries.
- ❏ People should always have dessert.
- ❏ Desserts should be banned.
- ❏ Everybody should play a sport.
- ❏ Sports are overrated.
- ❏ Jewelry is fun.
- ❏ Jewelry is expensive.

- ❏ Students should wear uniforms to school.
- ❏ Students should be allowed to dress the way they want.
- ❏ We should have more zoos.
- ❏ We should do away with zoos.
- ❏ More people should be eating vegetables.
- ❏ Vegetables should be banned from the earth.
- ❏ Amusement parks should be free.
- ❏ People need to pay to get into amusement parks.

In My Opinion . . .

An **opinion paragraph** is similar to a persuasive paragraph. In each, you have a point to make. With an opinion paragraph, you need to focus on your opinion, state what you think about something, and support your point with your reasons for having such an opinion. You don't need to convince the reader that you are right. You do need to be clear enough that the reader understands why you have the opinion. For practice, fill in the blanks below to complete this opinion paragraph.

There are several reasons why I (like, dislike) spiders. First, _____

_____

_____

Second, _____

_____

_____.

The most important reason why I _____ spiders is

_____

_____.

Therefore, _____

_____

_____.

Write an opinion paragraph below about an important belief or opinion you have. Your opinion will be your topic sentence. Then support your belief with strong reasons, saving the most important reason for last. Finally, sum up your opinion in the last sentence. (Some ideas for your opinion paragraph are *war, allowance, homework, religion, birthdays, equal rights, families, violence,* and *television.*)

_____

_____

_____

_____

_____

_____

_____

_____

Define This!

A **definitive paragraph** is a very important piece of writing because when we define things, we help others to understand our writing, our viewpoint, our opinion, and the point we wish to make. Usually when people think of a definition, they think of the dictionary. That's fine. Dictionaries are important and necessary, but do not use one for this activity. Instead, look inside your imagination and see if you can create a personal definition for each word below. Keep these questions in mind to help you write your definitions.

1. **What is it?**

2. **What does it look like?**

3. **How does it feel?**

4. **What does it smell like?**

5. **Does it have a sound?**

6. **What does it do?**

7. **How is it used?**

8. **How does it make me feel?**

9. **Does it have a purpose?**

10. **What thing or things is it completely different from or similar to?**

Now, do your best to complete the following beginning definitions. Each one will take several sentences to do a good job.

A shoe is_____

_____

_____

_____

A watermelon is _____

_____

_____

_____

Happiness is _____

_____

_____

_____

_____

_____

When I Grow Up

What kind of a career do you want to have when you grow up? There are many career ideas on this page. Choose one of these ideas or one of your own that you would like for a career. Write a paragraph about your choice.

❑ farmer   ❑ forest ranger
❑ architect   ❑ doctor
❑ teacher   ❑ engineer
❑ juggler   ❑ astronaut
❑ nurse   ❑ animal trainer
❑ musician   ❑ builder
❑ police officer   ❑ writer
❑ baseball player   ❑ lawyer
❑ clown   ❑ manager
❑ artist   ❑ designer
❑ actor   ❑ photographer
❑ pilot   ❑ firefighter
❑ computer scientist   ❑ filmmaker
❑ veterinarian   ❑ chef

My Career

I would like to be _____

for three reasons. The first reason is_____

_____

Another reason is _____

_____.

Finally, I would like to be _____

_____

because _____

_____

_____

_____

Sticky Glue

You placed your assignment on the table. You did not know that the table had sticky-icky glue on it. When you picked up your paragraph, ugh! Now you will need to rewrite it. First, choose your topic.

I learned how to . . .(*rollerskate, rollerblade, bicycle, sew, surf, ski, eat an artichoke, skateboard, paint, ride a horse, plant a garden, snowboard, bake cookies, etc.*).

Now rewrite your sticky assignment by completing the following parts that are still "readable."

I just learned how to _____

_____!

The first thing I did was _____

_____.

Next, I _____

_____.

After that, I_____

_____.

Finally, I _____

_____.

_____ is easy now!

Paragraph Starters

Use these paragraph starters when you need inspiration while practicing paragraph writing. You might want to use some of these ideas for writing an essay, a report, or a story.

Gorillas make good pets.	If I were my teacher, here are three things I would do.
There are many uses for popcorn.	It's a good idea for all students to invite the principal to dinner.
Collecting bugs is an interesting hobby.	Kids should be allowed to drive when they are 10 years old.
There are many things shaped like a circle.	There are lots of reasons why I am glad to be a member of my family.
I would like to be invisible.	I really like math (science, English, social studies, etc.).
I have three favorite foods.	I should have my own room.
I know my brother (sister) is an alien.	I deserve a raise in my allowance.
I would like to join the circus.	Eating is one of my favorite activities.
If I could stop time, there are three things I would do.	We should remember to wash our hands.
I would make a great president.	I would like to visit Mars.
I would like a giraffe for a pet.	It's a good idea to learn a foreign language.
It would be a good idea to build a roller-coaster in my backyard.	I love music.
Airplanes are not a good idea.	I would like to remodel my house.

Getting Your Paragraph Organized

Use this form to help you organize your paragraphs. Write a topic sentence in the circle at the top. Write three supporting ideas in the rectangles. Write your conclusion sentence in the triangle. Use these sentences to build your paragraph, adding any other words and details that you need to make it complete.

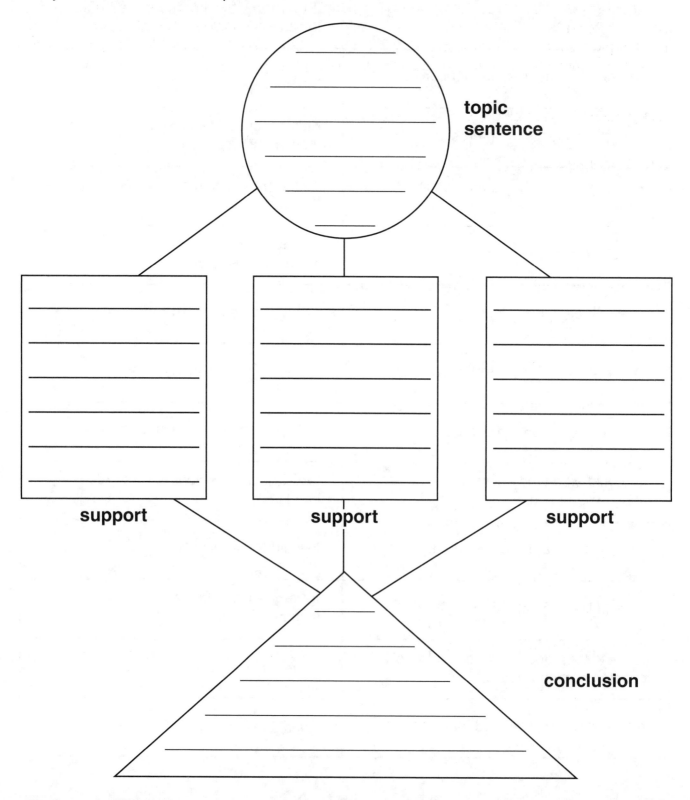

Writing by Sense

One of the best ways to write descriptively is to use your senses. Think about how something looks, smells, sounds, tastes, and feels, and then write about it, keeping those senses in mind. For example, instead of writing, "The flower smells nice," you can write, "The sweet nectar of the flowers tickles my nose." This gives an idea of exactly how the flower smells. For another example, instead of writing, "The puppies are cute," write, "The playful puppies roll over each other and tumble into a ball of fur and pink noses." This gives an idea of exactly how the puppies look. Sentences that use the senses to describe are much more interesting to read, and they make the images seem real for the reader.

Follow each direction below to write a sentence using sense writing.

1. Describe how a skyscraper **looks**._____

_____

_____

2. Describe how a freshly mowed lawn **smells**._____

_____

_____

3. Describe how a yipping dog **sounds**. _____

_____

_____

4. Describe how a lemon **tastes**. _____

_____

_____

5. Describe how a kitten **feels**._____

_____

_____

Similes

A **simile** is a figure of speech in which two things are compared by using the words *like* or *as*, such as in "The ice was as smooth as glass." Complete the following similes.

1. As deep as _____

2. As dark as _____

3. As hard as _____

4. As quiet as _____

5. As flat as_____

6. As sweet as _____

7. As silly as _____

8. As hot as _____

9. As soft as _____

10. As slow as _____

11. As strong as _____

12. As cold as_____

13. As loud as_____

14. As clear as _____

15. As bright as _____

More Similes

A **simile** is a figure of speech in which two unlike things are compared using the words *like* or *as*. (**Example:** He moved as quick as a wink.) Complete the following common similes.

1. As fresh as _____

2. As white as _____

3. As wise as _____

4. As fit as _____

5. As tall as _____

6. As lazy as _____

7. As hard as _____

8. As stubborn as _____

9. As cute as _____

10. As black as _____

11. As blind as _____

12. As happy as _____

13. As cool as _____

14. As stiff as _____

15. As clean as _____

16. As limp as _____

17. As busy as _____

18. As light as _____

19. As good as _____

20. As pretty as _____

Metaphors

Metaphors compare two different things without using *like* or *as*. (**Example:** His feet are giant boulders.) Use comparison words to complete the metaphors.

1. The clown is a _____

2. The bird is a _____

3. The elephant is a _____

4. The falcon is a _____

5. The moon was _____

6. The snow was _____

7. The baby was _____

8. The game was _____

9. The thunder and lightning were _____

10. The field was _____

11. The sand is _____

12. The river is _____

13. The grandparents were _____

14. The dress is _____

15. That hat is _____

Writing Stories in Parts

Use the next two pages to create a story about one of the following topics. Write the story in three parts: introduction, body, and conclusion.

- The Day That I Got Lost

- My Pet Saved the Day

- When I Grow Up

- Best Friends Have an Adventure

- My Adventures in Space

- The Most Unforgettable Day of My Life

Part One: introduction or beginning

_____

_____

_____

_____

_____

_____

Part Two: body or middle of the story

_____

_____

_____

_____

_____

_____

_____

Writing Stories in Parts (cont.)

Part Two (*cont.*):

_____

_____

_____

_____

Part Three: conclusion or ending of story

_____

_____

_____

_____

_____

Check yourself.

1. Did you begin the story with an attention-getter? ☐

2. In the beginning did you tell who was in the story? ☐

3. Did you give lots of details in the middle? ☐

4. Did you bring the story to a close in the ending? ☐

5. Did you check your spelling? ☐

6. Did you write neatly? ☐

Story Time!

Can you use your imagination to make a flow chart for a story? A story about a fierce dragon is started for you. Make up the rest of the story about this dragon. The last box is your ending. Write your words in the boxes on the left and draw some pictures in the boxes on the right that will go with your words.

Once upon a time, there was a very fierce dragon.	
The End	

Circus Balloon

Finish the story below. Use good descriptive words in your story.

A man from the circus filled the boy's large, red balloon with helium and tied it to a long, white string. The boy held the string tight in his hand and walked over to see the enormous, gray elephant. All of a sudden, a brisk wind . . .

_____

_____

_____

_____

_____

_____

_____

_____

_____

_____

Dreams

Describe a dream that you once had and draw a picture to go with it. Be sure to write complete sentences with subjects and predicates.

What a Success!

Imagine that one day you become very famous. Write a story about the success that brings you fame. Give your story a title. In the story, explain how and why you became famous. Also tell about what other important things you might do in the future.

_____

_____

_____

_____

_____

_____

_____

_____

_____

_____

_____

_____

_____

_____

_____

_____

_____

_____

_____

_____

_____

Draw the Antonyms

Antonyms are words that have opposite meanings.

Draw two pictures to illustrate each antonym pair.

wet, dry	day, night
happy, sad	few, many
big, little	cry, laugh

I Spy Homophones

Homonyms are words that sound alike
but are spelled differently.
Use the clues below to supply
the missing homophone pairs.

Example: *Hare* and *hair* are homophones.

You can use them to solve the first
problem.

1. a rabbit and something on your head

    _____   _____

2. belongs to us and a measurement of time

    _____   _____

3. used to make bread and a female deer

    _____   _____

4. opposite of yes and to understand

    _____   _____

5. past tense of read and a color

    _____   _____

6. a story and the end of a dog

    _____   _____

Letter Review

Trace the letters and then practice them on your own.

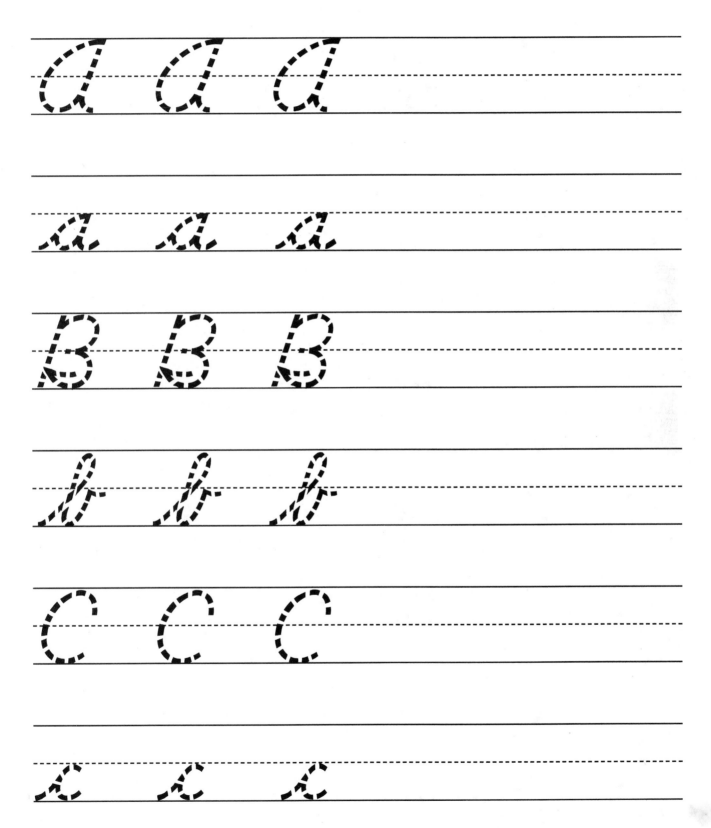

Letter Review (cont.)

Trace the letters and then practice them on your own.

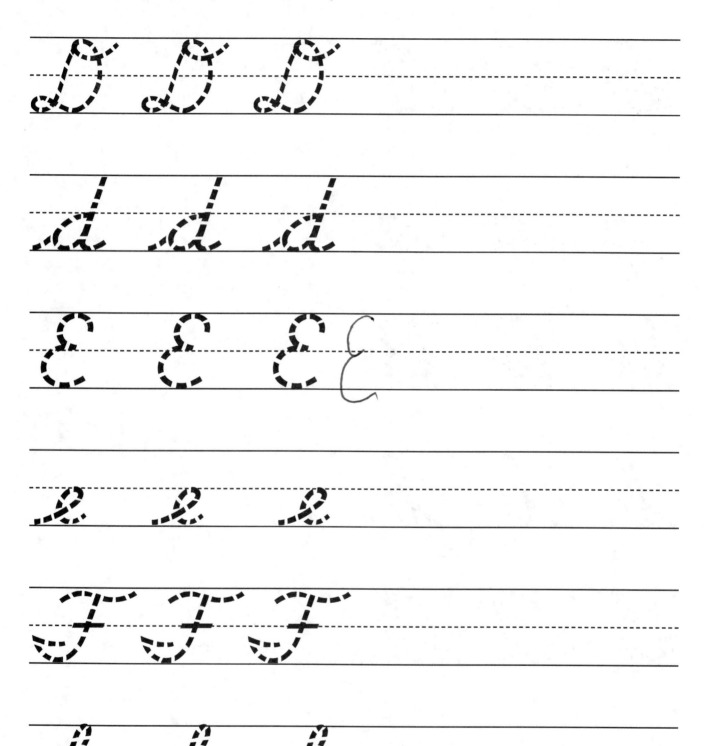

Letter Review (cont.)

Trace the letters and then practice them on your own.

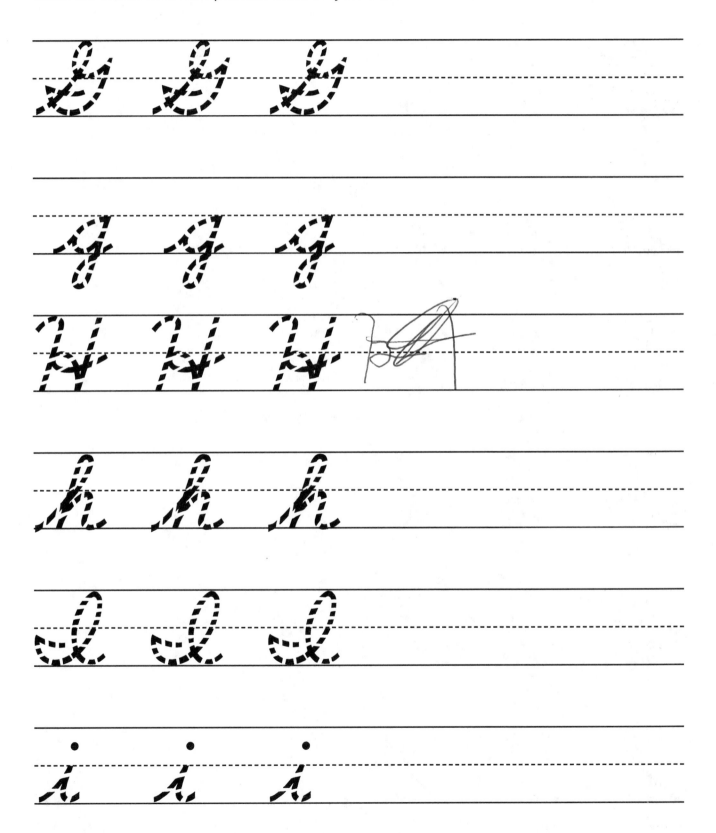

Letter Review (cont.)

Trace the letters and then practice them on your own.

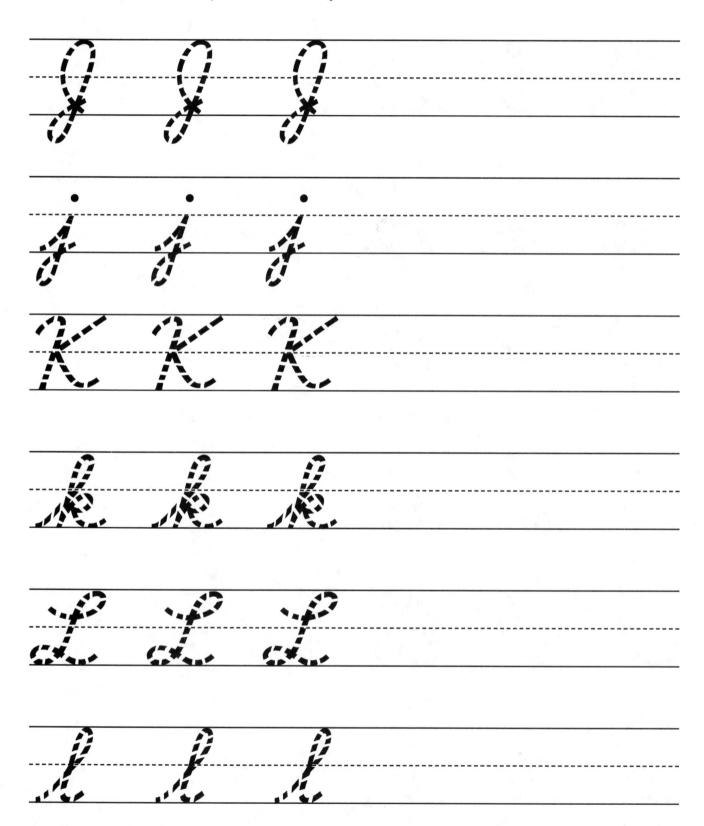

Letter Review (cont.)

Trace the letters and then practice them on your own.

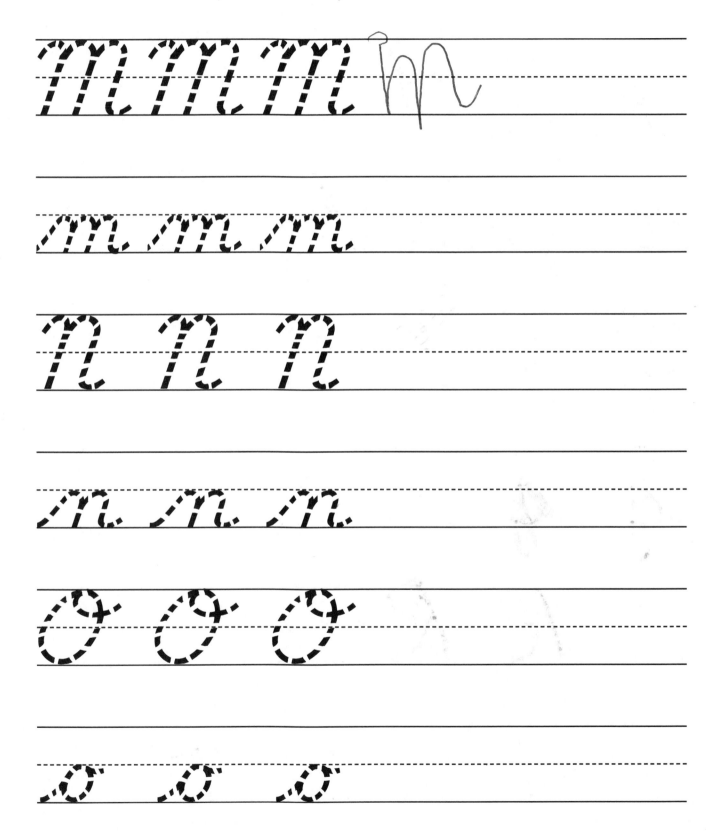

Letter Review (cont.)

Trace the letters and then practice them on your own.

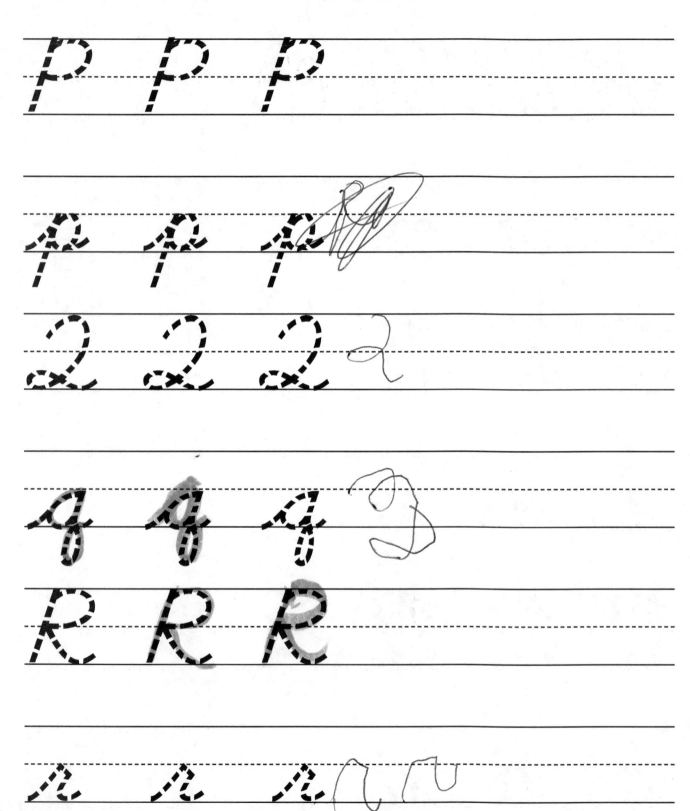

Letter Review (cont.)

Trace the letters and then practice them on your own.

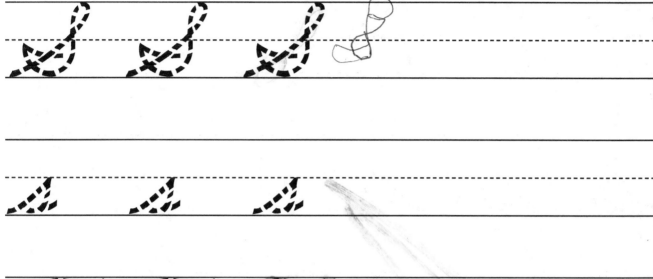

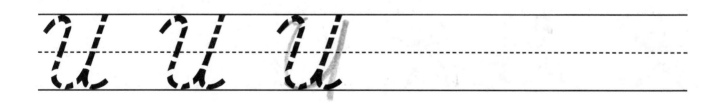

Letter Review (cont.)

Trace the letters and then practice them on your own.

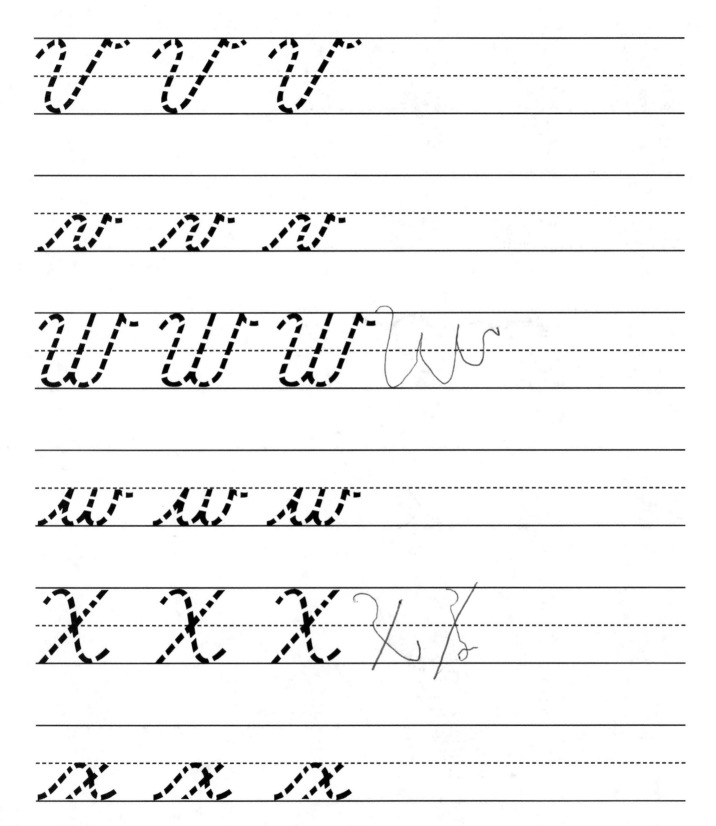

Letter Review (cont.)

Trace the letters and then practice them on your own.

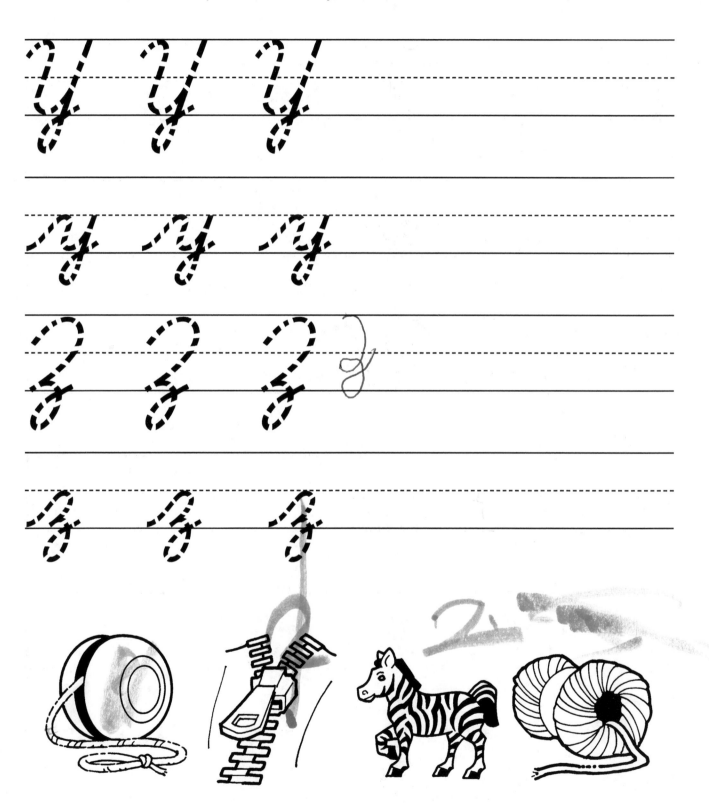

Add It Up

Find the sums for the addition problems below.

1. 1 + 3 = _____

2. 5 + 8 = _____

3. 3 + 7 = _____

4. 9 + 3 = _____

5. 6 + 1 = _____

6. 2 + 4 = _____

7. 1 + 2 = _____

8. 8 + 0 = _____

9. 0 + 3 = _____

10. 4 + 6 = _____

11. 7 + 7 = _____

12. 3 + 5 = _____

13. 4 + 2 = _____

14. 9 + 2 = _____

15. 6 + 9 = _____

16. 3 + 2 = _____

17. 2 + 0 = _____

18. 6 + 2 = _____

19. 9 + 5 = _____

20. 1 + 6 = _____

21. 8 + 9 = _____

22. 7 + 6 = _____

23. 9 + 4 = _____

24. 6 + 8 = _____

25. 5 + 5 = _____

26. 5 + 4 = _____

27. 4 + 8 = _____

28. 2 + 8 = _____

29. 3 + 6 = _____

30. 0 + 9 = _____

Mouse in the House

Cross out each answer in the computer as you solve the problems.

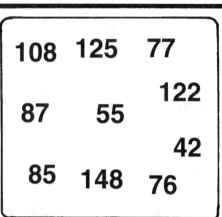

108	125	77
		122
87	55	
		42
85	148	76

a 40 + 68 =

b 12 + 73 =

c 32 + 23 =

d 35 + 42 =

e 61 + 15 =

f 57 + 30 =

g 70 + 78 =

h 82 + 43 =

i 21 + 21 =

j 101 + 21 =

How Much?

Use the prices to write addition problems. Find the sums.

a. 1 🧥 + 1 👟 =

＿ + ＿ = ＿

d. 1 👖 + 1 👟 =

＿ + ＿ = ＿

b. 1 👗 + 1 👖 =

＿ + ＿ = ＿

e. 1 ⌚ + 1 👒 + 1 🧥 =

＿ + ＿ + ＿ = ＿

c. 1 👒 + 1 ⌚ =

＿ + ＿ = ＿

f. 1 👗 + 1 👟 + 1 👖 =

＿ + ＿ + ＿ = ＿

Word Problems

Read each word problem. Write the number sentence it shows. Find the sum.

a

In the forest, Lisa counted 83 pine trees, 24 spider webs, and 16 chipmunks. How many things did she count in all?

b

In Bill's classroom there are 47 pencils, 21 pieces of chalk, and 33 bottles of glue. How many supplies are there in all?

c

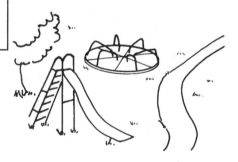

At the park, Carla counted 14 ducks, 32 children, and 24 roller skates. How many things did she count in all?

d

James counted 36 stars one night, 42 stars the next, and 87 on the third night. How many stars did he count in all?

Sum It Up

Find the sums.

a. $\begin{array}{r} 11 \\ + 50 \\ \hline \end{array}$	**g.** $\begin{array}{r} 69 \\ + 12 \\ \hline \end{array}$	**m.** $\begin{array}{r} 69 \\ + 16 \\ \hline \end{array}$	**s.** $\begin{array}{r} 36 \\ + 13 \\ \hline \end{array}$
b. $\begin{array}{r} 64 \\ + 42 \\ \hline \end{array}$	**h.** $\begin{array}{r} 72 \\ + 38 \\ \hline \end{array}$	**n.** $\begin{array}{r} 71 \\ + 59 \\ \hline \end{array}$	**t.** $\begin{array}{r} 29 \\ + 80 \\ \hline \end{array}$
c. $\begin{array}{r} 24 \\ + 93 \\ \hline \end{array}$	**i.** $\begin{array}{r} 48 \\ + 18 \\ \hline \end{array}$	**o.** $\begin{array}{r} 13 \\ + 68 \\ \hline \end{array}$	**u.** $\begin{array}{r} 51 \\ + 17 \\ \hline \end{array}$
d. $\begin{array}{r} 17 \\ + 20 \\ \hline \end{array}$	**j.** $\begin{array}{r} 52 \\ + 11 \\ \hline \end{array}$	**p.** $\begin{array}{r} 41 \\ + 96 \\ \hline \end{array}$	**v.** $\begin{array}{r} 19 \\ + 91 \\ \hline \end{array}$
e. $\begin{array}{r} 58 \\ + 72 \\ \hline \end{array}$	**k.** $\begin{array}{r} 15 \\ + 19 \\ \hline \end{array}$	**q.** $\begin{array}{r} 82 \\ + 30 \\ \hline \end{array}$	**w.** $\begin{array}{r} 31 \\ + 46 \\ \hline \end{array}$
f. $\begin{array}{r} 67 \\ + 14 \\ \hline \end{array}$	**l.** $\begin{array}{r} 31 \\ + 62 \\ \hline \end{array}$	**r.** $\begin{array}{r} 93 \\ + 90 \\ \hline \end{array}$	**x.** $\begin{array}{r} 87 \\ + 43 \\ \hline \end{array}$

Add Three

Find the sums.

a. 39 57 + 47	**g.** 39 12 + 72	**m.** 26 71 + 59	**s.** 17 79 + 54
b. 33 75 + 23	**h.** 51 24 + 88	**n.** 52 30 + 18	**t.** 39 95 + 48
c. 21 53 + 17	**i.** 42 84 + 19	**o.** 13 38 + 42	**u.** 27 77 + 70
d. 42 26 + 49	**j.** 23 14 + 92	**p.** 52 38 + 42	**v.** 59 44 + 16
e. 68 62 + 56	**k.** 84 36 + 65	**q.** 52 66 + 83	**w.** 51 36 + 24
f. 61 33 + 63	**l.** 34 42 + 30	**r.** 98 61 + 15	**x.** 67 73 + 30

Addition Challenge

Find the sums for the problems below.

1.   684
       792
  + 123

2.   485
       379
  + 369

3.   321
       831
  + 700

4.   680
       303
  + 425

5.   304
       262
  + 750

6.   421
       489
  + 492

7.   278
       915
  + 964

8.   409
       501
  + 961

9.   557
       627
  + 990

10.   863
       777
  + 421

11.   645
       129
  + 300

12.   789
       528
  + 450

Cup o' Tea

Cross out each answer in the teapot as you solve the problems.

a.
$$\begin{array}{r} 30 \\ -\ 16 \\ \hline \end{array}$$

b.
$$\begin{array}{r} 12 \\ -\ 11 \\ \hline \end{array}$$

c.
$$\begin{array}{r} 32 \\ -\ 25 \\ \hline \end{array}$$

d.
$$\begin{array}{r} 50 \\ -\ 36 \\ \hline \end{array}$$

e.
$$\begin{array}{r} 79 \\ -\ 49 \\ \hline \end{array}$$

f.
$$\begin{array}{r} 91 \\ -\ 50 \\ \hline \end{array}$$

g.
$$\begin{array}{r} 88 \\ -\ 62 \\ \hline \end{array}$$

h.
$$\begin{array}{r} 73 \\ -\ 43 \\ \hline \end{array}$$

i.
$$\begin{array}{r} 86 \\ -\ 26 \\ \hline \end{array}$$

j.
$$\begin{array}{r} 93 \\ -\ 52 \\ \hline \end{array}$$

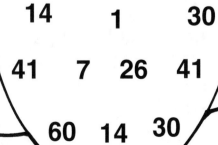

14   1   30

41   7   26   41

60   14   30

Word Problems

Read each word problem. Write the number sentence it shows. Find the difference.

a

Farmer Cole raised 93 bushels of wheat. Farmer Dale raised 68 bushels. What is the difference in the number of bushels each raised?

b

Dennis scored 43 points in his basketball game. Claire scored 40. What is the difference in points each earned?

c

Jason bought a pair of shoes for 53 dollars. Clark bought a pair for 28 dollars. What is the difference paid?

d

Jill counted 83 ants near an ant hill. Jack counted 62. What is the difference in the ants counted?

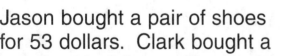
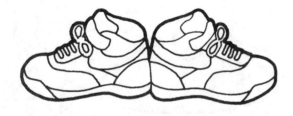

Subtraction Solutions

Fill in the puzzle by solving the subtraction problems. Use the word names in the Word List.

Word List				
eleven	thirteen	fifteen	seventeen	nineteen
twelve	fourteen	sixteen	eighteen	twenty

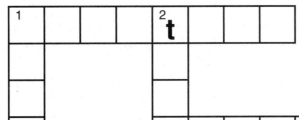

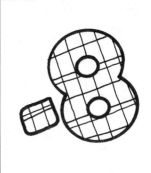

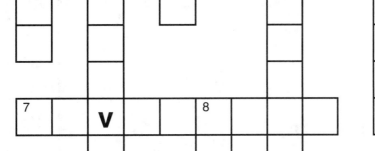

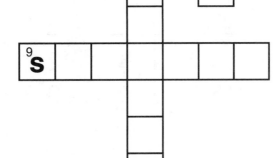

Across

1. 25 – 11 =
3. 40 – 21 =
7. 33 – 16 =
9. 51 – 35 =

Down

1. 46 – 31 =
2. 27 – 7 =
4. 22 – 4 =
5. 19 – 8 =
6. 44 – 32 =
8. 38 – 25 =

#3646 Practice and Learn

What's the Difference?

Find the differences.

a. $\begin{array}{r} 51 \\ -50 \\ \hline \end{array}$	**g.** $\begin{array}{r} 69 \\ -12 \\ \hline \end{array}$	**m.** $\begin{array}{r} 69 \\ -16 \\ \hline \end{array}$	**s.** $\begin{array}{r} 36 \\ -13 \\ \hline \end{array}$
b. $\begin{array}{r} 64 \\ -42 \\ \hline \end{array}$	**h.** $\begin{array}{r} 72 \\ -38 \\ \hline \end{array}$	**n.** $\begin{array}{r} 71 \\ -59 \\ \hline \end{array}$	**t.** $\begin{array}{r} 89 \\ -80 \\ \hline \end{array}$
c. $\begin{array}{r} 94 \\ -23 \\ \hline \end{array}$	**i.** $\begin{array}{r} 48 \\ -18 \\ \hline \end{array}$	**o.** $\begin{array}{r} 68 \\ -13 \\ \hline \end{array}$	**u.** $\begin{array}{r} 51 \\ -17 \\ \hline \end{array}$
d. $\begin{array}{r} 27 \\ -10 \\ \hline \end{array}$	**j.** $\begin{array}{r} 52 \\ -11 \\ \hline \end{array}$	**p.** $\begin{array}{r} 96 \\ -41 \\ \hline \end{array}$	**v.** $\begin{array}{r} 91 \\ -19 \\ \hline \end{array}$
e. $\begin{array}{r} 78 \\ -52 \\ \hline \end{array}$	**k.** $\begin{array}{r} 19 \\ -15 \\ \hline \end{array}$	**q.** $\begin{array}{r} 82 \\ -30 \\ \hline \end{array}$	**w.** $\begin{array}{r} 46 \\ -31 \\ \hline \end{array}$
f. $\begin{array}{r} 67 \\ -14 \\ \hline \end{array}$	**l.** $\begin{array}{r} 62 \\ -31 \\ \hline \end{array}$	**r.** $\begin{array}{r} 93 \\ -90 \\ \hline \end{array}$	**x.** $\begin{array}{r} 87 \\ -43 \\ \hline \end{array}$

Find the Difference

Find the differences.

a. 31 − 23	**g.** 79 − 32	**m.** 85 − 21	**s.** 69 − 37
b. 75 − 42	**h.** 57 − 51	**n.** 51 − 20	**t.** 98 − 34
c. 54 − 23	**i.** 88 − 44	**o.** 42 − 28	**u.** 87 − 28
d. 42 − 26	**j.** 63 − 23	**p.** 71 − 56	**v.** 69 − 43
e. 88 − 26	**k.** 86 − 14	**q.** 36 − 32	**w.** 46 − 41
f. 61 − 33	**l.** 53 − 32	**r.** 97 − 60	**x.** 77 − 63

What's the Scoop?

Fill in the missing number on each cone to complete the problem.

1.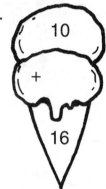
10
+
16

2.
17
− 8

3.
+ 4
17

4.
9
+
19

5.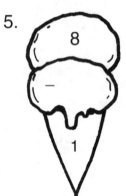
8
−
1

6.
15
+ 4

7.
− 11
7

8.
21
− 16

9.
20
+
29

10.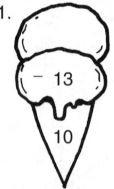
14
− 7

11.
− 13
10

12.
14
+
25

13.
14
− 6

14.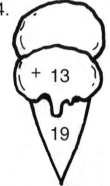
+ 13
19

15.
12
+ 12

16.
18
− 6

Sign In

Place + and – signs between the digits so that both sides of each equation are equal.

1.	6	4	1	2	6	2	=	15

2.	9	1	3	1	4	1	=	5

3.	9	3	4	1	2	3	=	14

4.	5	1	1	3	4	6	=	18

5.	9	8	6	3	5	3	=	8

6.	2	1	8	9	3	5	=	20

7.	5	3	2	4	1	5	=	12

8.	4	9	3	7	3	1	=	11

9.	7	6	2	8	7	1	=	3

10.	9	9	9	2	2	8	=	1

Times Tables

Complete the times tables.

0 x 0 = _____	1 x 6 = _____	2 x 12 = _____	4 x 5 = _____
0 x 1 = _____	1 x 7 = _____	3 x 0 = _____	4 x 6 = _____
0 x 2 = _____	1 x 8 = _____	3 x 1 = _____	4 x 7 = _____
0 x 3 = _____	1 x 9 = _____	3 x 2 = _____	4 x 8 = _____
0 x 4 = _____	1 x 10 = _____	3 x 3 = _____	4 x 9 = _____
0 x 5 = _____	1 x 11 = _____	3 x 4 = _____	4 x 10 = _____
0 x 6 = _____	1 x 12 = _____	3 x 5 = _____	4 x 11 = _____
0 x 7 = _____	2 x 0 = _____	3 x 6 = _____	4 x 12 = _____
0 x 8 = _____	2 x 1 = _____	3 x 7 = _____	5 x 0 = _____
0 x 9 = _____	2 x 2 = _____	3 x 8 = _____	5 x 1 = _____
0 x 10 = _____	2 x 3 = _____	3 x 9 = _____	5 x 2 = _____
0 x 11 = _____	2 x 4 = _____	3 x 10 = _____	5 x 3 = _____
0 x 12 = _____	2 x 5 = _____	3 x 11 = _____	5 x 4 = _____
1 x 0 = _____	2 x 6 = _____	3 x 12 = _____	5 x 5 = _____
1 x 1 = _____	2 x 7 = _____	4 x 0 = _____	5 x 6 = _____
1 x 2 = _____	2 x 8 = _____	4 x 1 = _____	5 x 7 = _____
1 x 3 = _____	2 x 9 = _____	4 x 2 = _____	5 x 8 = _____
1 x 4 = _____	2 x 10 = _____	4 x 3 = _____	5 x 9 = _____
1 x 5 = _____	2 x 11 = _____	4 x 4 = _____	5 x 10 = _____

Times Tables (cont.)

Complete the times tables.

5 x 11 = ____	7 x 4 = ____	8 x 10 = ____	10 x 3 = ____	11 x 9 = ____
5 x 12 = ____	7 x 5 = ____	8 x 11 = ____	10 x 4 = ____	11 x 10 = ____
6 x 0 = ____	7 x 6 = ____	8 x 12 = ____	10 x 5 = ____	11 x 11 = ____
6 x 1 = ____	7 x 7 = ____	9 x 0 = ____	10 x 6 = ____	11 x 12 = ____
6 x 2 = ____	7 x 8 = ____	9 x 1 = ____	10 x 7 = ____	12 x 0 = ____
6 x 3 = ____	7 x 9 = ____	9 x 2 = ____	10 x 8 = ____	12 x 1 = ____
6 x 4 = ____	7 x 10 = ____	9 x 3 = ____	10 x 9 = ____	12 x 2 = ____
6 x 5 = ____	7 x 11 = ____	9 x 4 = ____	10 x 10 = ____	12 x 3 = ____
6 x 6 = ____	7 x 12 = ____	9 x 5 = ____	10 x 11 = ____	12 x 4 = ____
6 x 7 = ____	8 x 0 = ____	9 x 6 = ____	10 x 12 = ____	12 x 5 = ____
6 x 8 = ____	8 x 1 = ____	9 x 7 = ____	11 x 0 = ____	12 x 6 = ____
6 x 9 = ____	8 x 2 = ____	9 x 8 = ____	11 x 1 = ____	12 x 7 = ____
6 x 10 = ____	8 x 3 = ____	9 x 9 = ____	11 x 2 = ____	12 x 8 = ____
6 x 11 = ____	8 x 4 = ____	9 x 10 = ____	11 x 3 = ____	12 x 9 = ____
6 x 12 = ____	8 x 5 = ____	9 x 11 = ____	11 x 4 = ____	12 x 10 = ____
7 x 0 = ____	8 x 6 = ____	9 x 12 = ____	11 x 5 = ____	12 x 11 = ____
7 x 1 = ____	8 x 7 = ____	10 x 0 = ____	11 x 6 = ____	12 x 12 = ____
7 x 2 = ____	8 x 8 = ____	10 x 1 = ____	11 x 7 = ____	
7 x 3 = ____	8 x 9 = ____	10 x 2 = ____	11 x 8 = ____	

Multiplication

Solve the problems.

2 x 2	12 x 5	6 x 1	6 x 3
3 x 8	7 x 5	7 x 7	7 x 9
5 x 1	11 x 8	9 x 0	9 x 2
10 x 0	10 x 4	10 x 6	10 x 8
2 x 3	11 x 10	11 x 12	12 x 1
11 x 5	6 x 0	6 x 2	6 x 4
7 x 4	7 x 6	7 x 8	10 x 7
10 x 8	12 x 8	9 x 1	9 x 3
10 x 3	10 x 5	10 x 7	10 x 9
11 x 9	11 x 11	12 x 0	12 x 2

Column Multiplication

Solve the problems.

96 x 16	68 x 88	56 x 75	22 x 67
90 x 13	33 x 31	84 x 28	74 x 17
47 x 19	20 x 62	70 x 96	26 x 93
25 x 11	24 x 19	58 x 75	14 x 72
26 x 16	41 x 40	50 x10	48 x 30
40 x 28	46 x 20	21 x 25	42 x 48
82 x 35	49 x 71	77 x 63	88 x 50
60 x 52	38 x 45	79 x 44	69 x 18
71 x 27	24 x 35	86 x 33	43 x 31
32 x 54	27 x 32	13 x 29	19 x 22

By Three

Solve the problems.

173 x 6	533 x 8	138 x 2	833 x 5
227 x 3	388 x 1	417 x 8	524 x 3
402 x 1	620 x 6	317 x 4	468 x 6
420 x 8	662 x 3	458 x 7	947 x 2
178 x 9	714 x 9	550 x 6	767 x 7
324 x 8	835 x 3	594 x 5	632 x 3
172 x 4	152 x 7	180 x 4	221 x 2
286 x 8	254 x 5	538 x 1	489 x 4
509 x 4	851 x 1	728 x 6	141 x 9
615 x 2	674 x 8	107 x 3	213 x 5

Double Time

Solve the problems.

23 x 16	13 x 38	89 x 57	44 x 76
90 x 39	31 x 11	24 x 23	22 x 51
17 x 79	41 x 96	74 x 19	16 x 39
35 x 15	14 x 79	48 x 79	25 x 17
14 x 63	80 x 54	70 x 71	28 x 93
56 x 82	34 x 24	21 x 26	58 x 48
73 x 50	46 x 27	67 x 64	99 x 56
50 x 28	68 x 40	39 x 42	64 x 48
81 x 76	34 x 83	96 x 30	34 x 23
51 x 44	23 x 36	18 x 28	36 x 20

#3646 Practice and Learn

Division Facts

Solve the problems.

$0 \div 0 =$ _____	$6 \div 1 =$ _____	$24 \div 12 =$ _____	$24 \div 4 =$ _____
$1 \div 0 =$ _____	$7 \div 1 =$ _____	$3 \div 3 =$ _____	$28 \div 4 =$ _____
$2 \div 0 =$ _____	$8 \div 1 =$ _____	$6 \div 3 =$ _____	$32 \div 4 =$ _____
$3 \div 0 =$ _____	$9 \div 1 =$ _____	$9 \div 3 =$ _____	$36 \div 4 =$ _____
$4 \div 0 =$ _____	$10 \div 1 =$ _____	$12 \div 3 =$ _____	$40 \div 4 =$ _____
$5 \div 0 =$ _____	$11 \div 1 =$ _____	$15 \div 3 =$ _____	$44 \div 4 =$ _____
$6 \div 0 =$ _____	$12 \div 1 =$ _____	$18 \div 3 =$ _____	$48 \div 4 =$ _____
$7 \div 0 =$ _____	$2 \div 2 =$ _____	$21 \div 3 =$ _____	$5 \div 5 =$ _____
$8 \div 0 =$ _____	$4 \div 2 =$ _____	$24 \div 3 =$ _____	$10 \div 5 =$ _____
$9 \div 0 =$ _____	$6 \div 2 =$ _____	$27 \div 3 =$ _____	$15 \div 5 =$ _____
$10 \div 0 =$ _____	$8 \div 2 =$ _____	$30 \div 3 =$ _____	$20 \div 5 =$ _____
$11 \div 0 =$ _____	$10 \div 2 =$ _____	$33 \div 3 =$ _____	$25 \div 5 =$ _____
$12 \div 0 =$ _____	$12 \div 2 =$ _____	$36 \div 3 =$ _____	$30 \div 5 =$ _____
$1 \div 1 =$ _____	$14 \div 2 =$ _____	$4 \div 4 =$ _____	$35 \div 5 =$ _____
$2 \div 1 =$ _____	$16 \div 2 =$ _____	$8 \div 4 =$ _____	$40 \div 5 =$ _____
$3 \div 1 =$ _____	$18 \div 2 =$ _____	$12 \div 4 =$ _____	$45 \div 5 =$ _____
$4 \div 1 =$ _____	$20 \div 2 =$ _____	$16 \div 4 =$ _____	$50 \div 5 =$ _____
$5 \div 1 =$ _____	$22 \div 2 =$ _____	$20 \div 4 =$ _____	$55 \div 5 =$ _____

Division Facts (cont.)

Solve the problems.

60 ÷ 5 = _____	42 ÷ 7 = _____	96 ÷ 8 = _____	60 ÷ 10 = ___	132 ÷ 11 = ___
6 ÷ 6 = _____	49 ÷ 7 = _____	9 ÷ 9 = _____	70 ÷ 10 = ___	12 ÷ 12 = _____
12 ÷ 6 = _____	56 ÷ 7 = _____	18 ÷ 9 = _____	80 ÷ 10 = ___	24 ÷ 12 = _____
18 ÷ 6 = _____	63 ÷ 7 = _____	27 ÷ 9 = _____	90 ÷ 10 = ___	36 ÷ 12 = _____
24 ÷ 6 = _____	70 ÷ 7 = _____	36 ÷ 9 = _____	100 ÷ 10 = __	48 ÷ 12 = _____
30 ÷ 6 = _____	77 ÷ 7 = _____	45 ÷ 9 = _____	110 ÷ 10 = __	60 ÷ 12 = _____
36 ÷ 6 = _____	84 ÷ 7 = _____	54 ÷ 9 = _____	120 ÷ 10 = __	72 ÷ 12 = _____
42 ÷ 6 = _____	8 ÷ 8 = _____	63 ÷ 9 = _____	11 ÷ 11 = _____	84 ÷ 12 = _____
48 ÷ 6 = _____	16 ÷ 8 = _____	72 ÷ 9 = _____	22 ÷ 11 = _____	96 ÷ 12 = _____
54 ÷ 6 = _____	24 ÷ 8 = _____	81 ÷ 9 = _____	33 ÷ 11 = _____	108 ÷ 12 = ___
60 ÷ 6 = _____	32 ÷ 8 = _____	90 ÷ 9 = _____	44 ÷ 11 = _____	120 ÷ 12 = ___
66 ÷ 6 = _____	40 ÷ 8 = _____	99 ÷ 9 = _____	55 ÷ 11 = _____	132 ÷ 12 = ___
72 ÷ 6 = _____	48 ÷ 8 = _____	108 ÷ 9 = ___	66 ÷ 11 = _____	144 ÷ 12 = ___
7 ÷ 7 = _____	56 ÷ 8 = _____	10 ÷ 10 = ___	77 ÷ 11 = ___	
14 ÷ 7 = _____	64 ÷ 8 = _____	20 ÷ 10 = ___	88 ÷ 11 = ___	
21 ÷ 7 = _____	72 ÷ 8 = _____	30 ÷ 10 = ___	99 ÷ 11 = ___	
28 ÷ 7 = _____	80 ÷ 8 = _____	40 ÷ 10 = ___	110 ÷ 11 = __	
35 ÷ 7 = _____	88 ÷ 8 = _____	50 ÷ 10 = ___	121 ÷ 11 = __	

239   #3646 Practice and Learn

Divide and Conquer

Solve the problems.

$16\overline{)400}$ $\qquad$ $15\overline{)225}$ $\qquad$ $18\overline{)234}$

$12\overline{)240}$ $\qquad$ $10\overline{)180}$ $\qquad$ $8\overline{)136}$

$5\overline{)95}$ $\qquad$ $8\overline{)248}$ $\qquad$ $2\overline{)112}$

$16\overline{)256}$ $\qquad$ $6\overline{)150}$ $\qquad$ $32\overline{)128}$

$16\overline{)288}$ $\qquad$ $9\overline{)171}$ $\qquad$ $11\overline{)231}$

240

Which Is It?

Read the number sentences. Add the correct math sign to each problem.

+	−	x	÷
add	subtract	multiply	divide

1. 5 _____ 7 = 12

2. 24 _____ 4 = 6

3. 9 _____ 3 = 12

4. 18 _____ 6 = 12

5. 4 _____ 9 = 13

6. 4 _____ 9 = 36

7. 10 _____ 8 = 80

8. 15 _____ 5 = 3

9. 11 _____ 4 = 7

10. 8 _____ 16 = 24

11. 2 _____ 8 = 16

12. 3 _____ 2 = 5

13. 22 _____ 6 = 16

14. 9 _____ 1 = 10

15. 3 _____ 3 = 9

16. 144 _____ 12 = 12

17. 21 _____ 3 = 7

18. 90 _____ 10 = 9

19. 12 _____ 11 = 132

20. 14 _____ 1 = 14

Picture Fractions

A **fraction** is a number that names part of a whole thing. The number at the top is the numerator. It tells how many parts of the whole are present. The number at the bottom is the denominator. It tells how many parts there are in all.

Examples

 $\frac{1}{2}$ (There are two parts in the circle. One part is gray. Therefore, the fraction is $\frac{1}{2}$.)

 $\frac{3}{4}$ (There are four parts in the square. Three parts are gray. The fraction is $\frac{3}{4}$.)

Write a fraction for each picture.

1. 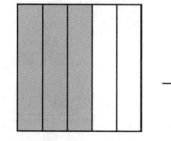 _____

5. 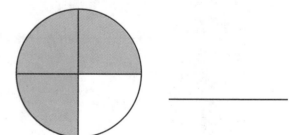 _____

2.  _____

6. 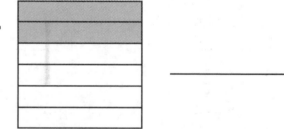 _____

3. 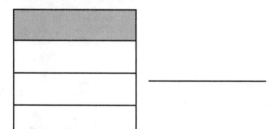 _____

7. 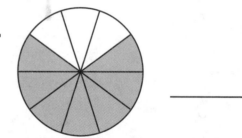 _____

4. 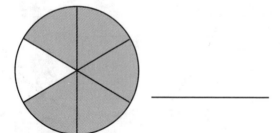 _____

8. 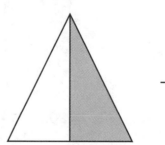 _____

Slice It Up!

In a **circle graph**, all the parts must add up to be a whole. Think of the parts like pieces that add up to one whole pie. Look at these pies and how they are divided into pieces.

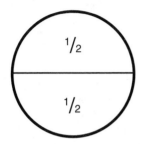

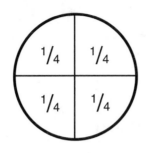

Make a circle graph to show how much pie a family ate. Here is the information you will need.

Mother ate 1/4 of the pie.

Sister ate 1/4 of the pie.

Father ate 1/4 of the pie.

Brother ate 1/8 of the pie.

Grandma ate 1/8 of the pie.

1/2 a pie

+ 1/2 a pie

2 halves =

1 whole pie

1/4 a pie

+ 1/4 a pie

+ 1/4 a pie

+ 1/4 a pie

4 fourths =

1 whole pie

Color the graph below using the Color Key.

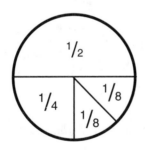

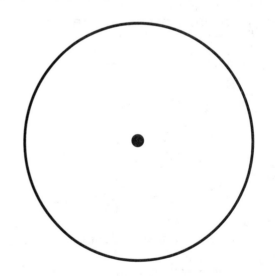

Pie My Family Ate

1/8 a pie

+ 1/8 a pie

+ 1/8 a pie

+ 1/8 a pie

+ 1/8 a pie

+ 1/8 a pie

+ 1/8 a pie

+ 1/8 a pie

8 eighths =

1 whole pie

1/2 a pie = 1 half

+ 1/4 a pie = 1 fourth

+ 1/8 a pie = 1 eighth

+ 1/8 a pie = 1 eighth

1 whole pie

Color Key

sister = orange   mother = pink

grandma = red   brother = yellow

father = blue

Circle Graph

Shown in this circle graph are the types of fruit sold at a produce stand in a week in July.

Fruits Sold at O'Henry's Fruit Stand July 1 to July 7

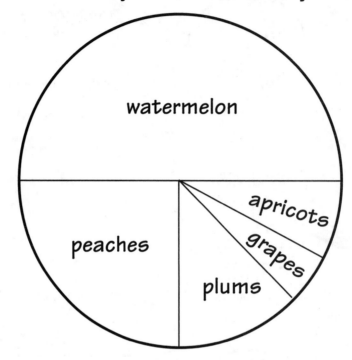

1. What fruit sold the most at O'Henry's Fruit Stand? _____`

2. What fruit sold the least? _____

3. Rank the order of the fruits that were sold. Number 1 will be the fruit that sold most, number 5, least.

   1. _____   2. _____   3. _____

            4._____   5. _____

4. Circle the correct fraction.

   Watermelon was   1/2   1/4   1/8   of all the fruit sold.

   Peaches were   1/2   1/4   1/8   of all the fruit sold.

   Plums were   1/2   1/4   1/8   of all the fruit sold.

5. Which of the fruits represented on the circle graph is your favorite?

_____

Slices

Look at this circle graph. It shows what Chris did during one hour of time at home.

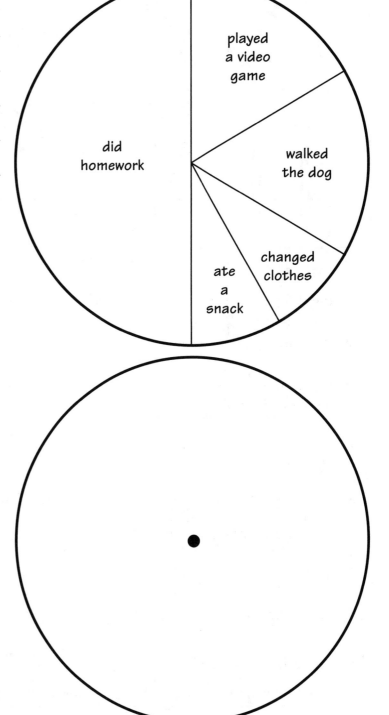

What Chris did from 4 to 5 P.M. on November 5

1. How many minutes did Chris spend . . .

    doing homework?_____

    eating a snack? _____

    changing clothes? _____

    playing a video game?_____

    walking the dog? _____

2. How did you figure out the number of minutes Chris did things?

    _____

    _____

Make a circle graph that shows what you did during one of your after-school hours.

Write the title of your graph here.

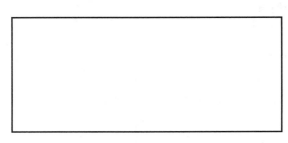

At the Playground

Using metric measurement, answer the questions below the playground map. Give all of your answers in meters. Draw lines between the areas and measure between the dots.

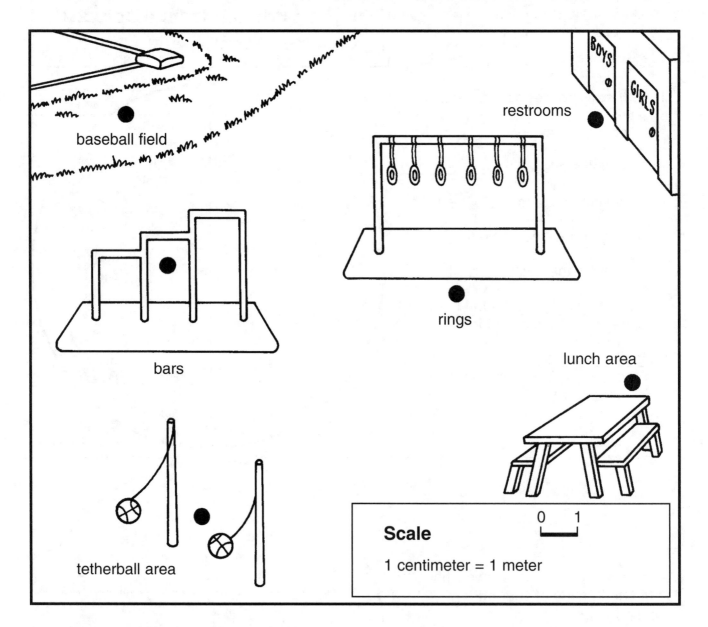

1. About how far is it from the bars to the baseball field? _____

2. About how far is it from the rings to the tetherball area? _____

3. About how far is it from the restrooms to the bars? _____

4. About how far is it from the lunch area to the bars? _____

5. About how far is it from the baseball field to the lunch area? _____

Measurement Choices

Measurement for a map scale can be given in inches, feet, and miles. This type of measurement is called **standard measure**.

Measurement for a map scale can also be given in centimeters, meters, and kilometers. This type of measurement is called **metric measure**.

On some map scales, both standard and metric measure are used. It is good to learn how to read and use both kinds of measurement systems.

When we choose a scale to use, it needs to be suited to the type of map we are making.

What do you think?

Decide on an appropriate scale to measure the size or distance of each of the following things. Use the scales in the box as your choices. Be ready to explain your choices.

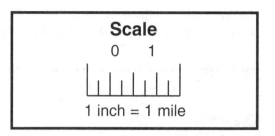

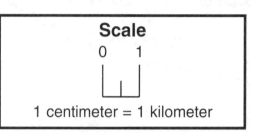

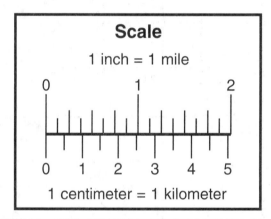

a. 1 centimeter = 1 centimeter	d. 1 inch = 1 foot
b. 1 centimeter = 1 meter	e. 1 inch = 1 mile
c. 1 centimeter = 1 kilometer	f. 1 inch = 100 miles

1. A cricket _____

2. Oregon to Texas _____

3. A bicycle race course _____

4. Your bedroom _____

5. Length of a sofa _____

6. Length of a horse's body _____

7. A swimming pool _____

8. The Mississippi River _____

9. The town park to your house _____

10. Your toes _____

                                             #3646 Practice and Learn

How to Measure

When you measure distances using a map scale, you can measure several different ways. The easiest and most accurate way is to use a standard measure or metric measure ruler.

You can also use a piece of string, paper, the joints of your fingers, a pencil or pen, or other things that could help you mark size.

Once you have chosen your measurement instrument, place it along the imaginary or real line between the distances you want to measure.

About how many miles is it between:

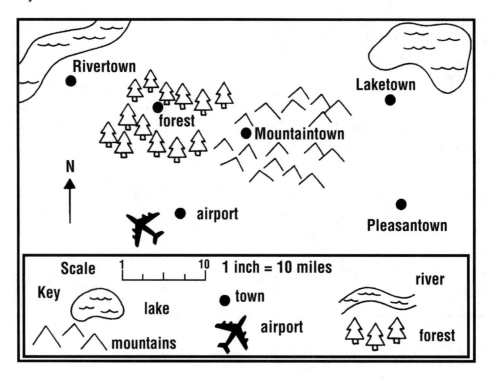

1. Rivertown and the airport? _____

2. Mountaintown and the forest? _____

3. Rivertown and Laketown? _____

4. Mountaintown and Pleasantown? _____

5. Laketown and Mountaintown? _____

6. Rivertown and the forest? _____

Is it farther from Pleasantown to Laketown or from Pleasantown to Mountaintown?

_____

From Here to There

Use this map scale and a metric ruler to answer the distance questions on this page. Use the center of the dots to measure.

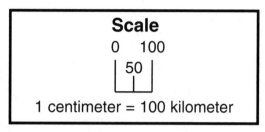

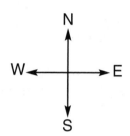

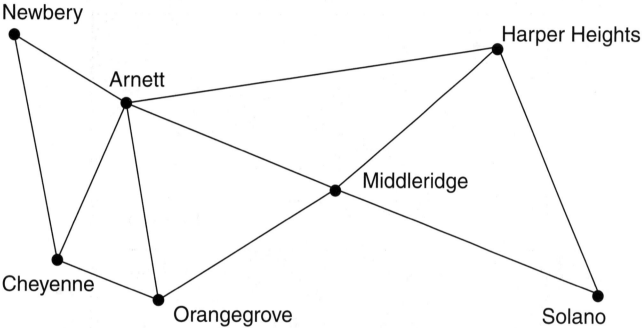

1. Newbery is _____ kilometers from Solano.

2. Middleridge is _____ kilometers from Orangegrove.

3. Cheyenne is _____ kilometers from Arnett.

4. Orangegrove is _____ kilometers from Harper Heights.

5. Arnett is _____ kilometers from Solano.

6. Harper Heights is _____ kilometers from Arnett.

7. Solano is _____ kilometers from Middleridge.

8. Middleridge is _____ kilometers from Harper Heights.

9. Newbery is _____ kilometers from Cheyenne.

10. Arnett is _____ kilometers from Middleridge.

How Much Is It Worth?

Read this money chart. Then answer the questions below.

Pennies, Nickels, and Dimes

1. A penny is worth _____.

2. A nickel is worth _____.

3. A dime is worth _____.

4. _____ pennies equal

    _____ nickel.

5. _____ nickels equal

    _____ dime.

6. _____ pennies equal

    _____ dime.

7. 5 pennies equal _____.

8. 2 nickels equal _____.

9. 10 pennies equal _____.

10. 1 dime, 1 nickel, and 1 penny

    equal _____.

Change, Please

List the coins you would give each person below to make change for his or her dollar.

1. Dolly wants 1 coin for her $1. _____

2. Zac wants 6 coins for his $1. _____

3. Holly wants 7 coins for her $1. _____

4. Andrew wants 10 coins for his $1. _____

5. Casie wants 15 coins for her $1. _____

6. Thomas wants 16 coins for his $1. _____

7. Chelsea wants 17 coins for her $1. _____

8. Austin wants 19 coins for his $1. _____

9. Marc wants 25 coins for his $1. _____

10. Roberto wants 28 coins for his $1. _____

Change for Fifty Cents

There are over 75 ways to make change for 50 cents. Work with a friend to list as many ways as you can. List the coins in order on each line, from largest to smallest. (**Hint:** Working from large to small coins will also help you find more ways to make change.) The list has been started for you. If you need more space, continue your list on the back of this paper.

Use the following abbreviations:

hd (half dollar)   **q** (quarter)   **d** (dime)   **n** (nickel)   **p** (penny)

1. _____ 1 hd _____   11. _____

2. _____ 2 q _____   12. _____

3. _____   13. _____

4. _____   14. _____

5. _____   15. _____

6. _____   16. _____

7. _____   17. _____

8. _____   18. _____

9. _____   19. _____

10. _____   20. _____

Change for a Dollar

There are over 200 ways to make change for a dollar. Work with a friend to list as many ways as you can. List the coins in order on each line, from largest to smallest. (*Hint:* Working from large to small coins will help you find more ways to make change, too.) The list has been started for you. If you need more space, continue your list on the back of this paper.

Use the following abbreviations:

hd *(half dollar)*   **q** *(quarter)*   **d** *(dime)*   **n** *(nickel)*   **p** *(penny)*

1. _____ 2hd _____
2. _____ 1hd and 2q _____
3. _____ 1hd and 5d _____
4. _____ 1hd and 10n _____
5. _____
6. _____
7. _____
8. _____
9. _____
10. _____
11. _____
12. _____
13. _____
14. _____
15. _____
16. _____
17. _____
18. _____
19. _____
20. _____
21. _____
22. _____
23. _____
24. _____
25. _____

26. _____
27. _____
28. _____
29. _____
30. _____
31. _____
32. _____
33. _____
34. _____
35. _____
36. _____
37. _____
38. _____
39. _____
40. _____
41. _____
42. _____
43. _____
44. _____
45. _____
46. _____
47. _____
48. _____
49. _____
50. _____

A.M. and P.M.

A.M. is the time after 12 o'clock midnight and before 12 o'clock noon. **P.M.** is the time after 12 o'clock noon and before 12 o'clock midnight. (Midnight itself is A.M. and noon itself is P.M.) Write **A.M.** or **P.M.** after each of these events to say what time it usually falls in.

1. dinner time _____

2. getting up _____

3. afternoon nap _____

4. after-school baseball game_____

5. before-school dance class _____

6. breakfast _____

7. evening movie _____

8. evening bath _____

9. after-dinner dessert_____

10. sunrise _____

11. going to school _____

12. sunset _____

13. lunch _____

14. morning cartoons _____

15. going to bed _____

16. after-school piano lessons _____

17. morning exercises_____

18. homework _____

19. afternoon reading _____

20. morning snack_____

Timely Chore

Each word in the time box refers to a specific time span. List the words in order from the shortest time span to the longest. Then, explain how long each time span is.

	Time Span	**How Long Is It?**
1.		
2.		
3.		
4.		
5.		
6.		
7.		
8.		
9.		
10.		
11.		
12.		

Time Box		
second	hour	millennium
fortnight	day	month
minute	score	century
year	decade	week

Exam Time

As Mr. Teran prepared to pass back the last spelling exam, five anxious students awaited their grades. Using the clues below, determine each child's grade. Mark an **X** in each correct box.

1. Lucy, who did not get an A on her test, scored higher than Martin and Gwen.

2. Cara and Gwen both scored higher than Donald.

3. Martin received a C on his test.

4. No two students received the same grade.

	A	B	C	C-	D
Lucy					
Gwen					
Cara					
Martin					
Donald					

Theodore

Mr. Martin has three boys in his science class who each go by a variation of the name Theodore. From the statements below, discover each boy's full name and age. Mark the correct boxes with an **X**.

1. Agee is younger than Dalton but older than Chin.

2. Ted is not the youngest or the oldest.

3. Theodore's last name is Chin.

4. None of the boys is the same age.

	Agee	Chin	Dalton	8	9	10
Ted						
Theodore						
Teddy						

Favorite Teams

Five boys root for five different baseball teams. Read the clues to determine which team each likes best. Mark the correct boxes with an **X**.

1. Will's bedroom is filled with posters and products from the A's.

2. Andrew's father is a big Cardinals fan, but Andrew is not.

3. Chad and Ryan like the Dodgers, the Reds, or the A's.

4. No boy's favorite team begins with the same letter as his name.

	Cardinals	Dodgers	A's	Reds	White Sox
Chad					
Danny					
Andrew					
Ryan					
Will					

A Visit to the Amusement Park

Katelyn, Kenny, Emily, and Howie recently visited their local amusement park to ride their favorite attractions—the roller coaster, the Ferris wheel, the carousel, and the bumper cars. While there, one ate a hamburger, another ate a corndog, another ate a hot dog, and the last ate bratwurst. Using the clues below, determine each person's favorite ride plus what each had to eat. Mark the correct boxes with an **X**.

	roller coaster	Ferris wheel	carousel	bumper cars	hamburger	corndog	hot dog	bratwurst
Katelyn								
Kenny								
Emily								
Howie								

1. The girls liked the roller coaster and bumper cars while the boys liked the Ferris wheel and the carousel.

2. Howie ate his food on a stick while Katelyn ate hers on a hot dog bun.

3. Katelyn's favorite ride has hills.

4. The boy who loved the Ferris wheel also loves hot dogs.

Softball Lineup

All nine players on the Tiger softball team are sitting on the bench in their batting order. Using the clues below, find their batting order. Record their batting order by putting an **X** in the correct box.

1. Jane is batting fifth, and Daisy will bat some time before Carrie.

2. Joanne sits between Daisy and Gertie, and Annie is to the right of Jane.

3. Gertie bats after Joanne but before Annie.

4. Penny sits next to Carrie.

5. Carrie and Tammy are at each end of the bench.

	1	2	3	4	5	6	7	8	9
Jane									
Daisy									
Carrie									
Joanne									
Gertie									
Annie									
Penny									
Tammy									
Lindsey									

Intermediate Points

Study this compass rose.

You are familiar with the four cardinal points, but there are times when directions can not be given using simply north, south, east, or west.

You need to be able to show points that come between the four primary directions. Intermediate points give a mapmaker just such a tool.

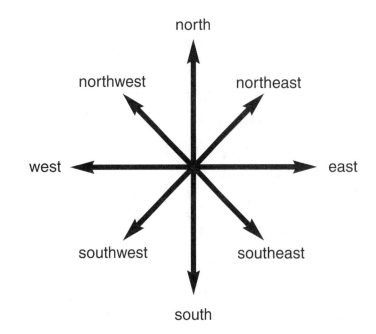

As you can see, the new direction words are made by combining the names of the cardinal points.

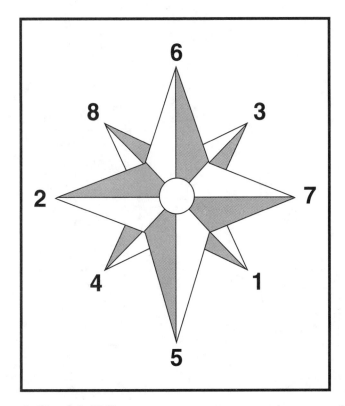

Using the cardinal and intermediate points, write the locations of the numbers in the box on the left.

1. _____

2. _____

3. _____

4. _____

5. _____

6. _____ **north** _____

7. _____

8. _____

Can You Find Home?

You are lost. Can you find your home by following the directions in the box below?

1. Begin in the most northwest home.
2. Move three houses east.
3. Move one house south.
4. Move two houses southwest.
5. Move one house west.
6. Move three houses northeast.
7. Move two houses southeast.
8. Move five houses west.
9. Move two houses north.
10. Move three houses southeast.

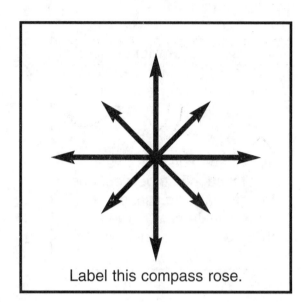

Label this compass rose.

Follow these directions. Color each of the houses you touch red. Color your home a different color.

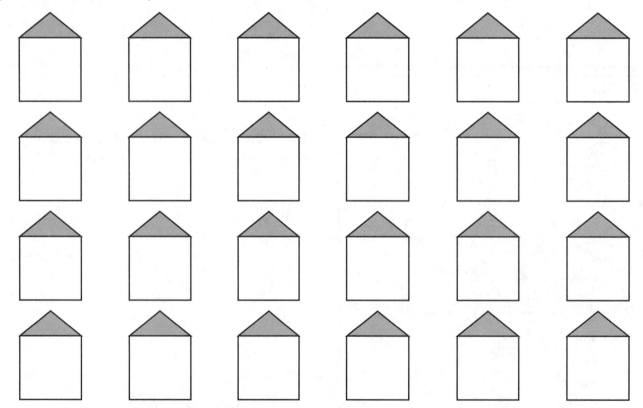

Can you rewrite the directions using fewer steps?

_____

_____

I've Got the Key!

Mapmakers draw the symbols they use in a map key. The map key explains what each symbol represents.

Look at this map and the map key. Use it to answer the questions below.

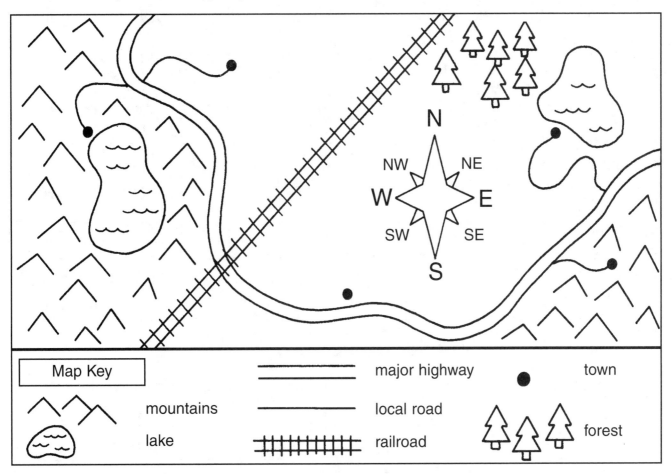

Answer true or false. If it is false, write the correct answer below it.

1. _____ A railroad track runs southwest to northeast.

2. _____ Mountains cover the northern section of the map.

3. _____ A lake and a forest are in the southeast.

4. _____ All towns can be reached by the major highway.

5. _____ Two towns are by lakes, and two towns are in the mountains.

6. _____ There are no towns along the railroad track.

7. _____ There is a large forest east of the lake and west of the railroad.

8. _____ The southernmost town is next to the major highway.

Grids

A **grid** is an arrangement of blocks that are made by vertical and horizontal lines intersecting on a page. Numbers and letters are used on the grid to help you name the blocks.

You can find something on a grid by putting a finger of your right hand on a number and a finger of your left hand on a letter. Then, slide your fingers together until they meet. When grid points are identified, the letter is written before the number.

Try it! What color is in block C4?

_____

	1	2	3	4
A	white	yellow	orange	gold
B	pink	green	tan	red
C	blue	purple	brown	silver
D	black	ivory	gray	lavender

Use the grid to name each of the colors identified below.

A1 _____   D3 _____   B4 _____   D2 _____

C4 _____   A2 _____   D1 _____   C2 _____

B3 _____   A4 _____   C3 _____   B1 _____

D4 _____   B2 _____   A3 _____   C1 _____

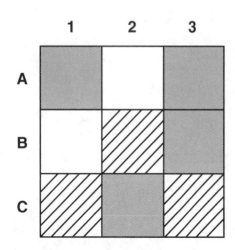

Use the grid on the left to answer these questions.

Which blocks are shaded?

_____

Which blocks are striped?

_____

Which blocks are unmarked?

_____

Where in This City?

Use the grid on the city map to find the places listed at the bottom of the page. Write the letter before the number for each place you find.

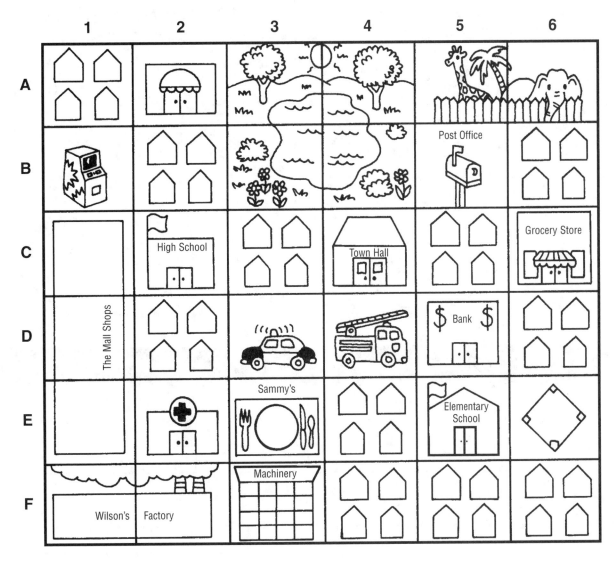

1. Medical Center _____

2. Machinery Warehouse _____

3. The Mall Shops _____, _____, and _____

4. Elementary School _____

5. Sammy's Restaurant _____

6. Green Park _____, _____, _____, and _____

7. Wilson's Factory _____, _____

8. City Zoo _____ and _____

9. City Bank _____

10. Town Hall _____

11. Ball Field _____

12. Arcade _____

13. Fire Station _____

14. Post Office _____

15. Grocery Store _____

16. High School _____

                        #3646 Practice and Learn

Where Is It?

Use the hemisphere maps on this page to help you locate the correct hemisphere for the places listed below.

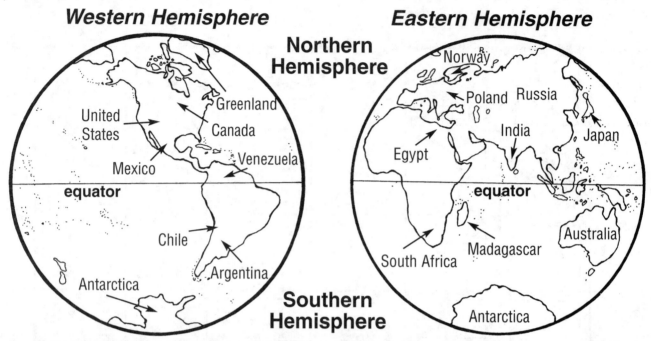

Place	Hemisphere (Northern or Southern)	Hemisphere (Eastern or Western)
1. South Africa		
2. Norway		
3. Venezuela		
4. Canada		
5. Japan		
6. Mexico		
7. Russia		
8. Egypt		
9. United States		
10. Argentina		
11. Poland		
12. Greenland		
13. India		
14. Chile		
15. Madagascar		
16. Australia		

How Many Degrees?

The intersection of Earth's latitude and longitude lines form a grid. All of these lines have degree markings. If you know the degrees of latitude and longitude of a certain place, you can easily find it on the map.

The map of Colorado below shows the latitude and longitude lines that divide the state. Use the map to answer these questions.

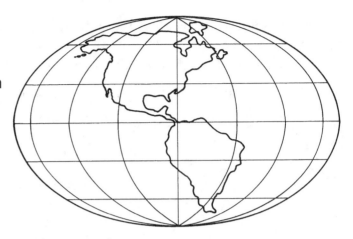

Which city is near . . .

1. 39 N, 109 W? _____

2. 41 N, 103 W? _____

3. 40 N, 105 W? _____

4. 38 N, 102 W? _____

5. 37 N, 108 W? _____

6. 39 N, 105 W? _____

7. 39 N, 107 W? _____

8. 37 N, 103 W? _____

9. 41 N, 108 W? _____

10. 39 N, 102 W? _____

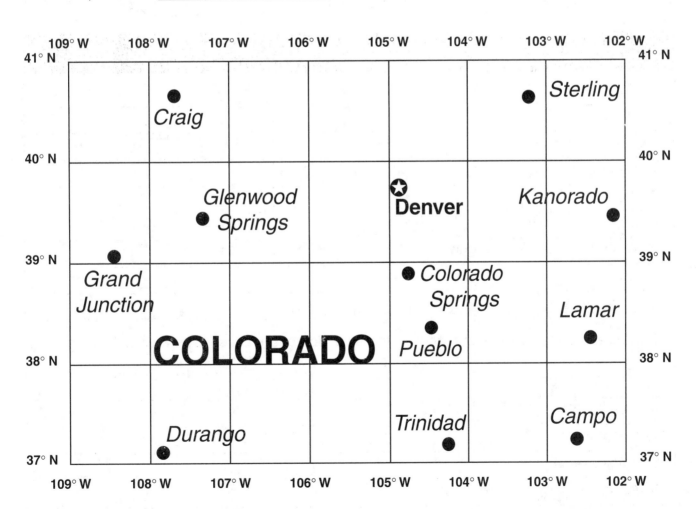

Road Maps

Road maps show the types of roads that are in a specific area. They also tell us other things we may need to know as we plan for travel, such as the distances from town to town, the locations of rest areas, and the availability of scenic routes.

After you read this map, answer the questions at the bottom of the page.

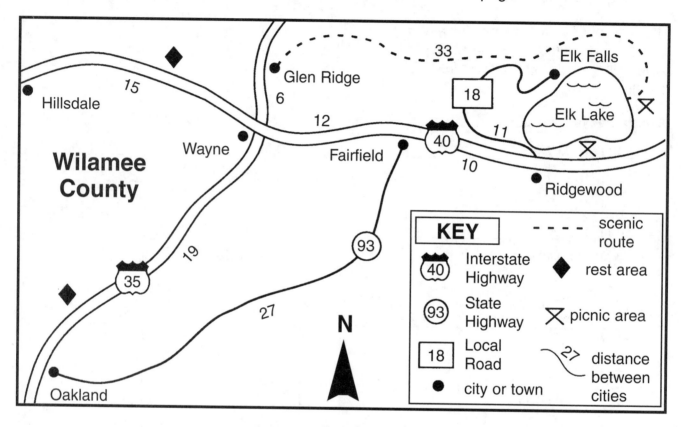

Distances Between Cities

1. Near what highways are the rest areas? _____

2. If you travel on State Highway 93, what is the distance from Oakland to Fairfield?

   _____

3. Interstate Highways 35 and 40 intersect at what city? _____

4. There is a scenic route that ends at the east side of Elk Lake. Where does it begin?

   _____

5. What is the distance from Hillsdale to:

   a. Wayne? _____   b. Ridgewood? _____

   c. Fairfield?_____   d. Elk Falls? _____

How Many Miles to Go?

Use the map on this page to answer the questions.

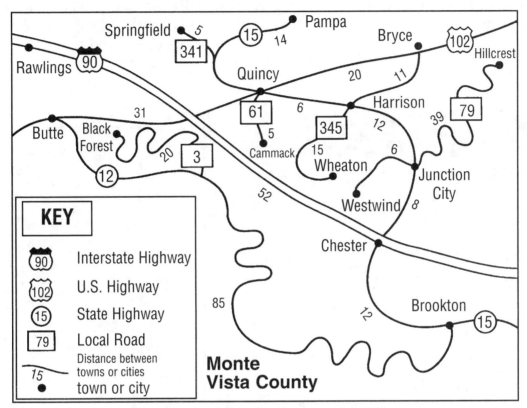

Distances Between Towns and Cities

1. You are in Butte. How far do you have to travel to

   a. Quincy? _____   b. Pampa? _____   c. Harrison? _____

   d. Hillcrest? _____   e. Bryce? _____   f. Brookton? _____

2. You are in Westwind. How far do you have to travel to

   a. Junction City? _____   b. Chester? _____   c. Bryce? _____

   d. Hillcrest? _____   e. Rawlings? _____   f. Cammack? _____

3. You are in Hillcrest. How far do you have to travel to

   a. Rawlings? _____   b. Bryce? _____   c. Wheaton? _____

   d. Brookton? _____   e. Westwind? _____   f. Pampa? _____

Challenge: Describe the route that would be fastest from Butte to Brookton.

_____

Why?_____

_____

Political Maps

One type of map that uses boundary lines is called a **political map**. A political map gives us information about county, province, state, and county boundaries as well as information about cities, towns, highways, roads, forest areas, and points of interest. Political maps also show oceans, rivers, and lakes, but they do not show the elevations of the land area as physical maps do.

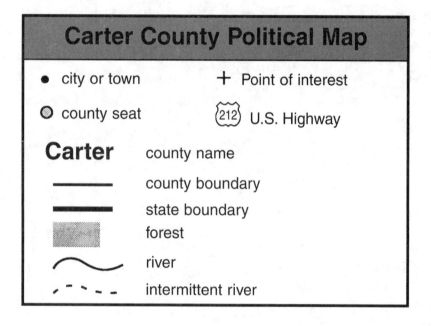

Carter County Political Map

- • city or town
- ◎ county seat
- + Point of interest
- ⟨212⟩ U.S. Highway

Carter   county name

———   county boundary

▬▬▬   state boundary

▨   forest

〰   river

- – - – -   intermittent river

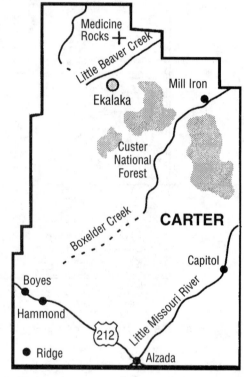

Use this political map of Carter County, Montana, to answer the questions below.

1. Which sides of Montana's border does Carter County help form? _____

   _____

2. What is the name of the county seat? _____

3. Through what three cities does the U.S. highway pass? _____

   _____

4. Name one intermittent river in Carter County. _____

5. What is the point of interest in this county? _____

On a separate piece of paper, make a political map of the county in which you live.

Historical Maps

There is another type of map that makes use of boundary lines. These maps are called **historical maps** and show something about the history of an area.

At the time of Columbus, there were about 300 Native American tribes in North America. These tribes are often divided into seven groups: Woodland, Plains, Southwestern, California-Intermountain, Pacific Coast, Far North, and Middle American.

Use this historical map to answer questions about the Native American of early North America.

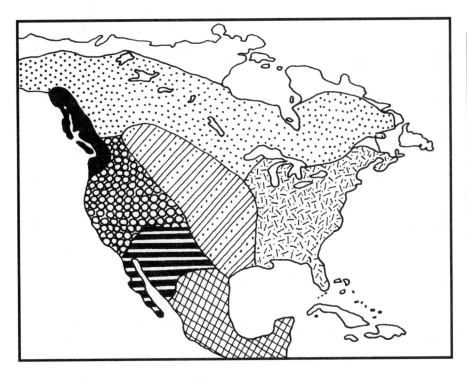

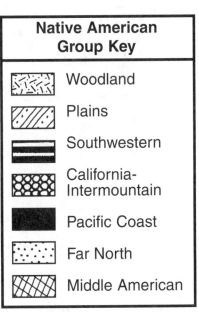

**Native American
Group Key**

Woodland

Plains

Southwestern

California-
Intermountain

Pacific Coast

Far North

Middle American

1. What group of Native Americans covered the largest North American area?

   _____

2. What group of Native Americans were both in Mexico and the United States?

   _____

3. What group of Native Americans covered the smallest North American area?

   _____

4. What Native Americans were the early inhabitants of North Dakota, South Dakota, Nebraska, and Kansas?

   _____

Product Maps

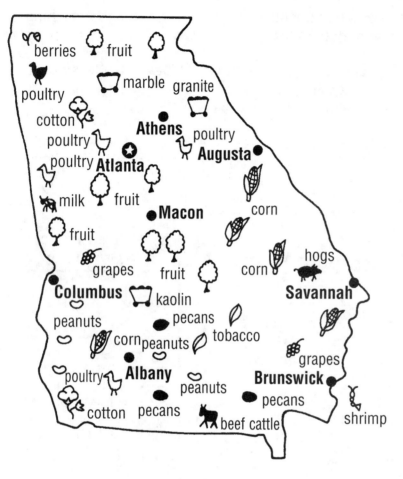

Sometimes maps can show us the types of things that are grown, raised, or mined in a certain place. These maps are called **product maps**.

Here are some of the products that are grown, raised, or mined in Georgia. Use the information on the map to answer the questions below.

1. Near what city are shrimp harvested? _____

2. What product is produced in great quantity near Macon? _____

3. What products are grown more in the southern part of Georgia than in the northern part? Name three.

   a. _____   b. _____   c. _____

4. What product is produced in the northwest corner of Georgia that is not produced in any great quantity in other locations in Georgia? _____

   _____

5. What food is grown between Augusta and Savannah? _____

6. What types of products are mined in the northern part of the state? _____

   _____

Challenge: After you have finished, use an encyclopedia or other source to find a product map of the place you live. Redraw it, selecting 10 to 20 products to draw on your map.

Population Maps

A **population map** shows the areas in which people live. This map shows the average number of people who live in certain areas of California. It is called a population density map.

Use the map to answer these questions. Write your answers on another piece of paper.

Population Density of California

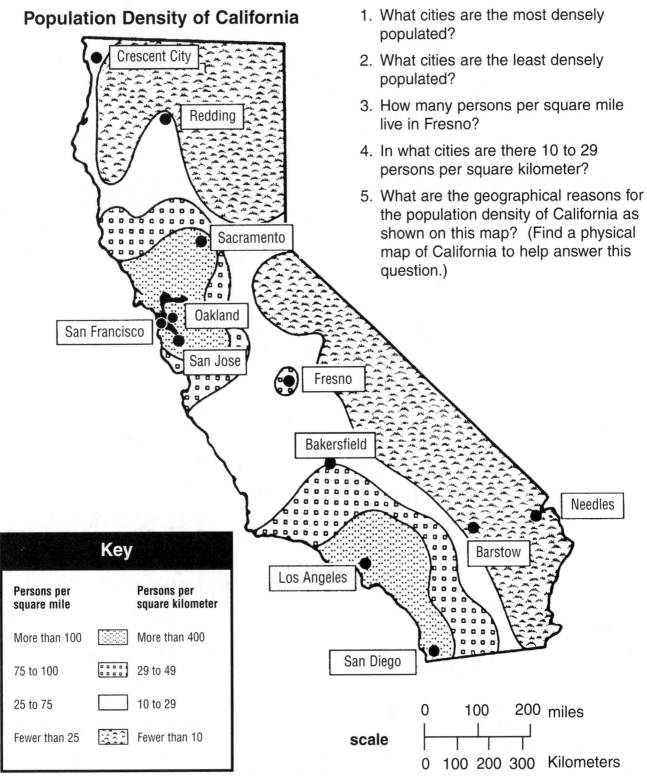

1. What cities are the most densely populated?

2. What cities are the least densely populated?

3. How many persons per square mile live in Fresno?

4. In what cities are there 10 to 29 persons per square kilometer?

5. What are the geographical reasons for the population density of California as shown on this map? (Find a physical map of California to help answer this question.)

Key

Persons per square mile		Persons per square kilometer
More than 100		More than 400
75 to 100		29 to 49
25 to 75		10 to 29
Fewer than 25		Fewer than 10

scale

0   100   200 miles

0 100 200 300   Kilometers

Weather Maps

Weather maps show what the weather of a specific area has been or could be. Weather patterns are shown on maps by using symbols or shading.

February Weather in Rainier County February, 19, 1988

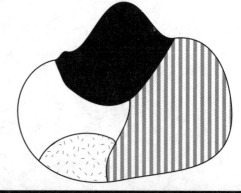

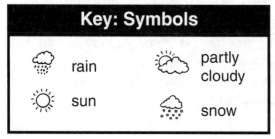

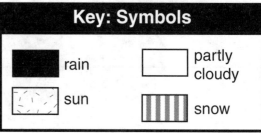

Weather maps can also show average temperatures in a specific area. Here is a map of the average January temperatures in Massachusetts.

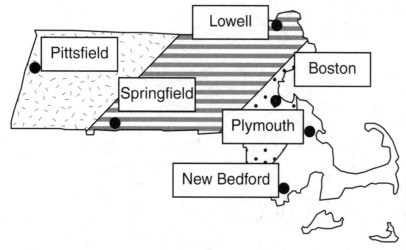

Key	
Degrees Fahrenheit	**Degrees Celsius**
Above 30	Above -1
26 to 30	-3 to -1
22 to 26	-6 to -3
Below 22	Below -6

1. Which city is coldest in January? _____

2. Which cities are in the region that has the mildest winters? _____

3. What is the average January temperature in

   a. Boston? _____   b. Lowell? _____   c. Pittsfield? _____

It All Adds Up!

The map skills you have learned in this book all add up! Can you read this map?

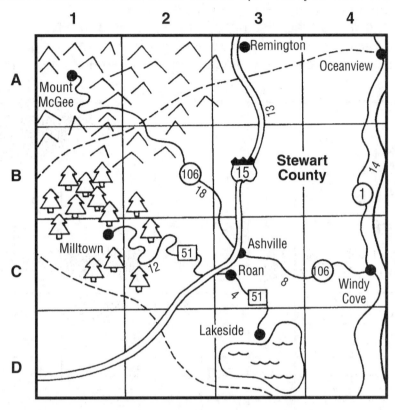

Key
- ● city or town
- ⋀⋀⋀ mountains
- county boundary
- 🌲🌲 forest
- 〰️ lake
- —— mileage between points
- 〰 coastline
- interstate highway
- ◯ state highway
- ▢ local road

1. At what gridpoints are the following places:

   a. Lakeside _____   b. Mount McGee _____   c. Ashville and Roan _____

2. What gridpoints are completely out of Stewart County? _____

3. What type of road leads from Windy Cove to Mount McGee? _____

4. Lumber products might be milled in what grid points? _____

5. What cities are not in Stewart County? _____

6. How many miles is it from:

   a. Lakeside to Milltown? _____   b. Oceanview to Ashville? _____

7. State Highway 1 parallels what kind of land? _____

How Far to New York?

Distance charts show you the distance between two places if you travel by road.

This distance chart shows the road distances in miles between ten North American cities. Look at the chart carefully. Read it by using two fingers and coming together to find the distance between cities. Practice. When you are comfortable using the chart, answer the questions below.

Ten City Distance Chart	Albuquerque	Boston	Chicago	Denver	Indianapolis	Los Angeles	Miami	Montreal	New York City
Boston	2172		963	1949	906	2779	1504	318	206
Chicago	1281	963		996	181	2054	1329	828	802
Denver	417	1949	996		1058	1059	2037	1815	1771
Indianapolis	1266	906	181	1058		2073	1148	840	713
Los Angeles	807	2779	2054	1059	2073		2687	2873	2786
Miami	1938	1504	1329	2037	1148	2687		1654	1308
Montreal	2087	318	828	1815	840	2873	1654		378
New York City	1979	206	802	1771	713	2786	1308	378	
Seattle	1440	2976	2013	1307	2194	1311	3273	2685	2815

Find the distances between these cities:

1. Los Angeles and New York: _____

2. Seattle and Albuquerque: _____

3. Boston and New York: _____

4. Denver and Miami: _____

5. New York City and Chicago: _____

6. Montreal and Indianapolis: _____

7. Chicago and Miami: _____

8. Indianapolis and Denver: _____

9. Montreal and Los Angeles: _____

10. Seattle and Boston:_____

11. Chicago and Boston:_____

12. Denver and Albuquerque: _____

Tables

A **table** is a type of chart that is organized in such a way as to make information easy to find.

Read this table about the three major classifications of rocks. Use the information in the table to answer the questions at the bottom of this page.

Three Major Classifications of Rocks			
Classification	**rock**	**color**	**structure**
Igneous Rock (forms from hardened magma)	granite	white to gray, pink to red	closely arranged medium-to-coarse crystals
	obsidian	black, sometimes with brown streaks	glassy, no crystals
	pumice	grayish-white	light, fine pores, floats on water
Sedimentary Rock (formed by hardening of plant, animal, and mineral materials)	coal	shiny to dull black	brittle, in seams of layers
	limestone	white, gray, and buff to black and red	dense, forms cliffs, and may contain fossils
	shale	yellow, red, gray, green, black	dense, fine particles, soft, smells like clay
Metamorphic Rock (formed by existing rock changing because of heat or pressure)	marble	many colors, often mixed	medium-to-coarse crystals
	quartzite	white, gray, pink, and buff	big, hard, and often glassy
	schist	white, gray, red, green, black	flaky, banded, sparkles with mica

1. What is the name of the igneous rock that is black and has a glassy appearance?

   _____

2. What classification of rock is most likely to contain fossils?

   _____

3. To which classification do schist and marble belong?

   _____

Chart the Read-a-Thon!

Students at Hudson Elementary School have been participating in a Read-a-Thon to raise money for their school library. Each student has tallied the number of books he or she has read and is ready to collect the pledge money.

This chart represents the reading and pledging of 15 students involved in the Read-a-Thon. After reading the chart, answer the questions at the bottom of the page.

Hudson Elementary School Read-a-Thon: Room 3			
Student's Name	**Total Books Read**	**Pledge per Book**	**Money Collected**
Acevedo, Jennifer	31	10¢	$3.10
Adams, Joseph	5	10¢	$.50
Barton, Michael	61	5¢	$3.05
Duran, Louis	17	15¢	$2.55
Edwards, Marylou	47	5¢	$2.35
Harrison, Trevor	11	25¢	$2.75
Lee, Rebecca	40	10¢	$4.00
Logan, Cassie	22	5¢	$1.10
Marshall, Barbara	9	50¢	$4.50
Peterson, David	102	5¢	$5.10
Ross, Kathryn	58	10¢	$5.80
Rublo, Anthony	83	5¢	$4.15
Shea, Sharon	39	10¢	$3.90
Tran, Alvan	14	10¢	$1.40
Yetter, Liz	75	5¢	$3.75
Total	614		$48.00

1. Which student read the most books?_____

2. What was the highest amount of money collected by one student? _____

3. Who had the highest pledge of money per book? _____

4. Was the person who read the most books the same as the person who collected the most money? _____

5. Was the person who had the highest pledge of money per book the same as the person who collected the most money?_____

6. What was the total number of books read by these students? _____

7. How much money did these students earn for the library? _____

Would a Read-a-Thon be a good way to raise money at your school?

Time Line

A **time line** is a way to show events that happened in the order they happened. You read time lines from left to right.

Read this time line and then answer the questions.

School Party Time Line

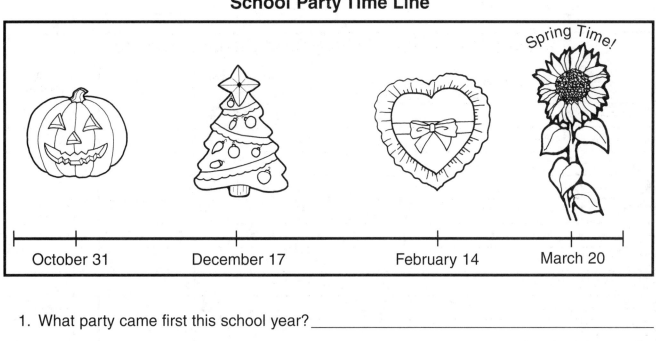

October 31	December 17	February 14	March 20

1. What party came first this school year?_____

2. What party came last this year?_____

3. What kind of party did the children have on February 14? _____

4. How many parties did the class have this year? _____

Make a time line using your birthday and the birthday dates of two other people in your family. Write the birthdays on the time line below. Illustrate your time line.

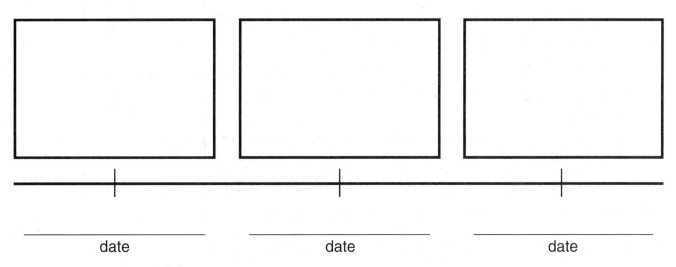

_____   _____   _____
       date   date   date

Events in My Life

Work with your family to find the dates for very special events in your life. Some events might have just your age or a grade level. Then choose the five events that you think are most important to you and write them on the time line below.

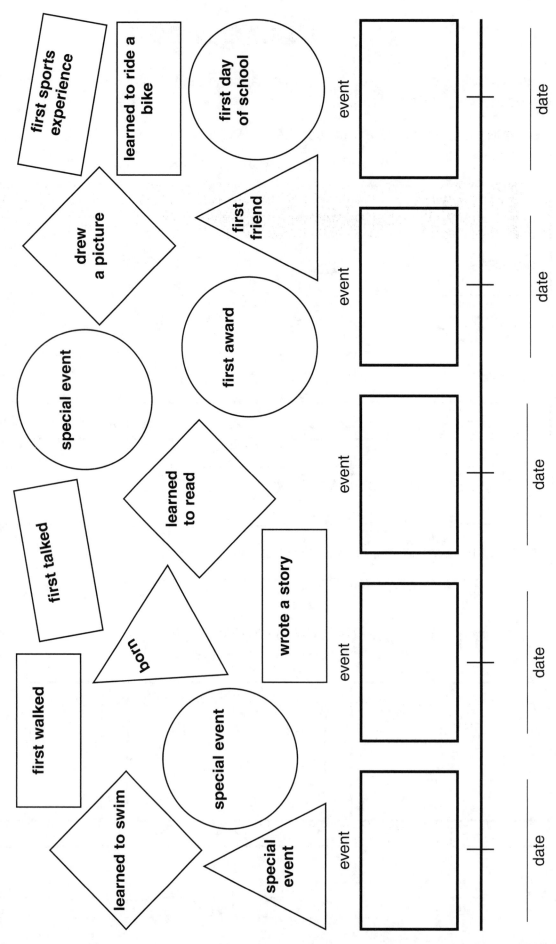

first sports experience

learned to ride a bike

first day of school

drew a picture

first friend

special event

first award

first talked

learned to read

born

wrote a story

first walked

special event

learned to swim

special event

event   date

event   date

event   date

event   date

event   date

Pictographs

One type of graph that gives us information is called a **pictograph**. In a pictograph, pictures are used instead of numbers.

Read this pictograph to find out the number and types of instruments sold in April at Harmony Music Store.

April Instrument Sales at Harmony Music Store

pianos	
flutes	
guitars	
drums	
trumpets	

Key: 1 instrument = 5 instruments

1. How many of each of these instruments were sold?

   pianos _____   flutes _____   guitars _____

   drums _____   trumpets _____

2. How many more guitars were sold than . . .

   pianos? _____   flutes? _____

   drums? _____   trumpets? _____

3. Do you think the piano sales or the guitar sales brought in more money for Harmony Music Store? Explain the reason(s) for your choice.

   _____

   _____

Diagrams

Diagrams are pictures that are labeled so that a reader can easily learn the parts of what is pictured.

Do you know anything about guitars? Did you know there are different types of guitars? Can you describe the similarities and differences between acoustic and electric guitars?

Study these diagrams. Then answer the questions at the bottom of the page.

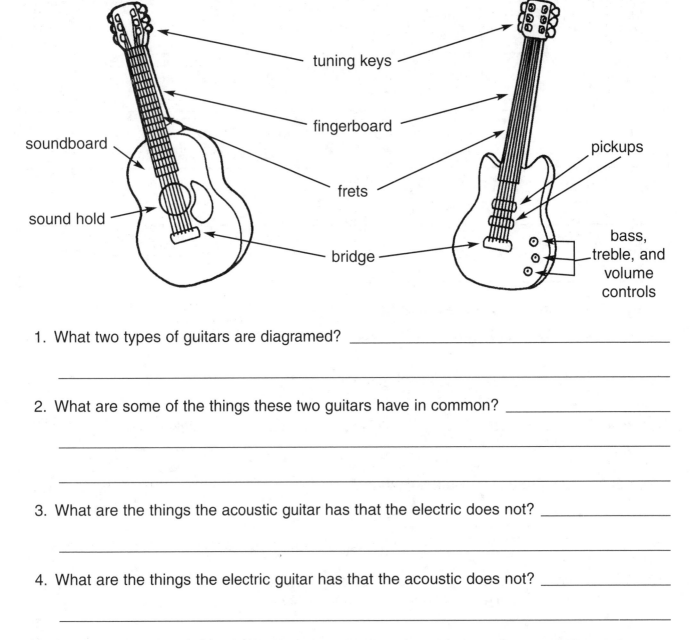

1. What two types of guitars are diagramed? _____

_____

2. What are some of the things these two guitars have in common? _____

_____

_____

3. What are the things the acoustic guitar has that the electric does not? _____

_____

4. What are the things the electric guitar has that the acoustic does not? _____

_____

*As an extension of this activity, research how a sound is made by each guitar. Then, if possible, bring acoustic and electric guitars to class for demonstration purposes.

Ant City!

Have you ever wondered what it looks like inside an ant hill? You will get an idea from studying this cutaway diagram.

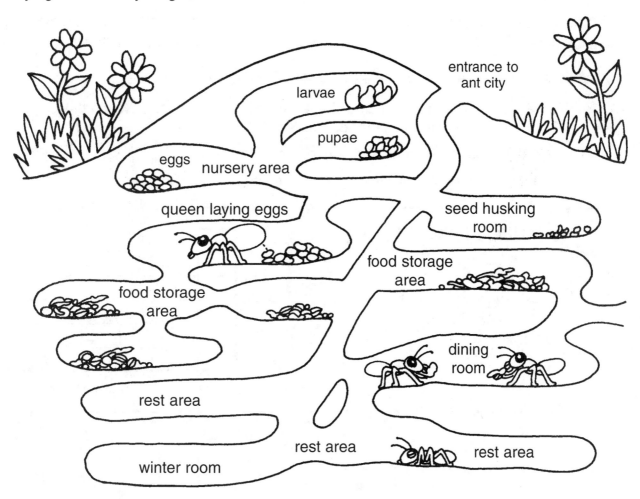

Use this color key to color the rooms of this ant hill.

yellow	nursery area (eggs, pupae, larvae)	**blue**	rest area	**orange**	food storage area
purple	winter room	**green**	seed husking room	**red**	dining room

Think about it: Why do you think the nursery is at the top of the ant city and the winter room is at the bottom?

_____

_____

_____

Graph Game

There are some letters of the alphabet hidden in these three graphs. Can you make the dots and draw the lines to find them?

Directions:

1. Begin on the left side of the graph.

2. Match the number in each pair with the number at the bottom. Match the letter in each pair with the letter on the left side of the graph.

3. Mark all the pairs with dots and connect the lines.

4. Write the name of the mystery letter on the line next to the graph.

Mystery Letter #1

Clues:

2,B   3,F   4,D   5,F   6,B

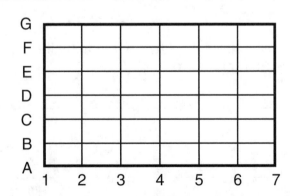

Mystery Letter #2

Clues:

2,F   3,B   4,D   5,B   6,F

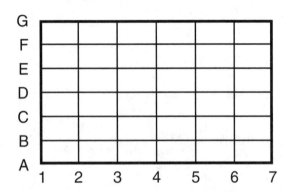

Mystery Letter #3

Clues:

3,F   4,B   5,F

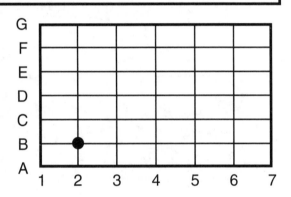

Movie Schedule

Sometimes a movie schedule is called a **timetable**. This is because the times that movies begin are listed together on a table. Look at the movie schedule. Use it to answer the questions below.

Movie	Starting Show Time
A Lad, Dan	11:00 AM, 2:00 PM, 4:30 PM
Free Billy	11:00 AM, 3:30 PM, 7:00 PM
The Sandy Lot	1:00 PM, 5:00 PM, 8:00 PM
The Mystery Garden	2:00 PM, 5:30 pm, 9:00 PM
The Adam's Farm	3:00 PM, 6:00 PM, 7:30 PM

1. Could you see *Free Billy* at 2:00 PM? _____

2. If you do not get out of church until 2:00 PM, when is the earliest you can see

   The Sandy Lot? _____

3. Is it true that three of the movies are shown in the morning? _____

   _____

4. Name the two movies that are shown at 2:00 PM. _____

   _____

5. Which movies begin after 7:30 PM? _____

   _____

6. Which movies would you like to see and at which times? _____

   _____

Go East!

Do you know where the states of the United States are in relation to each other? Now it is your chance to find out. Go east!

This is a maze game. The object of the game is to move geographically east through the states of the United States written here. Begin at Hawaii and end at Maine. You may move one space at a time right, left, or down. You may not move upward or diagonally. Move to the space with the state that is the closest and to the east. Trace your path as you go. Have a nice trip!

Start

South Carolina	Wisconsin	North Dakota	★ Hawaii	Washington	Alaska
Idaho	Virginia	New Jersey	Mississippi	Nevada	Oregon
Ohio	Colorado	South Dakota	Oklahoma	Wyoming	Montana
Maryland	Missouri	Illinois	Arkansas	Utah	California
Iowa	New Mexico	Kentucky	Georgia	Texas	North Carolina
Florida	Arizona	New York	West Virginia	Kansas	Louisiana
Maine ★	New Hampshire	Vermont	Nebraska	Indiana	Delaware

Finish

Go West!

Do you know where the countries of the world are in relation to each other? Now is your chance to find out. Go west!

This is a maze game. The object of the game is to move geographically west one space at a time through the countries of the world written here. Begin at Finland and end at Canada. You may not move upward or diagonally. Move to the space with the country that is closest and to the west. Trace your path as you go. Bon voyage!

Start

Russia	Spain	United States	Libya	★ Finland	Iran
Turkey	Peru	Venezuela	England	Germany	China
Nepal	Mexico	Algeria	Sudan	Japan	Brazil
Ecuador	New Zealand	Australia	Costa Rica	Thailand	Norway
Romania	Panama	Mongolia	India	Pakistan	Chile
Greece	Iraq	Sweden	Cuba	Saudi Arabia	Egypt
Chad	Canada ✪	Iceland	Ireland	France	Italy

Finish

Country and City Match

Match the city to its country by drawing a line between them.

Cities	Countries
Los Angeles	France
Glasgow	South Korea
Seoul	United States
Bombay	Japan
Nagano	Australia
Nice	Israel
Frankfurt	Portugal
Florence	Ireland
Toronto	Brazil
Lima	Peru
Rio de Janeiro	Colombia
Bogotá	Egypt
Lisbon	South Africa
Cairo	Canada
Jerusalem	Scotland
Copenhagen	Italy
Canberra	Denmark
Dublin	Mexico
Cape Town	Germany
Acapulco	India

Where Am I?

Here are clues to help you find a mystery state. When you have discovered the state, write its name on the bottom of the page.

1. I am east of California.

2. I am neither among the smallest nor the largest of the states in the United States.

3. I have a mild climate.

4. I contain all the raw materials for making steel—limestone, iron ore, and coal.

5. I am covered by forests on about two-thirds of my land.

6. I produce many chickens, eggs, and milk.

7. I am south of Michigan.

8. I have more than one famous cave.

9. I am crossed by the Tennessee River.

10. I am north of Florida.

11. I am a Southeast State.

12. I am surrounded by four states.

13. I have a belt of black clay soil that crosses me.

14. I am west of Georgia.

15. I touch the Gulf of Mexico.

I am _____!

Locate and then color the mystery state on the map below.

"State" My Name

Here are clues to help you find a mystery state. When you have discovered the state, write its name on the bottom of the page.

1. I am west of Virginia.

2. I am not among the smallest states in the United States.

3. I am home to buffalo, black bears, and tortoises.

4. I have a very large lake.

5. I am east of California.

6. I have rich mineral deposits, including oil shale.

7. I contain more than one national park.

8. I have snow-covered mountains.

9. I am south of Montana.

10. I am a Mountain West state.

11. I contain a huge desert.

12. I am crossed by the Colorado River.

13. I am surrounded by six states.

14. I have many famous canyons.

15. I am north of Arizona.

I am _____!

Locate and then color the mystery state on the map below.

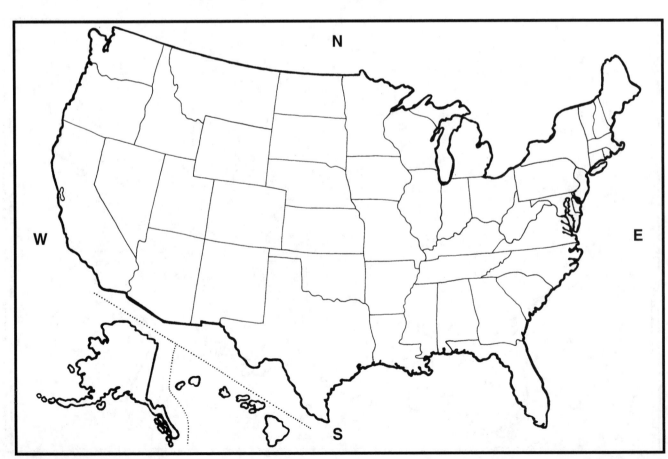

What Country Am I?

Here are clues to help you find a mystery country. When you have discovered the country, write its name on the bottom of the page.

1. I am in the Western Hemisphere.
2. I am south of Canada.
3. I am bordered by the Atlantic Ocean.
4. I am a leading producer of wheat.
5. I am north of Antarctica.
6. Early explorers came to find silver in my land.
7. I am a great world producer of cattle and sheep.
8. I am on the continent of South America.

9. I am bordered by the Andes Mountains.
10. I am in summer when the United States and Canada are in winter.
11. I am about a third the size of the United States.
12. I am bordered by the Uruguay River.
13. I have the highest and lowest elevations in South America.
14. Cape Horn is at my base.
15. I am east of Chile.

I am _____!

Use the map below to discover what the mystery country is.

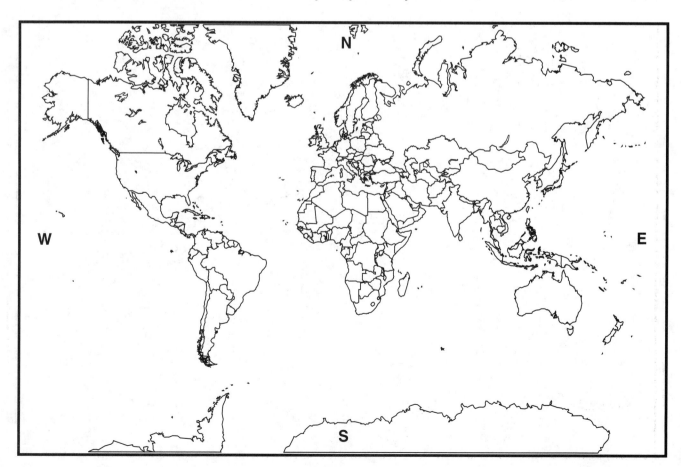

A Mystery Country

Here are clues to help you find a mystery country. When you have discovered the country, write its name on the bottom of the page.

1. I am in the Eastern Hemisphere.

2. I am not among the largest countries in the world.

3. I am west of Asia.

4. I am one of the world's leading producers and exporters of petroleum.

5. I am north of Angola.

6. Because of my nearness to the equator, I have a tropical climate.

7. I have many varied land regions.

8. I am on the continent of Africa.

9. Cacao, palm oil, and peanuts are some of my chief agricultural products.

10. I am on the west coast of Africa.

11. I rank among the world's largest nations in population.

12. Lake Chad forms part of my border.

13. I am surrounded by four countries.

14. I am crossed by the Niger River.

15. I am north of Cameroon.

I am _____!

Use the map below to discover what the mystery country is.

Answer Key

Page 7
1. dog, cat, tree
2. leaves, trees, wind
3. brother, baseball
4. pictures, paints
5. freedom, something, country.
6. love, family
7. electricity, light
8. student, story, rabbit, fox
9. soldiers, home, land
10. girl, money, bank
11. boys, desk, project
12. monkeys, vines, jungle
13. braid, ribbon
14. team, record, team
15. museum, exhibit

Page 8
Answers will vary.

Page 9
1. I live in the last (house) on Elm Street.
2. My (dog,) Max, and I went for a walk.
3. There are several Ryans in my (class.)
4. My (family) is planning a (trip) to the Grand Canyon.
5. "Mom, where is my yellow (shirt)?" Jenny asked her (mother.)
6. Where is Primrose Park?
7. The only (vegetable) I like is (broccoli.)
8. Our (cat) is named Sylvester.
9. My (teacher) is Mrs. Simms.
10. Ricky, Sam, and Tim played (football) in the (park.)
11. Katie and Emily live in Jasper City, but their (cousins) live in Walton.
12. My (brother) and his (friend) liked the (rollercoaster) at the Maple County Fair.
13. March was too windy this (year,) but April was a beautiful (month.)
14. Brent and Kenneth played (basketball) last Saturday.
15. Have the (children) ever seen *Star Wars*?

Page 10
There may be some variation in the answers; however, these are the likeliest choices.
1. clowder of cats
2. gang of elk
3. school of fish
4. tribe of monkeys
5. murder of crows
6. flight of swallows
7. pod of whales
8. crash of rhinoceroses

Page 11
1. markets
2. pencils
3. trucks
4. farmers
5. cupcakes
6. students
7. telephones
8. computers
9. pictures
10. penguins

Page 12
1. parties
2. companies
3. armies
4. countries
5. spies
6. puppies
7. liberties
8. flies
9. berries
10. factories
11. flurries
12. families
13. stories
14. victories
15. babies
16. ladies
17. monoplies
18. bodies

Page 13
1. dishes (*color*)
2. circuses (*color*)
3. parties
4. babies
5. buzzes (*color*)
6. inches (*color*)
7. keys
8. passes (*color*)
9. classes (*color*)
10. clowns
11. coaches (*color*)
12. watches (*color*)
13. fishes (*color*)
14. pitches (*color*)
15. finches (*color*)

Page 14
bush, bushes; pen, pens; bench, benches; egg, eggs; match, matches; miss, misses; valley, valleys; worry, worries; flower, flowers; princess, princesses; address, addresses; peach, peaches

Page 15
Sentences will vary.
1. men
2. women
3. children
4. sheep
5. mice
6. feet
7. oxen
8. geese

Page 16
1. doll's
2. Lena's
3. girls'
4. turtle's
5. Kate's
6. child's
7. boys'
8. penguin's
9. blouse's
10. pan's
11. man's
12. Jen's
13. lions'
14. toys'
15. play's

Page 17
1. plays
2. flies
3. makes
4. ran
5. popped
6. ran
7. fell
8. eat
9. stood
10. reads

Page 18
woke, jumped, landed, sat, rubbed, grumbled, fell, looked, wanted, see, ran, grabbed, blew, played, liked, sounded, heard, stopped, listened, came, like, grabbed, ran, sat, played, floated, felt, heard, stopped, listened, came, ran, played, liked, heard, called, went, took, put, put, told, went, tried, imagine, heard, stopped, listened, snored, moaned, stuck, heard, covered, fell

Page 19

Helping Verbs	Action Verbs
1. will	1. ride
2. is	2. ridden
3. were	3. pushed
4. can	4. move
5. has	5. driven
6. have	6. pulled
7. have	7. seen
8. will	8. go
9. is	9. going
10. will	10. drink

Page 20
1. painted
2. climbed
3. played
4. laughed
5. shouted
6. jumped
7. ran
8. saw
9. ate
10. came
11. made
12. built
13. slept
14. gave
15. took
16. brought
17. sang
18. held
19. went
20. wrote

Page 21
1. turned
2. cooked
3. rolled
4. watched
5. parked
6. filled
7. colored
8. folded
9. closed
10. looked
11. smile
12. fold
13. close
14. paint
15. climb
16. share
17. joke
18. match
19. laugh
20. play

Page 22
1. blew
2. came
3. sang
4. wore
5. took
6. cried
7. made
8. gave
9. fell
10. flew
11. catch
12. read
13. ride
14. drink
15. swing
16. shine
17. pay
18. write
19. sweep
20. tear

Page 23
1. was
2. were
3. was
4. were
5. was
6. were
7. were
8. was
9. were
10. was

Page 24
1. are
2. are
3. am
4. is
5. are
6. are
7. are
8. is
9. am
10. am

Page 25
1. S, has
2. P, run
3. P, jump
4. S, hops
5. P, sing
6. S, is
7. P, are
8. S, hops
9. S, is
10. S, has

Answer Key (cont.)

Page 26
1. unusual, front
2. playful
3. green, long
4. funny, old
5. new, gray
6. tall, pretty.
7. smart, funny
8. silly
9. happy, large
10. small, black, shiny
11. choir, colorful, lively
12. kind, generous
13. orange, yellow
14. little, imaginary
15. quiet, barn

Page 27
1. this; Which one?
2. old; What kind of?
3. French; What kind of?
4. Scottish; What kind of?
5. yellow; What kind of?
6. three; How many?
7. delicious, spinach; What kind of?
8. comic; What kind of?
9. soft; What kind of?
10. mean; What kind of?
11. clueless; What kind of?
12. those, black, small; What kind of?

Page 28
Adjectives will vary.

Page 29
1. a
2. an
3. a
4. an
5. a
6. a
7. an
8. an
9. a
10. a
11. An
12. a
13. a
14. An
15. A

Page 30
1. taller, tallest
2. sweeter, sweetest
3. smaller, smallest
4. messier, messiest
5. bigger, biggest
6. prettier, prettiest
7. harder, hardest
8. thicker, thickest

Page 31
1. how; quietly
2. when; tomorrow
3. when; later
4. where; here
5. how; fiercely
6. how; softly
7. how; gracefully
8. when; Yesterday
9. how; well
10. how; quickly

Page 32
Verbs and adverbs will vary.

Page 33
Answers may vary but here are some possibilities.
1. trustingly
2. calmly
3. sharply
4. permanently
5. truthfully
6. patiently
7. correctly
8. carefully
9. quietly
10. lightly

Page 34
1. He played baseball.
2. She swam across the pool.
3. They climbed the trees.
4. They rode their bikes to school.
5. The team surprised her with a trophy.
6. Kim saw it run across the street.
7. She read the new best seller.
8. He saw a strange shadow.
9. The girls walked to her house.
10. The family found them in a basket on their porch.
11. Where should I put them?
12. He put gas in the car.
13. They won the championship!
14. Where is it?
15. Please, give that to him.

Page 35
Answers will vary.

Page 36
1. busy, active
2. nibble, chew
3. flavorful, tasty
4. joyful, happy
5. fall, trip
6. huge, enormous
7. worried, anxious
8. mad, angry
9. talk, chat
10. cry, weep

Page 37
1. neat, spotless
2. sad, unhappy
3. thin, skinny
4. look, see
5. plain, simple
6. strong, powerful
7. cold, chilly
8. big, large
9. cheap, stingy
10. quiet, calm
11. poor, needy
12. little, small
13. sharp, pointed
14. loud, noisy
15. rich, wealthy

Page 38
1. like, similar
2. snip, cut
3. plump, fat
4. fly, soar
5. bark, yelp
6. clown, jester
7. huge, gigantic
8. real, true
9. entire, whole
10. baby, infant

Page 39
1. laugh, cry
2. fast, slow
3. hurt, heal
4. shiny, dull
5. wake, sleep
6. girl, boy
7. fire, water
8. truth, lie
9. ugly, pretty
10. hard, soft

Page 40
Answers will vary but may include:
1. hard
2. sour
3. cold
4. later
5. lie
6. mean
7. murky
8. west

Page 42
1. hare, hair
2. our, hour
3. dough, doe
4. no, know
5. read, red
6. tale, tail

Page 43
1. might
2. not
3. popular
4. plum
5. bare
6. bawl
7. banned
8. franc
9. cymbal
10. chilly
11. scent
12. hymn
13. bazaar
14. blue
15. cereal

Page 44
1. Weather Flash . . . heavy rains due in an hour.
2. Next, on *The World Turns* . . . Elizabeth is never seen again.
3. News Extra! A wild horse and deer escape from zoo.
4. Watch Muscle Man weekly lift weights on Channel 2.
5. Special Announcement! Ice skating pair wins gold medals!
6. Try a new cereal just for kids! *Awesome Oats!*

Page 45
1. S
2. S
3. A
4. S
5. A
6. A
7. A
8. S
9. S
10. S
11. A
12. A
13. S
14. S
15. A
16. A
17. S
18. A
19. A
20. S

Page 46
1. antonym
2. synonym
3. antonym
4. homophone
5. synonym
6. homophone
7. homophone
8. synonym
9. antonym
10. synonym
11. homophone
12. antonym
13. antonym
14. synonym
15. homophone
16. antonym
17. antonym
18. homophone
19. synonym
20. antonym

Answer Key (cont.)

Page 47

Some answers will vary.
Sunday, Monday, Tuesday, Wednesday, Thursday, Friday, Saturday

1. January
2. February
3. March
4. April
5. May
6. June
7. July
8. August
9. September
10. October
11. November
12. December

Page 48

Pacific Ocean, Grand Canyon, Mt. Rushmore, Amazon River, Sahara Desert, North Pole, San Diego Zoo, Lake Louise, Rocky Mountains, Hyde Park, Disneyland, Niagara Falls

Page 49

One, When, What, Mike, It's, Both, Ohhh, It's, Sure, Mike, Chris, Mike, He, The, Nobody, Mike, Chris, Next, The, No, You, Why, We, Well, The, They, They, George

Page 50

1. Uncle Jorge sat on the front porch.
2. I said, "Mom, what I really want to do is to stay home!"
3. My mom and my dad won't be home until 7 P.M.
4. His grandma made a quilt for his birthday.
5. My cousin and my grandma will be coming with my mom.
6. Our grandparents have a surprise for Aunt Aimee.
7. I wrote "Dear Grandma," at the top of my stationery.
8. I wish my aunt lived closer to us; she looks just like Mom.
9. Then Dad stopped and looked behind him.
10. I like to go to Grandmother Norton's house in the summer.
11. My favorite cousin is Jimmy because he makes me laugh.
12. At the wedding we saw Aunt Marsha and Cousin Brad.
13. My mom and dad are taking me to dinner after the awards assembly.
14. At the reunion I saw Aunt Edith, Uncle Jacques, and Cousins Kathy, Meredith, Hector, and Samantha.
15. For my birthday I'm inviting Cousin Sarah, Cousin Leigh, Aunt Susie, and my uncle, whose name is Mike.

Page 51

1. isn't
2. let's
3. can't
4. he'll
5. aren't
6. we've

Page 52

1. couldn't
2. haven't
3. can't
4. aren't
5. isn't
6. wouldn't

Page 53

1. do not
2. would not
3. will not
4. are not
5. should not
6. he is
7. I have
8. they have
9. we are
10. she is
11. you will
12. did not
13. is not
14. was not
15. we will
16. I would

Page 54

cannot, You are, Do not, will not, could not, it is, it is, that is, Let us, it is, will not, must have, I had, must have, she would, did not, There have, who have, must have, should not, could not, It is, would have, that is, I had, she had, she would, I will, would have, was not, were not, Who is, we are, would have, was not, could not, should not, would not, What is, must not, were not, would have, she had, had not, she had, she would, Here is, it is, She has, She has, I am, I will

Page 55

1. !
2. . or !
3. ?
4. .
5. .
6. ?
7. ?
8. !
9. .
10. . or !
11. !
12. ! or .
13. ?
14. .
15. ?

Page 56

1. . . . Amy, Katy, and Melissa.
2. . . . basketball, baseball, and volleyball.
3. Katy, Melissa, and Tommy . . .
4. . . . a geologist, an astronaut, or a chemist.
5. . . . Skip, Tiger, and Rags.
6. . . . math, science, and art.
7. Tommy, Amy, Katy, and Melissa . . .
8. . . . his parents, his sisters, and his dogs.
9. . . . three birds, two cats, and one dog.
10. . . . Tommy, Amy, and Manuel.

Page 57

1. Mrs. Burnett, may we go out to recess now?
2. Yes, we are going out to recess now, Jason.
3. Mary, will you swing with Tommy and me?
4. Sure, Jason, I love to swing.
5. Mary is going to swing with us, Tommy.
6. No, Jason, I'm sliding with Matt.
7. Matt can swing with us, Tommy.
8. Jason, we can all swing first, and then we can all slide.
9. Jason, do you want to go on the slide first?
10. Tommy, what time is recess over?

Page 58

1. Amy Jones, my best friend, has a very large family.
2. Joe, her oldest brother, works for an airline company.
3. The youngest in the family, Tony, is only three years old.
4. The oldest daughters, Karen and Sue, often help with the younger children.
5. My other good friend, Nicole, and I spend a great deal of time at Amy's house.
6. Mrs. Jones, Amy's mother, says that two more children are coming tomorrow.
7. Amy's dad, Mr. Jones, works hard to take care of seven children.
8. Rags and Slick, the Jones' pets, get a great deal of attention.

Page 59

1. Jerry was born on October 5, 1986.
2. My favorite Christmas was December 25, 1992.
3. Susan's mom came home from the hospital on April 6, 1994.
4. We took our summer vacation on July 21, 1993.
5. My grandfather was born on August 11, 1941.
6. On April 6, 1994, Susan's mom brought a new baby girl home from the hospital.
7. My grandfather remembers July 20, 1969, as an important date in history.
8. On July 21, 1993, my family went to Hawaii for our summer vacation.

Page 60

1. The state capital is in Austin, Texas.
2. My home is in Denver, Colorado.
3. Her grandparents live in Bangor, Maine.
4. Our tournament is in Ardmore, Oklahoma.
5. Disney World is in Orlando, Florida.
6. Her father is stationed in Fairbanks, Alaska.
7. Queen Elizabeth lives in London, England.
8. We rode the ferry in Seattle, Washington.

Page 61

1. April 15, 1972
2. July 27, 1640
3. September 13, 1910
4. Monday, January 31
5. Sunday, November 16
6. Anaheim, California
7. Albuquerque, New Mexico
8. Quebec, Canada
9. Bangor, Maine
10. Little Rock, Arkansas
11. Dear Joe,
12. Your friend,
13. Sincerely yours,
14. Love,
15. Yours truly,
16. All birds have feathers, wings, and beaks.
17. The Shetland pony is small, friendly, and gentle.
18. A friendly, playful dog makes a good pet.
19. I have three cats named Boots, Muffin, and Tiger.
20. I like to color with pencils, markers, and crayons.

Answer Key (cont.)

Page 62
1. No, Marlene does not like being squirted in the face.
2. Christopher, how long have you been on the telephone?
3. Well, just what did you have in mind?
4. Sure, Laura, I'd love another jelly donut.
5. My brother, the world's scariest boy, likes escargots.
6. The plane we are taking, a 747, will have plenty of room.
7. You realize, of course, that you will not be allowed out of the house in that outfit.
8. My orthodontist, Dr. Baugh, decorated his office for Halloween.
9. All right, if that's what you think, let's just eat all of the chocolate.
10. In the future we will be able to speak to our computers.
11. No kidding, you went rock climbing?
12. We went to Bouquet Canyon, a canyon near Valencia, to attend a harvest festival.
13. You could read, for example, some books about the historical period in which your novel takes place.
14. For Valentine's Day my dad gave me two pounds of my favorite treat, candy corn.
15. I don't care what you think, I'm going to go back there and help that little boy.

Page 63
1. cat's food
2. bird's nest
3. Miguel's bike
4. Kim's store
5. David's CD player
6. sister's book
7. brother's skateboard
8. baby's toys
9. teacher's desk
10. painter's brush
11. Nicky ran screaming into Manuel's house.
12. My dad knocked down a hornet's nest.
13. I wish I could drive my brother's car.
14. An alien ate Mariela's homework.
15. Grandpa's spaghetti is the best in the world.

Page 64
1. Ryan asked, "What do you want to play, Martha?"
2. Martha answered, "Let's play baseball."
3. "Okay, we'll play baseball first," said Ryan, "but let's play basketball after that."
4. Mom called, "The cookies are ready."
5. "Oh, boy," the boys yelled at the same time, "let's eat!"

Page 65
1. "What is that bizarre thing upon your head? It looks like an octopus," said Mr. Grimmy. (exact words)
2. The teacher told the students to read the poem, "The Raven" by Friday. (title)
3. I call my sister "Idget," but I have no idea why. (special word)

4. "Hey!" Jacques shouted, "Didn't you hear the coach? He said, 'Stop when you get to the fence!'" (quote within a quote)
5. "And then I will cover you with fragrant rose petals," Mama said, "and sing a lullaby." (exact words)
6. I found a book that said, "Dinosaurs may be more closely related to birds than to lizards." (exact words)
7. We have family nicknames, and my brother's is "Greasy Bear." (special word)
8. "Did you hear what Nicole said?" Amy asked us. "She said, `You guys are just too chicken to try it.' She doesn't know what she is talking about!" (quote within a quote)
9. I thought you would be too "cool" to go on the merry-go-round with me. (special word)
10. She watched *Somewhere in Time* so many times she wore out the tape. (no quotation marks)
11. My brother always talks in his sleep. Last night he said, "Hurry and purple it before the snails get it!" (exact words)
12. After we watched *Twister*, we couldn't stop watching the clouds. (no quotation marks)
13. "Come with us," Dad said, "and we can stop for ice cream on the way." (exact words)
14. I need to find the root word for "transient." (special word)
15. Mom says we shouldn't say "Where's he at?" because it is not proper English. (special words)

Page 66
Dear Pen Pal,

I love to go to the circus! On May 6, 1999, the circus came to my hometown of Jackson, Wyoming. A parade marched through our streets, and soon the big top could be seen. Ken, my brother, and I went to watch the performers prepare for opening night. We saw clowns, acrobats, and even the ringmaster. What a sight! Have you ever seen anything like it? You should go if you ever get the chance.

I also really enjoy playing baseball. My favorite team is the New York Yankees, but I also like the Cardinals. When I grow up I want to be a baseball pitcher, first baseman, or shortstop. Do you like baseball? What do you want to do when you grow up? I wish you could see my cool baseball card collection, but Ken's collection is even better.

Oh, I almost forgot to tell you about my family! There are four people in my family. They are my mom, my dad, my brother, and me. Scruffy, my cat, is also a family member. In August 2000 my grandpa will probably move in with us. I can't wait for that! Didn't you say your grandma lives with you? I'll bet you really like that.

Well, that's all for now. Please write back to me soon. See you!

Your pal,
Brent

Page 67
1. Blake
2. the paintbox
3. the colors
4. Blake
5. Green
6. Orange
7. Blake
8. Blake's favorite color
9. Mom
10. The painting

Page 68
1. Kids
2. Baseball
3. Swimming
4. I
5. Summertime
6. Jeremy
7. Mosquitoes
8. my skin, I
9. seashells
10. summer, it

Page 69
1. is very cold
2. jump into the water
3. splashes us
4. is cold
5. gets out of the water
6. does a handstand underwater
7. claps for him
8. has a leak in it
9. throws the inner tube onto the shore
10. sits on the inner tube
11. deflates with Tonia on it
12. laughs with Tonia
13. jumps into the water
14. swims as fast as he can
15. races Luke

Page 70
1. (Uncle Tony) invited us to the baseball game.
2. (His truck) carried us to the field.
3. (The parking lot) was crowded.
4. (We) finally found our seats.
5. (Uncle Tommy) bought popcorn and peanuts.
6. (Two batters) hit home runs.
7. (Our team) won the game.
8. (People) pushed to get out of the stadium.
9. (We) drove home late at night.
10. (My sister) was very tired.

Page 71–74
Answers will vary.

Page 75
1. Tuesday is the day we go to the library.
2. Who is your teacher?
3. The students in my class were reading.
4. What a wonderful day it is!
5. Jordan, come play with us.
6. Watch out, Michelle!
7. Do you like math?
8. I will paint today.
9. What time is lunch?
10. I got a sticker!

Page 76
1. Gorillas eat ripe bananas.
2. The magician opened the secret door.

Answer Key (cont.)

3. This sentence makes sense.
4. The egg broke on my head.
5. The tired dog took a nap.
6. The snake bit the zookeeper.
7. The boy sharpened his pencil.
8. The girl made a program for her computer.
9. I called my mother on the phone.
10. Susie watched the television.

Page 77

1. My books are on the table. My math book is on top.
2. They were closing the store. It was time to go home.
3. Watch out for the slippery ice! You could fall and hurt yourself.
4. I got a new blue dress. The blue shoes match perfectly.
5. My brother made the team! Will I be able to play baseball some day?
6. I like to go camping. The last time we went, we saw a bear.
7. My teacher was not at school. We had a substitute.
8. I don't like lima beans. I only want mashed potatoes.
9. Can you spend the night at my house? We can have pizza for dinner.
10. My dog has fleas. We had to get her some special medicine.

Page 78

Answers will vary.

Page 79

1. Bruce has many things in his room.
2. Answers will vary.
3. Is there a box of toys under the bed?
4. A rug is in front of the closet.
5. Answers will vary.
6. I can see trees from my window.
7. Answers will vary.
8. Answers will vary.
9. Answers will vary.
10. Latoya cleans her room every day.

Page 80

1. D
2. I
3. I
4. D
5. I
6. D
7. I
8. D
9. I
10. D

Page 81

1–5: Answers will vary
1. I am very tired.
2. Let's sit down here.
3. What a wonderful idea!
4. Ouch!
5. Watch where you throw that ball!
6. Well, then, let's have some lunch.
7. The sandwich is for you.
8. That lasagna is very hot! (*or*) That lasagna is very hot.
9. I didn't think you wanted lasagna.
10. Sue would like a hamburger, please.

11. Bob, you don't have to get so upset! (*or*) Bob, you don't have to get so upset.
12. This sandwich tastes good.
13. I love roast beef! (*or*) I love roast beef.
14. Take your brother to the park.

Page 82

I went to the store because I needed to get something for lunch. My stomach was growling so much that a little boy sitting in a shopping cart could hear it. "Mom," he said, "he has a rumbly tumbly!" "Shush," said his mother. I turned to the little boy and asked, "I have a what?" "A rumbly tumbly," he said and smiled shyly. "A rumbly tumbly, a rumbly tumbly," I said over and over again. The little boy started to giggle, and I was even hungrier than before. "Yikes!" I said to the little boy. "I have to get something to eat before my rumbly tumbly tumbles!" The little boy stopped giggling, pointed his finger at me, and said, "Go get something to eat right now before your rumbly tumbly tumbles!" "Okay!" I said as I rushed down the aisle toward the apples and bananas.

Page 83

1. C, baby
2. V, egg
3. V, apple
4. C, car
5. C, lollipop (or sucker)
6. V, ostrich
7. C, tree
8. C, girl

Page 84

Answers may include the following:
bl: block, blind, blue, blow
br: brown, brook, bright, bring
cl: clown, clap, clean, clutter
cr: cry, creep, cringe, crave
dr: drive, drink, drown, drip
fl: fly, flip, flounce, flit
fr: French, fry, free, frost
gl: glee, glean, glad, glow
gr: green, grass, grow, grape
pl: please, play, plot, plan
pr: pray, prim, promise, proper
sl: slow, slide, sled, slant
sp: space, spice, sport, speck
st: stand, stop, stick, stall
str: street, strand, strap, string
tr: train, trap, trim, trout

Page 85

1. chick or thick
2. choose
3. chop, shop, or whop
4. shape
5. math or mash
6. thank or shank
7. cheese
8. check
9. thirst
10. whistle or thistle
11. bath or bash
12. wish or with

13. whip, chip, or ship
14. bench
15. washing
16. trash

Page 86

yellow = mine, nice, find, try, sigh
purple = treat, eat, free, seem, he, she, sleep, meet, bee, team
red = tape, table, name, whale, ate
green = show, open, so
blue = you, fuse, huge, cube, rule

Page 87

green = club, nut, cup
purple = cat, and, fan
blue = men, when, met
yellow = stop, pot, nod, mob, off, on
red = thin, flip, bit

Page 88

short: bat, beg, bun, fish, hot, jack, let, moth, pump, tin
long: beach, boat, cake, eat, light, maid, mule, muse, note, write

Page 89

1. cane
2. site
3. cape
4. tube
5. dote
6. note
7. rate
8. lobe
9. bite
10. cube
11. grime
12. fine
13. bathe
14. vane
15. plane

Page 90

1. write
2. witch
3. whole
4. dumb
5. knot
6. notch
7. knew
8. comb
9. honest
10. lamb
11. ghost
12. whale
13. wrench
14. batch
15. whip
16. hour
17. catch
18. wrong
19. wrinkle
20. match
21. knight
22. knee
23. crumb
24. knife
25. thumb
26. knit

Page 91

1. alphabet
2. awful
3. cough
4. dolphin
5. elephant
6. elf
7. enough
8. fantastic
9. fish
10. fun
11. giraffe
12. laugh
13. muff
14. phonics
15. rough
16. taffy
17. telephone
18. tough

Page 92

f sound: cough, enough, rough, slough*, tough, trough
silent: daughter, dough, knight, light, naughty, night, right, sigh, sight, slough*, taught, though
*Note that slough can be pronounced both ways, and each way has a different meaning.

Page 93

1. ache
2. back
3. bank
4. beak
5. cane
6. cut
7. crumb
8. dock
9. jack
10. keep
11. key
12. kind
13. look
14. make
15. neck
16. nickel
17. pack
18. pocket
19. scare
20. school
21. skin
22. sock
23. spoke
24. stomach
25. walk
26. rake

Page 94

1. pig
2. bee or flea
3. snake
4. llama
5. bird
6. rabbit
7. horse
8. deer
9. fox or ox
10. dog, frog, or hog

1–4: Answers will vary but may include:
cat, rat, bat, gnat
goose, moose
whale, snail
hare, bear

Page 95

1. alone, known
2. bowl, roll
3. coat, wrote
4. home, roam
5. leak, week
6. maid, frayed
7. plate, great
8. seize, bees
9. sigh, fly
10. soap, rope
11. tail, bale
12. thought, taught

Page 96

1. paper
2. out
3. man
4. ball
5. moon
6. fall
7. light
8. out
9. table
10. book
11. over
12. day
13. room
14. up
15. cup

Page 97

goldfish, spotlight, sweatshirt, highway, cupcake, shoelace, railway, sunset, peppermint, football, ponytail, overlook, suitcase, jellyfish, windmill, silverware, tiptoe, rainbow, wristwatch, handlebar

Page 98

sunshine, flashlight, suitcase, tablecloth, football, raincoat, mailbox, butterfly, toothbrush, starfish, tabletop, sidewalk, mailman

Page 99

1. pil´-low
2. fel´-low
3. piz´-za
4. sup-pose´
5. sur-round´
6. scis´-sors
7. col-lect´
8. hur-rah´
9. ad´-dress or ad-dress´
10. sil´-ly

Page 100

1. tur´-tle
2. bee´-tle
3. bub´-ble
4. can´-dle
5. jug´-gle
6. hus´-tle
7. baf´-fle
8. cra´-dle
9. bot´-tle
10. trou´-ble

Page 101

1. car-toon´
2. cin´-der
3. drop´-let
4. ex´-tra
5. ex-press´
6. im-print´ or im´-print
7. jun´-gle
8. sal´-ad
9. mag´-ic
10. pic´-ture

Page 102

1. hu´-mor
2. a´-ble
3. be-gin´
4. ki´-wi
5. pa´-per
6. lo´-cate
7. o´-pen
8. pro´-file
9. ro-sette´
10. e-rupt´

Page 103

1. responsible
2. understand
3. meaning
4. worth
5. material
6. engage
7. aware
8. arrange
9. circle
10. week
11. mountain
12. cycle
13. angle
14. sense
15. admiral

Page 104

1. sail
2. run
3. farm
4. buy
5. pharmacy
6. direct
7. dance
8. science
9. photograph
10. analyze
11. choreograph
12. biography

Page 105

(un)- known, (re)- phrase, (dis)- respect, (re)- make, (pre)- cook, (mis)- align

Page 106

Answers will vary.

Page 107

1. reheat (*yellow*)
2. replay (*yellow*)
3. unsafe (*green*)
4. unlucky (*green*)
5. redo (*yellow*)
6. unfair (*green*)
7. reread (*yellow*)
8. rewrite (*yellow*)
9. uncover (*green*)

Page 108

overslept: slept too much
overstuffed: stuffed too much
underwatered: not watered enough
underfed: not fed enough
overflowed: flowed too much
undercooked: not cooked enough

Page 109

1. kind-(ness)
2. care-(ful)
3. help-(ful)
4. seed-(less)
5. clean-(ly)
6. health-(ful)

Page 110

Answers will vary.

Page 111

1. bucket; bucketful
2. spoon; spoonful
3. help; helpful
4. hand; handful
5. harm; harmful
6. pain; painful

Page 112

1. scenic
2. angelic
3. terrific
4. patriotic
5. majestic
6. traffic
7. Nomadic
8. antiseptic
9. scientific
10. volcanic

Page 113

Answers may vary but may include:

1. goose
2. summer
3. football
4. intelligence
5. doodle
6. buccaneer
7. bee
8. giraffe
9. beggar
10. moon
11. pepper
12. gaggle
13. wiggle
14. borrow
15. sorrow
16. sonnet
17. ballot
18. classic

Page 115

1. high
2. kayak
3. nitrogen
4. hopscotch
5. amnesia
6. maximum
7. dividend
8. neon
9. episode
10. hearth
11. aqua
12. newborn
13. moonbeam
14. arena
15. critic
16. Antarctica
17. Australia
18. Africa
19. Asia
20. Europe

Page 116

Answers will vary but may include:

1. canoe
2. pans
3. brain
4. low
5. lemon
6. spot
7. leaf
8. grin
9. rat
10. mug
11. earth
12. tab
13. wasp
14. pea
15. note
16. pat
17. pots
18. ton
19. rope
20. ewe

Page 117
Answers will vary.

Page 118
Answers will vary. Use a dictionary to check the spelling.

Page 119
Answers will vary. Use a dictionary to check the spelling.

Page 120
1. veteran or veterinarian
2. necktie
3. moving picture
4. champion
5. photograph
6. helicopter
7. referee
8. market
9. dormitory
10. examination
11. advertisement
12. doctor
13. laboratory
14. promenade
15. influenza
16. teenager
17. gasoline
18. statistic
19. luncheon
20. chrysanthemum

Page 121
One day the fourth-grade class went on a trip to the zoo. They took a bus to get there. Then everyone joined in groups to tour the zoo. The blue group went to see the bears, the red group went to the seals, and the yellow group walked to the monkey area. At noon, all the groups met for lunch. The children ate sandwiches and drank a lot of water. After lunch, they saw a bird show in the zoo theater. When the show was over, it was time to go home. The children piled into the bus and away they went. They had a great day!

Page 122
1. n	a. Blvd.
2. b	b. Mr.
3. h	c. yr.
4. e	d. Gov.
5. l	e. Dec.
6. j	f. tbs.
7. f	g. Tues.
8. a	h. St.
9. o	i. gal.
10. d	j. Capt.
11. m	k. Dr.
12. i	l. U.S.
13. k	m. Jr.
14. g	n. Wed.
15. c	o. Aug.

Page 123
1. president
2. as soon as possible
3. adjective
4. pounds
5. maximum
6. et cetera (and so forth)
7. September
8. Master of Arts
9. I owe you.
10. Bachelor of Arts
11. cash on delivery
12. répondez síl vous plaít. (Please reply.)
13. self-addressed, stamped envelope
14. South America
15. building
16. railroad
17. preposition
18. headquarters
19. district attorney
20. daylight-savings time

Page 124
1. record´	6. read (red)
2. de´sert	7. close (cloz)
3. content´	8. con´duct
4. con´test	9. sub´ject
5. refuse´	10. address´

Page 125
1. mat	6. feed
2. mate	7. us
3. tine	8. use
4. tin	9. meet
5. fed	10. met

Page 126
1. tail or tale	9. replay
2. most	10. wheel
3. trace	11. meter
4. hazy	12. motor
5. doe or dough	13. geese
6. duel	14. china
7. fray	15. love
8. trail	

Page 127
ape	kick	satisfy
apple	kiss	season
banana	laugh	state
bear	limb	town
carrot	list	tuna
cheese	many	tune
cornhusk	mote	umbrella
dandelion	mother	under
dandy	neck	underneath
egg	noise	very
eggplant	other	violin
friend	otter	voice
frond	over	wig
grapes	pout	wisdom
grass	put	wonder
heaven	putt	xylophone
house	quilt	yeast
hover	quit	yes
ice	quitter	yesterday
icicle	raise	zebra
juice	roast	zoo
jump	salt	zoology

Page 128
candy	grassy	rover
cane	house	salt
cart	join	same
cell	jump	science
cello	launch	scientist
dear	light	silent
deer	line	simple
dog	lion	sort
friend	loop	tune
gamble	lope	tunnel
game	lunch	umbrella
ghastly	moan	vest
ghost	moon	
grass	river	

Page 129
1. c	3. a	5. b
2. c	4. b	

Page 130
Definitions and sentences will vary.

Page 131
A. Answers will vary.
B. 1. Wash five small, empty food containers such as yogurt cartons or margarine tubs.
   2. In each container, mix 1 teaspoon of cold cream and 2 teaspoons of cornstarch.
   3. Add 1 teaspoon of water and a few drops of food coloring to each container. Blend carefully.
   4. Be sure to use a different color for each container: blue, green, red, yellow, and brown.
   5. After creating a batch of face paint, work with a partner and paint your faces to look like zoo creatures.
C. 1 teaspoon (of cold cream)
   2 teaspoons (of cornstarch)
   1 teaspoon (of water)

Page 134
1, 2, 3
2, 1, 3
2, 3, 1
3, 2, 1

Page 135
1. They cleaned their rooms.
2. They washed the family's car.
3. They got ready to go to the zoo.
4. They visted the sharks.
5. They went to the wolf den.
6. They met their mother at the alligator exhibit.

Page 136
I woke up one morning feeling strange.
I got out of bed and looked in the mirror.
What a shock I got when I saw a plant growing out of my ears!
I ran to my mother to show her what had happened.
She said, "Those seeds you swallowed yesterday have planted inside you."
Then she looked in the phone book for a good gardener to come over to trim me.
I am feeling better now, but I still have to water myself every day.

Answer Key (cont.)

Page 137
1. Bake cookies for school on Tuesday.
2. Go to baseball practice on Wednesday.
3. Write my book report on Thursday.
4. Practice the violin on Friday.
5. Call Janet on Saturday.

Page 138
A. 2, 1, 5, 4, 3
B. 1, 3, 5, 2, 4
C. 4, 2, 1, 5, 3
D. 3, 2, 4, 1, 5
E. 4, 2, 3, 1, 5
F. 3, 5, 1, 2, 4
G. 2, 1, 4, 3, 5
H. 3, 5, 1, 2, 4

Page 139
1. football field
2. bird
3. Beverly Hills
4. fortune cookies
5. diving board
6. towels
7. scissors
8. flowers
9. tomato soup
10. spaghetti

Page 142
Julie and Juan want to work at the zoo.

Page 143
Answers will vary but should reflect these ideas:
1. Lola
2. loves to watch parrots
3. They are her favorite animals.
4. Lola loves to watch the parrots because they are her favorite animals.

Page 144
Answers will vary, but they should reflect the following ideas:
Mrs. Lee and her class are late for the bus.
The children enjoyed watching the penguins.

Page 145
1. It is about a very young boy named Max.
2. He watches baby penguins hatch.
3. He is nearby when they hatch.
4. Sentences will vary.
5. Pictures will vary.

Page 146
1. It is about George Washington.
2. He was a great leader.
3. He was a good general and president.
4. Sentences will vary.
5. Paragraphs will vary.

Page 147
1. She climbed down her bedpost.
2. She is glad her mother did not see the mess under her bed.
3. She arranges the dollhouse furniture.
4. They eat the girls' leftover cookies from her bedtime snack.
5. She actually finds cookie crumbs in her dollhouse.

Page 148
1. He was excited to pitch in the big game.
2. He had been practicing his pitching.
3. He rode his bicycle to the ballpark.
4. He warmed up in the bullpen.
5. He was named Most Valuable Player.

Page 149
Answers may vary but may include:
1. Karly says that the rain is a mess.
2. She can barely get through the flood.
3. She complains.

Page 150
1. Jack and Wendy do not like the Fun House.
2. They think it is too scary, and they want to leave.
1. Mary really wants the dress, and she is jealous.
2. Mary says that she does not like the dress, but she wants to know if there are any more. Also, by asking so much about it, she leads others to believe that she is really interested.

Page 151
1. *Alike:* eight years old, best friends, teaching each other their primary language, do homework together, popcorn is favorite snack, love Pete, enjoy the park, swing and slide with Pete
2. *Different:* Marta doesn't speak much English, Marta is from Mexico, Marta speaks Spanish well and Janis does not, Janis has a little brother and Marta has no siblings, Marta is a good skater, Janis has a scooter

Page 152
1. rooster
2. movie
3. computer
4. rose
5. guitar

Page 154–155
Answers will vary.

Page 156
1. F
2. O
3. O
4. F
5. F
6. O
7. O
8. F
9. F
10. O
1. Answers will vary.
2. Answers will vary.

Page 157
The following statements should be underlined (biased): 2, 4, 7, 8, and 9.

Page 158
1. excited
2. sad
3. funny
4. worried
5. happy

Page 159
Answers will vary.

Page 160
1. two
2. Tracy and his father
3. Tracy
4. "he" in first sentence

Page 161
1. check
2. no check
3. check
4. check
5. no check

Page 162
1. 3
2. 1
3. 1
4. 3

Page 163
1. Alicia
2. Luke and Chris
3. movers
4. Sam
5. you and I
6. computer
7. Tom; sisters

Page 164
1. It scared or shocked her.
2. His father got serious and set rules or limits.
3. She was ready to leave.
4. He had not felt well.
5. He slept soundly.
6. He was going to be in trouble.
7. "Stop."
8. "Are you scared, nervous, or changing your mind?"
9. He loves to tell a story.
10. She doesn't know what is happening.

Page 165
1. Dinner is free.
2. John was in a bad mood.
3. My cousin can grow plants very well.
4. When I have money, I have to spend it.
5. One should apologize for wrongdoings.
6. Cathy didn't know how things were done yet.
7. Mother told us to clean the house.
8. Dad gets up early.
9. The child wasn't out of danger.
10. Crystal was sad.

Page 166
Some answers may vary.
1. Los Angeles
2. after noon
3. octagon
4. saw
5. Texas
6. bed
7. red
8. cherries
9. Easter
10. mother
11. pancakes
12. see
13. chicken
14. Egypt
15. temperature
16. 100
17. floor
18. pilot
19. hungry
20. hive

Page 167
Some answers may vary.
1. smell
2. tennis
3. Elizabeth
4. poem
5. driver
6. Roosevelt
7. foot
8. carpenter
9. den or cave
10. Frame
11. read
12. Braces
13. right
14. Swim
15. ankle
16. screwdriver
17. fin
18. fruit
19. Oink
20. queen

Answer Key (cont.)

Page 168

1. little
2. foot
3. bee
4. floor
5. Car
6. girl
7. Door
8. eat
9. books
10. bottom
11. Green
12. waist
13. pilot
14. read
15. tree
16. eye
17. Night
18. December
19. cub
20. Nephew

Page 169

Some answers may vary.

1. holidays
2. girls' names
3. countries
4. fruits
5. farm animals
6. shades of purple
7. writing instruments
8. Disney characters
9. circus performers
10. colleges
11. rivers
12. directions
13. nursery rhymes
14. artists
15. former U.S. presidents
16. numbers
17. letters
18. baked goods
19. last names
20. tools

Page 170

animals: sloth, snipe, quetzal, meerkat, phoebe, peccary, toucan

fruits: strawberry, mango, quince, loganberry, papaya, guava, pineapple

flowers: primrose, gardenia, carnation, iris, crocus, impatiens, sweet William

sports: lacrosse, soccer, rugby, football, Ping-Pong, triathlon, kayaking

instruments: violin, bassoon, harp, trumpet, flute, mandolin, cello

clothing: moccasin, parka, poncho, trousers, tux, cummerbund, gown

Pages 171–182

Answers will vary.

Page 183

Answers will vary for the subjects or predicates added to each sentence.

1. S
2. S
3. P
4. S
5. P
6. S
7. P
8. P
9. P
10. S
11. S
12. P
13. S
14. P
15. S

Page 184

Answers will vary.

Page 185

I love food, but I do not like to cook. First of all, I am not very good at cooking. I cut myself, I burn food, and I spill things that stain all my clothes. Then there is something about the ingredients that is a great mystery to me. I can follow a recipe very closely, but it never comes out right. The food might be too salty, too sweet, or just too weird. And then there's the mess. The food sticks to pots and pans and stains the sink. The floor, the dog, and I get covered in flour or onion juice. When I get finished with all that labor, I'm anxious to taste my masterpiece, but it is always a disappointment, and there are so many dishes that I don't have time to go out and get something really good to eat! I should just give up cooking altogether.

Page 186

1. tires, steering wheels, bumpers
2. refrigerators, ovens, frying pans
3. ears, knees, thumbs
4. lemons, dandelions, bananas

Pages 187–217

Writing will vary.

Page 218

1. 4
2. 13
3. 10
4. 12
5. 7
6. 6
7. 3
8. 8
9. 3
10. 10
11. 14
12. 8
13. 6
14. 11
15. 15
16. 5
17. 2
18. 8
19. 14
20. 7
21. 17
22. 13
23. 13
24. 14
25. 10
26. 9
27. 12
28. 10
29. 9
30. 9

Page 219

a. 108
b. 85
c. 55
d. 77
e. 76
f. 87
g. 148
h. 125
i. 42
j. 122

Page 220

a. 49 + 57 = $106
b. 26 + 32 = $58
c. 17 + 64 = $81
d. 32 + 57 = $89
e. 64 + 17 + 49 = $130
f. 26 + 57 + 32 = $115

Page 221

a. 83 + 24 + 16 = 123
b. 47 + 21 + 33 = 101
c. 14 + 32 + 24 = 70
d. 36 + 42 + 87 = 165

Page 222

a. 61
b. 106
c. 117
d. 37
e. 130
f. 81
g. 81
h. 110
i. 66
j. 63
k. 34
l. 93
m. 85
n. 130
o. 81
p. 137
q. 112
r. 183
s. 49
t. 109
u. 68
v. 110
w. 77
x. 130

Page 223

a. 143
b. 131
c. 91
d. 117
e. 186
f. 157
g. 123
h. 163
i. 145
j. 129
k. 185
l. 106
m. 156
n. 100
o. 93
p. 132
q. 201
r. 174
s. 150
t. 182
u. 174
v. 119
w. 111
x. 170

Page 224

1. 1599
2. 1233
3. 1852
4. 1408
5. 1316
6. 1402
7. 2157
8. 1871
9. 2174
10. 2061
11. 1074
12. 1767

Page 225

a. 14
b. 1
c. 7
d. 14
e. 30
f. 41
g. 26
h. 30
i. 60
j. 41

Page 226

a. 93 − 68 = 25
b. 43 − 40 = 3
c. 53 − 28 = 25
d. 83 − 62 = 21

Page 227

Across
1. fourteen
3. nineteen
7. seventeen
9. sixteen

Down
1. fifteen
2. twenty
4. eighteen
5. eleven
6. twelve
8. thirteen

Page 228

a. 1
b. 22
c. 71
d. 17
e. 26
f. 53
g. 57
h. 34
i. 30
j. 41
k. 4
l. 31
m. 53
n. 12
o. 55
p. 55
q. 52
r. 3
s. 23
t. 9
u. 34
v. 72
w. 15
x. 44

Answer Key (cont.)

Page 229

a. 8	i. 44	q. 4
b. 33	j. 40	r. 37
c. 31	k. 72	s. 32
d. 16	l. 21	t. 64
e. 62	m. 64	u. 59
f. 28	n. 31	v. 26
g. 47	o. 14	w. 5
h. 6	p. 15	x. 14

Page 230

1. 6	9. 9
2. 9	10. 7
3. 13	11. 23
4. 10	12. 11
5. 7	13. 8
6. 19	14. 6
7. 18	15. 24
8. 5	16. 12

Page 231

Possible Solutions:

1. $6 + 4 - 1 - 2 + 6 + 2 = 15$
2. $9 + 1 - 3 + 1 - 4 + 1 = 5$
3. $9 - 3 + 4 - 1 + 2 + 3 = 14$
4. $5 - 1 + 1 + 3 + 4 + 6 = 18$
5. $9 - 8 + 6 + 3 - 5 + 3 = 8$
6. $2 - 1 + 8 + 9 - 3 + 5 = 20$
7. $5 + 3 + 2 - 4 + 1 + 5 = 12$
8. $4 + 9 + 3 - 7 + 3 - 1 = 11$
9. $7 - 6 + 2 + 8 - 7 - 1 = 3$
10. $9 + 9 - 9 + 2 - 2 - 8 = 1$

Page 232

0 x 0 = 0	1 x 6 = 6	2 x 12 = 24	4 x 5 = 20
0 x 1 = 0	1 x 7 = 7	3 x 0 = 0	4 x 6 = 24
0 x 2 = 0	1 x 8 = 8	3 x 1 = 3	4 x 7 = 28
0 x 3 = 0	1 x 9 = 9	3 x 2 = 6	4 x 8 = 32
0 x 4 = 0	1 x 10 = 10	3 x 3 = 9	4 x 9 = 36
0 x 5 = 0	1 x 11 = 11	3 x 4 = 12	4 x 10 = 40
0 x 6 = 0	1 x 12 = 12	3 x 5 = 15	4 x 11 = 44
0 x 7 = 0	2 x 0 = 0	3 x 6 = 18	4 x 12 = 48
0 x 8 = 0	2 x 1 = 2	3 x 7 = 21	5 x 0 = 0
0 x 9 = 0	2 x 2 = 4	3 x 8 = 24	5 x 1 = 5
0 x 10 = 0	2 x 3 = 6	3 x 9 = 27	5 x 2 = 10
0 x 11 = 0	2 x 4 = 8	3 x 10 = 30	5 x 3 = 15
0 x 12 = 0	2 x 5 = 10	3 x 11 = 33	5 x 4 = 20
1 x 0 = 0	2 x 6 = 12	3 x 12 = 36	5 x 5 = 25
1 x 1 = 1	2 x 7 = 14	4 x 0 = 0	5 x 6 = 30
1 x 2 = 2	2 x 8 = 16	4 x 1 = 4	5 x 7 = 35
1 x 3 = 3	2 x 9 = 18	4 x 2 = 8	5 x 8 = 40
1 x 4 = 4	2 x 10 = 20	4 x 3 = 12	5 x 9 = 45
1 x 5 = 5	2 x 11 = 22	4 x 4 = 16	5 x 10 = 50

Page 233

5 x 11 = 55	7 x 4 = 28	8 x 10 = 80	10 x 3 = 30	11 x 9 = 99
5 x 12 = 60	7 x 5 = 35	8 x 11 = 88	10 x 4 = 40	11 x 10 = 110
6 x 0 = 0	7 x 6 = 42	8 x 12 = 96	10 x 5 = 50	11 x 11 = 121
6 x 1 = 6	7 x 7 = 49	9 x 0 = 0	10 x 6 = 60	11 x 12 = 132
6 x 2 = 12	7 x 8 = 56	9 x 1 = 9	10 x 7 = 70	12 x 0 = 0
6 x 3 = 18	7 x 9 = 63	9 x 2 = 18	10 x 8 = 80	12 x 1 = 12
6 x 4 = 24	7 x 10 = 70	9 x 3 = 27	10 x 9 = 90	12 x 2 = 24
6 x 5 = 30	7 x 11 = 77	9 x 4 = 36	10 x 10 = 100	12 x 3 = 36
6 x 6 = 36	7 x 12 = 84	9 x 5 = 45	10 x 11 = 110	12 x 4 = 48
6 x 7 = 42	8 x 0 = 0	9 x 6 = 54	10 x 12 = 120	12 x 5 = 60
6 x 8 = 48	8 x 1 = 8	9 x 7 = 63	11 x 0 = 0	12 x 6 = 72
6 x 9 = 54	8 x 2 = 16	9 x 8 = 72	11 x 1 = 11	12 x 7 = 84
6 x 10 = 60	8 x 3 = 24	9 x 9 = 81	11 x 2 = 22	12 x 8 = 96
6 x 11 = 66	8 x 4 = 32	9 x 10 = 90	11 x 3 = 33	12 x 9 = 108
6 x 12 = 72	8 x 5 = 40	9 x 11 = 99	11 x 4 = 44	12 x 10 = 120
7 x 0 = 0	8 x 6 = 48	9 x 12 = 108	11 x 5 = 55	12 x 11 = 132
7 x 1 = 7	8 x 7 = 56	10 x 0 = 0	11 x 6 = 66	12 x 12 = 144
7 x 2 = 14	8 x 8 = 64	10 x 1 = 10	11 x 7 = 77	
7 x 3 = 21	8 x 9 = 72	10 x 2 = 20	11 x 8 = 88	

Page 234

2 x 2 = 4	12 x 5 = 60	6 x 1 = 6	6 x 3 = 18
3 x 8 = 24	7 x 5 = 35	7 x 7 = 49	7 x 9 = 63
5 x 1 = 5	11 x 8 = 88	9 x 0 = 0	9 x 2 = 18
10 x 0 = 0	10 x 4 = 40	10 x 6 = 60	10 x 8 = 80
2 x 3 = 6	11 x 10 = 110	11 x 12 = 132	12 x 1 = 12
11 x 5 = 55	6 x 0 = 0	6 x 2 = 12	6 x 4 = 24
7 x 4 = 28	7 x 6 = 42	7 x 8 = 56	10 x 7 = 70
10 x 8 = 80	12 x 8 = 96	9 x 1 = 9	9 x 3 = 27
10 x 3 = 30	10 x 5 = 50	10 x 7 = 70	10 x 9 = 90
11 x 9 = 99	11 x 11= 121	12 x 0 = 0	12 x 2 = 24

Page 235

96 x 16 = 1,536	68 x 88 = 5,984	56 x 75 = 4,200	22 x 67 = 1,474
90 x 13 = 1,170	33 x 31 = 1,023	84 x 28 = 2,352	74 x 17 = 1,258
47 x 19 = 893	20 x 62 = 1,240	70 x 96 = 6,720	26 x 93 = 2,418
25 x 11 = 275	24 x 19 = 456	58 x 75 = 4,350	14 x 72 = 1,008
26 x 16 = 416	41 x 40 = 1,640	50 x 10 = 500	48 x 30 = 1,440
40 x 28 = 1,120	46 x 20 = 920	21 x 25 = 525	42 x 48 = 2,016
82 x 35 = 2,870	49 x 71 = 3,479	77 x 63 = 4,851	88 x 50 = 4,400
60 x 52 = 3,120	38 x 45 = 1,710	79 x 44 = 3,476	69 x 18 = 1,242
71 x 27 = 1,917	24 x 35 = 840	86 x 33 = 2,838	43 x 31 = 1,333
32 x 54 = 1,728	27 x 32 = 864	13 x 29 = 377	19 x 22 = 418

Page 236

173 x 6 = 1,038	533 x 8 = 4,264	138 x 2 = 276	833 x 5 = 4,165
227 x 3 = 681	388 x 1= 388	417 x 8 = 3,336	524 x 3 = 1,572
402 x 1 = 402	620 x 6 = 3,720	317 x 4 = 1,268	468 x 6 = 2,808
420 x 8 = 3,360	662 x 3 = 1,986	458 x 7 = 3,206	947 x 2 = 1,894
178 x 9 = 1,602	714 x 9 = 6,426	550 x 6 = 3,300	767 x 7 = 5,369
324 x 8 = 2,592	835 x 3 = 2,505	594 x 5 = 2,970	632 x 3 = 1,896
172 x 4 = 688	152 x 7 = 1,064	180 x 4 = 720	221 x 2 = 442
286 x 8 = 2,288	254 x 5 = 1,270	538 x 1= 538	489 x 4 = 1,956
509 x 4 = 2,036	851 x 1= 851	728 x 6 = 4,368	141 x 9 = 1,269
615 x 2 = 1,230	674 x 8 = 5,392	107 x 3 = 321	213 x 5 = 1,065

Page 237

23 x 16 = 368	13 x 38 = 494	89 x 57 = 5,073	44 x 76 = 3,344
90 x 39 = 3,510	31 x 11 = 341	24 x 23 = 552	22 x 51 = 1,122
17 x 79 = 1,343	41 x 96 = 3,936	74 x 19 = 1,406	16 x 39 = 624
35 x 15 = 525	14 x 79 = 1,106	48 x 79 = 3,792	25 x 17 = 425
14 x 63 = 882	80 x 54 = 4,320	70 x71 = 4,970	28 x 93 = 2,604
56 x 82 = 4,592	34 x 24 = 816	21 x 26 = 546	58 x 48 = 2,784
73 x 50 = 3,650	46 x 27 = 1,242	67 x 64 = 4,288	99 x 56 = 5,544
50 x 28 = 1,400	68 x 40 = 2,720	39 x 42 = 1,638	64 x 48 = 3,072
81 x 76 = 6,156	34 x 83 = 2,822	96 x 30 = 2,880	34 x 23 = 782
51 x 44 = 2,244	23 x 36 = 828	18 x 28 = 504	36 x 20 = 720

Page 238

0 ÷ 0 = 0	6 ÷ 1 = 6	24 ÷ 12 = 2	24 ÷ 4 = 6
1 ÷ 0 = 0	7 ÷ 1 = 7	3 ÷ 3 = 1	28 ÷ 4 = 7
2 ÷ 0 = 0	8 ÷ 1 = 8	6 ÷ 3 = 2	32 ÷ 4 = 8
3 ÷ 0 = 0	9 ÷ 1 = 9	9 ÷ 3 = 3	36 ÷ 4 = 9
4 ÷ 0 = 0	10 ÷ 1 = 10	12 ÷ 3 = 4	40 ÷ 4 = 10
6 ÷ 0 = 0	11 ÷ 1 = 11	15 ÷ 3 = 5	44 ÷ 4 = 11
7 ÷ 0 = 0	12 ÷ 1 = 12	18 ÷ 3 = 6	48 ÷ 4 = 12
8 ÷ 0 = 0	2 ÷ 2 = 1	21 ÷ 3 = 7	5 ÷ 5 = 1
9 ÷ 0 = 0	4 ÷ 2 = 2	24 ÷ 3 = 8	10 ÷ 5 = 2
10 ÷ 0 = 0	6 ÷ 2 = 3	27 ÷ 3 = 9	15 ÷ 5 = 3
11 ÷ 0 = 0	8 ÷ 2 = 4	30 ÷ 3 = 10	20 ÷ 5 = 4
12 ÷ 0 = 0	10 ÷ 2 = 5	33 ÷ 3 = 11	25 ÷ 5 = 5
1 ÷ 0 = 0	12 ÷ 2 = 6	36 ÷ 3 = 12	30 ÷ 5 = 6
1 ÷ 1 = 1	14 ÷ 2 = 7	4 ÷ 4 = 1	35 ÷ 5 = 7
2 ÷ 1 = 2	16 ÷ 2 = 8	8 ÷ 4 = 2	40 ÷ 5 = 8
3 ÷ 1 = 3	18 ÷ 2 = 9	12 ÷ 4 = 3	45 ÷ 5 = 9
4 ÷ 1 = 4	20 ÷ 2 = 10	16 ÷ 4 = 4	50 ÷ 5 = 10
5 ÷ 1 = 5	22 ÷ 2 = 11	20 ÷ 4 = 5	55 ÷ 5 = 11

Answer Key (cont.)

Page 239

60 ÷ 5 = 12	42 ÷ 7 = 6	96 ÷ 8 = 12	60 ÷ 10 = 6	132 ÷ 11 = 12
6 ÷ 6 = 1	49 ÷ 7 = 7	9 ÷ 9 = 1	70 ÷ 10 = 7	12 ÷ 12 = 1
12 ÷ 6 = 2	56 ÷ 7 = 8	18 ÷ 9 = 2	80 ÷ 10 = 8	24 ÷ 12 = 2
18 ÷ 6 = 3	63 ÷ 7 = 9	27 ÷ 9 = 3	90 ÷ 10 = 9	36 ÷ 12 = 3
24 ÷ 6 = 4	70 ÷ 7 = 10	36 ÷ 9 = 4	100 ÷ 10 = 10	48 ÷ 12 = 4
30 ÷ 6 = 5	77 ÷ 7 = 11	45 ÷ 9 = 5	110 ÷ 10 = 11	60 ÷ 12 = 5
36 ÷ 6 = 6	84 ÷ 7 = 12	54 ÷ 9 = 6	120 ÷ 10 = 12	72 ÷ 12 = 6
42 ÷ 6 = 7	8 ÷ 8 = 1	63 ÷ 9 = 7	11 ÷ 11 = 1	84 ÷ 12 = 7
48 ÷ 6 = 8	16 ÷ 8 = 2	72 ÷ 9 = 8	22 ÷ 11 = 2	96 ÷ 12 = 8
54 ÷ 6 = 9	24 ÷ 8 = 3	81 ÷ 9 = 9	33 ÷ 11 = 3	108 ÷ 12 = 9
60 ÷ 6 = 10	32 ÷ 8 = 4	90 ÷ 9 = 10	44 ÷ 11 = 4	120 ÷ 12 = 10
66 ÷ 6 = 11	40 ÷ 8 = 5	99 ÷ 9 = 11	55 ÷ 11 = 5	132 ÷ 12 = 11
72 ÷ 6 = 12	48 ÷ 8 = 6	108 ÷ 9 = 12	66 ÷ 11 = 6	144 ÷ 12 = 12
7 ÷ 7 = 1	56 ÷ 8 = 7	10 ÷ 10 = 1	77 ÷ 11 = 7	
14 ÷ 7 = 2	64 ÷ 8 = 8	20 ÷ 10 = 2	88 ÷ 11 = 8	
21 ÷ 7 = 3	72 ÷ 8 = 9	30 ÷ 10 = 3	99 ÷ 11 = 9	
28 ÷ 7 = 4	80 ÷ 8 = 10	40 ÷ 10 = 4	110 ÷ 11 = 10	
35 ÷ 7 = 5	88 ÷ 8 = 11	50 ÷ 10 = 5	121 ÷ 11 = 11	

Page 240

400 ÷ 16 = 25
225 ÷ 15 = 15
234 ÷ 18 = 13
240 ÷ 12 = 20
180 ÷ 10 = 18
136 ÷ 8 = 17
95 ÷ 5 = 19
248 ÷ 8 = 31
112 ÷ 2 = 56
256 ÷ 16 = 16
150 ÷ 6 = 25
128 ÷ 32 = 4
288 ÷ 16 = 18
171 ÷ 9 = 19
231 ÷ 11 = 21

Page 241

1. 5 + 7 = 12
2. 24 ÷ 4 = 6
3. 9 + 3 = 12
4. 18 − 6 = 12
5. 4 + 9 = 13
6. 4 x 9 = 36
7. 10 x 8 = 80
8. 15 ÷ 5 = 3
9. 11 ÷ 4 = 7
10. 8 + 16 = 24
11. 2 x 8 = 16
12. 3 + 2 = 5
13. 22 − 6 = 16
14. 9 + 1 = 10
15. 3 x 3 = 9
16. 144 ÷ 12 = 12
17. 21 ÷ 3 = 7
18. 90 ÷ 10 = 9
19. 12 x 11 = 132
20. 14 x 1 = 14

Page 242

1. 1/3
2. 1/4
3. 5/8
4. 3/5
5. 7/10
6. 2/6 = 1/3
7. 3/4
8. 1/2

Page 243

grandma (red) — 1/8
mother (yellow) — 1/4
brother (green) — 1/8
father (blue) — 1/4
sister (orange) — 1/4

Page 244

1. watermelon
2. grapes
3. 1) watermelon, 2) peaches, 3) plums, 4) apricots, 5) grapes
4. 1/2; 1/4; 1/8
5. Answers will vary.

Page 245

1. 30 minutes; five minutes; five minutes; 10 minutes; 10 minutes
2. Answers will vary.
Graphs will vary.

Page 246

Answers are approximate measurements.
1. 4 meters
2. 9 meters
3. 12.5 meters
4. 13 meters
5. 15.5 meters

Page 247

Answers will vary but may include:
1. a
2. f
3. c, e
4. b, d
5. d
6. d
7. b, d
8. f
9. c, e
10. a

Page 248

Answers are approximate measurements.
1. 18 miles
2. 10 miles
3. 35 miles
4. 18 miles
5. 16 miles
6. 10 miles
It is farther from Pleasantown to Mountaintown.

Answer Key (cont.)

Page 249

1. 1,750
2. 550
3. 450
4. 1,150
5. 1,400
6. 1,050
7. 850
8. 600
9. 600
10. 600

Page 250

1. one cent
2. five cents
3. ten cents
4. Answers will vary, but the first number should always be divided by five to get the second number.
5. Answers will vary, but the first number should always be divided by two to get the second number.
6. Answers will vary, but the first number should always be divided by ten to get the second number.
7. one nickel
8. one dime
9. one dime
10. 16 cents

Page 251

1. 1 silver dollar
2. 3 q, 2 d, 1 n
3. 2 q, 5 d
4. 10 d
5. 5 d, 10 n
6. 2 q, 4 d, 10 p
7. 7 d, 5 n, 5 p
8. 9 d, 10 p
9. 1 q, 3 d, 6 n, 15 p
10. 3 q, 25 p

Page 252

Answers will vary. Accept all that add to fifty cents.

Page 253

Answers will vary. Accept all that add to one dollar.

Page 254

1.	P.M.	11.	A.M.
2.	A.M.	12.	P.M.
3.	P.M.	13.	P.M.
4.	P.M.	14.	A.M.
5.	A.M.	15.	P.M.
6.	A.M.	16.	P.M.
7.	P.M.	17.	A.M.
8.	P.M.	18.	P.M.
9.	P.M.	19.	P.M.
10.	A.M.	20.	A.M.

Page 255

1. *second*: one-sixtieth of a minute
2. *minute*: 60 seconds
3. *hour*: 60 minutes
4. *day*: 24 hours
5. *week*: seven days
6. *fortnight*: two weeks
7. *month*: approximately four weeks (28–31 days)
8. *year*: 365 days
9. *decade*: 10 years
10. *score*: 20 years
11. *century*: 100 years
12. *millennium*: 1,000 years

Page 256

Lucy = B
Gwen = C-
Cara = A
Martin = C
Donald = D

Page 257

Ted Agee, 9
Theodore Chin, 8
Teddy Dalton, 10

Page 258

Chad = Reds
Danny = Cardinals
Andrew = White Sox
Ryan = Dodgers
Will = A's

Page 259

Katelyn—roller coaster, bratwurst
Kenny—Ferris wheel, hot dogs
Emily—bumper cars, hamburger
Howie—carousel, corndog

Page 260

Jane = 5
Daisy = 2
Carrie = 9
Joanne = 3
Gertie = 4
Annie = 6
Penny = 8
Tammy = 1
Lindsey = 7

Page 261

1. southeast
2. west
3. northeast
4. southwest
5. south
6. north
7. east
8. northwest

Page 262

Home = last row fourth house from the left

Page 263

1. true
2. false; western and southeastern
3. false; northeast
4. false; only one, the others are reached by local roads
5. true
6. true
7. false; west of lake, east of railroad
8. true

Page 264

example: silver
A1, white; D3, gray; B4, red; D2, ivory
C4, silver; A2, yellow; D1, black; C2, purple
B3, tan; A4, gold; C3, brown; B1, pink
D4, lavender; B2, green; A3, orange; C1, blue
shaded: A1, A3, B3, C2
striped: B2, C1, C3
unmarked: A2, B1

Page 265
1. E2
2. F3
3. C1, D1, E1
4. E5
5. E3
6. A3, A4, B3, B4
7. F1, F2
8. A5, A6
9. D5
10. C4
11. E6
12. B1
13. D4
14. B5
15. C6
16. C2

Page 266
1. Southern, Eastern
2. Northern, Eastern
3. Northern, Western
4. Northern, Western
5. Northern, Eastern
6. Northern, Western
7. Northern, Eastern
8. Northern, Eastern
9. Northern, Western
10. Southern, Western
11. Northern, Eastern
12. Northern, Western
13. Northern, Eastern
14. Southern, Western
15. Southern, Eastern
16. Southern, Eastern

Page 267
1. Grand Junction
2. Sterling
3. Denver
4. Lamar
5. Durango
6. Colorado Springs
7. Glenwood Springs
8. Campo
9. Craig
10. Kanorado

Page 268
1. 35 and 40
2. 27
3. Wayne
4. Glen Ridge, 33
5. a. 15
   b. 37
   c. 27
   d. 48

Page 269
1. a. 31
   b. 45
   c. 37
   d. 88
   e. 51
   f. 85
2. a. 6
   b. 14
   c. 29
   d. 45
   e. 66
   f. 29
3. a. 99
   b. 62
   c. 66
   d. 59
   e. 45
   f. 71

Page 270
1. east
2. Ekalaka
3. Boyes, Hammond, Alzada
4. Boxelder Creek
5. Medicine Rocks

Page 271
1. Far North
2. Southwestern
3. Pacific Coast
4. Plains

Page 272
1. Brunswick
2. fruit
3. pecans, peanuts, tobacco (Other choices are possible.)
4. berries
5. corn
6. marble, granite

Page 273
1. Sacramento, Oakland, San Francisco, San Jose, Los Angeles, San Diego
2. Needles, Barstow
3. 75 to 100
4. Crescent City, Redding, Bakersfield
5. Answers will vary. Accept logically explained answers, such as desert conditions in Needles and Barstow.

Page 274
1. Boston
2. Plymouth, New Bedford
3. Boston: Below 22 F, Below -6 C
   Lowell: 22 to 26 F, -6 to -3 C
   Pittsfield: 26 to 30 F, -3 to -1 C

Page 275
1. D3, A1, C3
2. A1, D1
3. State Highway 106
4. B1, B2, C1, C2
5. Mount McGee, Remington, Carlton
6. 16, 22
7. coastline

Page 276
Answers are in miles.
1. 2786
2. 1440
3. 206
4. 2037
5. 802
6. 840
7. 1329
8. 1058
9. 2873
10. 2976
11. 963
12. 417

Page 277
1. obsidian
2. sedimentary
3. metamorphic

Page 278
1. David Peterson
2. $5.80—Kathryn Ross
3. Barbara Marshall
4. no
5. no
6. 614
7. $48.00

Page 279
1. Halloween party
2. Spring Celebration
3. Valentine's Day party
4. 4

Page 280
Time lines will vary.

Page 281
1. 5 pianos, 10 flutes, 30 guitars, 15 drums, 5 trumpets
2. 25, 20, 15, 25
3. Accept any reasonable response.

Page 282
1. acoustic and electric guitar
2. tuning keys, fingerboard, frets, and bridge
3. soundboard and sound hole
4. pickups, base, treble, and volume controls

Page 284
#1 = M, #2 = W, #3 = V

Page 285
1. no
2. 5:00 P.M.
3. no
4. *A Lad*, *Dan*, and *The Mystery Garden*
5. *The Sandy Lot* and *The Mystery Garden*
6. Answers will vary.

Page 286
Alaska, Hawaii, Oregon, Nevada, Montana, South Dakota, Oklahoma, Arkansas, Illinois, Kentucky, Georgia, West Virginia, New York, Vermont, New Hampshire, Maine

Page 287
Finland, Germany, England, Venezuela, Peru, Mexico, New Zealand, Australia, Mongolia, India, Pakistan, Saudi Arabia, Egypt, Chad, Italy, France, Ireland, Iceland, Canada

Page 288
Los Angeles—United States
Glasgow—Scotland
Seoul—South Korea
Bombay—India
Nagano—Japan
Nice—France
Frankfurt—Germany
Florence—Italy
Toronto—Canada
Lima—Peru
Rio de Janeiro—Brazil
Bogota—Colombia
Lisbon—Portugal
Cairo—Egypt
Jerusalem—Israel
Copenhagen—Denmark
Canberra—Australia
Dublin—Ireland
Cape Town—South Africa
Acapulco—Mexico

Page 289
Alabama

Page 290
Utah

Page 291
Argentina

Page 292
Nigeria

#3646 Practice and Learn

Practice and Learn

Part 2

Part 2 Table of Contents

Introduction 310

Language Arts 311

Research

What is a Research Report? 311

Researching on the Internet 312

Using Encyclopedia Volumes 313

Facts and Opinions 314

Wild Animal Research 315

Parts of Speech

Nouns 321

Verbs 322

Tall Tale Pattern Story 323

Adjectives and Adverbs 324

Glad Libs 325

Make Your Own Word Search 326

Capitalization and Punctuation

Where's My List? 327

When and Where? 328

Days, Months, and Holidays 329

What's in a Name? 330

End Marks 331

Capitalization Review 332

Sentences and Paragraphs

Building Sentences 333

TV Review 334

What Happened Next? 336

Write Your Own Story 337

Paragraph Starters 339

Reading 341

Short Selections

Ben Franklin 341

Our National Anthem 342

Morse Code 343

Totem Poles 344

Frisbee™ 345

WD-40 346

Beatlemania 347

Butchart Gardens 348

Spider-Man 349

Olympics in the 1920s 350

Barbie Doll™ 351

Hula Hoop™ 352

The Endangered Sea Otter 353

Spider-Woman 354

The Walt Disney Story 355

The Amazon Rain Forest 356

Robin Hood 357

Kristi Yamaguchi 358

The Greatest Airship Ever Built 359

Judy Blume 360

Annie Oakley 361

Statue of Liberty 362

A. A. Milne 363

Constellations 364

Hercules 365

Neil Armstrong 366

Babe Ruth 367

Elvis Presley 368

Orel Hershiser 369

King Arthur 370

Ludwig van Beethoven 372

Novels

The Summer of the Swans 377

Shiloh 381

Math 385

Addition

Addition Facts Timed Practice 385

Single-Digit Addition: Three Rows 387

Single-Digit Addition: Four Rows 388

Single-Digit Addition: Eight Rows 389

Two Digits Plus One Digit 390

Two-Digit Addition: Two Rows 391

Two-Digit Addition: Three Rows 392

Table of Contents (cont.)

Addition (cont.)

Two-Digit Addition: Four Rows 393
Three-Digit Addition: Two Rows. 394
Three-Digit Addition: Three Rows 395
Three-Digit Addition: Four Rows 396
Four-Digit Addition: Two Rows. 397
Four-Digit Addition: Three Rows 398
Four-Digit Addition: Four Rows 399
Mixed Addition Practice 400

Subtraction

Subtraction Facts Timed Practice. 401
Two-Digits Minus One Digit 403
Three Digits Minus Two Digits 404
Four Digits Minus Three Digits. 406
Mixed Subtraction Practice 408

Multiplication

Multiplication Facts Timed Practice . . . 410
Two Digits Times One Digit 412
Two Digits Times Two Digits 414
Three Digits Times One Digit 416
Three Digits Times Two Digits 419
Mixed Multiplication Practice 421

Division

Division Facts Timed Practice 423
One Digit Divided by One Digit 425
Two Digits Divided by One Digit 427
Three Digits Divided by One Digit 429
Three Digits Divided by Two Digits . . . 432

Fractions

Changing Improper Fractions to
Mixed Numbers 435
Converting Mixed Numbers to Improper
Fractions. 436
Adding Fractions. 437
Subtracting Fractions. 441
Multiplying Fractions 443
Dividing Fractions. 445

Comparing Numbers

Greater Than and Less Than 448
McDonald's Math 449

Money

The Life of a Check 450
Check It Out! 451
Writing Checks. 453
Penny Wise 455

Charts and Graphs

Pictographs 457
Chocolate Consumers of the World . . . 458
Circle Graphs 460
Slices 461
Bar Graphs 462
Using Distance Charts. 463
Interpreting Charts 464
Using Chart Information 465
Locating Points on a Graph 467
Finding Coordinates on a Graph 468

Word Problems

Simple Addition Word Problems 469
Addition and Subtraction
Word Problems 470
Multiplication and Division
Word Problems 471
Division Word Problems 472

Science. 473

Gravity

Splat! 473
Whirlybirds. 475
Butterfly Balance 476

Motion

Facts About Motion. 478
Starting and Stopping 479
Racing Marbles 481
Impact Craters. 483

Table of Contents (cont.)

Rocketry

Making a Balloon Rocket 485

Blast Off! 486

Flight

Chutes Away 488

Make Flying Saucers 489

Magnetism and Electricity

Don't Give Me Any Static 493

Sound

Super Sound-Off 495

Phone Fun 496

Chemistry

The Best Bubble Maker 497

Facts About Chemical Reactions 498

Add Oxygen 499

Grow a Crystal Garden 501

Experimentation and Observation

Testing Towels 504

The Earth

The Earth 508

Shifting Crust 509

Cold Tracks 513

Plants

Invasion of the Mold 514

Moldy Old Cheese 516

The Sun's Energy 519

Get To the Root of It! 520

Growing, Growing, Grown 521

Flowers 522

Stems 525

How Does Your Garden Grow? 526

It's Not Easy Being Green 528

Social Studies 530

Geography

Cardinal Points 530

Through the Squares 531

Intermediate Points 532

Scale 533

How Far? 534

How to Measure 535

I've Got the Key! 536

Using Grids 537

Where in This City? 538

Your Map, Your Key 539

The Equator and Hemispheres 540

Where Is It? 541

Latitude and Longitude 542

Continents and Oceans 544

Test Your Map Skills 545

Geography Genius 548

U. S. History

Impact 565

A Colonial Word Search 566

Where Did It Happen? 567

Frontier Words 568

Identify the Locations 569

Time Zones and Daylight Savings 570

Time Zone Riddle 571

Famous Faces of WWI 572

Events of the Great War 573

Time Line of World Events, 1933-1945 . 574

In the Know 575

Which Came First? 576

Citizenship Test 577

What Do You Know? 578

American Social Studies Trivia 579

Famous Women 580

Presidents' First Names 581

Which President? 582

Answer Key 583

Introduction

To Teachers and Parents

The wealth of knowledge a person gains throughout his or her lifetime is impossible to measure, and it will certainly vary from person to person. However, regardless of the scope of knowledge, the foundation for all learning remains a constant. All that we know and think throughout our lifetimes is based upon fundamentals, and these fundamentals are the basic skills upon which all learning develops.

Within this book are hundreds of pages designed to teach and reinforce the skills that are mandatory for a successful completion of fifth-grade curricular standards. To use this resource effectively, simply refer to the contents list to find the practice sheets that correspond to the desired skills.

Skills are reinforced in these areas:

- Language Arts
- Reading
- Math
- Science
- Social Studies

The practice sheets within this book are ideal for both use at home and in the classroom. Research shows us that skill mastery comes with exposure and drill. To be internalized, concepts must be reviewed until they become second nature. Parents may certainly foster the classroom experience through exposing their children to the necessary skills whenever possible, and teachers will find that these pages perfectly complement their classroom needs.

In addition to this resource, there are many hands-on materials that will prove vital when reinforcing basic skills. These include math flash cards, measuring spoons, cups, weights, Celsius and Fahrenheit thermometers, a clock or a stop watch, a variety of math manipulatives, a globe, maps, charts, and graphs. Kinesthetic learners will also benefit from items they can manipulate and use for figuring and writing, and every child will enjoy hands-on science experiences of all kinds.

Keep in mind that skills can be reinforced in nearly every situation, and such reinforcement need not be forced. As parents, consider your use of basic skills throughout your daily business, and include your children in the process. For example, while grocery shopping, let your child manage the coupons, finding the correct products and totaling the savings. Also, allow your child to measure detergent for the washing machine or help prepare a meal by measuring the necessary ingredients. You might even consider as a family the time you spend viewing television and calculate how much of the allotted time goes to advertisements. Likewise, there are countless ways that teachers can reinforce skills throughout a school day. For example, assign each child a number and when taking roll, call out math problems with those numbers as the answers. The children will answer "present" when they calculate the problems and realize that their numbers are the answers. You might also play the game of bingo with parts of speech, matching problems, or vocabulary words.

Since basic skills are utilized every day in untold ways, make the practice of them part of your children's or students' routines. Such work done now will benefit them in countless ways throughout their lives.

What is a Research Report?

A research report presents information that the writer has learned through a detective-like search for the facts. Facts are found in books, magazines, newspapers, encyclopedias, atlases, computer programs, and even in personal interviews. You will become an expert on your topic by the time you are done.

How do you choose a subject?

Find something that interests you and something that you would like to learn more about. You might want to spend time in the library to see how much information is available on your topic. If you are having a problem deciding on a topic, keep reading.

Ideas for Subjects

Read the possible topics below. Circle all those that interest you.

- dogs
- trains
- baseball
- football
- basketball
- space exploration
- pets
- movie stars

- inline skates
- ocean
- fish
- presidents
- government
- a country
- a wild animal
- a state

- Grand Canyon
- historical event
- cars
- a famous person
- world wars
- Frisbee

Choose four favorite topics from above and write them on the lines below. After each, write a more specific topic that might make your report more manageable.

Favorite Topic   **More Specific Topic**

Example: Planets   Mars

1. _____   _____

2. _____   _____

3. _____   _____

4. _____   _____

Researching on the Internet

As Robert Louis Stevenson says, "The world is full of a number of things . . . ." And they can all be found on the Internet!"

The Internet is a network of computers that are all connected so they can "talk" to each other. For example, ten-year-old Matthew needs to write a research report about life on the Mississippi River during the times of Tom Sawyer because his class just read the book *The Adventures of Tom Sawyer.* Since Matt is at school using the computer lab, he decides to look up his topic on the Internet. He manages to connect with a university library in another state and finds more information than he can use.

Sounds great! However, before you go "online," keep in mind some important safety rules.

Be Safe and Not Sorry Online

1. Never give any personal information about yourself or your family, such as your full name, where you live, or your telephone number.

2. You will meet many friendly people online, but remember—they are strangers.

3. If you find yourself having an online conversation that makes you uncomfortable, report that person to your online service.

4. Never give away your password.

5. Never agree to meet anyone you've chatted with online unless your parents agree to the meeting and go with you to a public place.

6. Don't send someone you've met online your picture or anything else without first checking with your parents.

Whether you have access to the Internet at your local public library, your school, or at home, you will want to have some practice in researching a topic if you are new to Internet research. Even if you have experience, practice will enable you to research a topic faster. You will be able to find more information within the time limitations necessary when going online.

Using Encyclopedia Volumes

An encyclopedia is a set of books or a CD-Rom with an encyclopedia on it, which contains information on just about everything in the world. The books contain information that is arranged in alphabetical order, beginning with the A's in the first volume and ending with the Z's in the last volume. Your library will have an encyclopedia; it may have several. Many CD-Rom encyclopedias will allow you to click on a table of contents or an index to help you search for a topic, or you can type an idea into a box to find related topics. Most will have a list of books to read at the end of the article. Your school library will probably have them also. An encyclopedia is a good place to find information for your research paper.

Write each of the subjects below on the spine of the encyclopedia volume in which they would be found.

- photography
- dinosaurs
- Hawaii
- chocolate
- rattlesnakes
- lightning
- wildflowers
- computers
- The Beatles
- volcanoes
- space shuttle
- gorillas

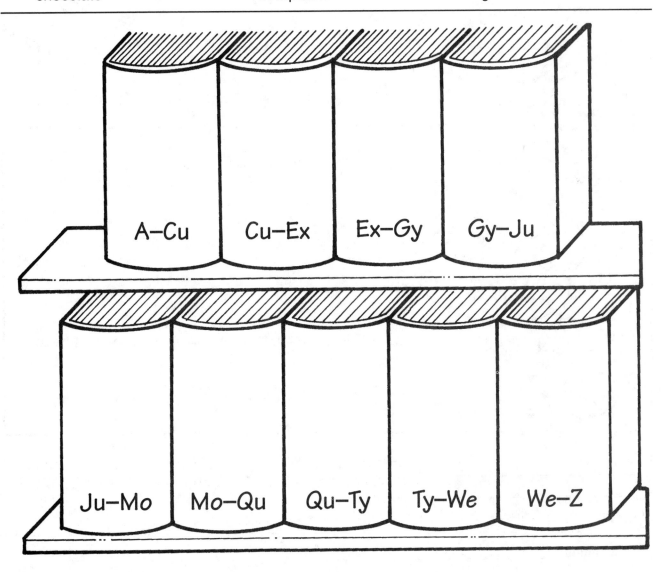

Facts and Opinions

When you write a research paper, you must be very careful to stick to the facts. A research paper is written to give people information that is true or that can be proven true.

Is this a fact?

"France is the best place in the world to live."

Whether you agree or not, it is just someone's opinion. It is not a fact.

In the blanks before each sentence below, write **F** for fact or **O** for opinion.

_____ 1. The moon orbits the earth.

_____ 2. The moon is inspirational to all who see it.

_____ 3. A banana tastes disgusting.

_____ 4. A banana is a fruit.

_____ 5. Abraham Lincoln was killed.

_____ 6. Abraham Lincoln was the best president.

_____ 7. Canada has the most beautiful lakes in the world.

_____ 8. Canada has many lakes.

_____ 9. Red and yellow mixed together make orange.

_____ 10. Orange is the prettiest color.

Many plants have thorns. (fact)

Thorny plants are not good in gardens. (opinion)

Now write one fact and one opinion about your school.

1. Fact: _____

2. Opinion: _____

Wild Animal Research

Directions for Writing

1. Choose six wild animals from the pictures on pages 14–16 and create your own book about them. Each page will represent one of the animals.

2. List the animals on which you wish to report.

_____   _____

_____   _____

_____   _____

3. Do some research to find interesting facts about the animals you have chosen. Use page 12 to record your findings.

4. Write a paragraph about each animal on six different wild animals. Use the form on page 13.

5. When you make your actual book, be sure to use your best writing skills—grammar, punctuation, and spelling—so your readers will understand and enjoy what you have written.

6. Cut out the pictures from pages 14–16 of the animals you chose. Glue each on the appropriate wild animal book form (page 13). As an alternative, you may wish to illustrate the animal yourself. Fill in the background of your picture with the animal's habitat

7. Make a front and back cover for your book. Complete your book by stapling the covers and pages together.

8. Share your animal books with someone.

Wild Animal Research (cont.)

Animal_____

Description (size, color, etc.) _____

Habitat (where it lives) _____

Its food _____

Its enemies _____

Caring for its young _____

Other interesting facts _____

Animal_____

Description (size, color, etc.) _____

Habitat (where it lives) _____

Its food _____

Its enemies _____

Caring for its young _____

Other interesting facts _____

Animal_____

Description (size, color, etc.) _____

Habitat (where it lives) _____

Its food _____

Its enemies _____

Caring for its young _____

Other interesting facts _____

Wild Animal Research (cont.)

_____

(animal)

Wild Animal Research (cont.)

You may choose from these pictures to illustrate your book.

Kangaroo

Rhinoceros

Gorilla

Tiger

Wild Animal Research (cont.)

You may choose from these pictures to illustrate your book.

Polar Bear

Koala

Sloth

Penguin

Wild Animal Research (cont.)

You may choose from these pictures to illustrate your book.

Panda

Wolf

Elephant

Alligator

Nouns

Nouns are words that name a person, place, thing, or idea.

- **Persons** include both names of people and categories.

  Mr. Blue   children   policemen   teacher   girl   boy

- **Places** can name both specific and general places.

  New York   school   park   department stores   homes

- **Things** refer to objects.

  door   shoes   newspaper   table   globe

- **Ideas** tell about feelings or thoughts.

  love   pain   philosophy   care   liberty   freedom   belief   rules

---

A. Underline the nouns in the following sentences. The number at the end of the sentence tells how many nouns to look for.

1. Summer is a wonderful time of the year. (3)

2. The weather is hot and many children enjoy swimming. (4)

3. Most schools are closed and people have time to go on vacations. (4)

4. The days are longer and we have more hours of sunlight. (4)

5. It is wonderful to go to the pool, beach, or lake. (4)

6. My teacher, Mr. Dawson, visited the Metropolitan Museum of Art in New York City in July. (5)

7. He said that great care and concern are shown by visitors. (4)

8. My friends, Tim and Carol, went to the Statue of Liberty and to Ellis Island. (5)

9. The scent of beautiful flowers drifts across Central Park as we eat our lunch outside. (5)

10. We like to cook hamburgers on the grill and picnic in the backyard. (4)

B. Use the back of this paper to write each of the following words under the correct heading of **person**, **place**, **thing**, or **idea**.

• France	• shoelaces	• city	• loyalty	• love	• building
• happiness	• bicycles	• Ms. Litz	• glasses	• table	• fairness
• clouds	• science	• sounds	• Dr. Forest	• pain	• Texas

Verbs

Verbs are words that express action or being.

An *action verb* describes physical action, that which can be seen.

   Example: Tom collected stamps and coins.

Sometimes the verb expresses mental action, that which cannot be seen.

   Example: Candice knew all the answers on the test.

A *linking verb* joins or links the subject of a sentence with a word or words in the predicate. It tells that something *is* or *was*.

   Example: The pot on the stove was hot!

Common Linking Verbs include the following:

am	*be*	*feel*	*has been*	*is*	*been*	*sound*
have been	*are*	*being*	*taste*	*was*	*will be*	*look*
had been	*were*	*become*	*appear*	*seem*		

Directions: In each of the sentences below, underline the verb. Label each verb *action* or *linking*.

_____   1. Lightning flashed across the sky.

_____   2. The quarterback raced down the field.

_____   3. The winner crossed the finish line.

_____   4. The crackling fire looked beautiful!

_____   5. The roasting marshmallows smelled delicious!

_____   6. The hunters captured a turkey and a deer.

_____   7. Hailstones are little ice balls.

_____   8. Fog covered the airport, preventing the planes from landing.

_____   9. Trucks skidded on the snow-covered highways.

_____   10. Dew formed on the grass in the early morning.

_____   11. The magician pulled a bouquet of flowers from the scarf.

_____   12. Mike appears frail after his operation.

_____   13. Kitty seems to be the fastest runner in the sixth grade.

_____   14. The young boys became excellent ranch hands.

Tall Tale Pattern Story

Use the form below to create a tall tale. Fill in the blanks with the correct words. Then illustrate the tall tale and share it with someone.

Many years ago _____ was born in

(hero)

_____ . _____was so big

(place)   (hero)

that he/she slept in a _____ . Each morning.

(noun)

_____ ate _____ ,

(hero)   (noun)

_____ , and _____ for breakfast. As

(noun)   (noun)

_____ grew older, he/she decided to learn to

(hero)

_____ . He/She became so good at

(verb)

_____ that he/she could _____

(verb)   (adverb)

beat anything or anybody. One day _____ found a/an

(hero)

_____ and rescued it from

(animal)

_____ . _____ named his/her new

(noun)   (hero)

friend _____ . People were amazed when they saw

(name)

_____ traveling with a/an _____

(hero)   (animal)

Then the two rescued _____ from a

(famous person)

_____ . Since then, _____

(danger)   (hero)

and _____ have become favorites of people everywhere.

(animal name)

Adjectives and Adverbs

> **Adjectives** describe nouns and pronouns.
>
> **Adverbs** modify verbs, adjectives, and other adverbs.

A. Cross out the word on the right that **cannot** be used to describe the word on the left.

1. sing   joyfully, beautiful, well, loudly
2. train   fast, yellow, electric, slowly
3. Ms. Woods   thinly, jumpy, comical, kindly
4. freedom   more powerful, limited, very, desired

B. Circle the adjectives.

1. pretty glass   6. round ball
2. big dog   7. wet towel
3. green door   8. excellent work
4. happy boy   9. broken pencil
5. thin cookie   10. smelly shoe

C. Circle the adverbs.

1. running slowly   6. writing sloppily
2. turning quickly   7. watching closely
3. quickly hit   8. sipping loudly
4. falling down   9. driving badly
5. joyfully leaping   10. throwing wildly

D. Think of three nouns and write them below. Write an adjective to go with each noun on the line next to it.

Noun	Adjective
1. _____	_____
2. _____	_____
3. _____	_____

E. Think of three verbs and write them below. Think of an adverb. Write the adverb on the line next to each verb.

Verb	Adverb
1. _____	_____
2. _____	_____
3. _____	_____

Glad Libs

With a partner, fill in each blank with the appropriate part of speech. When all the blanks have been filled in, read the story aloud. Try writing your own story on the back of the paper.

Fairy Tales Can Come True

Once upon a _____, there was a(n) _____
                    (noun)   (adjective)

little girl named _____. She _____ reading
                        (proper noun)   (verb)

_____ fairy tales. One morning she _____ ran to her
         (adjective)   (adverb)

bookshelf where, much to her surprise, she saw a (an) _____ fairy god-
                                                                (adjective)

_____. "_____!" she said, "You startled me!"
         (noun)   (exclamation)

"Nonsense!" said the fairy, "I'm here to grant you _____ wishes; but first,
                                                              (number)

you must guess my name, fit into the golden _____, and
                                                        (noun)

_____ dangle your long _____ hair out of the window.
        (adverb)   (adjective)

"Easy," replied the girl. "Your name is _____, this item fits like a glove,
                                                    (proper noun)

and I will _____ dangle my hair out the window."
                (adverb)

She was granted her wishes. The first things she did were _____,
                                                                        (verb)

_____, and _____. Then everyone lived happily ever
        (verb)   (verb)

after!

Make Your Own Word Search

Choose 10 or more words to build the puzzle. The words must all be nouns, verbs, adverbs, or adjectives. Write your words in the word box. Fill the words in the grid below. Put other letters in the empty boxes until they are all full. Give the word search to another person to solve.

Word Box

_____ _____ _____

_____ _____ _____

_____ _____ _____

Where's My List?

A comma is used between words in a series. Three or more things together make a series.

Example: *We will be talking today about muffins, kittens, and lollipops.*

Add the missing commas to the sentences below.

1. All birds have feathers wings and beaks.

2. My sister is sleepy grumpy and clueless.

3. I would have done my homework, but I was abducted by aliens was left in Siberia and had to wait for the Marines to rescue me.

4. I ordered a pizza with cheese pickles and sliced cherries.

5. Please go to the store and get flypaper chopsticks and kumquats.

6. I went to the door with rollers in my hair a mud mask on my face and wearing my bathrobe.

7. My dog has brown spots a short tail and fuzzy feet.

8. My little brother can't go anywhere without his blanket his stuffed duck and his rabbit's foot key chain.

9. When I go to college, I am taking a stereo a microwave and a treadmill.

10. For her birthday, Mindy wants some edible flowers sparkly socks and a pony.

✧   ✧   ✧

A comma is also used between two or more describing words (adjectives).

Example: *A friendly, playful dog makes a good pet.*

Add the missing commas to the sentences below.

1. My rabbit has long floppy ears.

2. A large heavy sparrow could weigh 200 pounds.

3. My teacher has a green pointy nose.

4. My dad used to have curly frizzy hair.

5. A friendly playful giraffe ate all my spaghetti.

When and Where?

A comma is used when writing a date. The comma separates the date and the year. It is also used to separate the day and the date.

A. Insert commas where needed in the sentences below.
1. My parents bought their first home on January 13 1976.
2. My mom was born on March 31 1948.
3. We went to Disneyland on Tuesday August 18 and it was really crowded!
4. My brother's birthday is November 17 1973.
5. On Saturday April 19, we are flying to my grandma's house.
6. I get my tonsils out on Monday September 16 and then I can eat lots of ice cream.
7. Our puppies were born on February 14 1997.
8. It rained cats and dogs on January 18 1995.

B. Write these dates using commas correctly.
1. today's date and year_____
2. today's day and date _____
3. your birthday _____
4. your favorite day of the year (besides your birthday)_____
5. the birthdate of a member of your family (and tell who)

Use a comma between the city and state (country or province) in an address.

C. Add commas to the following sentences.
1. Yesterday, I met a girl from Canberra Australia.
2. A hurricane went on shore at Acapulco Mexico.
3. I've never been to Seattle Washington.
4. It can get very cold in Buffalo New York.
5. Yesterday, I received e-mail from Bordeaux France.
6. Many movie stars live in La Canada-Flintridge California.
7. Alexandria Virginia, is an interesting historic town.
8. You can take a great train ride in Durango Colorado.
9. Have you been on the roller coasters in St. Louis Missouri?
10. The mountains are really high in Vail Colorado.

D. Answer the following with the name of a city and state or a city and province.
1. Where were you born? _____
2. Where was your mother born? _____
3. Where do you live today? _____
4. Name where one of your grandparents lives. _____
5. Where is the last place you visited? _____

Days, Months, and Holidays

Capitalize the words on this page by changing a lowercase letter to a capital letter where it is needed. As you capitalize each **holiday**, color its first letter in the circle.

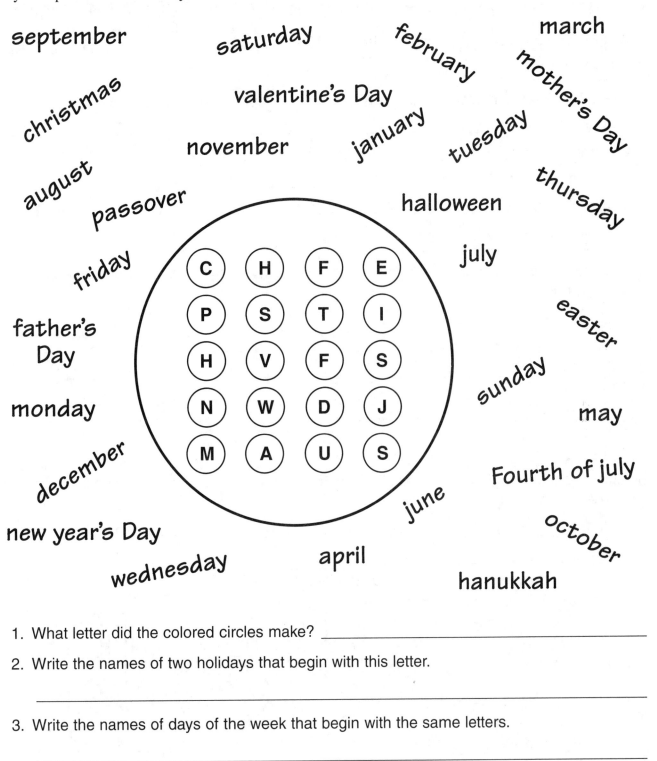

september

saturday

march

february

mother's Day

christmas

valentine's Day

november

january

tuesday

thursday

august

passover

halloween

friday

july

father's Day

easter

monday

sunday

may

december

Fourth of july

new year's Day

october

wednesday

april

june

hanukkah

C H F E
P S T I
H V F S
N W D J
M A U S

1. What letter did the colored circles make? _____

2. Write the names of two holidays that begin with this letter.

_____

3. Write the names of days of the week that begin with the same letters.

_____

4. Write the names of months that begin with the same letters.

_____

What's in a Name?

Did you know that your name is a proper noun? It is, and **you should always capitalize your first and last names and middle name if you have one**. And what about your pet snake? If you call your snake "George," "Rex," or "Samantha Slither," you should capitalize that, too. And if your stuffed animal is named "Old MacDonald" that name should be capitalized, with the M of Mac (or Mc) capitalized and the D of Donald also capitalized. Your little brother has the nickname, "Punkin"? That would also be capitalized.

Rewrite the following names so that they are properly capitalized.

1. amanda panda _____

2. jeffrey r. hardy_____

3. carlos custard appleseed _____

4. gilbert mcgillicutty_____

5. leslie q. presley_____

Do you have any pets at home? If you do, write the names of your pets (or any other pets you know) here.

_____

_____

_____

_____

_____

Here are some pets without names. Think of a name for each pet. The names can be fancy or simple, long or short, but they should all be capitalized. The first one has been done as an example.

Malcolm Angus McCollie McDuff   _____   _____   _____

_____   _____   _____

Extension: Make a *Names Notebook*. In a small notebook, write all the creative names you can think of in alphabetical order. Be sure to capitalize! Keep your notebook handy. The next time you write a story, you will have lots of interesting names from which to choose.

End Marks

Every sentence must end with a punctuation mark. As you have been learning, **a sentence may end with a period, a question mark, or an exclamation point**.

- A **period** comes at the end of a sentence that tells something.

  Examples: I have a purple bicycle. Turn left at the corner.

- A **question mark** comes at the end of a sentence that asks a question.

  Examples: What color is your bicycle? Is that your house?

- An **exclamation point** comes at the end of a sentence that contains a strong feeling.

  Examples: Watch out for that car! What a wonderful surprise!

The following sentences need end marks. Think about which end punctuation each sentence needs. Then write the correct punctuation mark at the end of each sentence.

1. I love my purple bicycle ☐

2. I saved enough money to buy it last year ☐

3. Would you like to try it ☐

4. My brother has a blue bicycle ☐

5. One time he crashed into me, and I fell off my bike ☐

6. Have you ever fallen off your bike ☐

7. Did you skin your knee ☐

8. I was so mad at my brother ☐

9. He told me he was sorry ☐

10. I'm so glad that my bike did not break ☐

11. Watch out for the glass in the road ☐

12. Don't ride your bike in the street ☐

13. Can you park a bike right here ☐

14. I have to go inside now ☐

15. Will I see you tomorrow ☐

Capitalization Review

It is time to see how much you have learned about capitalization. Circle all the letters below that should be capitals. (*Hint:* There are 63 of them.)

1. the first day of school is exciting.

2. freddy wilson's frog peepers hopped into mrs. woolsey's purse.

3. as i walked outside, i smelled smoke.

4. In the play, robin hood was played by lieutenant bronksy.

5. the fourth thursday in november is thanksgiving.

6. i like halloween best when it is on a saturday.

7. aunt susan went to yellowstone national park.

8. connie lives on maple street in bismark, north dakota.

9. brazil, argentina, and peru are in south america.

10. the mediterranean sea and the atlantic ocean touch spain.

11. the letter was signed, "love always, esther."

12. davis medical center opened in january last year.

13. one of the religions practiced by many african people is islam.

14. italians and germans belong to the caucasian race.

15. last tuesday ruben walked his dog spotty down tulip street to central park.

Building Sentences

Writing sentences can be fun. The following sentences are all about someone special–you! Add words to complete each of the sentences. When you are finished, cut out the box, glue it to a piece of decorative paper, and add a photograph of yourself.

1. My favorite sport is _____ because _____
   _____ .

2. My favorite song is _____ because _____
   _____ .

3. My favorite animal is _____ because _____
   _____ .

4. My favorite class at school is _____ because_____
   _____ .

5. My favorite TV show is _____ because_____
   _____ .

6. My favorite place to go is _____ because_____
   _____ .

7. My favorite dessert is _____ because_____
   _____ .

8. My favorite story is _____ because_____
   _____ .

9. My favorite time of the day is _____ because_____
   _____ .

10. My favorite movie is _____ because _____
    _____ .

TV Review

Complete the following TV program review. Then use the space on page 31 to write about the program and your reactions to it based on the information on this page.

Name of Program _____

1. Summary of episode _____

2. Explain how the show depicts the mother. _____
   _____

3. Explain how the show depicts the father. _____
   _____

4. Name and describe a child who is a main character in the episode. _____
   _____

   a. What problem or dilemma does he or she face in this episode? _____
      _____

   b. How is it resolved? _____

5. Name and describe a second child character. _____
   _____

   a. How is he or she related to the other character you described?_____
      _____

   b. What role did this character play in the main character's problem? ____
      _____

6. Do you think the program portrays a realistic family? Explain your answer._____
   _____

7. How is your family like this TV family? _____
   _____

   How is it different? _____
   _____

8. Would you like to be a part of this TV family? Explain why or why not. ____
   _____

TV Review (cont.)

_____

Title

PaPe

What Happened Next?

When you write about something that happened to you or something that you do, it must be in the right time order. Another name for this is *chronology*. The things you write about in a paragraph should usually be in *chronological* (or time) *order* to make sense.

Here are some lists of events that are out of order. Put them in chronological order by marking them from first (1) to last (5). The first one has been done for you.

A.

2	eat breakfast
1	get up
5	go to school
4	go out the door
3	brush teeth

E.

_____	slap your arm
_____	see a mosquito
_____	feel a bite
_____	hear a buzz
_____	scratch a bump

B.

_____	bait a hook
_____	clean a fish
_____	eat a fish
_____	catch a fish
_____	cook a fish

F.

_____	buy popcorn
_____	leave the theater
_____	stand in line
_____	buy a ticket
_____	watch a movie

C.

_____	mail the letter
_____	put the letter in an envelope
_____	write a letter
_____	wait for an answer
_____	seal the letter

G.

_____	find an old Halloween mask
_____	clean up your room
_____	sneak up on your brother
_____	put it on
_____	jump out at him

D.

_____	write a book report
_____	click on word processing
_____	turn on the printer
_____	turn on the computer
_____	print the book report

H.

_____	snap on the leash
_____	guide your dog back home
_____	get the leash
_____	whistle for your dog
_____	walk your dog

Choose one of the lists above and, on a separate piece of paper, make it into a paragraph. Be sure to write a good topic sentence.

Extension: Using the lists above, make sets of cards (five cards in a set). On each card write a phrase, such as "sneak up on your brother," and illustrate it. Take the cards to the children in younger grades and have them put the cards in order.

Write Your Own Story

Choose one of the following story ideas. Follow the steps to develop your ideas into a several-paragraph story. Illustrate the story if you wish.

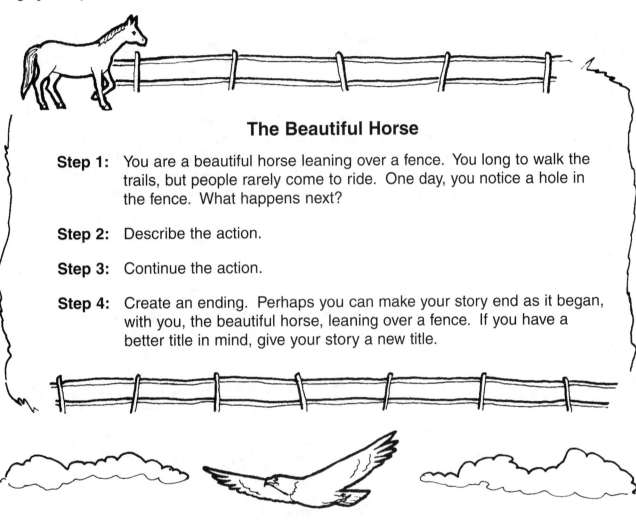

The Beautiful Horse

Step 1: You are a beautiful horse leaning over a fence. You long to walk the trails, but people rarely come to ride. One day, you notice a hole in the fence. What happens next?

Step 2: Describe the action.

Step 3: Continue the action.

Step 4: Create an ending. Perhaps you can make your story end as it began, with you, the beautiful horse, leaning over a fence. If you have a better title in mind, give your story a new title.

The Eagle

Step 1: You are an eagle perched high on a rock crag. Far below, you spot a gray and brown jackrabbit. What is going to happen?

Step 2: Describe the action.

Step 3: Continue the action.

Step 4: Tell how it ends. Make your story end where it began, with you, the eagle, perched on your rocky crag. If you have a better title in mind, give your story a new title.

Write Your Own Story (cont.)

Choose one of the following story ideas. Follow the steps to develop your ideas into a several-paragraph story. Illustrate the story if you wish.

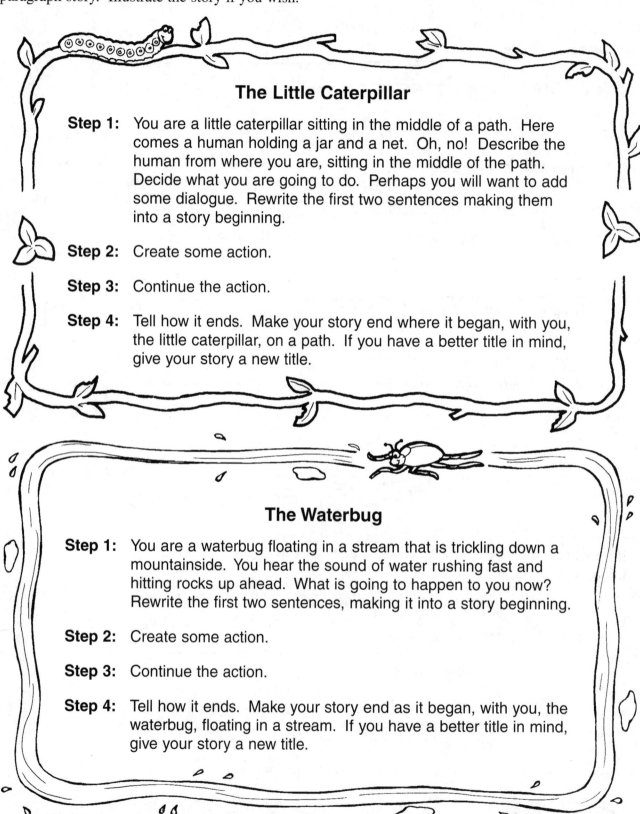

The Little Caterpillar

Step 1: You are a little caterpillar sitting in the middle of a path. Here comes a human holding a jar and a net. Oh, no! Describe the human from where you are, sitting in the middle of the path. Decide what you are going to do. Perhaps you will want to add some dialogue. Rewrite the first two sentences making them into a story beginning.

Step 2: Create some action.

Step 3: Continue the action.

Step 4: Tell how it ends. Make your story end where it began, with you, the little caterpillar, on a path. If you have a better title in mind, give your story a new title.

The Waterbug

Step 1: You are a waterbug floating in a stream that is trickling down a mountainside. You hear the sound of water rushing fast and hitting rocks up ahead. What is going to happen to you now? Rewrite the first two sentences, making it into a story beginning.

Step 2: Create some action.

Step 3: Continue the action.

Step 4: Tell how it ends. Make your story end as it began, with you, the waterbug, floating in a stream. If you have a better title in mind, give your story a new title.

Paragraph Starters

You might want to set a goal for yourself of writing each day. You will see your writing improve if you do this. You will find ideas on what to write about below and on page 36. Look them over and circle the ones about which you would like to write. Use these paragraph starters when you need inspiration while practicing paragraph writing. You might want to use some of these ideas for writing an essay, a report, or a story.

Gorillas make good pets.	If I were my teacher, here are three things I would do.
There are many uses for popcorn.	It's a good idea for all students to invite the principal to dinner.
Collecting bugs is an interesting hobby.	Kids should be allowed to drive when they are 10 years old.
There are many things shaped like a circle.	There are lots of reasons why I am glad to be a member of my family.
I would like to be invisible.	I really like math (science, English, social studies, etc.).
I have three favorite foods.	I should have my own room.
I know my brother/sister is an alien.	I deserve a raise in my allowance.
I would like to join the circus.	Eating is one of my favorite activities.
If I could stop time, there are three things I would do.	We should remember to wash our hands.
I would make a great president.	I would like to visit Mars.
I would like a giraffe for a pet.	It's a good idea to learn a foreign language.
It would be a good idea to build a roller coaster in my backyard.	I love music.
Airplanes are not a good idea.	I would like to remodel my house.

Paragraph Starters (cont.)

A smelly monster lives under my bed.	Snakes make great pets.
People should not be expected to wear matching shoes and socks.	I make the best peanut butter sandwiches.
It would be a good idea if we all lived in tents.	A woman should be president.
Gravity is a good idea.	I don't like earthquakes.
We should be allowed to bring our pets to school every day.	I love to read because . . .
Eating is a very weird thing to do.	I am afraid of the ocean.
We need pocket computers.	There are three good reasons for wearing a hat.
Anyone can draw.	Red is the best color for food.
I would rather starve than . . .	It's hard to wake up in the morning.
I put ketchup on everything.	I love roller coasters.
I don't like fish.	Even when I'm sick, there are some interesting things to do.
Rainy days are the best.	I think we need three arms and three hands instead of just two of each.
I would not like to lose my big toe.	It would be better if the sun stayed up all the time.

Ben Franklin

Preview the words in exercise A before reading the following selection. Then complete the exercises below.

Benjamin Franklin was a great American. He had many outstanding accomplishments in his lifetime. He was a printer, a publisher, a writer, an inventor, a scientist, a diplomat, a statesman, and an inspiration to those he met.

At age 42, Franklin decided to devote himself to the study of science. During this time, he was one of the world's greatest scientists, inventing and experimenting and loving his work. He proved that lightning was electricity and that things could be positively or negatively charged with electricity. Among the many things he made were the world's first battery, lightning rod, bifocal glasses, and an energy-efficient, wood-burning stove. However, he never patented any of his inventions. He preferred, instead, to share what he had learned freely with the world.

A. These words were used in the selection you just read. Match the words from the list on the left with their proper meaning.

_____ 1. diplomat

_____ 2. devote

_____ 3. inspiration

_____ 4. statesman

_____ 5. patent

a. official rights to the inventor

b. wise or experienced leader

c. a person who represents a country

d. give attention

e. sudden or original idea

B. Use the back of this paper to answer the following questions.

1. What are some of the many outstanding accomplishments Ben Franklin achieved in his lifetime? List three of them.

2. What did he decide to do when he was 42 years old?

3. What did he prove about lightning?

4. Did he patent any of his inventions? Why?

5. Which one of his inventions do you feel helped the world the most and why?

Our National Anthem

Preview the words in exercise A before reading the following selection. Then complete the exercises below.

In 1814, Francis Scott Key composed a poem, "The Defense of Fort McHenry," as he watched the bombardment of Ft. McHenry during the War of 1812. Later, Key's words were set to the tune of a popular English drinking song, "The Anacreaon in Heaven." Although the United States had been using the song in ceremonies for many years, it did not become the official national anthem until March 3, 1931, when President Herbert Hoover signed the bill that made "The Star-Spangled Banner" our national anthem.

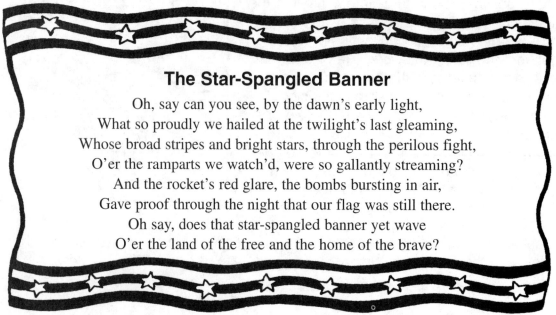

The Star-Spangled Banner
Oh, say can you see, by the dawn's early light,
What so proudly we hailed at the twilight's last gleaming,
Whose broad stripes and bright stars, through the perilous fight,
O'er the ramparts we watch'd, were so gallantly streaming?
And the rocket's red glare, the bombs bursting in air,
Gave proof through the night that our flag was still there.
Oh say, does that star-spangled banner yet wave
O'er the land of the free and the home of the brave?

A. These words were used in the selection you just read. Match the words from the list on the left with their proper meanings.

_____ 1. defense   a. in a position of authority

_____ 2. bombardment   b. song of patriotism or praise

_____ 3. ceremonies   c. protection from attack or harm

_____ 4. official   d. continued attacking

_____ 5. anthem   e. formal acts performed as a ritual

B. Use the back of this paper to answer the following questions.

1. What was the name of the poem that Francis Scott Key wrote?

2. What was happening when he wrote it?

3. When did it become the official national anthem?

4. Who was the president that signed the bill?

5. Do you think that this song is the right one for our national anthem? Explain your answer.

Morse Code

Preview the words in exercise A before reading the following selection. Then complete the exercises below.

Today, we commonly use telephones when we want to transmit a message over a long distance. However, before the use of telephones, other means of communications were used. Messages were often sent on paper. More urgent messages may have been sent by Morse code.

Morse code is a system of dashes and dots. Each combination of dashes and dots represents a different letter in the alphabet. Samuel F. B. Morse developed this language in 1835 to send messages over long distances with a telegraph machine. Morse code is still commonly used in emergencies by people today when telephone services are interrupted or unavailable.

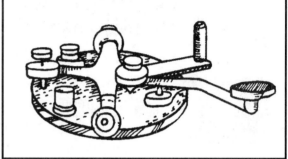

The telegraph is used to send messages over long distances.

A. These words were used in the selection you just read. Match the words from the list on the left with their proper meanings.

_____ 1. transmit   a. series of symbols

_____ 2. interrupt   b. to send from one person to another

_____ 3. unavailable   c. to stop

_____ 4. message   d. not able to obtain or get

_____ 5. code   e. words sent from one person to another

B. Use the back of this paper to answer the following questions.

1. What symbols are used in Morse code?

2. Who developed this code?

3. Is a telephone used to send messages with Morse code?

4. Who most commonly uses Morse code today?

5. Describe when you might need to use Morse code and what you could use to send the message?

Totem Poles

Preview the words in exercise A before reading the following selection. Then complete the exercises below.

As you travel through Vancouver and Victoria, British Columbia, you can see many totem poles. Stanley Park in Vancouver and Thunderbird Park in Victoria, British Columbia, each has a wonderful collection of totem poles.

Totem poles have been used by many Native Americans as a way to record history. Tribes, clans, and families used them as a symbol. A totem pole is a carving of animals, birds, fish, plants, or other natural objects that represent a Native American tribe.

A family would place its totem pole in front of its home. At the top of the pole was the family totem or symbol. When a totem pole was erected, there was a festival called a potlatch.

A. These words were used in the selection you just read. Match the words from the list on the left with their proper meanings.

_____ 1. clan   a. something that stands for something else

_____ 2. carving   b. group of people (usually related)

_____ 3. potlatch   c. a shape made by cutting with a sharp object

_____ 4. collection   d. group of objects

_____ 5. symbol   e. festival

B. Use the back of this paper to answer the following questions.

1. Where can you find a wonderful collection of totem poles?

2. What is the purpose of totem poles?

3. What is carved on a totem pole?

4. What was put at the top of the totem pole?

5. Describe what your family's totem pole would look like. You can draw it on another piece of paper.

Frisbee™

Preview the words in exercise A before reading the following selection. Then complete the exercises below.

The Frisbee™ story began in the late 1800s with the Frisbee Pie Company in Bridgeport, Connecticut. Their pies, which came in a ten-inch-wide round tin with a raised edge and wide brim, were popular with students at nearby Yale University. At some point, pie-tin catch had become a fad among the young collegians. The fad continued into the 1950s but was changed forever with the introduction of a plastic flying dish called Flyin' Saucer invented by Walter Frederick Morrison. First marketed as the Pluto Platter, the toy's name was officially changed to Frisbee when Wham-O's president saw Yale students throwing and catching Frisbee pie plates. However, not until the 1960s did sales of the Frisbee take off. Today it remains a popular toy and sport.

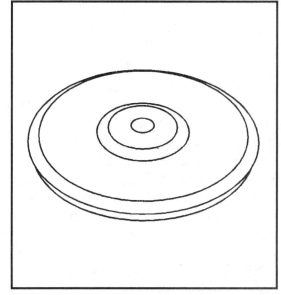

A. These words were used in the selection you just read. Match the words from the list on the left with their paper meanings.

_____ 1. fad   a. thin round object

_____ 2. collegians   b. to make something that has not been made before

_____ 3. marketed   c. something that is popular for a short time

_____ 4. disk   d. college students

_____ 5. invent   e. sold or offered for sale

B. Use the back of this paper to answer the following questions.

1. When did the Frisbee Pie Company begin?

2. What did the college students do with pie tins?

3. What name was the Flyin' Saucer marketed as before it was changed to Frisbee?

4. When did the sales of the Frisbee take off?

5. What would you have called this toy and why?

WD-40

Preview the words in exercise A before reading the following selection. Then complete the exercises below.

During the early 1950s, the aerospace industry began looking for a product to eliminate moisture from electrical circuitry and to prevent corrosion on airplanes. A satisfactory product was invented by Norman Larsen, who was the president and head chemist at the Rocket Chemical Company. His water displacement formula was developed on his fortieth try, thus the name WD-40. When it was discovered that WD-40 worked well to quiet squeaky doors and unstick stuck locks, a number of employees began sneaking the product home. In 1958, the product was made available to the public.

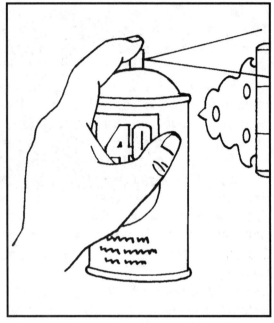

The WD-40 Company makes more than one million gallons of the lubricant each year. When astronaut John Glenn circled the earth in Friendship VII in 1964, the spacecraft was covered with WD-40 from top to bottom.

A. These words were used in the selection you just read. Match the words from the list on the left with their proper meanings.

_____ 1. corrosion   a. vehicle designed to travel into space

_____ 2. displacement   b. slippery substance used to lubricate parts

_____ 3. lubricant   c. person trained to travel into space

_____ 4. astronaut   d. act of wearing away (i.e., rusting)

_____ 5. spacecraft   e. to take the place of

B. Use the back of this paper to answer the following questions.

1. During the early 1950s, what was the aerospace industry looking for?

2. Who invented the formula later called WD-40?

3. How did it get its name?

4. What spacecraft was covered from top to bottom with this product?

5. What would you have called it and why?

Beatlemania

Preview the words in exercise A before reading the following selection. Then complete the exercises below.

Just how did four boys from Liverpool make it so big? Their story began in 1957 when John Lennon invited 15-year-old Paul McCartney to join his group, "The Quarrymen." Guitarist George Harrison and drummer Pete Best had joined the group by August 1961. In 1962, Best was replaced by Ringo Starr. After record store owner Brian Epstein became their manager, they signed with a recording company. It was not long before the Beatles became England's biggest-ever idols. Their live performances were accompanied by hordes of screaming fans. After their February 1964 appearance on *The Ed Sullivan Show*, "The Fab Four," as they were sometimes called, became transatlantic chart-toppers. While their first album had combined pop-soul songs with some of Lennon's and McCartney's original compositions, later albums reflected the whole group's efforts.

A. These words were used in the selection you just read. Match the words from the list on the left with their proper meanings.

_____ 1. transatlantic   a. person in charge of someone's business

_____ 2. combined   b. joined together

_____ 3. compositions   c. crossing the Atlantic Ocean

_____ 4. hordes   d. works of art, literature, or music

_____ 5. manager   e. large crowds of people

B. Use the back of this paper to answer the following questions.

1. Who first started the group?

2. What was the name of the first group?

3. Who replaced Pete Best?

4. What show made them famous in America?

5. Why do you think that this group was so popular all over the world?

Butchart Gardens

Preview the words in exercise A before reading the following selection. Then complete the exercises below.

One of the most beautiful flower gardens in the world is located in Victoria, British Columbia. This garden spreads out over many acres and features a Japanese garden, a rose garden, and a sunken garden.

In most of Canada, spring-like weather does not arrive until after St. Patrick's Day on March 17. However, before spring arrives in Victoria, Flower Count Week is celebrated. During this week people all over the city go out and actually count how many flowers and buds they see. Children are given an hour off from school to help count. There are special centers to which the numbers are called, and a graph of the number of flowers counted is posted at Eaton Centre, a large shopping mall downtown.

A. Match the words from the list on the left with their proper meanings.

_____ 1. acre   a. placed information for others to see

_____ 2. celebrate   b. garden below the ground level

_____ 3. locate   c. area of ground equal to 4,840 square yards

_____ 4. posted   d. to observe a special occasion

_____ 5. sunken garden   e. to find

B. Use the back of this paper to answer the following questions.

1. Where is Butchart Gardens located?

2. What are three of the types of gardens that you can find there?

3. What do people do during Flower Count Week?

4. What special privilege do children get?

5. If you could plant a garden, would it be a flower or vegetable garden? Explain your answer.

Spider-Man

Preview the words in exercise A before reading the following selection. Then complete the exercises below.

Spider-Man's real identity is Peter Parker, the freelance photographer. Peter was not born with any special powers or talents. However, when he was a teenager, he was accidentally bitten by a spider that had been exposed to huge amounts of radiation. As a result, Peter became strong and agile like a spider and was able to cling to any surface, including walls and ceilings.

He made a red and blue uniform for himself and created a mechanism for shooting a web. He decided to call himself the "Amazing Spider-Man," making sure to keep his real identity a secret. After Spider-Man's uncle was killed by a burglar, he quit his acting career and was determined to devote his life to fighting crime.

A. These words were used in the selection you just read. Match the words from the list on the left with their proper meanings.

_____ 1. freelance   a. parts that make a machine work

_____ 2. identity   b. able to move quickly

_____ 3. radiation   c. works independently

_____ 4. agile   d. who a person is

_____ 5. mechanism   e. waves or particles emitted by radioactivity.

B. Use the back of this paper to answer the following questions.

1. What is Spider-Man's true identity?

2. How did he get his special powers?

3. What did he wear when he wanted to be Spider-Man?

4. Why did he give up his career to become a full-time Spider-Man?

5. What do you think Peter's life would have been like if he had never been bitten by the spider?

Olympics in the 1920s

Preview the words in exercise A before reading the
following selection. Then complete the exercises
below.

The Olympic Games are the world's greatest sports
contest. A tradition begun in ancient Greece in 776
B.C. and abolished in A.D. 394, the games did not
begin again until 1896. Since then, the modern
Olympiads have undergone numerous changes.
Some sports, like rugby, have come and gone while
others, like track and field, have remained constant.

During the 1920s there were two important changes
in the Olympics. The now familiar Olympic flag first
appeared in 1920. In 1924, the first winter Olympic
games were held in Chamonix, France. Originally
held in the same year as the traditional games, the
schedule changed in the 1990s, with the summer and
winter games held two years apart.

A. Match the words from the list on the left with their proper meanings.

_____ 1. tradition   a. first; the source

_____ 2. ancient   b. the passing of customs to the next generation

_____ 3. numerous   c. form of football

_____ 4. Rugby   d. many; a lot

_____ 5. original   e. very old

B. Use the back of this paper to answer the following questions.

1. When were the first Olympics?

2. Have they stayed the same all these years?

3. Where were the first Olympic Games held?

4. Are the winter games and summer games held in the same year?

5. What sport would you like to participate in at the Olympics and why?

Barbie™ Doll

Preview the words in exercise A before reading the following selection. Then complete the exercises below.

In 1959, the Barbie™ Doll made her debut. Today, she is the best-selling toy in American history. Her inventor is Ruth Handler, a former secretary and housewife. Ruth noticed that her daughter preferred to play with teenage dolls rather than those designed for her own age group. The problem was that the teenage dolls available at that time were paper cutouts. Ruth designed a more grown-up doll that would wear fashionable clothing and be a little girl's dream of things to come. Barbie™, named after Handler's daughter, made her debut at the 1959 New York Toy Show. A huge success, it sold $500 million worth in its first eight years. Ruth Handler went on to become vice president and then president of Mattel, Inc., the company that manufacturers Barbie™.

A. These words were used in the story you just read. Match the words on the left with their proper meanings.

_____ 1. debut   a. a good result

_____ 2. designed   b. liked better

_____ 3. fashionable   c. in the latest style

_____ 4. preferred   d. made a plan for

_____ 5. success   e. seen in public for the first time

B. Use the back of this paper to answer the following questions.

1. When did Barbie make her debut?

2. Who invented Barbie?

3. Why did she invent Barbie?

4. Who went on to become president of Mattel, Inc., the company that manufacturers Barbie?

5. Do you think Barbie is a doll that should be sold in toy stores? Explain your answer.

Hula Hoop™

Preview the words in exercise A before reading the following selection. Then complete the exercises below.

The Wham-O toy company manufactured the Hula Hoop™ in the 1950s. For six months it enjoyed great success as the Hula Hoop became the fastest-selling toy in history. Just as quickly, however, the craze seemed to die down. Every generation since then has seen a resurgence of the unusual toy. Based on a wooden hoop used by Australian youths, the plastic Hula Hoop was invented by Richard Knerr, a partner in the Wham-O toy manufacturing company.

A. These words were used in the selection you just read. Match the words on the left with their proper meanings.

_____ 1. manufactured   a. popular for a short time

_____ 2. craze   b. a circular frame

_____ 3. resurgence   c. people who grew up and lived at the same time

_____ 4. generation   d. made

_____ 5. hoop   e. having become popular again

B. Use the back of this paper to answer the following questions.

1. How long was the Hula-Hoop the fastest selling toy in history?

2. Did the craze last for a long time?

3. What was the Hula Hoop based on?

4. Who invented the Hula Hoop?

5. Invent a game you could play with the Hula Hoop. Briefly describe how to play.

The Endangered Sea Otter

Preview the words in exercise A before reading the following selection. Then complete the exercises below.

In the mid-1800s, the fur trade was thriving. Hunters up and down the West Coast were trapping and trading furs for goods. Demand for precious furs was high. Unfortunately, the sea otter was one of the animals prized for its pelt. Hunters traveled from Alaska to Southern California to capture them. As a result, the playful sea otters were hunted almost to extinction by the late 1800s. Since then, the government has taken an interest in sea otters and has placed a ban on the hunting of these creatures. Although there are still hunters who illegally poach these animals for their fur, the population of sea otters off the coast of California is increasing.

A. These words were used in the selection you just read. Match the words from the list on the left with their proper meanings.

_____ 1. thriving   a. against the law

_____ 2. endangered   b. no longer exists

_____ 3. illegally   c. group of the same kind of animal

_____ 4. extinct   d. healthy

_____ 5. species   e. to be in danger

_____ 6. pelt   f. animal skin

B. Use the back of this paper to answer the following questions.

1. What kind of trade was thriving in the mid 1800s?

2. Why did the hunters want the sea otters?

3. Why can't people hunt sea otters today?

4. What is happening to the sea otters off the coast of California today?

5. Do you think that we should be able to hunt seal otters today? Explain your reasons.

Spider-Woman

Preview the words in exercise A before reading the following selection. Then complete the exercises below.

No one knows the real identity of Spider-Woman. She kept it a well-guarded secret. She refuses to reveal her identity because she wants to protect the people she cares about from being harmed by her enemies. Unlike Spider-Man, it is unknown whether Spider-Woman was born with special powers or if she acquired them later in life.

Spider-Woman has extraordinary strength, endurance, and agility. Spider-Woman can move her body like a spider, climbing up walls and across ceilings. Spider-Woman's intuition is only average. She is not able to sense danger any better than the ordinary person. However, her psychic ability is exceptional. She can create a web by concentrating intensely and does not need any kind of device. Spider-Woman uses the web to trap criminals. One problem with the web is that it becomes increasingly weaker the further away it is from Spider-Woman. Therefore, a criminal can easily break loose if caught in the outer boundaries of the web. If Spider-Woman loses consciousness, she cannot create or maintain a web.

A. These words were used in the selection you just read. Match the words from the list on the left with their proper meanings.

_____ 1. identity   a. lines or limits where something ends

_____ 2. extraordinary   b. who a person is

_____ 3. psychic   c. able to read another's mind

_____ 4. concentrate   d. with utmost strain

_____ 5. intensely   e. beyond what is ordinary

_____ 6. boundaries   f. focus on common center

B. Use the back of this paper to answer the following questions.

  1. Who is the real Spider-Woman?

  2. How did she get her special powers?

  3. How does she create a web?

  4. Can she sense danger like an ordinary person can?

  5. How can a criminal break loose from her web?

  6. What super power would you add to Spider-Woman?

The Walt Disney Story

Preview the words in exercise A before reading the following selection. Then complete the exercises below.

Walter Elias Disney was born on December 5, 1901, the fourth of five children. Disney's early years were spent on a farm in Missouri, where he developed an interest in drawing.

In 1919, Disney and a friend formed an art company and made some animated cartoons.

Four years later he moved to California, where he and his brother, Roy, began Walt Disney Productions. Disney created a character he called Mortimer the Mouse. His wife, Lillian, suggested a name that was less stuffy, and Mickey was born. In 1928, with Disney providing his voice, Mickey Mouse starred in *Steamboat Willie*. The success of Mickey Mouse was only the beginning. In the thirties, Mickey acquired a number of cartoon pals, including Donald Duck, Pluto, Minnie Mouse, and Goofy. Walt Disney died in 1966, but the studio he founded continues the Disney tradition, bringing new technology to films. Disney's spirit lives on in his memorable characters and theme parks.

A. These words were used in the selection you just read. Match the words from the list on the left with the proper meanings.

_____ 1. stuffy   a. made to seem alive

_____ 2. develop   b. dull

_____ 3. founded   c. use of scientific knowledge

_____ 4. animated   d. to cause to grow; get better

_____ 5. technology   e. brought into being; established

B. Use the back of this paper to answer the following questions.

1. When was Walter Elias Disney born?

2. Where did the name Mickey Mouse come from?

3. Who did Walt go into business with to form Walt Disney Productions?

4. What was the first movie that Mickey Mouse starred in?

5. Describe a character that you would create if you had your own movie company.

The Amazon Rain Forest

Preview the words in exercise A before reading the following selection. Then complete the exercises below.

In 1971, construction began in Brazil for a major trans-Amazon highway to open up and remove areas of the rain forest for settlement and development. Huge areas of the Amazon rain forest were cut down and burned to make way for about one million new settlers. Because the large cities were so overcrowded and most people were unable to find work there, the government offered lucrative incentives to families who moved to the Amazon. Each family would be given a 240-acre piece of land, housing, and a small salary for a few months. Plans were made to build schools, health facilities, and other services. Thousands made the move but had to give up after only a few months because life in the rain forest was so difficult. The project failed, and it led to the destruction of a great deal of the Amazon rain forest. The result of this devastation was that much of the rain forest habitat was lost forever, and the soil eroded and turned into poor agricultural land.

A. These words were used in the selection you just read. Match the words from the list on the left with their proper meanings.

_____ 1. lucrative

_____ 2. facilities

_____ 3. habitat

_____ 4. incentive

_____ 5. devastation

_____ 6. agricultural

a. destruction

b. that which relates to producing crops or raising livestock

c. producing wealth, profitable

d. buildings used for activities

e. something used to make someone do better

f. place where an animal lives

B. Use the back of this paper to answer the following questions.

1. What did construction begin for in 1971?

2. What happened to large areas of the Amazon rain forest?

3. What was each family offered if they moved there?

4. What services would be available to these families?

5. Was this project a success? Explain your answer.

6. Is the rain forest important to the ecology of the rest of the world? Explain your answer.

Robin Hood

Preview the words in exercise A before reading the
following selection. Then complete the exercises below.

Robin Hood is a legendary English hero whose rebellious
nature made him a popular character in stories and
ballads beginning sometime during the 1300s. To this day,
no one knows for sure whether or not he really existed.

The legend begins when Robin Hood is rescued by a
group of outlaws who live in Sherwood Forest. He finds
that he has much more in common with these outlaws
than anyone else so he becomes their leader. Robin
Hood's followers include the beautiful Maid Marian, the
love of his life; Friar Tuck, a good-hearted priest; and Little
John, a seven-foot giant of a man.

Robin Hood's popularity comes from the way he fights
corruption and injustice. He treats corrupt officials, such
as the sheriff of Nottingham, with contempt. However, he treats women and poor people with
respect. He and his band of outlaws steal from the rich and give to the poor. The commoners
praise him as a hero, while authority figures proclaim him an outlaw.

A. These words were used in the selection you just read. Match the words on the left with
   their proper meanings.

_____ 1. legend	a. a feeling of honor
_____ 2. rebellious	b. resisting authority
_____ 3. ballads	c. dishonesty
_____ 4. commoners	d. ordinary people
_____ 5. corruption	e. poems or songs that tell a story
_____ 6. respect	f. story handed down from the past

B. Use the back of this paper to answer the following questions.

   1. Who is Robin Hood?

   2. Who rescues Robin Hood in the forest?

   3. Who are his faithful followers?

   4. How does he treat corrupt officials such as the sheriff of Nottingham?

   5. How does he treat women and poor people?

   6. Do you think Robin Hood was a real person? Explain your answer.

Kristi Yamaguchi

Preview the words in exercise A before reading the following selection. Then complete the exercises below.

Kristi Tsuya Yamaguchi was born in Hayward, California, in 1971. She was born with a clubfoot, but she did not let that stand in the way of her ambitions. She started skating at the age of six and was competing within two years.

When Yamaguchi was 12 years old, she started skating with Rudi Galindo. Together they won the 1985 national junior pairs championships.

In 1990, Yamaguchi and Galindo decided they wanted to concentrate on their singles careers rather than continue with their pairs skating. This gave Yamaguchi more time to devote to her singles training. As a result, her singles skating improved. She started working to make her routines more complicated. This paid off because she was able to become the world champion in figure skating in 1991 and 1992.

Yamaguchi went to Albertville, France, for the 1992 Winter Olympics. She knew that the competition was going to include many excellent skaters. She chose a routine that was technically difficult. She skated with perfection, and the judges rated her routine the highest. Yamaguchi won a gold medal. It had been 16 years since an American woman had won a gold medal in the singles event.

A. These words were used in the selection you just read. Match the words from the list on the left with their proper meanings.

_____ 1. clubfoot   a. deformity of the foot

_____ 2. concentrate   b. strong desire to achieve something

_____ 3. routine   c. a series of regular activities

_____ 4. champion   d. winner of game or contest

_____ 5. ambition   e. to direct ones thoughts on something

B. Use the back of this paper to answer the following questions.

1. Where and when was Kristi born?

2. How old was she when she started skating?

3. What did she decide to do in 1990?

4. What medal did she win at the 1992 Winter Olympics?

5. Would you prefer to be a singles skater or a pairs skater? Explain your answer.

The Greatest Airship Ever Built

Preview the words in exercise A before reading the following selection. Then complete the exercises below.

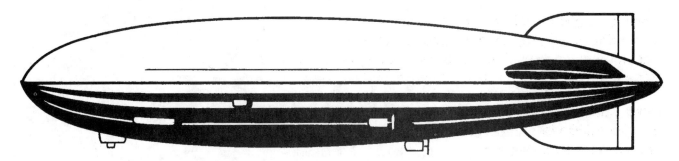

You have probably seen helium-filled blimps gracefully making their way across the sky. These ships are quiet, safe, and fuel efficient, but their cousins, the zeppelins, did not possess all of these qualities. During the 1930s, huge zeppelins more than 40 times the size of modern blimps carried passengers across the oceans.

The largest and most luxurious zeppelin ever built was the Hindenburg. A magnificent airship, it contained observation decks and private sleeping rooms and offered gourmet dining to its rich passengers.

On Monday, May 3, 1937, at 7:30 A.M. the Hindenburg began a routine journey to America. It reached America on May 6. After delays due to bad weather, it finally landed. Suddenly, there was a loud thump, and the tail section exploded into flames. The fire spread rapidly throughout the rest of the craft, and within half a minute the blazing air ship was on the ground. With that unfortunate mishap, the age of the zeppelin came to a complete and abrupt halt.

A. These words were used in the selection you just read. Match the words from the list on the left with their proper meanings.

_____ 1. helium	a. a good result without waste
_____ 2. blazing	b. very splendid and comfortable
_____ 3. efficient	c. a very light gas
_____ 4. routine	d. brightly-burning flame
_____ 5. luxurious	e. regular or standard

B. Use the back of this paper to answer the following questions.

1. How much bigger were zeppelins than blimps?

2. What was the largest and most luxurious zeppelin ever built?

3. Where was the Hindenburg going in 1937?

4. What happened to the Hindenburg as it landed?

5. Would you like to ride in a blimp or zeppelin? Explain your answer.

Judy Blume

Preview the words in exercise A before reading the following selection. Then complete the exercises below.

Beginning with the introduction of her book *Are You There God? It's Me, Margaret* in 1970, Judy Blume became a leading children's author.

Judy Sussman Blume was born on February 12, 1938, in Elizabeth, New Jersey. As a child, Judy Sussman was an A student and did exactly as she was told, even though on the inside she wished she could rebel. She loved to read Nancy Drew mysteries, biographies, and horse stories but also longed to read about characters who shared problems that she and other young people were facing. She attended New York University, and in 1960, the year before she graduated, she married John W. Blume, an attorney.

Since her first book was published in 1969, Judy Blume has received awards from all over the United States. In addition to writing several juvenile fiction books, Judy Blume has written young adult and adult books. Blume also contributed to the project *Free to Be You and Me* for the Mrs. Foundation in 1974.

In recent years, Judy Blume founded KIDS Find and remains on the council of advisors for the National Coalition of Censorship.

A. These words were used in the selection you just read. Match the words from the list on the left with their proper meanings.

_____ 1. rebel   a. resist or fight authority

_____ 2. biographies   b. people who consult or give advice

_____ 3. juvenile   c. completed a course of study

_____ 4. advisors   d. childish

_____ 5. graduated   e. true stories about someone, written by
                                         another person

B. Use the back of this paper to answer the following questions.

1. What was the name of the first book that made her famous?

2. What kind of student was she as a child?

3. What kind of books did she like to read as a child?

4. Why did she change her name to Judy Blume?

5. What would be a subject for a book that you would like her to write about?

Annie Oakley

Preview the words in exercise A before reading the
following selection. Then complete the exercises
below.

Annie Oakley was born in 1860 in Darke County,
Ohio. Her name at birth was Phoebe Ann Moses.
By the age of eight, she had learned to shoot and
helped her family by hunting animals for food. Annie
was a professional marksman by the time she was
15. She participated in many shooting contests that
took place in Cincinnati. She beat Frank Butler in a
shooting match, which sparked a romance between
them. Annie and Frank were married in 1876. Soon
afterwards, Annie started calling herself Annie
Oakley. In 1885, Annie joined Buffalo Bill's Wild
West Show. She gave a fascinating performance with the assistance of her husband. She
would shoot a dime that was in his hand or a cigarette that was in his mouth. Annie also did a
trick during which her husband, who was standing 90 feet (27 m) away from her, threw a
playing card into the air and she shot it. Annie's accuracy amazed audiences. She was often
called "Little Sure Shot," a nickname that was given to her by Sitting Bull, a Sioux Indian chief.

A. These words were used in the selection you just read. Match the words from the list on
   the left with their proper meanings.

   _____ 1. marksman   a. feelings of love toward someone

   _____ 2. assistance   b. person skilled in shooting a gun or rifle

   _____ 3. accuracy   c. having the power to charm

   _____ 4. fascinating   d. to help

   _____ 5. romance   e. freedom from error

B. Use the back of this paper to answer the following questions.

   1. How did she help her family when she was eight years old?

   2. How did she meet her husband?

   3. Describe one of the tricks that she could do.

   4. What was her nickname?

   5. Why do you think that Annie's performance was so popular?

Statue of Liberty

Preview the words in exercise A before reading the following
selection. Then complete the exercises below.

The Statue of Liberty has always been a symbol of welcome
and a promise of freedom for immigrants to the United States
of America. The statue was given to the United States by the
people of France in 1884. They wanted to have it ready by the
Centennial in 1876, but it was delayed because France was
involved in a war with Prussia. Frédéric Bartholdi designed
and sculpted the statue. He was sent to America to complete
his plans. As he sailed into the harbor at Bedloe's Island, he
knew that was where the statue should be. He decided to
make the statue a lady as a symbol of liberty and that she
would face the ocean with a greeting and a promise. He
decided to call it Liberty Enlightening the World. Bartholdi
talked to President Grant, and it was agreed that France would
built the statue and the United States would build the base and
pedestal.

The seven spikes in the statue's crown reach out to the seven
seas and the seven continents. The seven spikes also stand
for seven liberties.

A. These words were used in the selection you just read. Match the words from the list on
   the left with their proper meanings.

   _____ 1. immigrants   a. long, pointed piece of metal or wood

   _____ 2. sculpted   b. settlers from another country

   _____ 3. statue   c. rights or freedoms

   _____ 4. spikes   d. shaped or designed

   _____ 5. liberties   e. likeness of something that has been sculpted
                                    out of another material such as clay

B. Use the back of this paper to answer the following questions.

   1. What does the Statue of Liberty symbolize?

   2. Who gave the United States the statue and when?

   3. Who designed it?

   4. What did the designer decide to name the statue?

   5. What do the seven spikes in the crown stand for?

A. A. Milne

Preview the words in exercise A before reading the following selection. Then complete the exercises below.

Alan Alexander Milne, better known as A. A. Milne, is the author of Winnie-the-Pooh stories for children. He was born on January 18, 1882, in London, England, and was the youngest of three boys. An unambitious student, he discovered writing when his brother bet him he couldn't compose a verse as well as he could. But Milne surprised his brother with a well-written poem, and the two collaborated on verse for a couple of years.

During World War I Milne joined the Royal Warwickshire Regiment, a reserve battalion, and served in France. In his spare time he was able to write his first children's book and a play to entertain the troops. When he returned to civilian life, he continued with his writing career. On August 21, 1920, his only son, Christopher Robin, was born. The book that established him as a major children's author was the 1926 story *Winnie-the-Pooh*.

Winnie, Eeyore, and Christopher Robin have become some of children's favorite storybook characters. In recent years they were immortalized on screen by the Walt Disney Company, which made its first motion picture about *Winnie-the-Pooh* in 1965.

A. These words were used in the selection you just read. Match the words from the list on the left with their proper meanings.

_____ 1. unambitious   a. groups of soldiers

_____ 2. collaborated   b. one section of a poem or song

_____ 3. verse   c. not eager to succeed

_____ 4. entertain   d. worked with someone on a project

_____ 5. troops   e. to hold someone's attention

B. Use the back of this paper to answer the following questions.

1. How did A. A. Milne became a writer?

2. During World War I, what did he do in his spare time?

3. What book did he write in 1926?

4. Who made the first motion picture about the book written in 1926?

5. What would happen if *Winnie-the-Pooh* took place in Japan? Explain your answer.

Constellations

Preview the words in exercise A before reading the following selection. Then complete the exercises below.

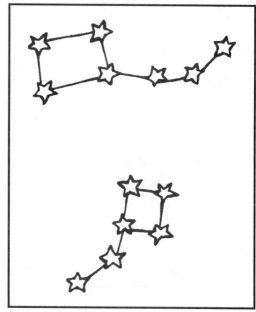

People have been using stars to guide their way and lives for centuries. Without the use of landmarks, mariners of old depended solely upon compass and stars to direct their ships. Since the stars served such an important role for people, names were given to groups of stars to help chart the night sky. We call these star groupings constellations. The constellations have been known by many different names by different groups of people. A good example of this is the Big Dipper. The Big Dipper is known as the Bear by the ancient Greeks, the Wagon by the ancient Romans, and the Plow by many European people today. To the Hindus, the Big Dipper represents the Seven Rishis.

Many of the constellation names were based on ancient stories and myths. The following is a story from Greek mythology which explains the constellation Cassiopeia.

Cassiopeia claimed that she was more beautiful than the lovely sea nymphs. The nymphs became angry and complained to Poseidon, god of the sea. Poseidon decided to punish Cassiopeia for her vanity by sending a sea monster to destroy her kingdom. He then demanded that Cassiopeia's daughter be sacrificed to the sea monster. Fortunately, the young girl was rescued by Perseus before the sea monster could kill her. Cassiopeia was changed into a constellation at her death and was placed into the night sky for all to remember.

A. These words were used in the selection you just read. Match the words from the list on the left with their proper meanings.

_____ 1. mariners	a. to rely upon
_____ 2. compass	b. ones who navigate a ship
_____ 3. European	c. natives of India who believes in Hinduism
_____ 4. Hindu	d. instrument used to tell geographic locations
_____ 5. depended	e. from Europe
_____ 6. nymphs	f. female spirits who live in woods or water

B. Use the back of this paper to answer the following questions.

1. What did ancient people use the stars for?
2. What do we call star groupings?
3. What is the name of one of the constellations written about in the article?
4. What were many of the stars' names based on?
5. What did Cassiopeia think about herself?

Hercules

Preview the words in exercise A before reading the following selection. Then complete the exercises below.

Hercules is a great hero in Greek mythology. He was the son of Zeus, king of the gods of Olympia.

When Hercules was just a baby, he began showing that he had great strength by killing two serpents who were about to attack him. As he grew up, he became famous for his strength and his kindness to those in need. He learned wrestling, archery, and fencing. Although Hercules was basically a good person, he had one serious problem. He had a terrible temper. His temper was so uncontrollable that he had been banished from Thebes. Hercules was told that the only way he could make up for his behavior was to serve King Eurystheus for 12 years. During this time, Hercules was given many difficult tasks to accomplish. With strong determination, he was able to accomplish all of them

A. These words were used in the selection you just read. Match the words from the list on the left with their proper meanings.

_____ 1. banished   a. tendency to become angry

_____ 2. accomplish   b. sport using swords

_____ 3. mythology   c. to carry out

_____ 4. temper   d. made-up stories about people, gods, and
                                ancestors

_____ 5. fencing   e. forced to leave

B. Use the back of this paper to answer the following questions.

1. Who was Hercules' father?

2. What unusual thing did Hercules do when he was just a baby?

3. What are the names of two activities that he liked to do when he was growing up?

4. Why was he banished from Thebes?

5. What did he have to do to make up for his bad behavior?

6. What lesson do you think Hercules learned from his 12-year experience?

Neil Armstrong

Preview the words in exercise A before reading the following selection. Then complete the exercises below.

Neil Alden Armstrong was born in 1930 in Wapakoneta, Ohio. During the Korean War, Armstrong was a pilot for the United States Navy. After the war, he studied at Purdue University where he graduated in 1955. Then Armstrong became a civilian test pilot for what is now called the National Aeronautics and Space Administration (NASA). In 1962, Armstrong started training to be an astronaut, making him the first civilian to join the program.

In 1966, Armstrong climbed aboard Gemini 8 to make his first flight into space. Although the mission was a success, it did encounter a serious problem. After docking the two spacecrafts, it went into a violent roll. Fortunately, he and his partner were able to deal with the crisis and safely return to Earth.

In July 1969, Armstrong was chosen as the commander of the Apollo 11 mission. People from all around the world watched as Armstrong made history on July 20, 1969, by being the first person to walk on the moon.

Armstrong retired from NASA in 1971 to become an aerospace engineering professor.

A. These words were used in the selection you just read. Match the words from the list on the left with their proper meanings.

_____ 1. aerospace   a. to meet unexpectedly

_____ 2. civilian   b. a crucial situation

_____ 3. docking   c. science that deals with space flight

_____ 4. crisis   d. guiding or coming to a dock

_____ 5. encounter   e. a person not in the armed forces

B. Use the back of this paper to answer the following questions.

1. What job did Neil Armstrong do for the Navy?

2. What was the name of the first flight that he took?

3. What was the problem they faced on the Gemini 8 flight?

4. When did he retire, and what did he do?

5. How do you think Armstrong felt about being the first person to walk on the moon? Explain your answer.

Babe Ruth

Preview the words in exercise A before reading the following selection. Then complete the exercises below.

Born in 1895, George Herman Ruth grew up on the streets of Baltimore, fending for himself, and by the age of eight had gotten into trouble. Young George was sent to a Catholic boys' home, where he played baseball. An invaluable team member, he could play just about any position.

In 1914 Ruth began his career with the Baltimore Orioles, at that time a minor league team. Later that year, Ruth joined the Boston Red Sox. There he served as a pitcher while also showing his prowess as a hitter. Because he could hit the ball harder and farther than any other team member, he held two positions—in some games he pitched and in other games he played in the outfield. By 1918, Babe Ruth was recognized as the best left-handed pitcher in baseball. He also led the American League in home runs. Boston's owner, in need of money, sold Ruth to the New York Yankees after the 1919 season. As a Yankee, Ruth concentrated solely on hitting and playing the outfield, and immediately, he shattered a number of records and brought baseball to a new level.

Formerly, baseball had been a pitcher's game, but Ruth changed all that; now it was a hitter's game. Ruth set many records that stood unchanged for years. In 1920 he broke the 1884 record of 24 home runs in one season by hitting 54. The next year he hit 59 homers and scored a total of 177 runs. In 1927 Ruth hit 60 home runs, a record that stood for 34 years. Attendance at games increased so much that the Yankees built Yankee Stadium, sometimes known as "the house that Ruth built."

A. These words were used in the selection you just read. Match the words from the list on the left with their proper meanings.

_____ 1. fending	a. superior skill or ability
_____ 2. invaluable	b. to provide for
_____ 3. concentrated	c. home runs
_____ 4. attendance	d. priceless
_____ 5. prowess	e. focused
_____ 6. homers	f. number of people at an event

B. Use the back of this paper to answer the following questions.

1. Where was George Herman Ruth born?
2. What was his childhood like?
3. During his lifetime, what positions did he play?
4. What record did he break in 1920?
5. What was the other name for Yankee Stadium?
6. If you met him on the street today, what would you say to him?

Elvis Presley

Preview the words in exercise A before reading the following selection. Then complete the exercises below.

Elvis Presley has been called the King of rock and roll. Born on January 8, 1935, in Tupelo, Mississippi, Presley won his first talent contest when he was just eight years old. In 1954, he recorded his first song as a present for his mother. The owner of the recording service had recently started his own record company, Sun, and signed Presley as a new talent. Presley did not have much success with Sun and after a year left for RCA. Thanks in large part to television and appearances on programs such as *The Ed Sullivan Show*, Presley became a huge star all across America.

In 1955, Colonel Tom Parker became Presley's manager and signed him to RCA Records at a cost of $40,000. One year later, Presley had a number-one hit with "Heartbreak Hotel." A string of hits continued with "Hound Dog," "Don't Be Cruel," and "Love Me Tender."

Presley entered the film industry and starred in a number of musicals until he was drafted by the U.S. Army. For two years he served his country, and he was proud to do so. His return to civilian life meant a return to acting, but his singing career was not as hot as it once was. Pop artists of the sixties began to replace his now-dated style.

During the seventies, Presley started live tours, and his singing career picked up. On August 16, 1977, Elvis Presley died. He left behind an impressive 94 gold singles and over 40 gold albums. Today, he remains one of the biggest influences on 20th century pop culture and is an enduring idol in the world of rock and roll.

A. These words were used in the selection you just read. Match the words from the list on the left with their proper meanings.

1. success   a. making a strong impression
2. enduring   b. long lasting
3. manager   c. popular singers
4. drafted   d. to be selected for military service
5. pop artists   e. having achieved something
6. impressive   f. a person who is in charge of a business or person

B. Use the back of this paper to answer the following questions.

1. What did Elvis win when he was eight years old?
2. Why did he record his first song?
3. Why did he stop starring in movies?
4. How did Elvis help his career in the seventies?
5. How many albums did he make in his lifetime?
6. If Elvis were alive today, do you think you would like to go to see him in a concert? Explain your answer.

Orel Hershiser

Preview the words in exercise A before reading the following selection. Then complete the exercises below.

When Orel Hershiser was young, he enjoyed playing a variety of sports, such as racquetball, tennis, golf, and hockey. However, baseball was his favorite. At the age of eight, Hershiser entered a contest that was held in Yankee Stadium in New York. In the contest, he had to throw, hit, and run. He competed against boys from all across America. Hershiser came in third place.

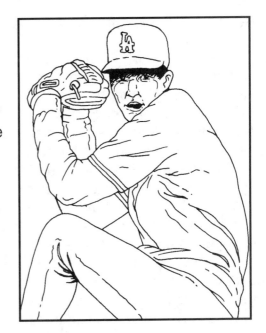

Hershiser had a great deal of difficulty playing baseball in high school and college. In high school, he started out playing, but he was cut from the team. In college, he was not allowed to join the baseball team because his grades and his playing were not good enough. Rather than give up, Hershiser worked to improve his grades and his baseball skills. His grades went up, and he increased the speed of his pitches by five miles per hour. As a result, he made the college team.

Hershiser started playing professional baseball as a pitcher for the Los Angeles Dodgers' minor-league team. His playing ability was only fair, and he often felt discouraged. However, his coach, trainer, and manager felt Hershiser had potential so they convinced him to keep working on his pitch. That is exactly what Hershiser did, and eventually he became a starring pitcher in the major leagues.

A. These words were used in the selection you just read. Match the words from the list on the left with their proper meanings.

_____ 1. convinced   a. possibility; promise

_____ 2. variety   b. number of different kinds

_____ 3. ability   c. persuaded to do something

_____ 4. potential   d. skill

_____ 5. discouraged   e. to lack confidence or hope

B. Use the back of this paper to answer the following questions.

1. What was Orel's favorite sport as a child?

2. Did he play baseball in college?

3. Where did he start playing professional baseball?

4. Was baseball easy for him as an adult? Explain your answer.

5. Why do you think he kept on playing baseball even though he was not a great player and was often discouraged?

King Arthur

Read the following story and then complete the exercises on page 371.

King Arthur was and continues to be one of the great British heros of medieval times. Although it is believed that there really was an Arthur, the adventure stories that have been told about him for nearly 1,000 years are generally thought to be legend. According to the Latin versions of the story, King Uther Pendragon, Arthur's father was not allowed to raise Arthur himself because he had made a special pact with Merlin, a magician. As a result, Merlin raised Arthur as his own son and never told him that his father was a king.

According to the legend, there was a sword embedded in a stone that was located in a churchyard. The sword, called Excalibur, was said to be magical, and anyone who could remove it from the stone would become the king of Britain. Many nobles and knights tried to remove it, but they could not. Then Arthur tried and easily pulled Excalibur from the stone. This amazing feat proved that he was royalty, so he became Britain's king. At some point after Arthur became king, he fell in love with Princess Guinevere and married her. Although they had several castles to choose from, Arthur preferred to stay at Camelot, which was located somewhere in southern England.

Arthur tried to rule with fairness and wisdom. As a result, most knights greatly respected Arthur and wanted to serve him. They came from many countries in hopes of being chosen as a knight of the Round Table. This table was round in shape and could seat 1,600 knights without any one knight having a better seat than the others. Arthur felt that this was the best way to prevent his knights from arguing.

The legend of King Arthur tells about his many heroic adventures. He is said to have conquered most of western Europe by defeating the Roman Empire. Unfortunately, while he was away, his nephew, Mordred, captured his kingdom. When Arthur returned home, he fought and killed Mordred. Although he was victorious, he received wounds during this battle and later died. Some say that Arthur never died but was taken to the mystical island of Avalon so that his wounds would heal. Many believe that he will return someday.

King Arthur (cont.)

A. These words were used in the selection you just read. Match the words from the list on the left with their proper meanings.

_____ 1. British   a. very brave or daring

_____ 2. legend   b. the people of Great Britain

_____ 3. medieval   c. members of a royal family (i.e., king or queen)

_____ 4. embedded   d. story handed down from earlier times

_____ 5. royalty   e. relating to the Middle Ages

_____ 6. heroic   f. firmly enclosed

B. Use the space below and on the back of this paper to answer the following questions.

1. According to legend, who raised King Arthur as his own son?

2. What did Arthur do with the sword embedded in the stone?

3. What kind of ruler was King Arthur?

4. Describe the table that he had built and why he chose the shape that he did?

5. What circumstances could have caused his death?

6. What would you have done if you had been able to pull Excalibur from the stone?

_____

_____

_____

_____

_____

_____

_____

Ludwig van Beethoven

Read the selection below. When you are finished, answer the questions on page 373 and complete the activities on pages 374–376.

Ludwig van Beethoven was born in Bonn, Germany, in 1770. When he was only four years old, he was practicing on the violin and the clavier (a keyboard) for many hours each day. His father was determined to turn the boy into a musician.

He learned so quickly that he went on his first concert tour at the age of 11. When Beethoven was 17, Mozart, a great musician and composer of the time, heard him play and was impressed with his ability.

A few years later, Beethoven went to Vienna, Austria, to study with Haydn, another great musician and composer. It was not long before Beethoven was writing music, too. In his lifetime, he wrote about 300 pieces of music. Beethoven's compositions included sonatas, symphonies, concertos, and operas. (Sonatas are long musical compositions that are divided into several parts or "movements." Symphonies are sonatas written for the orchestra. Concertos are sonatas written for an instrument soloist and orchestra. Operas are plays in which the words are sung to music.)

After an illness at the age of 31, Beethoven gradually lost his hearing. Despite this terrible tragedy, he was somehow able to keep the melody or tune, the harmony of the chords, and the tempo or beat of the music inside his head. He wrote some of his most beautiful music after that time. Yet, he was never able to hear what he had written!

Toward the end of his life, Beethoven had to be turned toward the audience to see the applause because he could not hear it. He died in 1827 at the age of 57 and is considered one of the greatest composers who ever lived.

Ludwig van Beethoven (cont.)

What did you learn about Ludwig van Beethoven? Answer the following questions in complete sentences.

1. Where and when was Beethoven born? _____

2. How old was he when he began to study music?

   _____

3. Who wanted him to be a musician?

   _____

4. How old was Beethoven when he went on his first concert tour?

   _____

5. How old was Beethoven when Mozart heard him play?

   _____

6. Where did Beethoven go to study music?

   _____

7. With whom did he study?

   _____

8. About how many musical compositions did Beethoven write?

   _____

9. What types of compositions did he write?

   _____

10. What great tragedy befell Beethoven?

   _____

Ludwig van Beethoven (cont.)

It is important to be able to read and spell the different words connected with the study of Beethoven. Here are some of the words you might be using.

composer	symphony	Mozart	violin
Austria	melody	concerto	Haydn
Bonn	composition	harmony	sonata
orchestra	Germany	notation	tempo
opera	piano	Vienna	musician

Using words in different ways helps you learn to read them and to spell them. Practice these skills by writing the words in alphabetical order on the lines below.

1. _____

2. _____

3. _____

4. _____

5. _____

6. _____

7. _____

8. _____

9. _____

10. _____

11. _____

12. _____

13. _____

14. _____

15. _____

16. _____

17. _____

18. _____

19. _____

20. _____

Ludwig van Beethoven (cont.)

Use these words to solve the word search.

composer	symphony	Mozart	violin
Austria	melody	concerto	Haydn
Bonn	composition	harmony	sonata
orchestra	Germany	notation	tempo
opera	piano	Vienna	musician

```
S D F G H J K P Q W E A U S T R I A X C
A C O M P O S I T I O N Z X C S T V O P
M O O N B V C A C E X Z O V I O L I N I
L M K N J H G N G F M D S T A N Q E E R
U P Y T C T R O S E R P F G A A H N H U
B O N N M E L O D Y A S O D F T H N A Y
G S T O P E R A R G M E D C V A I A Y T
A E S D F G H T K L E P M N B V C O D A
Q R W E R T Y O O I O R H P L K J H N C
A M U S I C I A N Q U I M O Z A R T S D
A S D F G H J K L P O I U A N Y T R E W
O R C H E S T R A H A R M O N Y A S D F
Q A Z X S W E D C V F R T G B Y J U I L
```

375

Ludwig van Beethoven (cont.)

Imagine that you are Beethoven, the great composer. Use what you have learned from the previous selection and activities to complete this writing exercise. Write a letter to your best friend, expressing your feelings about losing your hearing while you still have so much more music to write.

Use the correct form for a personal letter and your best writing skills—grammar, punctuation, and spelling—so your readers will understand and enjoy what you have written.

Date your letter sometime in 1801, the year Beethoven suffered the loss of his hearing.

_____

_____

_____

_____

_____

_____

_____

_____

_____

_____

_____

_____

_____

The Summer of the Swans

The following questions are based on the book, *The Summer of the Swans* by Betsy Byers (Scholastic, 1970).

Read the book in chapter groups as follows: 1-4, 5-9, 10-14, 15-18, and 19-20. Stop after each group of chapters to answer the questions below and on pages 74 and 75.

After you have completed the book, answer the book review questions on page 76.

Chapters 1-4

1. Why is Sara so negative about herself?

_____

_____

_____

2. Who is Charlie?

_____

_____

3. Why does Aunt Willie live with and care for Sara, Charlie, and Wanda?

_____

_____

_____

4. What does Sara compare her life to and why?

_____

_____

_____

_____

5. What is Sara's main frustration with her siblings?

_____

_____

_____

The Summer of the Swans (cont.)

Chapters 5-9

1. Why is Charlie's wristwatch such a pleasure for him?

_____

2. How does Charlie indicate that he sees the swans?

_____

_____

3. Where do the swans live most of the time?

_____

4. Why does Sara say she dislikes Frank? What might be another reason?

_____

_____

Chapters 10-14

1. Why does Sara go back to the lake?

_____

_____

2. How does Sara feel when she does not find Charlie with the swans?

_____

_____

3. What promise did Aunt Willie make to the children's mother?

_____

4. Why does Sara feel that she has lost her father, too?

_____

_____

5. How do we know that Sara is really a fair person?

_____

_____

The Summer of the Swans (cont.)

Chapters 15-18

1. How does Sara find out she is wrong about Joe Melby?

_____

2. Why does Sara want to run away when she sees Joe Melby coming?

_____

_____

3. How does Joe make it easier for Sara to apologize?

_____

4. What causes Charlie even more stress, and how does he handle it?

_____

5. How does Joe prove what a good friend he is?

_____

Chapters 19-20

1. What does Sara do to help relieve her anxiety?

_____

_____

2. What makes Charlie feel safe and well?

_____

3. How does Joe help comfort Charlie?

_____

4. How can we tell Charlie loves Aunt Willie?

_____

5. In what ways does Sara change over this summer?

_____

_____

The Summer of the Swans (cont.)

Book Review

Matching: Match the descriptions with the correct people.

_____ 1. Sara	a. raises three children.
_____ 2. Sam	b. works in Ohio.
_____ 3. Charlie	c. is called "Little One."
_____ 4. Aunt Willie	d. is unhappy with her life.
_____ 5. Wanda	e. gets lost.

True or False: Write true or false next to each statement below.

_____ 1. Charlie follows the swans and gets lost.

_____ 2. Sara has low self-esteem.

_____ 3. Aunt Willie likes to ride Frank's motor scooter.

_____ 4. Wanda works as a teacher's guide.

_____ 5. Mary is more worried about the party than finding Charlie.

Short Answer: Answer these questions using complete sentences.

1. How do you know how Sara feels about herself?

   _____

2. Why does Aunt Willie live with the children?

   _____

3. What happened to Charlie when he was only three years old?

   _____

4. What things about her family cause Sara distress and dissatisfaction?

   _____

5. Why is apologizing to Joe Melby so hard for Sara?

   _____

Shiloh

The following questions are based on the book *Shiloh* by Phyllis Reynolds Naylor (Dell, 1991).

Read the book in chapter groups as follows: 1-3, 4-7, 8-11, and 12-15.

Stop after each group of chapters to answer the questions below and on pages 78 and 79.

After you have completed the book, answer the book review questions on page 80.

Chapters 1-3

1. Briefly describe how Marty and Shiloh first meet. How does Shiloh behave?

_____

_____

_____

_____

2. List the names of the three Preston children and their ages.

_____

_____

_____

3. In what town and state does the story take place? What season is it?

_____

_____

4. How does Judd treat Shiloh after Marty returns him? How does Marty respond?

_____

_____

_____

_____

5. How does Marty try to raise money?

_____

_____

_____

_____

Shiloh (cont.)

Chapters 4-7

1. What promise does Marty make to Shiloh?

   _____

2. How does Marty keep Dara Lynn off the hill where he is hiding Shiloh?

   _____

3. What do we learn about Judd Travers' childhood?

   _____

   _____

4. What does Marty purchase at Mr. Wallace's corner store and why?

   _____

5. Although he feels badly about it, Marty must lie in order to keep Shiloh safe. List at least three different lies Marty tells in Chapter 4-7.

   _____

   _____

Chapters 8-11

1. After Mrs. Preston discovers Shiloh, Marty comes up with a plan to find his beloved beagle a safe home. What is his plan?

   _____

   _____

2. Briefly describe how Shiloh gets hurt.

   _____

   _____

3. Describe what takes place at Doc Murphy's house.

   _____

   _____

4. How does Marty feel after he tells David Howard the truth about Shiloh? How does David respond?

   _____

   _____

5. What agreement do the Prestons make with Judd concerning Shiloh?

   _____

Shiloh (cont.)

Chapters 12-15

1. All along, Marty is certain Judd mistreats his animals. Why not, then, just report Judd to the proper authorities?

_____

_____

_____

_____

2. Judd works Marty very hard. List three of Marty's chores.

_____

_____

_____

3. What word does Judd leave out of the contract? Why does Marty insist that he include it?

_____

_____

_____

4. According to Judd, the contract between him and Marty is no good. Why not?

_____

_____

_____

5. After Marty completes his side of the bargain, Judd presents him with a gift. What does he give him? Why is it an important gesture?

_____

_____

_____

_____

Shiloh (cont.)

Book Review

Matching: Match the descriptions of the characters with their names.

1. Marty Preston	a. gentle but frank mother of three
2. Mrs. Preston	b. Marty's friend from Friendly
3. Mr. Preston	c. grocery story owner
4. Judd Travers	d. a teacher, likes to talk about politics
5. Mr. Wallace	e. 11-year-old boy in love with a beagle
6. Doc Murphy	f. 7 years old, curious but afraid of snakes
7. David Howard	g. Shiloh's personal veterinarian
8. Mrs. Howard	h. chews tobacco, had a tough childhood
9. Dara Lynn	i. youngest of the Prestons
10. Becky	j. postman, hardworking father of three

True or False: Answer true or false in the blanks below.

_____ 1. The Prestons live in North Carolina.

_____ 2. Shiloh is a hunting dog.

_____ 3. Judd and Marty's relationship ends on a sour note.

_____ 4. David Howard has a pet hermit crab.

_____ 5. The Prestons have street lights near their home.

Sequence: Arrange these events in order by writing numbers 1 to 5 on the lines.

_____ Marty's mom catches Marty and Shiloh.

_____ Judd gives Marty a dog collar.

_____ Marty builds the pen for Shiloh.

_____ Mr. Baker's German shepherd attacks Shiloh.

_____ Marty goes on the postal route with his dad.

Short Answer: On the back of this paper, write a brief response to each question.

1. Name a three of the towns in Tyler County.

2. What will Marty do if Shiloh is not allowed in heaven?

3. To what call does Shiloh respond when Marty finds him?

Addition Facts Timed Practice

When you practice basic addition facts for speed and accuracy, you improve your ability to solve problems in which addition computations are needed.

You will need a pencil and a timer with a second hand.   Set the timer . . . and go.

1. 6 + 9	2. 8 + 1	3. 8 + 9	4. 9 + 4	5. 5 + 0
6. 8 + 0	7. 5 + 9	8. 6 + 1	9. 8 + 8	10. 5 + 5
11. 7 + 6	12. 5 + 1	13. 0 + 6	14. 4 + 1	15. 4 + 4
16. 3 + 1	17. 6 + 5	18. 6 + 4	19. 7 + 0	20. 9 + 3
21. 5 + 2	22. 9 + 9	23. 4 + 2	24. 3 + 5	25. 6 + 6
26. 6 + 7	27. 6 + 8	28. 5 + 6	29. 0 + 7	30. 4 + 6
31. 9 + 6	32. 2 + 2	33. 9 + 0	34. 9 + 5	35. 0 + 1
36. 7 + 7	37. 3 + 6	38. 9 + 8	39. 7 + 3	40. 4 + 9
41. 9 + 1	42. 0 + 9	43. 3 + 9	44. 7 + 2	45. 3 + 0
46. 6 + 0	47. 5 + 3	48. 8 + 5	49. 9 + 7	50. 4 + 7

Addition Facts Timed Practice (cont.)

51.	7 + 1	52.	8 + 3	53.	4 + 10	54.	4 + 3	55.	1 + 3
56.	2 + 0	57.	7 + 8	58.	3 + 3	59.	1 + 1	60.	6 + 2
61.	5 + 7	62.	2 + 7	63.	1 + 2	64.	8 + 4	65.	7 + 9
66.	0 + 5	67.	4 + 5	68.	7 + 4	69.	3 + 2	70.	1 + 8
71.	1 + 6	72.	1 + 9	73.	0 + 4	74.	8 + 6	75.	2 + 9
76.	2 + 3	77.	4 + 8	78.	5 + 4	79.	8 + 2	80.	1 + 4
81.	0 + 0	82.	3 + 4	83.	8 + 7	84.	3 + 7	85.	2 + 1
86.	0 + 2	87.	6 + 3	88.	1 + 7	89.	2 + 4	90.	3 + 8
91.	5 + 8	92.	2 + 6	93.	0 + 3	94.	1 + 9	95.	2 + 5
96.	0 + 8	97.	1 + 5	98.	2 + 8	99.	0 + 2	100.	7 + 5

How long did it take you to complete the page? _____

How many did you get correct? _____

Single-Digit Addition: Three Rows

1.   1
         2
     + 3

2.   1
         2
     + 9

3.   3
         1
     + 1

4.   6
         6
     + 1

5.   1
         6
     + 3

6.   3
         2
     + 6

7.   5
         8
     + 4

8.   7
         3
     + 9

9.   8
         5
     + 2

10.   5
         8
     + 3

11.   8
         6
     + 0

12.   9
         3
     + 7

13.   1
         7
     + 2

14.   7
         0
     + 5

15.   9
         6
     + 5

16.   5
         2
     + 9

Single-Digit Addition: Four Rows

1.   7
      9
      5
    + 5
    _____

2.   1
      2
      2
    + 1
    _____

3.   5
      4
      8
    + 1
    _____

4.   5
      6
      0
    + 4
    _____

5.   1
      7
      0
    + 1
    _____

6.   4
      5
      7
    + 1
    _____

7.   3
      6
      5
    + 1
    _____

8.   7
      3
      7
    + 5
    _____

9.   1
      7
      5
    + 5
    _____

10.   6
       8
       8
     + 1
     _____

11.   2
       6
       9
     + 3
     _____

12.   8
       4
       6
     + 2
     _____

Single-Digit Addition: Eight Rows

1.
```
    7
    3
    5
    7
    9
    5
    9
  + 7
  ___
```

2.
```
    6
    8
    5
    3
    6
    8
    5
  + 8
  ___
```

3.
```
    8
    7
    4
    7
    9
    6
    8
  + 3
  ___
```

4.
```
    1
    3
    6
    3
    3
    9
    5
  + 8
  ___
```

5.
```
    3
    1
    8
    4
    5
    6
    3
  + 3
  ___
```

6.
```
    3
    8
    3
    7
    2
    1
    4
  + 7
  ___
```

7.
```
    4
    9
    5
    2
    6
    2
    7
  + 7
  ___
```

8.
```
    7
    5
    3
    8
    6
    6
    5
  + 6
  ___
```

9.
```
    9
    1
    9
    9
    2
    4
    7
  + 9
  ___
```

10.
```
    2
    7
    8
    6
    5
    1
    7
  + 2
  ___
```

11.
```
    8
    6
    4
    8
    7
    1
    8
  + 4
  ___
```

12.
```
    2
    8
    2
    1
    7
    8
    1
  + 2
  ___
```

13.
```
    6
    2
    3
    3
    6
    4
    9
  + 4
  ___
```

14.
```
    8
    7
    1
    3
    6
    7
    4
  + 4
  ___
```

15.
```
    3
    2
    5
    0
    1
    3
    8
  + 0
  ___
```

16.
```
    9
    0
    5
    2
    3
    0
    1
  + 7
  ___
```

Two Digits Plus One Digit

1. 14
+ 5

2. 16
+ 4

3. 14
+ 3

4. 47
+ 2

5. 55
+ 5

6. 52
+ 1

7. 26
+ 4

8. 68
+ 7

9. 75
+ 3

10. 82
+ 5

11. 39
+ 6

12. 60
+ 1

13. 52
+ 6

14. 20
+ 2

15. 61
+ 2

16. 15
+ 4

17. 29
+ 6

18. 79
+ 8

19. 78
+ 9

20. 48
+ 2

21. 51
+ 6

22. 37
+ 5

23. 96
+ 1

24. 48
+ 8

25. 91
+ 7

Two-Digit Addition: Two Rows

1. 36
    + 85
    ———

2. 59
    + 95
    ———

3. 88
    + 43
    ———

4. 54
    + 40
    ———

5. 55
    + 26
    ———

6. 57
    + 32
    ———

7. 28
    + 16
    ———

8. 79
    + 41
    ———

9. 35
    + 56
    ———

10. 14
    + 25
    ———

11. 38
    + 86
    ———

12. 34
    + 13
    ———

13. 65
    + 60
    ———

14. 76
    + 62
    ———

15. 71
    + 36
    ———

16. 99
    + 97
    ———

17. 43
    + 68
    ———

18. 21
    + 46
    ———

19. 15
    + 39
    ———

20. 82
    + 45
    ———

21. 73
    + 47
    ———

22. 66
    + 53
    ———

23. 64
    + 96
    ———

24. 58
    + 77
    ———

25. 61
    + 12
    ———

Two-Digit Addition: Three Rows

1. 76
    16
    + 77
    ⎯⎯

2. 79
    40
    + 98
    ⎯⎯

3. 64
    93
    + 34
    ⎯⎯

4. 78
    67
    + 12
    ⎯⎯

5. 42
    72
    + 18
    ⎯⎯

6. 99
    21
    + 59
    ⎯⎯

7. 48
    29
    + 34
    ⎯⎯

8. 54
    45
    + 49
    ⎯⎯

9. 12
    85
    + 91
    ⎯⎯

10. 19
    98
    + 78
    ⎯⎯

11. 82
    70
    + 29
    ⎯⎯

12. 14
    16
    + 51
    ⎯⎯

13. 69
    81
    + 68
    ⎯⎯

14. 54
    57
    + 81
    ⎯⎯

15. 68
    41
    + 78
    ⎯⎯

16. 78
    16
    + 82
    ⎯⎯

Two-Digit Addition: Four Rows

1.
```
    55
    77
    71
  + 63
  _____
```

2.
```
    75
    72
    82
  + 71
  _____
```

3.
```
    58
    16
    96
  + 12
  _____
```

4.
```
    61
    52
    79
  + 73
  _____
```

5.
```
    53
    36
    48
  + 45
  _____
```

6.
```
    73
    87
    50
  + 36
  _____
```

7.
```
    65
    62
    69
  + 16
  _____
```

8.
```
    15
    71
    20
  + 42
  _____
```

9.
```
    91
    99
    82
  + 86
  _____
```

10.
```
    31
    88
    98
  + 86
  _____
```

11.
```
    76
    96
    64
  + 12
  _____
```

12.
```
    45
    17
    13
  + 16
  _____
```

Three-Digit Addition: Two Rows

1. 286
    + 612
    _____

2. 442
    + 383
    _____

3. 141
    + 931
    _____

4. 321
    + 552
    _____

5. 313
    + 675
    _____

6. 182
    + 837
    _____

7. 445
    + 891
    _____

8. 158
    + 703
    _____

9. 146
    + 243
    _____

10. 794
    + 323
    _____

11. 694
    + 396
    _____

12. 323
    + 298
    _____

13. 197
    + 646
    _____

14. 795
    + 607
    _____

15. 661
    + 351
    _____

16. 693
    + 977
    _____

17. 594
    + 229
    _____

18. 894
    + 928
    _____

19. 621
    + 346
    _____

20. 321
    + 617
    _____

21. 756
    + 492
    _____

22. 324
    + 601
    _____

23. 388
    + 235
    _____

24. 824
    + 123
    _____

25. 575
    + 739
    _____

Three-Digit Addition: Three Rows

1.   779
     864
+ 392
	2. 156
	     732
	+ 991
		3. 297
		     948
		+ 915
			4. 862
			     734
			+ 367

5.   887
     228
+ 316
	6. 875
	     593
	+ 294
		7. 483
		     114
		+ 663
			8. 879
			     814
			+ 582

9.   423
     384
+ 854
	10. 986
	     382
	+ 376
		11. 918
		     782
		+ 294
			12. 893
			     453
			+ 276

13.   544
     218
+ 938
	14. 587
	     293
	+ 952
		15. 493
		     571
		+ 949
			16. 224
			     688
			+ 111

                                                                             #3646 Practice and Learn

Three-Digit Addition: Four Rows

1.   757
      213
      141
  + 293

2.   414
      563
      951
  + 747

3.   486
      152
      342
  + 116

4.   775
      256
      675
  + 118

5.   954
      913
      529
  + 788

6.   495
      394
      525
  + 411

7.   994
      292
      197
  + 188

8.   181
      579
      957
  + 493

9.   555
      923
      986
  + 592

10.   288
      953
      842
  + 276

11.   885
      563
      836
  + 394

12.   384
      925
      881
  + 171

Four-Digit Addition: Two Rows

1. 7418
    + 9921

2. 5335
    + 9155

3. 5721
    + 9778

4. 4199
    + 1538

5. 7932
    + 5284

6. 4141
    + 6194

7. 5425
    + 1444

8. 6422
    + 9623

9. 1274
    + 3411

10. 7983
    + 6375

11. 3323
    + 7196

12. 2497
    + 4839

13. 5489
    + 3121

14. 6758
    + 1565

15. 7788
    + 4456

16. 2626
    + 5161

17. 1457
    + 6296

18. 6582
    + 1458

19. 3951
    + 5146

20. 7835
    + 4196

21. 5476
    + 2939

22. 1942
    + 8844

23. 9255
    + 7622

24. 2558
    + 4571

25. 2719
    + 2447

Four-Digit Addition: Three Rows

1.	1865 8935 + 8755	2.	2315 9165 + 2537	3.	4978 1918 + 2259	4.	6731 6579 + 2253
5.	4732 9287 + 2133	6.	5772 9105 + 2675	7.	2843 7503 + 6823	8.	2459 7737 + 5192
9.	5874 3316 + 6627	10.	7664 3491 + 1638	11.	4178 2877 + 7131	12.	6772 7966 + 9466
13.	8473 6825 + 9351	14.	8245 3306 + 6149	15.	9341 8816 + 6919	16.	8741 3687 + 1393

Four-Digit Addition: Four Rows

1.   5263
       5752
       7852
  + 8921

2.   7446
       2885
       7729
  + 9767

3.   6788
       4986
       2338
  + 9924

4.   8354
       2276
       8213
  + 6972

5.   6194
       1685
       3392
  + 1543

6.   8356
       9424
       3734
  + 7751

7.   3355
       8421
       5896
  + 7818

8.   7148
       5845
       2516
  + 8148

9.   9972
       4365
       7942
  + 5965

10.   1744
       5556
       1545
  + 3956

11.   3417
       7299
       8892
  + 5524

12.   6459
       5281
       4952
  + 1446

                                                             #3646 Practice and Learn

Mixed Addition Practice

1.   55
  + 21

2.   5
  + 6

3.   83
  + 37

4.   5
  + 4

5.   8
  + 7

6.   4662
  + 8

7.   18
  + 21

8.   9
  + 8

9.   85
  + 96

10.   1769
  + 9

11.   92
  + 48

12.   5
  + 14

13.   85
  + 95

14.   1839
  + 4

15.   7
  + 11

16.   7
  + 9

17.   79
  + 79

18.   88
  + 13

19.   3445
  + 4

20.   63
  + 47

Subtraction Facts Timed Practice

When you practice your basic subtraction facts for speed and accuracy, you improve your ability to solve problems in which subtraction computations are needed.

You will need a pencil and a timer with a second hand. Set the timer . . . and go.

1. 13 − 4	2. 17 − 9	3. 9 − 1	4. 15 − 9	5. 5 − 0
6. 8 − 0	7. 14 − 9	8. 7 − 1	9. 16 − 8	10. 10 − 5
11. 13 − 6	12. 6 − 1	13. 6 − 6	14. 5 − 1	15. 8 − 4
16. 4 − 1	17. 11 − 5	18. 10 − 4	19. 7 − 0	20. 12 − 3
21. 7 − 2	22. 18 − 9	23. 6 − 2	24. 8 − 5	25. 12 − 6
26. 13 − 7	27. 14 − 8	28. 11 − 6	29. 7 − 0	30. 10 − 6
31. 15 − 6	32. 4 − 2	33. 9 − 0	34. 14 − 5	35. 1 − 0
36. 14 − 7	37. 9 − 6	38. 17 − 8	39. 10 − 3	40. 13 − 9
41. 10 − 1	42. 9 − 9	43. 12 − 9	44. 9 − 2	45. 3 − 0
46. 6 − 0	47. 8 − 3	48. 13 − 5	49. 16 − 7	50. 11 − 7

              #3646 Practice and Learn

Subtraction Facts Timed Practice (cont.)

51. 8
    − 1

52. 11
    − 3

53. 4
    − 0

54. 7
    − 3

55. 4
    − 3

56. 2
    − 0

57. 15
    − 8

58. 6
    − 3

59. 2
    − 1

60. 8
    − 2

61. 12
    − 7

62. 9
    − 7

63. 3
    − 2

64. 12
    − 4

65. 16
    − 9

66. 5
    − 5

67. 9
    − 5

68. 11
    − 4

69. 5
    − 2

70. 9
    − 8

71. 7
    − 6

72. 10
    − 9

73. 4
    − 4

74. 14
    − 6

75. 11
    − 9

76. 5
    − 3

77. 12
    − 8

78. 9
    − 4

79. 10
    − 2

80. 5
    − 4

81. 0
    − 0

82. 7
    − 4

83. 15
    − 7

84. 10
    − 7

85. 3
    − 1

86. 11
    − 2

87. 9
    − 3

88. 8
    − 7

89. 6
    − 4

90. 11
    − 8

91. 13
    − 8

92. 8
    − 6

93. 3
    − 3

94. 1
    − 0

95. 7
    − 5

96. 8
    − 8

97. 6
    − 5

98. 10
    − 8

99. 2
    − 2

100. 12
    − 5

How long did it take to complete the page? _____

How many did you get correct? _____

Two Digits Minus One Digit

1. 41
    − 6

2. 21
    − 7

3. 41
    − 7

4. 51
    − 7

5. 47
    − 6

6. 84
    − 9

7. 17
    − 4

8. 83
    − 2

9. 98
    − 7

10. 93
    − 8

11. 97
    − 9

12. 48
    − 2

13. 99
    − 5

14. 58
    − 8

15. 57
    − 4

16. 71
    − 1

17. 47
    − 6

18. 27
    − 6

19. 68
    − 1

20. 59
    − 6

21. 38
    − 6

22. 88
    − 9

23. 14
    − 6

24. 99
    − 9

25. 29
    − 4

Three Digits Minus Two Digits

1. 411
    − 51

2. 666
    − 41

3. 256
    − 37

4. 417
    − 68

5. 613
    − 32

6. 879
    − 56

7. 595
    − 62

8. 319
    − 72

9. 571
    − 37

10. 439
    − 99

11. 174
    − 56

12. 462
    − 81

13. 551
    − 94

14. 293
    − 31

15. 958
    − 28

16. 831
    − 67

17. 352
    − 13

18. 967
    − 88

19. 577
    − 44

20. 617
    − 22

21. 773
    − 95

22. 382
    − 25

23. 732
    − 75

24. 879
    − 53

25. 575
    − 22

Three Digits Minus Two Digits (cont.)

1. 917 – 72	2. 241 – 82	3. 335 – 78	4. 918 – 97	5. 952 – 64
6. 274 – 73	7. 246 – 13	8. 783 – 24	9. 498 – 92	10. 485 – 24
11. 543 – 11	12. 568 – 13	13. 188 – 21	14. 237 – 14	15. 755 – 47
16. 681 – 96	17. 923 – 36	18. 266 – 33	19. 876 – 36	20. 864 – 48
21. 178 – 32	22. 834 – 86	23. 326 – 76	24. 779 – 71	25. 484 – 41

Four Digits Minus Three Digits

1. 4556
   − 343

2. 3722
   − 411

3. 2983
   − 661

4. 4349
   − 122

5. 4986
   − 813

6. 2991
   − 131

7. 4965
   − 714

8. 9589
   − 257

9. 1757
   − 145

10. 1995
    − 164

11. 5375
    − 213

12. 2558
    − 427

13. 6649
    − 344

14. 9371
    − 321

15. 7978
    − 848

16. 9356
    − 123

17. 7955
    − 321

18. 3796
    − 166

19. 7379
    − 133

20. 8976
    − 734

21. 2566
    − 332

22. 8759
    − 647

23. 7887
    − 317

24. 9998
    − 358

25. 1499
    − 328

Four Digits Minus Three Digits (cont.)

1.   9487
   – 156
	2. 1896
	   – 653
		3. 9238
		   – 121
			4. 5886
			   – 235
				5. 8736
				   – 424

6.   4648
   – 523
	7. 2698
	   – 247
		8. 7774
		   – 651
			9. 9953
			   – 112
				10. 6697
				   – 544

11.   4776
   – 735
	12. 3598
	   – 352
		13. 1894
		   – 361
			14. 4758
			   – 248
				15. 5678
				   – 348

16.   8268
   – 253
	17. 6553
	   – 242
		18. 3497
		   – 226
			19. 7488
			   – 314
				20. 6646
				   – 242

21.   4598
   – 445
	22. 1416
	   – 657
		23. 2413
		   – 766
			24. 4515
			   – 249
				25. 7279
				   – 646

Mixed Subtraction Practice

1. $\begin{array}{r} 68 \\ -\ 6 \\ \hline \end{array}$
2. $\begin{array}{r} 53 \\ -\ 29 \\ \hline \end{array}$
3. $\begin{array}{r} 334 \\ -\ 4 \\ \hline \end{array}$
4. $\begin{array}{r} 794 \\ -\ 9 \\ \hline \end{array}$

5. $\begin{array}{r} 7192 \\ -\ 46 \\ \hline \end{array}$
6. $\begin{array}{r} 8495 \\ -\ 47 \\ \hline \end{array}$
7. $\begin{array}{r} 84 \\ -\ 9 \\ \hline \end{array}$
8. $\begin{array}{r} 2794 \\ -\ 6 \\ \hline \end{array}$

9. $\begin{array}{r} 9689 \\ -\ 84 \\ \hline \end{array}$
10. $\begin{array}{r} 8927 \\ -\ 5 \\ \hline \end{array}$
11. $\begin{array}{r} 186 \\ -\ 61 \\ \hline \end{array}$
12. $\begin{array}{r} 7851 \\ -\ 84 \\ \hline \end{array}$

13. $\begin{array}{r} 15 \\ -\ 7 \\ \hline \end{array}$
14. $\begin{array}{r} 6688 \\ -\ 94 \\ \hline \end{array}$
15. $\begin{array}{r} 1157 \\ -\ 9 \\ \hline \end{array}$
16. $\begin{array}{r} 823 \\ -\ 8 \\ \hline \end{array}$

17. $\begin{array}{r} 45 \\ -\ 5 \\ \hline \end{array}$
18. $\begin{array}{r} 861 \\ -\ 7 \\ \hline \end{array}$
19. $\begin{array}{r} 38 \\ -\ 9 \\ \hline \end{array}$
20. $\begin{array}{r} 76 \\ -\ 8 \\ \hline \end{array}$

Mixed Subtraction Practice (cont.)

1. $\begin{array}{r} 5 \\ -\ 5 \\ \hline \end{array}$

2. $\begin{array}{r} 355 \\ -\ 186 \\ \hline \end{array}$

3. $\begin{array}{r} 5 \\ -\ 3 \\ \hline \end{array}$

4. $\begin{array}{r} 876 \\ -\ 344 \\ \hline \end{array}$

5. $\begin{array}{r} 5 \\ -\ 3 \\ \hline \end{array}$

6. $\begin{array}{r} 2312 \\ -\ 479 \\ \hline \end{array}$

7. $\begin{array}{r} 9224 \\ -\ 667 \\ \hline \end{array}$

8. $\begin{array}{r} 5792 \\ -\ 9 \\ \hline \end{array}$

9. $\begin{array}{r} 433 \\ -\ 318 \\ \hline \end{array}$

10. $\begin{array}{r} 7 \\ -\ 2 \\ \hline \end{array}$

11. $\begin{array}{r} 333 \\ -\ 124 \\ \hline \end{array}$

12. $\begin{array}{r} 7 \\ -\ 2 \\ \hline \end{array}$

13. $\begin{array}{r} 742 \\ -\ 553 \\ \hline \end{array}$

14. $\begin{array}{r} 3211 \\ -\ 7 \\ \hline \end{array}$

15. $\begin{array}{r} 4718 \\ -\ 266 \\ \hline \end{array}$

16. $\begin{array}{r} 888 \\ -\ 364 \\ \hline \end{array}$

17. $\begin{array}{r} 5261 \\ -\ 5143 \\ \hline \end{array}$

18. $\begin{array}{r} 9 \\ -\ 6 \\ \hline \end{array}$

19. $\begin{array}{r} 3918 \\ -\ 2 \\ \hline \end{array}$

20. $\begin{array}{r} 6766 \\ -\ 8 \\ \hline \end{array}$

#3646 Practice and Learn

Multiplication Facts Timed Practice

When you practice basic multiplication facts for speed and accuracy, you improve your ability to solve problems in which multiplication computations are needed.

You will need a pencil and a timer with a second hand. Set the timer . . . and go.

1. 9 X 4	2. 3 X 0	3. 7 X 3	4. 7 X 4	5. 8 X 9
6. 6 X 8	7. 5 X 7	8. 4 X 3	9. 0 X 5	10. 6 X 5
11. 8 X 1	12. 6 X 6	13. 7 X 2	14. 3 X 2	15. 4 X 2
16. 6 X 2	17. 0 X 4	18. 3 X 5	19. 5 X 1	20. 6 X 9
21. 1 X 7	22. 4 X 4	23. 3 X 7	24. 7 X 1	25. 5 X 6
26. 4 X 5	27. 7 X 6	28. 6 X 7	29. 9 X 6	30. 1 X 2
31. 5 X 5	32. 7 X 8	33. 2 X 7	34. 6 X 0	35. 3 X 1
36. 9 X 9	37. 1 X 9	38. 6 X 3	39. 8 X 3	40. 4 X 9
41. 0 X 7	42. 1 X 8	43. 3 X 9	44. 4 X 0	45. 3 X 3
46. 5 X 3	47. 2 X 3	48. 5 X 2	49. 9 X 7	50. 2 X 4

Multiplication Facts Timed Practice (cont.)

51. 1 × 1

52. 8 × 7

53. 8 × 8

54. 8 × 6

55. 3 × 6

56. 9 × 0

57. 1 × 6

58. 4 × 1

59. 2 × 2

60. 0 × 9

61. 8 × 0

62. 2 × 6

63. 4 × 7

64. 3 × 4

65. 5 × 8

66. 9 × 5

67. 7 × 9

68. 7 × 0

69. 0 × 6

70. 9 × 3

71. 1 × 3

72. 9 × 1

73. 2 × 9

74. 6 × 4

75. 4 × 6

76. 8 × 4

77. 3 × 8

78. 7 × 7

79. 5 × 9

80. 8 × 5

81. 5 × 0

82. 6 × 1

83. 2 × 0

84. 9 × 8

85. 1 × 0

86. 0 × 3

87. 1 × 4

88. 8 × 2

89. 5 × 4

90. 4 × 8

91. 0 × 0

92. 0 × 1

93. 9 × 2

94. 1 × 1

95. 7 × 5

96. 0 × 2

97. 2 × 8

98. 1 × 5

99. 0 × 8

100. 2 × 5

How long did it take you to complete the pages? _____

How many did you get correct? _____

Two Digits Times One Digit

1. 42 X 9	2. 99 X 8	3. 32 X 9	4. 15 X 6	5. 73 X 8
6. 81 X 5	7. 45 X 1	8. 88 X 7	9. 88 X 2	10. 33 X 7
11. 75 X 5	12. 92 X 6	13. 18 X 2	14. 76 X 4	15. 81 X 7
16. 25 X 9	17. 18 X 6	18. 18 X 2	19. 48 X 3	20. 35 X 2
21. 18 X 5	22. 98 X 5	23. 96 X 9	24. 25 X 6	25. 68 X 4

Two Digits Times One Digit (cont.)

1.   11
   X 4

2.   91
   X 3

3.   69
   X 4

4.   59
   X 5

5.   26
   X 4

6.   17
   X 3

7.   42
   X 6

8.   97
   X 3

9.   22
   X 2

10.   71
   X 4

11.   12
   X 7

12.   26
   X 3

13.   25
   X 7

14.   85
   X 3

15.   58
   X 5

16.   97
   X 4

17.   18
   X 9

18.   33
   X 1

19.   86
   X 3

20.   16
   X 6

21.   65
   X 7

22.   38
   X 7

23.   43
   X 8

24.   24
   X 8

25.   95
   X 3

Two Digits Times Two Digits

1. $\begin{array}{r} 35 \\ \times\ 22 \\ \hline \end{array}$
2. $\begin{array}{r} 23 \\ \times\ 77 \\ \hline \end{array}$
3. $\begin{array}{r} 11 \\ \times\ 44 \\ \hline \end{array}$
4. $\begin{array}{r} 58 \\ \times\ 53 \\ \hline \end{array}$
5. $\begin{array}{r} 94 \\ \times\ 55 \\ \hline \end{array}$

6. $\begin{array}{r} 48 \\ \times\ 67 \\ \hline \end{array}$
7. $\begin{array}{r} 74 \\ \times\ 35 \\ \hline \end{array}$
8. $\begin{array}{r} 91 \\ \times\ 88 \\ \hline \end{array}$
9. $\begin{array}{r} 11 \\ \times\ 51 \\ \hline \end{array}$
10. $\begin{array}{r} 53 \\ \times\ 73 \\ \hline \end{array}$

11. $\begin{array}{r} 93 \\ \times\ 34 \\ \hline \end{array}$
12. $\begin{array}{r} 99 \\ \times\ 82 \\ \hline \end{array}$
13. $\begin{array}{r} 47 \\ \times\ 62 \\ \hline \end{array}$
14. $\begin{array}{r} 12 \\ \times\ 93 \\ \hline \end{array}$
15. $\begin{array}{r} 28 \\ \times\ 45 \\ \hline \end{array}$

16. $\begin{array}{r} 78 \\ \times\ 99 \\ \hline \end{array}$
17. $\begin{array}{r} 87 \\ \times\ 29 \\ \hline \end{array}$
18. $\begin{array}{r} 32 \\ \times\ 76 \\ \hline \end{array}$
19. $\begin{array}{r} 71 \\ \times\ 66 \\ \hline \end{array}$
20. $\begin{array}{r} 39 \\ \times\ 28 \\ \hline \end{array}$

21. $\begin{array}{r} 18 \\ \times\ 29 \\ \hline \end{array}$
22. $\begin{array}{r} 61 \\ \times\ 56 \\ \hline \end{array}$
23. $\begin{array}{r} 31 \\ \times\ 23 \\ \hline \end{array}$
24. $\begin{array}{r} 59 \\ \times\ 22 \\ \hline \end{array}$
25. $\begin{array}{r} 75 \\ \times\ 97 \\ \hline \end{array}$

Two Digits Times Two Digits (cont.)

1. 16 X 98	2. 44 X 88	3. 36 X 74	4. 98 X 31	5. 16 X 36
6. 37 X 98	7. 77 X 54	8. 29 X 49	9. 47 X 82	10. 92 X 19
11. 67 X 56	12. 39 X 76	13. 82 X 34	14. 59 X 44	15. 96 X 24
16. 91 X 71	17. 73 X 77	18. 22 X 87	19. 29 X 77	20. 98 X 48
21. 95 X 31	22. 36 X 75	23. 58 X 71	24. 73 X 95	25. 82 X 52

#3646 Practice and Learn

Three Digits Times One Digit

1.   385
   X 8

2.   775
   X 5

3.   252
   X 5

4.   617
   X 9

5.   599
   X 9

6.   467
   X 6

7.   214
   X 6

8.   991
   X 2

9.   155
   X 6

10.   202
   X 5

11.   641
   X 6

12.   869
   X 2

13.   908
   X 2

14.   854
   X 5

15.   144
   X 6

16.   588
   X 6

17.   301
   X 2

18.   683
   X 9

19.   331
   X 8

20.   458
   X 8

21.   532
   X 9

22.   121
   X 9

23.   957
   X 7

24.   859
   X 2

25.   474
   X 5

Three Digits Times One Digit (cont.)

1.	283 X 7	2.	346 X 6	3.	923 X 8	4.	796 X 2	5.	596 X 4
6.	811 X 5	7.	231 X 8	8.	206 X 6	9.	179 X 6	10.	853 X 3
11.	682 X 8	12.	117 X 9	13.	636 X 2	14.	884 X 9	15.	929 X 4
16.	393 X 1	17.	346 X 7	18.	802 X 5	19.	597 X 1	20.	955 X 8
21.	864 X 2	22.	832 X 4	23.	273 X 8	24.	375 X 3	25.	681 X 5

Three Digits Times One Digit (cont.)

1. 283
   X 9

2. 746
   X 6

3. 985
   X 1

4. 123
   X 6

5. 224
   X 4

6. 783
   X 7

7. 486
   X 9

8. 735
   X 3

9. 797
   X 8

10. 453
    X 4

11. 514
    X 2

12. 733
    X 6

13. 709
    X 6

14. 998
    X 6

15. 261
    X 1

16. 536
    X 5

17. 228
    X 1

18. 651
    X 5

19. 192
    X 3

20. 765
    X 6

21. 166
    X 3

22. 572
    X 7

23. 109
    X 1

24. 641
    X 9

25. 646
    X 7

Three Digits Times Two Digits (cont.)

1.   911
   X 41

2.   748
   X 63

3.   128
   X 41

4.   667
   X 36

5.   843
   X 38

6.   156
   X 76

7.   497
   X 22

8.   898
   X 33

9.   473
   X 72

10.   444
    X 86

11.   971
    X 24

12.   691
    X 84

13.   903
    X 93

14.   621
    X 85

15.   692
    X 45

16.   459
    X 56

17.   133
    X 69

18.   333
    X 15

19.   794
    X 17

20.   638
    X 25

21.   775
    X 27

22.   315
    X 43

23.   671
    X 52

24.   489
    X 52

25.   592
    X 13

Three Digits Times Two Digits (cont.)

1. 261
    X 71

2. 243
    X 17

3. 951
    X 31

4. 785
    X 66

5. 864
    X 25

6. 232
    X 19

7. 235
    X 69

8. 871
    X 92

9. 785
    X 98

10. 637
     X 44

11. 693
     X 77

12. 967
     X 27

13. 928
     X 37

14. 822
     X 51

15. 346
     X 46

16. 165
     X 81

17. 724
     X 45

18. 644
     X 84

19. 783
     X 63

20. 278
     X 26

21. 323
     X 32

22. 937
     X 15

23. 827
     X 31

24. 812
     X 39

25. 372
     X 55

Mixed Multiplication Practice

1.   9
   X 5
   _____

2.   27
   X 6
   _____

3.   46
   X 8
   _____

4.   9
   X 3
   _____

5.   32
   X 69
   _____

6.   3
   X 2
   _____

7.   5
   X 54
   _____

8.   31
   X 5
   _____

9.   4
   X 15
   _____

10.   4
   X 97
   _____

11.   76
   X 92
   _____

12.   46
   X 5
   _____

13.   5
   X 34
   _____

14.   1
   X 9
   _____

15.   47
   X 79
   _____

16.   28
   X 5
   _____

17.   8
   X 11
   _____

18.   8
   X 7
   _____

19.   57
   X 2
   _____

20.   5
   X 7
   _____

Mixed Multiplication Practice (cont.)

1.   125
    X 69

2.   28
    X 91

3.   783
    X 62

4.   8
    X 7

5.   5
    X 5

6.   347
    X 3171

7.   238
    X 98

8.   878
    X 98

9.   55
    X 35

10.   718
    X 61

11.   4883
    X 737

12.   269
    X 47

13.   9
    X 6

14.   81
    X 89

15.   9
    X 3

16.   43
    X 68

17.   378
    X 99

18.   4
    X 3

19.   3
    X 4

20.   5
    X 9

Division Facts Timed Practice

When you practice basic division facts for speed and accuracy, you improve your ability to solve problems in which division computations are needed.

You will need a pencil and a timer with a second hand. Set the timer . . . and go.

1. $1\overline{)5}$ 2. $8\overline{)56}$ 3. $2\overline{)16}$ 4. $3\overline{)21}$ 5. $6\overline{)30}$

6. $9\overline{)72}$ 7. $9\overline{)54}$ 8. $3\overline{)9}$ 9. $4\overline{)20}$ 10. $0\overline{)6}$

11. $7\overline{)28}$ 12. $5\overline{)40}$ 13. $2\overline{)10}$ 14. $4\overline{)28}$ 15. $1\overline{)4}$

16. $2\overline{)18}$ 17. $0\overline{)5}$ 18. $8\overline{)48}$ 19. $2\overline{)14}$ 20. $5\overline{)25}$

21. $3\overline{)6}$ 22. $6\overline{)42}$ 23. $3\overline{)27}$ 24. $6\overline{)54}$ 25. $7\overline{)14}$

26. $2\overline{)12}$ 27. $8\overline{)64}$ 28. $6\overline{)24}$ 29. $0\overline{)8}$ 30. $1\overline{)3}$

31. $5\overline{)45}$ 32. $2\overline{)8}$ 33. $8\overline{)32}$ 34. $4\overline{)12}$ 35. $9\overline{)81}$

36. $3\overline{)18}$ 37. $8\overline{)72}$ 38. $7\overline{)63}$ 39. $9\overline{)45}$ 40. $9\overline{)63}$

Division Facts Timed Practice (cont.)

41. $8\overline{)8}$ 42. $9\overline{)36}$ 43. $4\overline{)32}$ 44. $1\overline{)1}$ 45. $5\overline{)15}$

46. $6\overline{)18}$ 47. $7\overline{)7}$ 48. $5\overline{)30}$ 49. $2\overline{)0}$ 50. $5\overline{)10}$

51. $8\overline{)24}$ 52. $1\overline{)9}$ 53. $1\overline{)3}$ 54. $7\overline{)35}$ 55. $4\overline{)16}$

56. $3\overline{)0}$ 57. $4\overline{)24}$ 58. $1\overline{)0}$ 59. $6\overline{)36}$ 60. $4\overline{)8}$

61. $5\overline{)35}$ 62. $4\overline{)36}$ 63. $9\overline{)27}$ 64. $3\overline{)12}$ 65. $2\overline{)6}$

66. $4\overline{)0}$ 67. $6\overline{)12}$ 68. $1\overline{)6}$ 69. $6\overline{)48}$ 70. $3\overline{)3}$

71. $7\overline{)0}$ 72. $9\overline{)9}$ 73. $7\overline{)56}$ 74. $8\overline{)40}$ 75. $7\overline{)42}$

76. $1\overline{)7}$ 77. $8\overline{)16}$ 78. $5\overline{)20}$ 79. $3\overline{)24}$ 80. $3\overline{)15}$

81. $7\overline{)21}$ 82. $1\overline{)8}$ 83. $9\overline{)18}$ 84. $5\overline{)5}$ 85. $6\overline{)6}$

86. $4\overline{)4}$ 87. $9\overline{)0}$ 88. $2\overline{)4}$ 89. $7\overline{)49}$ 90. $2\overline{)2}$

How long did it take you to complete this practice? _____

How many did you get correct? _____

One Digit Divided by One Digit

1. $2\overline{)7}$ 2. $5\overline{)7}$ 3. $3\overline{)4}$ 4. $1\overline{)5}$

5. $3\overline{)6}$ 6. $3\overline{)8}$ 7. $2\overline{)4}$ 8. $3\overline{)4}$

9. $6\overline{)9}$ 10. $4\overline{)9}$ 11. $3\overline{)7}$ 12. $1\overline{)4}$

13. $5\overline{)6}$ 14. $1\overline{)6}$ 15. $3\overline{)9}$ 16. $5\overline{)8}$

17. $4\overline{)4}$ 18. $4\overline{)7}$ 19. $2\overline{)2}$ 20. $1\overline{)9}$

One Digit Divided by One Digit (cont.)

1. $1 \overline{)4}$ 2. $3 \overline{)8}$ 3. $7 \overline{)7}$ 4. $2 \overline{)8}$

5. $5 \overline{)7}$ 6. $5 \overline{)8}$ 7. $2 \overline{)7}$ 8. $3 \overline{)6}$

9. $7 \overline{)9}$ 10. $4 \overline{)6}$ 11. $1 \overline{)7}$ 12. $6 \overline{)9}$

13. $4 \overline{)7}$ 14. $3 \overline{)7}$ 15. $4 \overline{)9}$ 16. $7 \overline{)8}$

17. $1 \overline{)4}$ 18. $1 \overline{)6}$ 19. $2 \overline{)3}$ 20. $3 \overline{)5}$

Two Digits Divided by One Digit

1. $1 \overline{)19}$ 2. $5 \overline{)56}$ 3. $3 \overline{)81}$ 4. $8 \overline{)77}$

5. $3 \overline{)32}$ 6. $4 \overline{)85}$ 7. $4 \overline{)24}$ 8. $1 \overline{)93}$

9. $7 \overline{)38}$ 10. $2 \overline{)54}$ 11. $4 \overline{)67}$ 12. $3 \overline{)62}$

13. $6 \overline{)94}$ 14. $2 \overline{)42}$ 15. $7 \overline{)66}$ 16. $2 \overline{)44}$

17. $9 \overline{)13}$ 18. $4 \overline{)58}$ 19. $9 \overline{)82}$ 20. $5 \overline{)67}$

#3646 Practice and Learn

Two Digits Divided by One Digit (cont.)

1. $5 \overline{)25}$ 2. $4 \overline{)19}$ 3. $8 \overline{)94}$ 4. $9 \overline{)97}$

5. $5 \overline{)44}$ 6. $4 \overline{)61}$ 7. $5 \overline{)49}$ 8. $8 \overline{)71}$

9. $3 \overline{)62}$ 10. $5 \overline{)69}$ 11. $4 \overline{)46}$ 12. $5 \overline{)82}$

13. $2 \overline{)92}$ 14. $2 \overline{)75}$ 15. $3 \overline{)76}$ 16. $7 \overline{)92}$

17. $7 \overline{)53}$ 18. $8 \overline{)22}$ 19. $2 \overline{)67}$ 20. $6 \overline{)71}$

Three Digits Divided by One Digit

1. $2\overline{)884}$ 2. $3\overline{)933}$ 3. $2\overline{)539}$ 4. $7\overline{)868}$

5. $1\overline{)725}$ 6. $6\overline{)187}$ 7. $2\overline{)467}$ 8. $3\overline{)399}$

9. $7\overline{)946}$ 10. $5\overline{)854}$ 11. $9\overline{)818}$ 12. $6\overline{)476}$

13. $8\overline{)418}$ 14. $6\overline{)282}$ 15. $3\overline{)572}$ 16. $4\overline{)766}$

17. $9\overline{)962}$ 18. $4\overline{)489}$ 19. $5\overline{)814}$ 20. $6\overline{)725}$

Three Digits Divided by One Digit (cont.)

1. 7$\overline{)295}$ 2. 6$\overline{)668}$ 3. 8$\overline{)641}$ 4. 7$\overline{)391}$

5. 9$\overline{)163}$ 6. 9$\overline{)839}$ 7. 4$\overline{)157}$ 8. 3$\overline{)159}$

9. 8$\overline{)398}$ 10. 4$\overline{)474}$ 11. 7$\overline{)658}$ 12. 3$\overline{)563}$

13. 3$\overline{)251}$ 14. 6$\overline{)553}$ 15. 1$\overline{)515}$ 16. 7$\overline{)323}$

17. 6$\overline{)234}$ 18. 2$\overline{)839}$ 19. 2$\overline{)436}$ 20. 9$\overline{)969}$

Three Digits Divided by One Digit (cont.)

1. $9 \overline{)331}$ 2. $9 \overline{)229}$ 3. $9 \overline{)231}$ 4. $4 \overline{)317}$

5. $3 \overline{)326}$ 6. $4 \overline{)514}$ 7. $6 \overline{)398}$ 8. $4 \overline{)699}$

9. $6 \overline{)661}$ 10. $4 \overline{)739}$ 11. $2 \overline{)711}$ 12. $3 \overline{)577}$

13. $8 \overline{)622}$ 14. $5 \overline{)238}$ 15. $5 \overline{)175}$ 16. $7 \overline{)483}$

17. $6 \overline{)798}$ 18. $3 \overline{)653}$ 19. $9 \overline{)839}$ 20. $6 \overline{)468}$

Three Digits Divided by Two Digits

1. 47) 454

2. 77) 456

3. 85) 783

4. 35) 263

5. 36) 736

6. 19) 656

7. 31) 561

8. 82) 627

9. 77) 715

10. 33) 533

11. 78) 957

12. 81) 525

13. 43) 855

14. 63) 139

15. 49) 223

16. 89) 942

17. 41) 434

18. 62) 384

19. 73) 436

20. 69) 374

Three Digits Divided by Two Digits (cont.)

1. $26 \overline{)235}$

2. $43 \overline{)519}$

3. $22 \overline{)137}$

4. $18 \overline{)895}$

5. $16 \overline{)921}$

6. $82 \overline{)881}$

7. $35 \overline{)209}$

8. $17 \overline{)921}$

9. $28 \overline{)777}$

10. $55 \overline{)801}$

11. $42 \overline{)841}$

12. $53 \overline{)207}$

13. $19 \overline{)221}$

14. $15 \overline{)822}$

15. $21 \overline{)625}$

16. $25 \overline{)927}$

17. $12 \overline{)225}$

18. $18 \overline{)355}$

19. $62 \overline{)994}$

20. $17 \overline{)631}$

Three Digits Divided by Two Digits (cont.)

1. 72 ⟌ 672   2. 69 ⟌ 531   3. 57 ⟌ 242   4. 32 ⟌ 834

5. 91 ⟌ 787   6. 68 ⟌ 921   7. 88 ⟌ 318   8. 94 ⟌ 599

9. 49 ⟌ 895   10. 24 ⟌ 656   11. 26 ⟌ 684   12. 81 ⟌ 956

13. 58 ⟌ 658   14. 36 ⟌ 578   15. 19 ⟌ 246   16. 15 ⟌ 678

17. 64 ⟌ 667   18. 71 ⟌ 241   19. 33 ⟌ 358   20. 89 ⟌ 441

Changing Improper Fractions to Mixed Numbers

Write each of these improper fractions as a mixed number. Simplify where possible.

1. $\dfrac{7}{4}$	2. $\dfrac{15}{7}$	3. $\dfrac{12}{5}$	4. $\dfrac{7}{5}$
5. $\dfrac{5}{3}$	6. $\dfrac{16}{9}$	7. $\dfrac{10}{3}$	8. $\dfrac{14}{13}$
9. $\dfrac{12}{11}$	10. $\dfrac{9}{2}$	11. $\dfrac{4}{3}$	12. $\dfrac{7}{2}$
13. $\dfrac{13}{8}$	14. $\dfrac{6}{5}$	15. $\dfrac{8}{3}$	16. $\dfrac{5}{4}$
17. $\dfrac{16}{5}$	18. $\dfrac{19}{10}$	19. $\dfrac{15}{12}$	20. $\dfrac{7}{6}$
21. $\dfrac{12}{9}$	22. $\dfrac{9}{6}$	23. $\dfrac{5}{2}$	24. $\dfrac{16}{12}$
25. $\dfrac{18}{11}$	26. $\dfrac{9}{5}$	27. $\dfrac{9}{8}$	28. $\dfrac{6}{4}$
29. $\dfrac{8}{7}$	30. $\dfrac{9}{7}$	31. $\dfrac{11}{5}$	32. $\dfrac{6}{5}$
33. $\dfrac{14}{9}$	34. $\dfrac{3}{2}$	35. $\dfrac{5}{4}$	36. $\dfrac{18}{13}$
37. $\dfrac{7}{6}$	38. $\dfrac{9}{8}$	39. $\dfrac{19}{8}$	40. $\dfrac{7}{2}$

#3646 Practice and Learn

Converting Mixed Numbers to Improper Fractions

Write each of the mixed numbers as an improper fraction.

1. $4\frac{4}{5}$ 2. $3\frac{1}{5}$ 3. $2\frac{5}{7}$ 4. $7\frac{1}{3}$ 5. $9\frac{1}{4}$

6. $1\frac{5}{7}$ 7. $9\frac{1}{2}$ 8. $9\frac{4}{5}$ 9. $2\frac{5}{8}$ 10. $9\frac{3}{5}$

11. $4\frac{6}{8}$ 12. $1\frac{6}{9}$ 13. $8\frac{3}{9}$ 14. $7\frac{5}{8}$ 15. $8\frac{3}{6}$

16. $5\frac{8}{9}$ 17. $2\frac{5}{6}$ 18. $4\frac{3}{5}$ 19. $3\frac{4}{6}$ 20. $1\frac{4}{5}$

21. $4\frac{2}{6}$ 22. $9\frac{8}{9}$ 23. $7\frac{1}{6}$ 24. $1\frac{1}{3}$ 25. $4\frac{2}{3}$

26. $5\frac{3}{6}$ 27. $8\frac{3}{7}$ 28. $6\frac{3}{9}$ 29. $3\frac{2}{4}$ 30. $6\frac{1}{8}$

31. $9\frac{1}{3}$ 32. $7\frac{1}{9}$ 33. $2\frac{3}{6}$ 34. $8\frac{1}{2}$ 35. $9\frac{6}{7}$

36. $1\frac{5}{8}$ 37. $6\frac{3}{4}$ 38. $5\frac{7}{8}$ 39. $8\frac{1}{9}$ 40. $6\frac{4}{5}$

Adding Fractions

Add the fractions and write your answer in simplest form where possible.

1. $1\frac{1}{2}$
    $+\ 1\frac{1}{2}$

2. $2\frac{1}{3}$
    $+\ 1\frac{1}{3}$

3. $5\frac{1}{6}$
    $+\ 2\frac{2}{6}$

4. $1\frac{1}{8}$
    $+\ \ \frac{3}{8}$

5. $6\frac{1}{9}$
    $+\ \ \frac{2}{9}$

6. $3\frac{2}{3}$
    $+\ 1\frac{1}{3}$

7. $5\frac{1}{4}$
    $+\ \ \frac{2}{4}$

8. $9\frac{1}{2}$
    $+\ 1\frac{1}{2}$

9. $2\frac{1}{6}$
    $+\ 1\frac{2}{6}$

10. $4\frac{2}{3}$
    $+\ 3\frac{1}{3}$

11. $2\frac{1}{8}$
    $+\ 1\frac{2}{8}$

12. $7\frac{1}{7}$
    $+\ 1\frac{3}{7}$

13. $2\frac{2}{8}$
    $+\ 3\frac{1}{8}$

14. $13\frac{1}{3}$
    $+\ 1\frac{2}{3}$

15. $22\frac{4}{5}$
    $+\ \ \frac{1}{5}$

16. $101\frac{1}{6}$
    $+33\frac{2}{6}$

Adding Fractions (cont.)

Add the fractions and write your answer in simplest form where possible.

1. $\frac{2}{3}$
$+ \frac{7}{8}$

2. $\frac{7}{8}$
$+ \frac{5}{7}$

3. $\frac{1}{3}$
$+ \frac{2}{6}$

4. $\frac{4}{5}$
$+ \frac{7}{8}$

5. $\frac{3}{5}$
$+ \frac{3}{9}$

6. $\frac{4}{5}$
$+ \frac{3}{9}$

7. $\frac{1}{6}$
$+ \frac{4}{5}$

8. $\frac{6}{7}$
$+ \frac{2}{3}$

9. $\frac{7}{9}$
$+ \frac{2}{8}$

10. $\frac{1}{9}$
$+ \frac{3}{5}$

11. $\frac{4}{5}$
$+ \frac{8}{9}$

12. $\frac{7}{8}$
$+ \frac{2}{5}$

13. $\frac{4}{6}$
$+ \frac{4}{5}$

14. $\frac{4}{7}$
$+ \frac{1}{6}$

15. $\frac{7}{9}$
$+ \frac{2}{7}$

16. $\frac{5}{9}$
$+ \frac{6}{8}$

Adding Fractions (cont.)

Add the fractions and write your answer in simplest form where possible.

1. $\frac{4}{7}$ 2. $\frac{7}{8}$ 3. $\frac{3}{8}$ 4. $\frac{4}{5}$

$+ \frac{2}{4}$ $+ \frac{2}{4}$ $+ \frac{4}{9}$ $+ \frac{2}{3}$

5. $\frac{2}{8}$ 6. $\frac{1}{2}$ 7. $\frac{3}{4}$ 8. $\frac{3}{7}$

$+ \frac{3}{8}$ $+ \frac{5}{7}$ $+ \frac{1}{3}$ $+ \frac{2}{8}$

9. $\frac{4}{5}$ 10. $\frac{3}{8}$ 11. $\frac{6}{7}$ 12. $\frac{2}{7}$

$+ \frac{5}{9}$ $+ \frac{2}{3}$ $+ \frac{1}{2}$ $+ \frac{6}{7}$

13. $\frac{1}{6}$ 14. $\frac{1}{6}$ 15. $\frac{5}{8}$ 16. $\frac{1}{5}$

$+ \frac{2}{3}$ $+ \frac{1}{5}$ $+ \frac{5}{7}$ $+ \frac{6}{7}$

Adding Fractions (cont.)

Add the fractions and write your answer in simplest form where possible.

1. $1\frac{5}{9}$
   $+\ 5\frac{2}{4}$

2. $3\frac{3}{4}$
   $+\ 9\frac{4}{8}$

3. $6\frac{2}{5}$
   $+\ 6\frac{1}{5}$

4. $3\frac{4}{6}$
   $+\ 4\frac{7}{9}$

5. $1\frac{3}{9}$
   $+\ 9\frac{6}{9}$

6. $9\frac{1}{9}$
   $+\ 1\frac{5}{8}$

7. $1\frac{8}{9}$
   $+\ 5\frac{6}{7}$

8. $2\frac{3}{7}$
   $+\ 7\frac{7}{9}$

9. $1\frac{1}{3}$
   $+\ 2\frac{7}{8}$

10. $6\frac{2}{6}$
    $+\ 1\frac{2}{4}$

11. $2\frac{3}{9}$
    $+\ 6\frac{2}{8}$

12. $5\frac{2}{6}$
    $+\ 4\frac{3}{7}$

13. $2\frac{4}{6}$
    $+\ 3\frac{5}{6}$

14. $8\frac{2}{9}$
    $+\ 8\frac{4}{6}$

15. $2\frac{5}{9}$
    $+\ 5\frac{3}{8}$

16. $6\frac{1}{5}$
    $+\ 9\frac{5}{6}$

Subtracting Fractions

Subtract the fractions and write your answer in simplest form where possible.

1. $\dfrac{4}{12}$

    $-\dfrac{3}{12}$

2. $\dfrac{7}{8}$

    $-\dfrac{2}{8}$

3. $\dfrac{13}{16}$

    $-\dfrac{7}{16}$

4. $\dfrac{3}{6}$

    $-\dfrac{1}{6}$

5. $\dfrac{5}{6}$

    $-\dfrac{1}{6}$

6. $\dfrac{2}{3}$

    $-\dfrac{2}{3}$

7. $\dfrac{9}{10}$

    $-\dfrac{1}{10}$

8. $\dfrac{5}{8}$

    $-\dfrac{1}{8}$

9. $\dfrac{3}{4}$

    $-\dfrac{1}{4}$

10. $\dfrac{2}{5}$

    $-\dfrac{1}{5}$

11. $\dfrac{10}{11}$

    $-\dfrac{2}{11}$

12. $\dfrac{9}{10}$

    $-\dfrac{3}{10}$

13. $\dfrac{9}{10}$

    $-\dfrac{8}{10}$

14. $\dfrac{11}{16}$

    $-\dfrac{7}{16}$

15. $\dfrac{7}{12}$

    $-\dfrac{3}{12}$

16. $\dfrac{13}{14}$

    $-\dfrac{12}{14}$

Subtracting Fractions (cont.)

Subtract the fractions and write your answer in simplest form where possible.

1. $\dfrac{4}{7}$
  $-\dfrac{1}{2}$

2. $\dfrac{6}{9}$
  $-\dfrac{2}{5}$

3. $\dfrac{4}{5}$
  $-\dfrac{7}{9}$

4. $\dfrac{7}{9}$
  $-\dfrac{1}{3}$

5. $\dfrac{3}{4}$
  $-\dfrac{2}{9}$

6. $\dfrac{5}{8}$
  $-\dfrac{3}{7}$

7. $\dfrac{5}{7}$
  $-\dfrac{1}{3}$

8. $\dfrac{2}{7}$
  $-\dfrac{1}{5}$

9. $\dfrac{1}{5}$
  $-\dfrac{1}{8}$

10. $\dfrac{5}{6}$
  $-\dfrac{2}{6}$

11. $\dfrac{2}{3}$
  $-\dfrac{2}{4}$

12. $\dfrac{5}{8}$
  $-\dfrac{5}{9}$

13. $\dfrac{5}{6}$
  $-\dfrac{1}{6}$

14. $\dfrac{7}{9}$
  $-\dfrac{1}{3}$

15. $\dfrac{8}{9}$
  $-\dfrac{7}{8}$

16. $\dfrac{5}{8}$
  $-\dfrac{2}{6}$

Multiplying Fractions

Multiply the fractions and write your answer in simplest form where possible.

1. $\dfrac{2}{4} \times \dfrac{2}{5}$ 2. $\dfrac{4}{9} \times \dfrac{5}{6}$ 3. $\dfrac{1}{6} \times \dfrac{3}{5}$ 4. $\dfrac{4}{8} \times \dfrac{2}{3}$

5. $\dfrac{4}{7} \times \dfrac{4}{9}$ 6. $\dfrac{8}{9} \times \dfrac{3}{4}$ 7. $\dfrac{3}{8} \times \dfrac{6}{8}$ 8. $\dfrac{1}{8} \times \dfrac{4}{9}$

9. $\dfrac{4}{8} \times \dfrac{4}{5}$ 10. $\dfrac{3}{4} \times \dfrac{1}{2}$ 11. $\dfrac{2}{3} \times \dfrac{7}{9}$ 12. $\dfrac{7}{8} \times \dfrac{2}{6}$

13. $\dfrac{6}{9} \times \dfrac{5}{9}$ 14. $\dfrac{1}{6} \times \dfrac{3}{6}$ 15. $\dfrac{2}{5} \times \dfrac{3}{9}$ 16. $\dfrac{4}{9} \times \dfrac{3}{4}$

17. $\dfrac{4}{7} \times \dfrac{3}{4}$ 18. $\dfrac{1}{7} \times \dfrac{2}{5}$ 19. $\dfrac{4}{5} \times \dfrac{1}{3}$ 20. $\dfrac{1}{6} \times \dfrac{4}{9}$

21. $\dfrac{7}{9} \times \dfrac{4}{7}$ 22. $\dfrac{1}{4} \times \dfrac{2}{6}$ 23. $\dfrac{3}{6} \times \dfrac{3}{8}$ 24. $\dfrac{2}{3} \times \dfrac{3}{4}$

           #3646 Practice and Learn

Multiplying Fractions (cont.)

Multiply the fractions and write your answer in simplest form where possible.

1. $\frac{4}{7} \times \frac{6}{9}$ 2. $\frac{4}{5} \times \frac{1}{2}$ 3. $\frac{8}{9} \times \frac{1}{6}$ 4. $\frac{1}{5} \times \frac{1}{4}$

5. $\frac{3}{9} \times \frac{5}{6}$ 6. $\frac{3}{8} \times \frac{5}{9}$ 7. $\frac{2}{5} \times \frac{5}{7}$ 8. $\frac{7}{8} \times \frac{2}{8}$

9. $\frac{5}{6} \times \frac{7}{8}$ 10. $\frac{2}{3} \times \frac{3}{9}$ 11. $\frac{8}{9} \times \frac{7}{9}$ 12. $\frac{4}{9} \times \frac{2}{9}$

13. $\frac{6}{9} \times \frac{1}{4}$ 14. $\frac{4}{7} \times \frac{2}{6}$ 15. $\frac{1}{3} \times \frac{3}{4}$ 16. $\frac{4}{6} \times \frac{5}{9}$

17. $\frac{1}{2} \times \frac{2}{4}$ 18. $\frac{3}{8} \times \frac{1}{6}$ 19. $\frac{5}{7} \times \frac{3}{6}$ 20. $\frac{5}{9} \times \frac{2}{5}$

21. $\frac{2}{3} \times \frac{4}{8}$ 22. $\frac{7}{8} \times \frac{1}{3}$ 23. $\frac{1}{2} \times \frac{2}{8}$ 24. $\frac{3}{5} \times \frac{1}{9}$

Dividing Fractions

Divide the fractions and write your answer in simplest form where possible.

1. $\dfrac{1}{5} \div \dfrac{4}{8}$ 2. $\dfrac{3}{9} \div \dfrac{1}{7}$ 3. $\dfrac{2}{7} \div \dfrac{4}{5}$ 4. $\dfrac{3}{5} \div \dfrac{7}{9}$

5. $\dfrac{5}{9} \div \dfrac{4}{6}$ 6. $\dfrac{1}{7} \div \dfrac{4}{9}$ 7. $\dfrac{3}{6} \div \dfrac{4}{5}$ 8. $\dfrac{1}{8} \div \dfrac{2}{5}$

9. $\dfrac{4}{5} \div \dfrac{7}{8}$ 10. $\dfrac{3}{8} \div \dfrac{7}{8}$ 11. $\dfrac{2}{4} \div \dfrac{3}{5}$ 12. $\dfrac{1}{8} \div \dfrac{6}{9}$

13. $\dfrac{1}{7} \div \dfrac{3}{7}$ 14. $\dfrac{8}{9} \div \dfrac{4}{7}$ 15. $\dfrac{1}{2} \div \dfrac{5}{6}$ 16. $\dfrac{1}{5} \div \dfrac{4}{5}$

17. $\dfrac{3}{8} \div \dfrac{2}{6}$ 18. $\dfrac{4}{6} \div \dfrac{1}{2}$ 19. $\dfrac{2}{6} \div \dfrac{1}{5}$ 20. $\dfrac{1}{4} \div \dfrac{5}{6}$

21. $\dfrac{9}{10} \div \dfrac{3}{5}$ 22. $\dfrac{5}{9} \div \dfrac{2}{6}$ 23. $\dfrac{4}{5} \div \dfrac{3}{7}$ 24. $\dfrac{4}{9} \div \dfrac{2}{6}$

Dividing Fractions (cont.)

Divide the fractions and write your answer in simplest form where possible.

1. $\dfrac{3}{4} \div \dfrac{1}{8}$ 2. $\dfrac{8}{9} \div \dfrac{2}{3}$ 3. $\dfrac{2}{6} \div \dfrac{4}{7}$ 4. $\dfrac{3}{4} \div \dfrac{4}{6}$

5. $\dfrac{5}{6} \div \dfrac{5}{9}$ 6. $\dfrac{1}{2} \div \dfrac{1}{6}$ 7. $\dfrac{6}{7} \div \dfrac{5}{6}$ 8. $\dfrac{7}{8} \div \dfrac{2}{9}$

9. $\dfrac{7}{8} \div \dfrac{3}{4}$ 10. $\dfrac{1}{8} \div \dfrac{5}{8}$ 11. $\dfrac{4}{7} \div \dfrac{6}{9}$ 12. $\dfrac{2}{6} \div \dfrac{1}{5}$

13. $\dfrac{5}{9} \div \dfrac{4}{7}$ 14. $\dfrac{2}{9} \div \dfrac{2}{9}$ 15. $\dfrac{4}{8} \div \dfrac{5}{6}$ 16. $\dfrac{3}{9} \div \dfrac{3}{5}$

17. $\dfrac{6}{8} \div \dfrac{2}{3}$ 18. $\dfrac{5}{6} \div \dfrac{2}{3}$ 19. $\dfrac{1}{5} \div \dfrac{3}{8}$ 20. $\dfrac{3}{4} \div \dfrac{7}{9}$

21. $\dfrac{6}{7} \div \dfrac{4}{7}$ 22. $\dfrac{1}{8} \div \dfrac{2}{8}$ 23. $\dfrac{2}{4} \div \dfrac{6}{9}$ 24. $\dfrac{2}{9} \div \dfrac{7}{8}$

Dividing Fractions (cont.)

Divide the fractions and write your answer in simplest form where possible.

1. $\dfrac{1}{8} \div \dfrac{2}{3}$ 2. $\dfrac{5}{8} \div \dfrac{6}{8}$ 3. $\dfrac{8}{9} \div \dfrac{3}{9}$ 4. $\dfrac{1}{7} \div \dfrac{6}{9}$

5. $\dfrac{3}{8} \div \dfrac{2}{6}$ 6. $\dfrac{5}{6} \div \dfrac{4}{7}$ 7. $\dfrac{4}{5} \div \dfrac{4}{6}$ 8. $\dfrac{5}{9} \div \dfrac{4}{9}$

9. $\dfrac{1}{2} \div \dfrac{7}{9}$ 10. $\dfrac{4}{9} \div \dfrac{2}{3}$ 11. $\dfrac{3}{6} \div \dfrac{6}{8}$ 12. $\dfrac{3}{8} \div \dfrac{1}{3}$

13. $\dfrac{3}{4} \div \dfrac{1}{2}$ 14. $\dfrac{3}{4} \div \dfrac{1}{3}$ 15. $\dfrac{4}{9} \div \dfrac{3}{9}$ 16. $\dfrac{5}{8} \div \dfrac{1}{8}$

17. $\dfrac{8}{9} \div \dfrac{2}{4}$ 18. $\dfrac{7}{8} \div \dfrac{4}{8}$ 19. $\dfrac{1}{2} \div \dfrac{3}{4}$ 20. $\dfrac{4}{6} \div \dfrac{6}{7}$

21. $\dfrac{1}{8} \div \dfrac{3}{4}$ 22. $\dfrac{6}{9} \div \dfrac{2}{6}$ 23. $\dfrac{7}{8} \div \dfrac{4}{5}$ 24. $\dfrac{1}{4} \div \dfrac{1}{4}$

                                                                   #3646 Practice and Learn

Greater Than and Less Than

Complete each problem to show greater than or less than. (Write > or < in the spaces.)

1. 14   49

2. 91   47

3. 34   72

4. 98   39

5. 86   22

6. 57   73

7. 27   38

8. 48   39

9. 98   78

10. 57   51

11. 46   65

12. 16   69

13. 43   33

14. 44   87

15. 61   41

16. 37   49

17. 46   31

18. 95   54

19. 36   54

20. 32   24

21. 42   86

22. 24   42

23. 74   83

24. 29   76

25. 33   66

26. 42   67

27. 34   46

28. 22   52

29. 62   22

30. 89   32

31. 69   64

32. 64   41

33. 22   82

McDonald's Math

The data in the box below is taken from dietary sheets provided by McDonald's restaurants. Read through the data box and use the information provided to figure out which side of each inequality has the greater number of calories. Place a < or > sign on the line to complete each problem.

Data

These figures reflect the number of calories in each item.

 hamburger—270   hot fudge sundae—290

cheeseburger—320   apple pie—260

 fish sandwich—360   1% milk—100

 small French fries—210   small cola—150

 garden salad—80   chocolate shake—340

---

1. 2 hamburgers   2 hot fudge sundaes

2. 1 fish sandwich   4 garden salads

3. 5 small colas   3 fish sandwiches

4. 3 chocolate shakes   12 1% milks

5. 2 apple pies   7 garden salads

6. 3 cheeseburgers   5 small French fries

7. 2 garden salads + 3 cheeseburgers   4 hamburgers

8. 4 fish sandwiches   6 small French fries + 1 garden salad

9. 2 small colas + 1 chocolate shake   2 apple pies + 3 1% milks

10. 2 hot fudge sundaes   2 small French fries + 3 garden salads

11. 6 1% milks + 2 cheeseburgers   4 small French fries + 1 shake

12. 2 apple pies + 2 fish sandwiches   3 cheeseburgers + 3 small French fries

In the space below write two more inequalities using the data from the box above.

1. _____

2. _____

The Life of a Check

Use the information in the flow chart below to answer the questions at the bottom of the page.

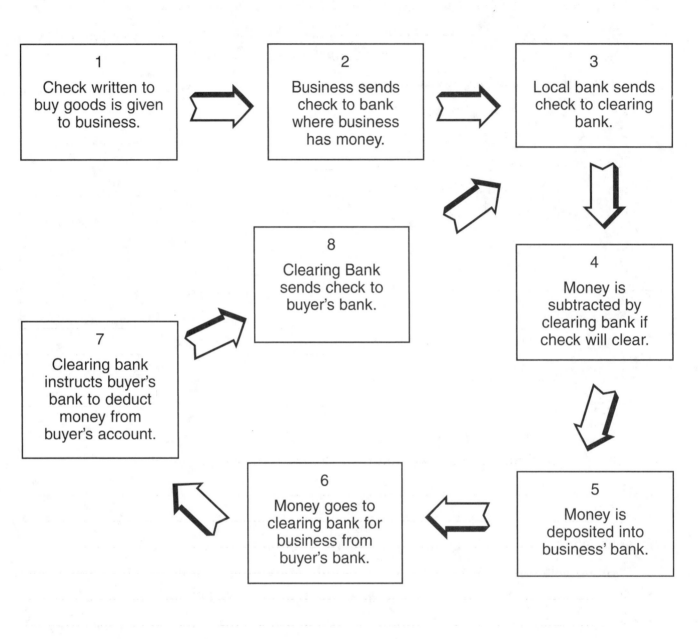

A. Where does the check go after you pay the business for what you bought?

_____

B. In which step does the check go to the buyer's bank?

_____

C. Do you have to have money in your own bank in order to write a check?

_____

Check It Out!

One way that you can purchase something if you do not have the cash in your pocket is to write a check. You will need to know how to write numbers out in words in order to be able to use checks properly. The exercises below will help you to do this.

A. Write in dollars and cents the value for each of the following amounts. For example, the amount, one dollar and thirty-five cents would be written $1.35.

  1. four dollars and twenty-seven cents _____

  2. nine dollars and sixty-two cents _____

  3. one dollar and ninety-nine cents _____

  4. eight dollars and twenty-two cents _____

  5. three dollars and sixteen cents _____

  6. sixteen dollars and sixty-six cents _____

B. Write in words the value for each of the following amounts. For example, $1.43 would be written one dollar and forty-three cents.

  1. $3.99 _____

  2. $9.33 _____

  3. $5.87 _____

  4. $2.22 _____

  5. $6.48 _____

  6. $8.72 _____

C. Using section **B** above, write how many dollars are represented in #1-6.

  1. _____

  2. _____

  3. _____

  4. _____

  5. _____

  6. _____

D. Using section **B** above, write how many cents are represented in #1-6.

  1. _____

  2. _____

  3. _____

  4. _____

  5. _____

  6. _____

Check It Out! (cont.)

A check tells your bank how much you want them to pay from your bank account into someone else's bank account. Study the check below to see how a check is written.

You must always have enough money in your checking account when you write a check. Paying by check gives you proof that you have paid a bill. Review the parts of a check and what is required on each line to make a check valid.

1. Your name, address, and phone number (usually pre-printed).

2. The name of the person or company you want to pay.

3. The date you are writing the check.

4. The amount in numbers.

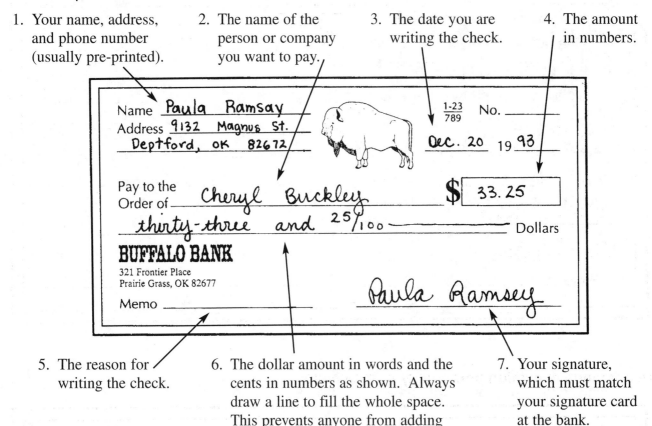

5. The reason for writing the check.

6. The dollar amount in words and the cents in numbers as shown. Always draw a line to fill the whole space. This prevents anyone from adding anything to the amount.

7. Your signature, which must match your signature card at the bank.

Activity: Practice filling out a check. You may write it to anyone you want for any amount you want. Refer to the sample above to guide you.

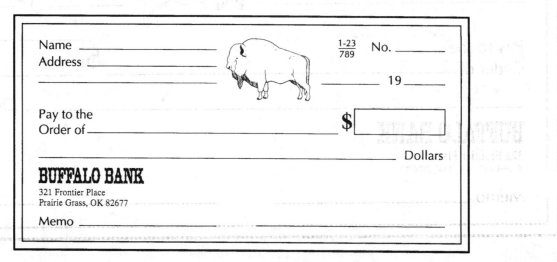

Writing Checks

A check tells your bank how much you want them to pay from your bank account to someone else. Fill in the blank checks to the person listed above each check.

To a relative:

Name _____
Address _____
_____

$\frac{1\text{-}23}{789}$ No. _____

_____ 19 _____

Pay to the
Order of _____ $ [   ]

_____ Dollars

BUFFALO BANK

321 Frontier Place
Prairie Grass, OK 82677

Memo _____ _____

To a famous television personality or movie star:

Name _____
Address _____
_____

$\frac{1\text{-}23}{789}$ No. _____

_____ 19 _____

Pay to the
Order of _____ $ [   ]

_____ Dollars

BUFFALO BANK

321 Frontier Place
Prairie Grass, OK 82677

Memo _____ _____

          #3646 Practice and Learn

Writing Checks (cont.)

A check tells your bank how much you want them to pay from your bank account to someone else. Fill in the blank checks to the person listed above each check.

To a friend:

Name _____ $\frac{1\text{-}23}{789}$ No. _____

Address _____

_____   _____ 19 _____

Pay to the
Order of _____ $ _____

_____ Dollars

BUFFALO BANK

321 Frontier Place
Prairie Grass, OK 82677

Memo _____   _____

To a friend:

Name _____ $\frac{1\text{-}23}{789}$ No. _____

Address _____

_____   _____ 19 _____

Pay to the
Order of _____ $ _____

_____ Dollars

BUFFALO BANK

321 Frontier Place
Prairie Grass, OK 82677

Memo _____   _____

Penny Wise

Budgeting your money is a very important skill for everyone. If you receive an allowance, you should decide how and on what to spend your money. Will you spend part of it and save the rest? Are there upcoming events or activities for which you will need extra money?

When you become an adult, you will need to think very carefully about how to spend your money. Here is something you can do with an adult to help you understand more about keeping a budget. You are going to help with the grocery shopping today. You have $52.00 to spend, and you need to find out if you have enough money to purchase what is needed. You will need a pencil, a calculator, and a clipboard.

At Home: Make a list of six items that you need to get at the grocery store. Make these real items on your grocery list.

At the Store: Write the cost of each item next to it.

Item (List at home.)   Cost (Write this at the store.)

1. _____   _____

2. _____   _____

3. _____   _____

4. _____   _____

5. _____   _____

6. _____   _____

How much would you spend? _____   Can you get all of the items?

_____

What is the amount of money that you either need or have extra? _____

Extension: Imagine that you are going to make one of the recipes on page 152. First, check at home to see which ingredients you already have. (Be sure you have enough of each ingredient.) Make a list of the ingredients you need to buy. On a piece of paper, write down how much you think the ingredients will cost. Go to the store and check out the prices. How well did you estimate the cost? (With adult permission and help, you may wish to make one of the recipes.)

Penny Wise (cont.)

Applesauce

Ingredients:

- 4 large apples
- 1 tablespoon (15 mL) water
- 2 tablespoons (30 mL) sugar
- cinnamon (optional)

Utensils:

- 2-quart (2 L) saucepan with lid
- vegetable peeler
- table knife
- potato masher

Directions:

Peel apples and cut into fourths. Remove cores. Put apples into saucepan. Add water. Cover saucepan with lid. Cook over high heat until water begins to boil. Reduce heat to low. Simmer for 20 minutes until apples are soft. Remove from heat. Use potato masher to mash apples and sugar together. Eat applesauce hot or cold. Sprinkle cinnamon on top if desired.

Applesauce Drop Cookies

Ingredients:

- ½ cup (125 mL) butter, margarine, or softened shortening
- 1 cup (250 mL) sugar
- 1 egg
- 1 cup (250 mL) flour
- 1 tablespoon (15 mL) baking powder
- ½ teaspoon (2.5 mL) salt

- 1 teaspoon (5 mL) cinnamon
- ½ teaspoon (2.5 mL) cloves
- ½ teaspoon (2.5 mL) nutmeg
- 1 cup (250 mL) applesauce
- 1 cup (250 mL) raisins
- 1 ¾ cup (438 mL) quick rolled oats

Utensils:

- large bowl
- wire whisk
- mixing spoon or large spoon

- teaspoon
- baking sheet

Directions:

Mix butter and sugar until creamy. Beat in egg. Add all dry ingredients except rolled oats and raisins. Blend well. Stir in applesauce, raisins, and rolled oats. Drop by teaspoonsful onto greased baking sheet. Bake at 375°F (190°C) about 15 minutes or until lightly browned.

Pictographs

One type of graph that gives us information is called a *pictograph*. In a pictograph, pictures are used instead of numbers.

Read this pictograph to find out the number and types of pets sold in April at Harmony Pet Store.

April Pet Sales at Harmony Pet Store	
birds	
fish	
dogs	
cats	
rabbits	
Key: 1 picture = 5 pets	

1. How many of each of these animals were sold?

   birds _____ fish _____ dogs _____ cats _____ rabbits _____

2. How many more dogs were sold than each of the following?

   birds _____ fish _____ cats _____ rabbits _____

3. Which category of animals do you think brought in more money for Harmony Pet Store? Explain the reason(s) for your choice.

   _____

   _____

   _____

   _____

   _____

Chocolate Consumers of the World

There are chocolate lovers all over the world! Listed below are some of the major chocolate-consuming countries of the world. Beside each country is the average number of pounds/kilograms (lbs/kg) of chocolate eaten per person each year. (Metric conversions, rounded to the nearest tenth, are listed for those using metric measurement.)

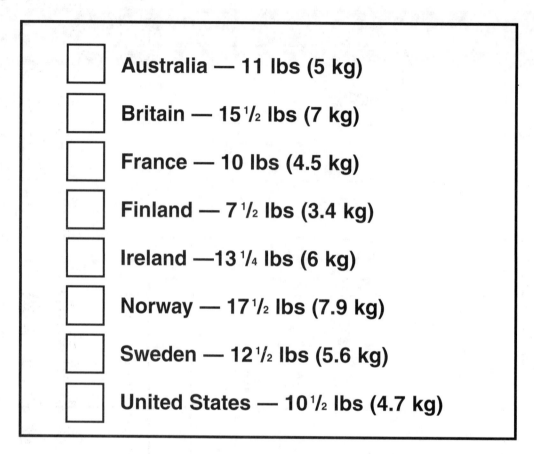

- Australia — 11 lbs (5 kg)
- Britain — 15 ½ lbs (7 kg)
- France — 10 lbs (4.5 kg)
- Finland — 7 ½ lbs (3.4 kg)
- Ireland — 13 ¼ lbs (6 kg)
- Norway — 17 ½ lbs (7.9 kg)
- Sweden — 12 ½ lbs (5.6 kg)
- United States — 10 ½ lbs (4.7 kg)

Activity

A pictograph is a graph in which pictures or symbols represent information. The graph's key shows the value that each symbol or picture represents. The key on page 459 indicates that one chocolate candy symbol represents one pound of chocolate for each person in a year. Create a pictograph on the "Chocolate Consumers of the World" chart on page 459.

Directions

1. Arrange the countries in order from 1-8, with 1 representing the country that consumes the most chocolate and 8 representing the country with the least amount of chocolate consumed. Write the order in the boxes above. Copy the countries (in order) on the chart on page 459.

2. Cut out the correct number of candies from the bottom of page 459 to represent each country's chocolate consumption. (Use the key to determine how many chocolates to cut out.)

3. Complete the pictograph by gluing the correct number of chocolates next to each country. (Be sure to use half of a chocolate to represent ½ pound, one quarter of a chocolate to show ¼ of a pound, etc. Do the same for kilograms.)

Chocolate Consumers of the World (cont.)

Chocolate Consumption*

Country							

Key: * Each candy represents 1 pound (.45 kg) per person per year.

Circle Graphs

One type of graph that gives us information is called a *circle graph*. In a circle graph, you can show how things are divided into the parts of a whole.

Shown in this circle graph are the types and amounts of fruit sold at a produce stand in a week in July.

Fruits Sold at O'Henry's Fruit Stand

| July 1 to July 7 |

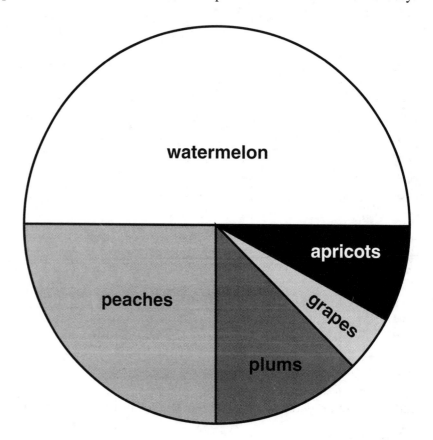

1. What fruit sold the most at O'Henry's Fruit Stand? _____

2. What fruit sold the least? _____

3. Rank the order of the fruits that were sold. Number 1 will be the fruit that sold the most and number 5 the least.

    1. _____   2. _____   3. _____

    4. _____   5. _____

4. Circle the correct fraction.

    Watermelon was $^1/_2$ $^1/_4$ $^1/_8$ of all the fruits sold.

    Peaches were $^1/_2$ $^1/_4$ $^1/_8$ of all the fruits sold.

    Plums were $^1/_2$ $^1/_4$ $^1/_8$ of all the fruits sold.

5. Which of the fruits represented on the circle graph is your favorite?

_____

Slices

In a *circle graph*, all the parts must add up to be a whole. Think of the parts as pieces that add up to one whole pie.

Look at the circle graph below that shows what Chris did at home between 4 P.M. and 5 P.M. on November 5.

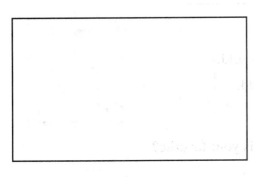

1. How many minutes did Chris spend on the following things?

   doing homework   _____

   eating a snack   _____

   changing clothes   _____

   playing a video game   _____

   walking the dog   _____

2. How did you figure out the number of minutes Chris did things?

   _____

   _____

   _____

Make a circle graph that shows what you did during one of your after-school hours.

   did homework   _____

   played a video game   _____

   walked the dog   _____

   changed clothes   _____

   ate a snack   _____

Write the title of your graph here.

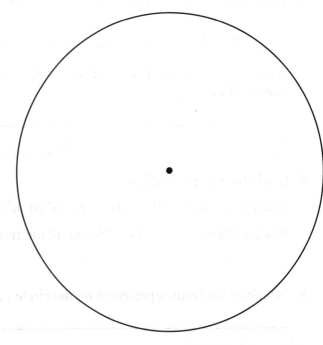

Bar Graphs

One type of graph that gives us information is called a *bar graph*. A bar graph shows us many different types of things by the height or length of the bars.

Sam has to plan ahead to store food for the winter months. The graphs below show two ways Sam could organize his food. Use the graphs to answer the questions.

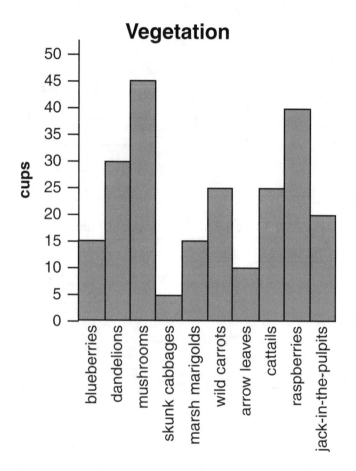

Vegetation

(**Hint:** 2 cups = 1 pint; 2 pints = 1 quart)

1. How many cups of cattails does Sam have? _____
2. How many cups of berries are there? _____
3. How many quarts of raspberries have been stored? _____
4. There are 10 cups of arrow leaves. How many more cups of dandelions than arrow leaves are there? _____
5. How many pints of jack-in-the-pulpits are there? _____
6. If Sam made bread and used one pint of cattails to make flour, how many cups would he have left? _____
7. Which plant has Sam stored the least amount of? _____
8. Which plant has Sam stored the greatest amount of? _____
9. If Sam ate half his store of wild carrots by January, how many cups would he have left for the spring months? _____

(**Hint:** 16 ounces = 1 pound)

1. How many pounds of squirrel are there? _____
2. How many ounces of rabbit meat does Sam have stored? _____
3. How many more pounds of venison than fish are there? _____
4. If Sam used 24 ounces of turtle to make soup, how many pounds would he have left? _____
5. How many pounds of meat does Sam have in all? _____

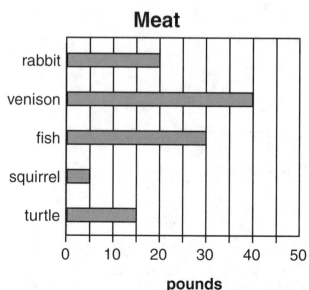

Meat

pounds

Using Distance Charts

Distance charts show you the distance between two places if you travel by road.

This distance chart shows the miles between 10 North American cities. Look at the chart carefully. Read it by locating the two cities and moving one finger across and one finger down until the two fingers come together to show the distance between cities. Practice. When you are comfortable using the chart, answer the questions below.

Ten-City Distance Chart	Albuquerque	Boston	Chicago	Denver	Indianapolis	Los Angeles	Miami	Montreal	New York City
Boston	2172		963	1949	906	2779	1504	318	206
Chicago	1281	963		996	181	2054	1329	828	802
Denver	417	1949	996		1058	1059	2037	1815	1771
Indianapolis	1266	906	181	1058		2073	1148	840	713
Los Angeles	807	2779	2054	1059	2073		2687	2873	2786
Miami	1938	1504	1329	2037	1148	2687		1654	1308
Montreal	2087	318	828	1815	840	2873	1654		378
New York City	1979	206	802	1771	713	2786	1308	378	
Seattle	1440	2976	2013	1307	2194	1131	3273	2685	2815

Find the distances between these cities.

1. Boston and New York City _____

2. Seattle and Montreal _____

3. Boston and Los Angeles _____

4. Denver and Miami _____

5. New York City and Chicago _____

6. Montreal and Indianapolis _____

7. Chicago and Seattle _____

8. Indianapolis and Denver _____

9. Montreal and Los Angeles _____

10. New York City and Miami _____

11. Chicago and Boston _____

12. Denver and Albuquerque _____

Interpreting Charts

Students at Hudson Elementary School have been participating in a Read-a-Thon to raise money for their school library. Each student has tallied the number of books he or she has read and is now ready to collect the pledge money.

This chart represents the reading and pledges of 15 students involved in the Read-a-Thon. After reading the chart, answer the questions at the bottom of the page.

Wilson Elementary School Read-a-Thon: Room 3			
Student's Name	**Total Books Read**	**Pledge per Book**	**Money Collected**
Alvarez, Jennifer	33	10¢	$3.30
Andrews, Joey	5	10¢	$ .50
Brooks, Joe	61	5¢	$3.05
Duran, Nicholas	17	15¢	$2.55
Edwards, Marylou	47	5¢	$2.35
Harrison, Taylor	11	25¢	$2.75
Lewis, Rebecca	38	10¢	$3.80
Logan, Cassie	22	5¢	$1.10
Marshall, Barbara	9	50¢	$4.50
Peterson, Daniel	102	5¢	$5.10
Ross, Kathryn	58	10¢	$5.80
Rublo, Anthony	85	5¢	$4.25
Shea, Sharon	39	10¢	$3.90
Tran, Alvin	13	10¢	$1.30
Yetter, Liz	75	5¢	$3.75
TOTAL	**615**	——	**$48.00**

1. Which student read the most books?_____

2. What was the highest amount of money collected by one student? _____

   Which student?_____

3. Who had the highest pledge of money per book? _____

4. Was the person who read the most books the same as the person who collected the most money? _____

5. Was the person who had the highest pledge of money per book the same as the person who collected the most money?_____

6. What was the total number of books read by these students? _____

7. What was the average number of books read by each student?_____

8. What was the average amount of money pledged per book? _____

Using Chart Information

How much do you weigh? Your weight depends upon where you are. If you are in orbit around Earth, far away from Earth's gravitational pull, you would be weightless and would float. Mass is the amount of matter that makes up an object. The gravitational pull depends upon mass. Even a pencil has mass. Thus, it has a gravitational pull, but since it is far less than Earth's mass, it falls to the ground when you drop it.

If you were to visit planets and moons with more or less mass than Earth's, a scale would show you weighed a different amount than you do on Earth. Complete the chart to find out how much you would weigh on the planets in our solar system and on the Moon.

Planet	Surface Gravity		Your Weight on Earth	New Weight
Mercury	.38	x		
Venus	.90	x		
Earth	1.00	x		
Mars	.38	x		
Jupiter	2.64	x		
Saturn	1.13	x		
Uranus	.89	x		
Neptune	1.13	x		
Pluto	.06	x		
Earth's Moon	.17	x		

Using Chart Information (cont.)

Make a graph to show the results of the calculations from your data-capture sheet (page 161).

MY WEIGHT ON THE PLANETS AND THE MOON

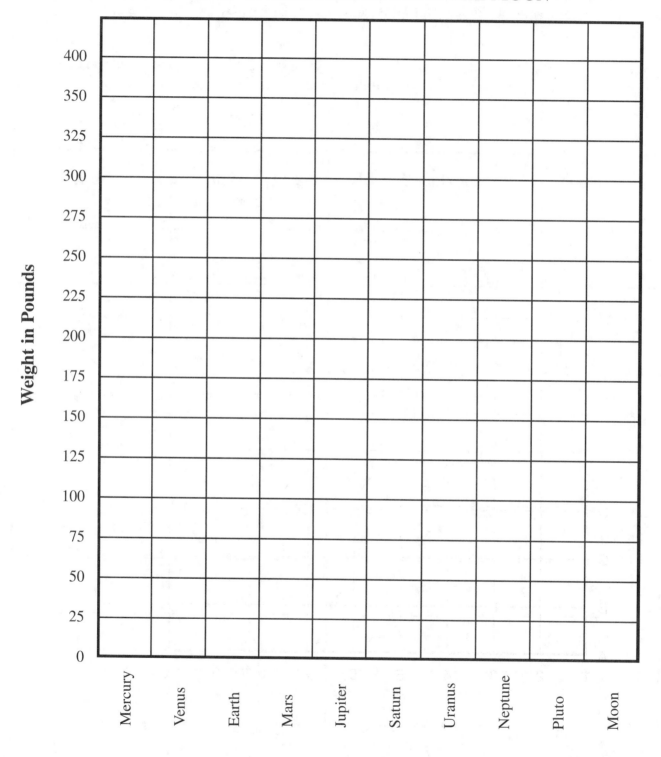

Locating Points on a Graph

Jim earned a terrific prize for winning first place in the community talent show. The prize he won is spelled out in this graph.

Find the points on the graph that are identified below. Can you discover what Jim won? Each point you find will give you a letter of the hidden prize.

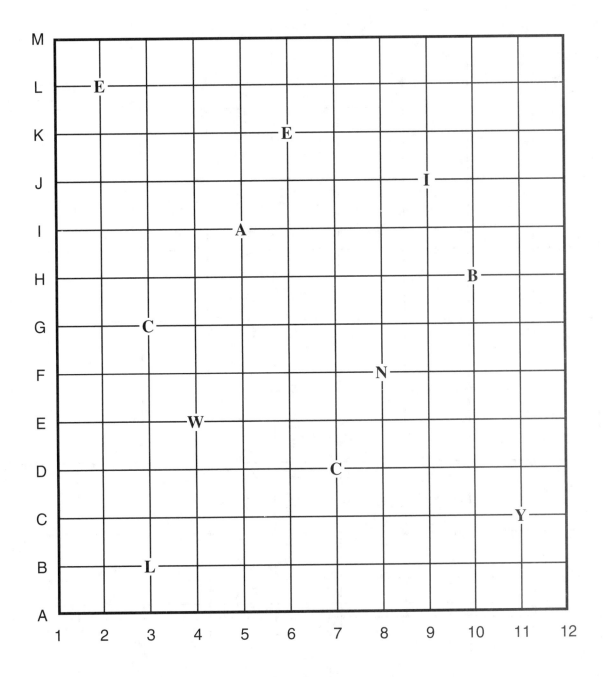

$\overline{\text{5,I}}$ $\qquad$ $\overline{\text{8,F}}$ $\overline{\text{2,L}}$ $\overline{\text{4,E}}$ $\qquad$ $\overline{\text{10,H}}$ $\overline{\text{9,J}}$ $\overline{\text{3,G}}$ $\overline{\text{11,C}}$ $\overline{\text{7,D}}$ $\overline{\text{3,B}}$ $\overline{\text{6,K}}$

Finding Coordinates on a Graph

How Do You Make a Hot Dog Stand?

The answer to this riddle is written in a special code at the bottom of this page. Each pair of numbers stands for a point on the graph. Write the letter shown at the point near the intersection of each pair of numbers. Read numbers across and then up. The letters will spell out the answer to the riddle.

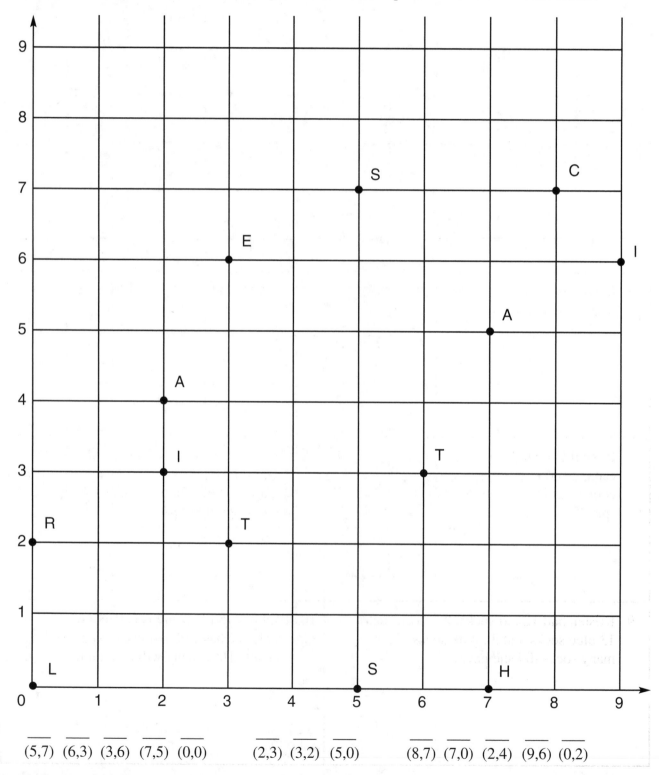

$\overline{\hspace{1em}}$ $\overline{\hspace{1em}}$ $\overline{\hspace{1em}}$ $\overline{\hspace{1em}}$ $\overline{\hspace{1em}}$ $\overline{\hspace{1em}}$ $\overline{\hspace{1em}}$ $\overline{\hspace{1em}}$ $\overline{\hspace{1em}}$ $\overline{\hspace{1em}}$ $\overline{\hspace{1em}}$ $\overline{\hspace{1em}}$ $\overline{\hspace{1em}}$

(5,7) (6,3) (3,6) (7,5) (0,0)   (2,3) (3,2) (5,0)   (8,7) (7,0) (2,4) (9,6) (0,2)

468

Simple Addition Word Problems

Read each word problem and then answer the questions.

1. Daniel bought 2 candy bars at 47 cents each. How much did he spend?	2. Laura had 92 cents. She wanted to buy a 35 cent juice and a 49 cent hog dog. How much did she spend? How much change does she receive?
3. Jim put his pennies into 2 small boxes. He put 1396 pennies into each box. How many pennies did he have?	4. The Wilson's drove their car 10,483 miles one year and 19,768 miles the next year. How far did they drive during the two years?
5. Robyn had 296 marbles in one box and 187 marbles in another box. How many marbles did she have?	6. In 1959, the population of Happyville was 28,746. During the next 20 years the population increased by 19,658. What was the population then?
7. Russell bought 4 bags of chips at 60 cents each, 2 sodas at 35 cents each and 2 cookies at 25 cents each. How much did he spend?	8. Tamra wanted to go bowling. She rented shoes for $10.00, paid for 2 games at $2.00 a game and bought one soda for $0.35. How much did she spend?
9. Kristen had 12 red socks, 27 green socks, 13 blue socks and 32 pink socks. How many socks did she have?	10. Paul has 75 rocks in his collection. His Uncle Joe has 139 and wants to give them to Paul. How many will he then have?

Addition and Subtraction Word Problems

Read the following problems. Circle the important facts you need to solve them. Use the space provided to find the solution to each problem.

1. There were 76 students in a school jog-a-thon. Twenty-six of them were in 3rd grade, 28 of them were in 4th grade, and 22 of them were in 5th grade.

   a. How many 4th- and 5th-grade students were in the jog-a-thon? _____

   b. Which grade had the most students in the jog-a-thon? _____

2. The jog-a-thon route covered 150 kilometers. There were 4 rest stops for the runners. Niki ran 52 kilometers and stopped at the second rest stop.

   a. How much further does Niki have to run to complete the route? _____

   b. Had she gone at least half the distance? _____

3. Melita's team wanted to collect a total of $325.00. They collected $208.75 from the jog-a-thon and $76.20 from a candy sale.

   a. How much money did they collect? _____

   b. Would they collect more money from 3 candy sales than from 1 jog-a-thon? _____

4. Twenty team members had lunch together at the third rest stop. They had traveled 70 kilometers. Thirteen team members drank milk with their lunch and the rest drank grape juice.

   a. How many team members drank grape juice? _____

   b. How many team members did not drink grape juice? _____

5. Bill, Holly, and Katie collected contributions from their neighbors. Bill collected $13.78, Holly collected $16.85, and Katie collected $12.34.

   a. How much more did Holly collect than Bill? _____

   b. How much did Holly and Katie collect together? _____

6. To get ready, Carol bought new shoes for $36.00 and a new water bottle for $1.36. Her mom gave her $47.00 to spend.

   a. How much did she spend for the shoes and water bottle? _____

   b. How much more were the shoes than the water bottle? _____

Multiplication and Division Word Problems

Read each problem and then answer the questions.

The Bailey family runs a small market that not only sells but also grows fresh fruit and vegetables. They sell gardening tools, seeds, and plants. They help their customers with questions about picking which plants to grow and how to best care for them.

1. Two hundred fifteen watermelon seeds were planted in the ground. Five seeds were planted in each small hole. How many small holes were there?	2. The gardeners at Bailey's Market planted 48 onions in each of 12 rows. How many onions were planted?
3. A clerk sold Garrett a rake for $7.75 and a shovel for $13.77. He paid half and had his brother pay the other half. How much did each pay?	4. Tim bought 2,000 carrot seeds on Monday and 3,985 seeds on Tuesday. He needs to plant all of the seeds. He plants 7 seeds in each hole. How many holes will he have when he is done?
5. Randy planted 7 rows of corn and each row had 8 plants in it. He needed to wrap them into bundles of 4. How many bundles would he have?	6. Two customers each bought 25 potatoes for a pot luck supper. They made 10 pots of stew and used all of the potatoes. How many potatoes did they use in each stew?
7. Each seed packet cost $.79. Robyn bought 9 of them. How much did she spend?	8. Each seed packet has 135 seeds in it. Robyn will need to plant 15 seeds in a row. How many rows will she plant?
9. What will be the total cost of 2 bags of grapes at $2.00 each, 1 bag of potatoes at $1.99 each, and 4 baskets of strawberries at $3.46 each?	10. The workers need to move the display case that has the apples in it. There are 6 different bins of apples. Each bin has 44 apples in it. How many apples are there in the display case?

Division Word Problems

Read each problem and then answer the questions.

1. You deliver 630 newspapers each week. You deliver the same amount each day. How many papers do you deliver each day?	2. You have a roll of film that will take 24 pictures. How many rolls would you need to take 120 pictures?
3. Patti has 396 gum balls and 12 friends to share them with. How many will each friend get?	4. You have collected 3,960 pennies in an old pickle jar. You have 22 friends that you want to give them to. How many would each friend receive?
5. Doug has 657 decals in his desk drawer. He wants to split them among his 9 friends. How many would each one receive?	6. Chris has 5,987 soccer cards. He wants to sell them in packages of 24. How many packages would he have? Would he have any left over? If so, how many?
7. Mike collects rocks. He has 627 in his collection. He wants to store them in 8 boxes. How many will he have in each box? How many will be left over?	8. Cathy was organizing her photographs and found that she had 156 vacation pictures. If she arranges eight pictures on a photo album page, how many pages will she need?
9. Susan's grandmother was making cookies for Susan's classroom. She made 90 cookies. There are 29 students in Susan's class and one teacher. How many cookies would each person get?	10. The pet store had 78 birds that they had to put in 13 cages. How many birds would be in each cage?

Splat!

Learn about the force of gravity.

Materials

- washable ink or thin paint

- eyedropper

- meter stick or yardstick

- large sheet of white paper (Butcher paper is best.)

- newspapers

- masking tape

- data-capture sheet (page 170), one per student

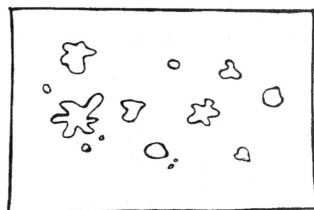

Procedure

1. Place newspapers down in the work area. Secure with masking tape.

2. In the center of the newspapers, tape a large sheet of white paper.

3. You will be dropping paint from different heights onto the paper. Release one drop of paint from each height. Practice with the eyedropper over the container of paint until you are able to release just one drop.

4. Drop paint from 4" (10 cm), 8" (20 cm), 12" (30 cm), 16" (40 cm), 20" (50 cm), 24" (60 cm), 28" (70 cm), 32" (80 cm), 36" (90 cm), and 40" (100 cm)

5. After each drop has landed, label it so that you know the height from which it was dropped.

6. Try to keep the splatters separated on the paper.

7. Answer the questions on your data-capture sheet (page 170).

The Big Why

Gravity forces the droplets to fall faster and faster the higher they are dropped. This create a larger and larger amount of energy upon impact. The energy causes the molecules of the droplets to scatter.

Splat! (cont.)

Data Capture Sheet

Compare your splats. Are they the same?

_____

_____

Did the splatters continue to break apart more explosively as you increased the height? Explain.

_____

_____

Was there a limit of how much splatter you were able to produce?

_____

_____

If so, where was the limit reached?

_____

_____

_____

What forces kept the paint together as it fell and also tried to resist the splat?

_____

_____

_____

As the paint was dropped from greater heights, what pattern did the resultant splats display?

_____

_____

Whirlybirds

Learn about gravity, air resistance, and whirlybirds.

Materials

- construction or index paper
- scissors
- small paperclips
- large paper clips
- index cards
- manila folder
- markers or crayons

Procedure

1. Cut along the dotted lines.

2. Fold along the dark lines.

3. Add one paper clip to the fuselage.

4. Fold one rotor back. Fold the other rotor forward.

5. Hold the whirlybird by the top of the rotors as high off the ground as you can reach.

6. Release the model. Observe how the whirlybird falls. Do several trials.

7. Use a marker or crayon to color one rotor. Drop the whirlybird and use the colored rotor as an aid in counting how many times the rotors turn before it lands.

8. Do several trials and keep a record of your results. Make a graph to compare your results.

The Twister

You can make a model that twirls faster by using a smaller design. Reduce the design illustrated and repeat the directions above.

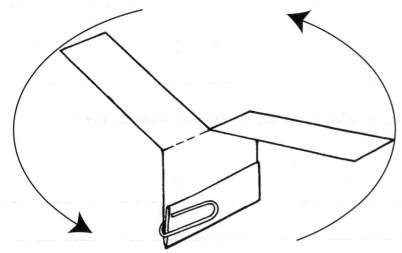

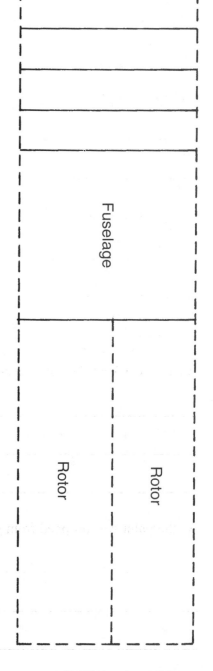

Fuselage

Rotor   Rotor

Butterfly Balance

Learn about the center of gravity.

Materials

- heavy paper or card stock

- reproducible butterfly design (page 173)

- scissors

- pencil that has never been sharpened

- small ball of clay to use as a base

- two pennies

- rubber cement

- markers or crayons for decorating the butterfly

Procedure

1. Trace the butterfly pattern onto heavy paper. Cut out the design.
2. Decorate the butterfly.
3. Use the clay to form a sturdy base for the pencil. Be sure the pencil is perfectly straight.
4. Glue the pennies on the butterfly where indicated.
5. Balance the butterfly on the eraser of the pencil. The butterfly should balance on its "nose." It might take a little adjustment of the pennies to obtain a stable balance.

The Big Why

Artists use the center of gravity concept to create interesting effects. By manipulating where the weight is located (in this case by using coins), we change the point where the corner of gravity lies. This can cause the illusion of a balancing act that seems to defy gravity.

Butterfly Balance (cont.)

Use this pattern to make your balancing butterfly.

Facts About Motion

Refer to the information below as you complete the activities on pages 175-180.

Everything from the smallest atom to the largest sun is in motion! Movement is the mechanism that makes life possible. Newton's First Law deals with a fundamental principle that objects in motion will stay in motion, and objects at rest will stay at rest, unless a force acts upon them.

The First Law of Motion is a description of the property of *inertia*. Everybody has inertia. It is the lazy property. Inertia likes everything to stay the same. If a rock is lying on the ground and you want to move it, you will find that it is harder to start moving the rock than it is to keep it moving. That is because inertia says, "Leave me alone! I like what I am doing." On the other hand, if that same rock is traveling through space, it takes energy to get it to stop. Once again, the rock wants to be left alone to continue what it is doing.

The motion of an object is very easy to measure. When something is moving, we are interested in how much distance is covered in what period of time. For this reason, the units for motion are the units of distance divided by a unit of time. In the U.S. customary system of measurement, we most commonly use miles per hour. In the metric system, speed is measured in kilometers per hour or meters per second.

The word *speed* has been used on purpose throughout this activity. The concept of *velocity* is a very specific quantity that includes not only speed but also direction. It takes both speed and direction to describe velocity.

To understand motion, an important concept is the frame of reference. When we are measuring the speed of an object, we are always measuring in reference to ourselves or a particular spot on the surface of the earth. The ancients got into trouble with frame of reference when they thought that everything revolved around the earth. To them, the earth was the most important body in the heavens and, therefore, must be the stable, fixed point around which everything moved. This idea of reference point is key to Einstein's Theory of Relativity. In essence, Einstein said that we cannot know if we are standing still and the object is moving or the object is standing still and we are moving. It all depends on our point of view! All motion is relative.

Starting and Stopping

Learn about Newton's First Law.

Materials

- five blocks
- a wooden hammer or ruler
- data-capture sheet (page 176)
- safety glasses

Procedure

1. Stack the blocks on top of each other.

2. Put on your safety glasses. (**Note:** For safety purposes, be sure that other people are at a safe distance from moving blocks.) Slowly hit the bottom block away from the pile. Record the results on your data-capture sheet.

3. Set up the blocks again.

4. Strike the bottom again. This time hit it fast and hard. Record the results on your data capture sheet.

5. Set up the blocks again. Slowly strike the middle block. Record the results on your data-capture sheet.

6. Set up the blocks again. Strike the middle block hard and fast. Record the results on your data-capture sheet.

7. Review the results on your data-capture sheet. Then, read the information below. Does your experiment support the facts about inertia and Newton's First Law?

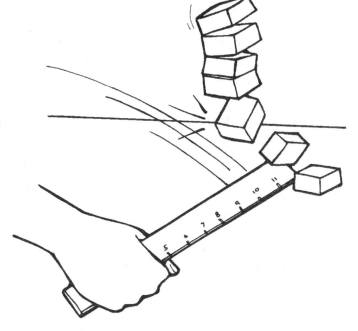

The Big Why

If something is at rest, it wants to stay that way, so it takes more force to move it. If something is moving, it wants to remain moving at the same speed and in the same direction, so it takes another force to stop it or change its direction. When you strike the blocks hard and fast, the inertia of the top blocks holds them in place. When you strike the blocks slowly, the force can be slowly applied to all the blocks, overcoming inertia and producing movement for all of the blocks.

Starting and Stopping (cont.)

Data-Capture Sheet

What happened when you hit the bottom block slowly?

_____

What happened when you hit the bottom block hard and fast?

_____

What happened when you hit the middle block slowly?

_____

What happened when you hit the middle block hard and fast?

_____

_____

_____

Using what you have observed in this experiment, explain why you think a magician can pull a tablecloth out from under a set of dishes and not break or disturb the table setting.

Newton's First Law of Motion states that an object at rest will remain at rest and an object in motion will remain in motion at constant velocity unless acted upon by another force. Inertia is the basis for this law. The word *inertia* comes from the Latin word *iners* which means "lazy" or "idle." In your own words, explain what inertia is.

_____

_____

_____

_____

_____

_____

_____

Racing Marbles

Learn about measuring speed.

Materials

- any book that is 1" (2.5 cm) or more thick

- plastic, 12" (30 cm) ruler that has a groove down the center

- a game marble

- smooth surface to work on (An uncarpeted floor is the best.)

- piece of chalk

- stopwatch

- calculator

- data-capture sheet (page 178), one per student

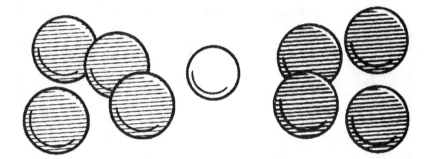

Procedure

1. Mark a starting point on the floor. From the starting point, measure and mark a distance of 20" (50 cm), 40" (100 cm), and 60" (150 cm)

2. Make an incline by placing one end of the ruler on the starting point and the other on a book. The incline will be directed toward the distance marks.

3. Place a marble at the top of the incline and let it accelerate down the ruler.

4. Begin timing when the marble crosses the starting point.

5. Time how long it takes until the marble crosses the 20" (50 cm) mark.

6. Repeat two more times.

7. Do a total of three trials for 20" (50 cm), three trials for 40" (100 cm), and three trials for 60" (150 cm).

8. Complete your data-capture sheet on page 178.

The Big Why

Speed is a measure of change—the change in distance over a particular time period.

Racing Marbles (cont.)

As you race your marbles, fill in the data below. Then calculate the average time for the three trials.

20 in. (50 cm)	Trial 1	Trial 2	Trial 3	Average
Time:				
40 in. (100 cm)	Trial 1	Trial 2	Trial 3	Average
Time:				
60 in. (150 cm)	Trial 1	Trial 2	Trial 3	Average
Time:				

Calculate Speed

Use the average time for each distance. Calculate the speed the marble was traveling as it covered the three distances. Record your answers below, using a calculator and the following equation:

$$\textbf{speed = distance} \div \textbf{time}$$

For 20" (50 cm) Speed = _____ inches (cm)/second

For 40" (100 cm) Speed = _____ inches (cm)/second

For 60" (150 cm) Speed = _____ inches (cm)/second

For Further Thought

Why are the speeds for the three distances different?

Impact Craters

Learn about force and acceleration.

Materials

- medium and large rocks

- sandy area or boxes filled with sand

- straight piece of cardboard for smoothing the sand

- ruler

- data-capture sheet (page 180)

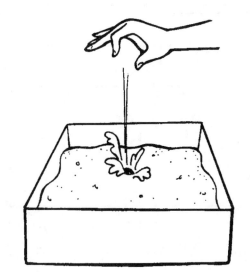

Procedure

1. Pick an area of sand and smooth it with the cardboard.

2. The object is to drop the rocks from various heights and measure the craters made. Smooth the sand after each rock and record information on your data-capture sheet.

3. Throw the rocks straight down, one at a time, into the sand. Observe how the craters formed. Smooth the sand after each landing and record information on your data-capture sheet.

4. Throw the rocks down at an angle. Observe how the craters formed. Smooth the sand after each rock is thrown and record information on the back of your data-capture sheet.

The Big Why

When objects slow down or come to an abrupt stop, there must be a force applied to produce this change. When the change is abrupt, as in this experiment, the change in velocity produces a large amount of energy that is absorbed by the ground. This energy causes the dirt to move, hence an impact crater. Often there is enough energy to produce an explosion!

Impact Craters (cont.)

Data-Capture Sheet

Trial	Rock Size	How Dropped	Describe the Crater
1			
2			
3			
4			
5			
6			

Draw a picture of the crater made by dropping the largest rock straight down.

Draw a picture of the crater made by throwing a large rock into the sand at an angle.

What is different about each crater?

_____

_____

As the rocks came to a stop, they did not stop instantly. There was a period of deceleration or slowing down. What evidence is there of the forces involved in stopping an object?

_____

Making a Balloon Rocket

Learn about propulsion.

Materials

- long balloon
- thin string or yarn
- large straw with a short piece cut off
- tape
- measuring tape

Procedure

1. Place the string or yarn through the longer piece of straw. Attach the string or yarn to each side of the room.

2. Blow up the balloon. Do not let the air out. You may wish to use something to clamp the neck of the balloon closed.

3. Tape the longer piece of straw to the balloon, making sure not to let the air out of the balloon.

4. Place the shorter piece of straw into the neck of the balloon and tape it into place.

5. Stand at one end of the room and let the air out of the balloon. As the air rushes out, the balloon should travel along the string or yarn.

6. Launch your balloon rocket three times. Use the measuring tape to see how far your balloon rocket moves each time. Record your measurements on the back of this paper.

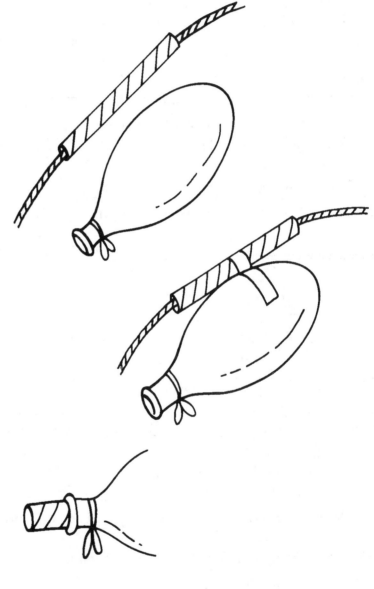

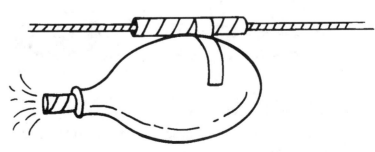

Blast Off!

Learn about trajectory.

Materials

- balloons of several shapes and sizes
- index cards or tagboard
- ruler
- markers
- colored pencils or crayons
- tape
- fishline

Procedure

1. Use an index card or tagboard to make a rocket like the one shown in the illustration.
2. Color the rocket pattern and roll it into a cylinder. Tape the cylinder together.
3. Blow up a balloon and hold it in the inflated condition as a partner gently tapes the rocket model to the top or side of the balloon.
4. Take the balloon rocket to the designated launch area preferrably outside the classroom.
5. Set the balloon rocket on the launching pad, lean away from the rocket, and release the balloon.

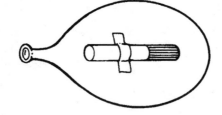
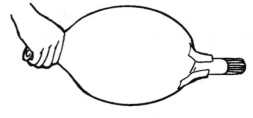

- How well did your rocket work?
- Try launching the rocket again with a different balloon. Try long balloons, twisties, very large spherical balloons, and any other sizes and shapes available.
- Try the slender design shown here. This design curls into a long, slender tube. It can be attached to the top or side of the balloon.
- With which balloon did this model work best?
- Design your own rocket version. Modify one of the two designs shown on this page or create an entirely new design.
- Try launching your design, using your favorite type of balloon.

- Test it on other balloon sizes.
- Compare your design with those launched by other class members.
- Why do you think that thin, cylindrical models often work best?

Blast Off! (cont.)

Guided Rockets

You can often get greater distance by guiding the launch.

1. Cut a 30-foot (9-meter) piece of fishline. Tie one end to the shaft of a pushpin and pin that end into a bulletin board about four feet (122 cm) off the floor or to a tree or pole outdoors.

2. Extend the string across the room or playground to the farthest distance possible. Keep the fishline out of the path of students and tape it against a wall until you are ready to launch.

3. Copy the design shown below onto an index card, manila folder, or similar thick paper. Color it with markers or crayons.

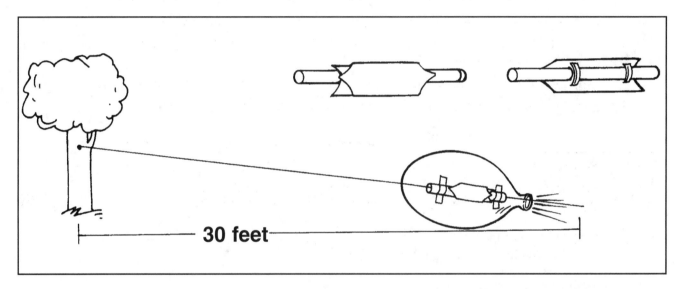

4. Tape the rocket design onto a straw in two places.

5. Thread the end of the fishline through the straw and hold it in place while a partner blows up a balloon and tapes it onto the rocket model.

6. Hold the string and model so that the straw sits easily on the fishline and the fishline is aimed slightly higher than where it is pinned.

7. Release the balloon and observe how well the rocket travels. Did it get to the end of the fishline?

   • Did the straw catch or run freely along the fishline? Did the balloon seem to run out of air before the rocket reached the end of the line?

   • Do several trials of your rocket. Use balloons of different styles and sizes. Hold the fishline at different angles to get the maximum amount of speed.

   • Create a model rocket of your own. Use a different style or type of rocket. Make your rocket longer or shorter, wider or narrower.

   • Try several different versions. Use different balloons and test each of your models.

   • Try mounting your rocket onto a double-length straw that you have hooked together.

   • Try making a cylinder to go around the straw.

Chutes Away

Learn about air resistance.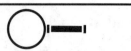

Materials

- fishline
- paper
- newspaper
- small trash bags
- construction paper

- large paper clips
- manila folder or tagboard
- plastic bottles
- boxes

- hole punch or pushpin
- masking tape
- scissors

The Basic Chute

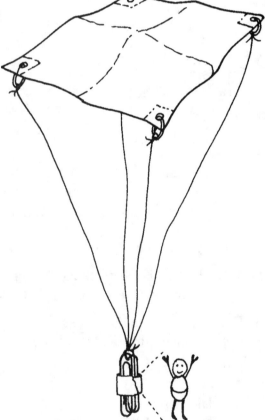

1. Fold an 8½" x 11" (22 cm x 28 cm) piece of paper in fourths

2. Push out the side folded in so that all four folds face up.

3. Cover each corner on both sides with a piece of masking tape.

4. Use a hole punch or pushpin to make a hole at all four corners. Make the hole right through the tape.

5. Cut four pieces of fishline each about 16" (41 cm) long.

6. Tie one piece of fishline at each corner.

7. Tape three large paper clips together. Draw a small figure of a parachutist to tape onto the paper clips.

8. Tie all four ends of the fishline together at an even distance from the corners. Tie or tape them to the paper clip parachutist.

9. Hold your parachute as high as you can by the chute or canopy and drop it. Note how fast it falls and whether the canopy slows the fall.

10. Stand on a chair, stairs, or a stage (if available), and drop the chute from a higher level.

11. Try folding the entire chute and throwing it high into the air. Does it unfold in time or fall too soon?

Make Flying Saucers

Learn about the principles of flight.

Materials

- tagboard or manila folders
- paper fasteners (brads)
- large paper clips
- glue
- clear tape
- scissors
- math compass
- ruler

Procedure

1. Use a compass to make a circle with a radius of four inches (10 cm) on a piece of tagboard or a manila folder. This will make a circle with a diameter (distance across) of eight inches (20 cm).

2. Cut out the circle. This will be the base of the saucer.

3. Use the compass to make a second circle with a radius of three inches (8 cm). This will create a circle with a diameter of six inches (15 cm). Cut out this circle.

4. Use the compass to draw four more circles. Make each circle smaller than the one before it. Cut out each circle.

5. Arrange the circles in a concentric pattern as shown in the illustration below.

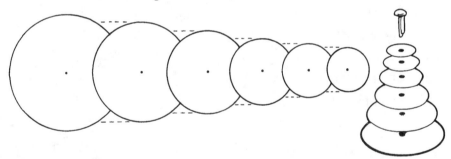

6. Glue each of the circles to the one below it in the stack.

7. Use a pushpin and the point of a compass to make a hole through the center of the stack so that a paper fastener (brads) can be pushed through the layers.

8. Fold the blades of the paper fastener down, and tape them onto the back of the largest circle.

9. Arrange six, large paper clips around the edges of the saucer as shown below, and tape them securely to the back of the largest circle.

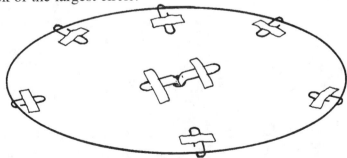

10. Take the flying saucer outdoors and launch it with a swift, Frisbee-like snap of the wrist. Do several trials. Try different ways of throwing your saucer into the air. Observe how your saucer flies.

Make Flying Saucers (cont.)

The Ring Flyer

1. Set the compass for a four-inch (10 cm) radius to draw a circle eight inches (20 cm) in diameter. Cut out the circle.

2. Set the compass for a two-inch (5 cm) radius and draw a smaller circle with a four-inch (10 cm) diameter in the center of the larger circle you just cut out.

3. Cut the smaller circle out from the inside of the tagboard to make a ring as shown in the illustration.

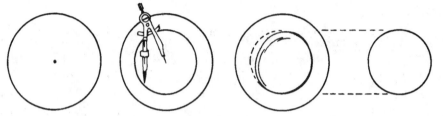

4. Set the compass for a three-inch (8 cm) radius to draw a circle six inches (15 cm) in diameter. Cut out the circle.

5. Set the compass for a two-inch (5 cm) radius, and draw a smaller circle with a four-inch (10 cm) diameter in the center of the larger circle you just cut out.

6. Cut out the smaller circle from the inside to make a smaller ring.

7. Glue the smaller ring onto the larger ring as shown in the illustration.

8. Arrange six large paper clips around the inside of the ring. Arrange six large paper clips around the outside of the ring in alternate spaces as shown.

9. Tape down the paper clips to the bottom of the larger ring.

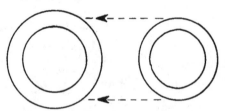 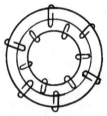

10. Launch the ring with a snap of the wrist like tossing a Frisbee or toss it into the air with a strong overhand throw. Do several trials. Observe how it flies. How does its flight differ from the flying saucer model (page 185)?

Unbalanced Saucers

Place six small paper clips between the large clips on your flying saucer. Tape them down on the bottom layer of the saucer. Throw this model into the air with a snap of the wrist. Does it fly better with the extra paper clips?

Rearrange the large paper clips and the small ones so that the weight on the saucer is unbalanced. You could have four or five paper clips of each size on one side of the saucer and only one or two clips on the other side.

Launch this model and observe what happens.

Make Flying Saucers (cont.)

Larger Saucers

1. Set your compass gauge at the five-inch (13 cm) mark to create a circle with a radius of five inches. Make a circle on a manila folder or tagboard. The circle will have a diameter across the center of 10 inches (25 cm).

2. Use tagboard, manila folders, or construction paper to make nine more circles, each progressively smaller than the one before.

3. Carefully arrange each circle in a concentric pattern with the smallest on top. Glue each circle to the one below it.

4. Use a pushpin to make a hole through the center of the stack and then make the hole large enough with the compass point until you can push a paper fastener through the stack.

5. Arrange six large paper clips evenly around the edges of the saucer. Arrange six small paper clips in between the large clips.

6. Securely tape the blades of the paper fastener (brads) and the paper clips to the back of the largest circle.

7. Launch your flying saucer with a snap of the wrist. Compare your results with the basic flying saucer and the ring flyer (pages 185 and 186).

Pyramid Saucer

Copy or cut out the pattern for a square pyramid illustrated below. Make the model pyramid from tagboard or a folder. Fold along the lines of the square to make the pyramid. Tape the edges of the pyramid and securely tape the pyramid onto the center of the flying saucer.

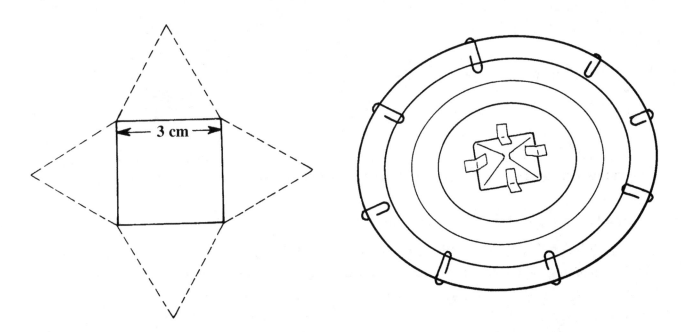

Launch your pyramid saucer. Do several trials. Compare your results with the results of other saucers and ring flyers.

Make Flying Saucers (cont.)

Domed Saucers

Use your best flying saucer or make a new one and mount a dome on the saucer as you did with the square pyramid. Use a plastic, Styrofoam, or paper cup, margarine or cup lids, bottle caps, or create a dome shape from a piece of tagboard or manila folder. The illustrations show several examples for you to try.

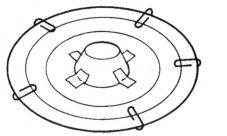 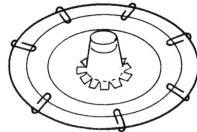 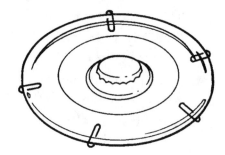

Launch each model. Do several trials. Compare your results. Which domed model works best?

Loaded Saucers

The illustrations here show several unusual models of flying saucers for you to try.

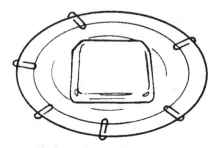 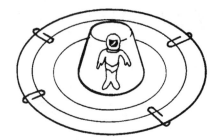 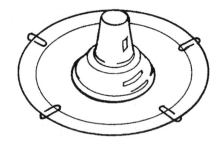

Use your own imagination and your experience in building flying saucers to create the best saucer you can make.

- Try different materials, such as paper plates, for the base.
- Try putting a load both underneath and above the saucer.
- Try changing the edge of the saucer to create a Frisbee-like curve along the edge.
- Try unbalanced saucers and saucers with shapes that aren't circular.
- Be imaginative!
- Test each model.
- Determine your best model.

Don't Give Me Any Static

Learn about static charges.

Materials

- salt
- pepper
- plastic comb
- piece of wool (or flannel) cloth
- small, clear dish
- data-capture sheet (page 190)

Procedure

1. Place a small amount of salt and a small amount of pepper in the glass dish.

2. Rub the comb vigorously with the wool cloth.

3. Move the comb slowly down over the salt and pepper mixture.

4. Move the comb even closer without touching the mixture. Finally, touch the comb to the mixture.

5. Record your observations on your data-capture sheet.

6. Test other items in the room to see what else is attracted by static forces.

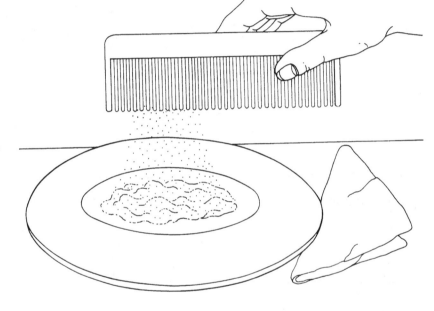

The Big Why

By rubbing the plastic comb with the wool or flannel cloth, it is charged with electrons. Free-moving electrons from the material are transferred to the comb. The comb becomes negatively charged and acts similar to a magnet. The comb, however, does not have a north and south pole. The pepper rises first because it is lighter. If you come close enough, some of the salt will also jump to the comb.

The attraction is caused by the movement of electrons on the surface of the pepper. The negatively-charged comb forces the electrons on the pepper to move away from the comb. The pepper becomes charged by induction; that is, it now has a negative side (away from the comb) and a positive side (closest to the comb). Since opposite charges attract, the pepper is drawn to the comb. Another way to separate the salt and pepper is to put them both in a small amount of water. The salt will sink to the bottom (it is heavier), and the pepper will float.

Don't Give Me Any Static (cont.)

Data-Capture Sheet

Draw a picture of the top of the small clear dish after it was charged and then flipped over.

[blank box]

Where did the pepper stick?

_____

_____

Why did the pepper stick to the rubbed areas?

_____

_____

What charge did the plastic surface have?

_____

_____

Explain how this principle can be used in a photocopy machine.

_____

_____

Super Sound-Off

Learn about how sound is created.

Simple Sound Maker

Materials

- tagboard or manila folder
- index cards
- newspaper
- newsprint paper
- copy paper
- construction paper
- scissors
- ruler
- tape

Procedure

1. Use the ruler to measure a four-inch (10 cm) square on an index card, manila folder, or piece of tagboard.
2. Use the scissors to cut out the square.
3. Use the ruler to draw a diagonal line across the square, then fold along the diagonal, using the ruler or scissors to sharply crease the fold.
4. Use the ruler to measure a six-inch (15 cm) square on a piece of plain white paper. Cut out the square.
5. Draw one diagonal line across the square, dividing it in two.
6. Cut along the diagonal line. Set one piece aside for later use.
7. Lay the first square inside the two shorter sides of the triangle with the fold of the square between the two sides.
8. Fold up about one centimeter along the two shorter sides of the triangle, and tape the folds in place as shown in the illustration.

 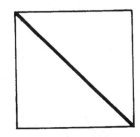 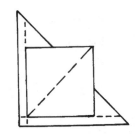 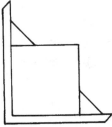

9. Fold the square again and place your thumb and forefinger along the untaped end of the folded figure.
10. Hold the figure above your head, and whip the model through the air as fast as you can. There should be a loud sound as the inner paper pops out of the folded square.
11. Practice holding and snapping the model in different positions. Try to make the loudest crack possible.
12. Try whipping the model sideways.
13. Try holding the model upside down.

Watch what happens to the paper as the sound is made. A wave of compressed air creates the sound as it is forced out by the inner paper.

Where do you have to hold your fingers to make the model crack?

Phone Fun

Learn how sound travels.

Basic Phone Model

Materials

- fishline
- small paper cups
- pushpins
- paper clips

Procedure

- Use a pushpin to make a hole in the bottom of each of two small paper cups.
- Cut a piece of nylon fishline about 20 feet (6 m) long.
- Feed one end of the fishline through the bottom of the cup and tie one small paper clip to the line.
- Pull the line and paper clip firmly against the inside bottom of the cup.
- Feed the other end of the fishline through the bottom of the second cup, tie another small paper clip to the line, and pull it firmly against the inside bottom of the cup.

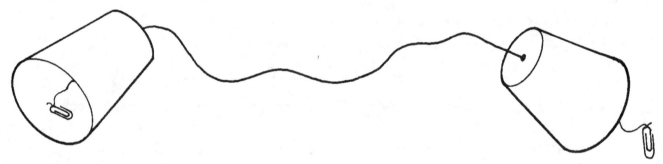

- One partner should hold the cup over one ear while the other person talks into the cup.
- The line must be kept tight, or the phone will not work.

The Big Way

The speaker's voice vibrates molecules of air inside the cup. These vibrations are picked up by the bottom of the cup, which acts as a diaphragm. The line transfers the vibrations to the bottom of the second cup, which also acts as a diaphragm that vibrates the molecules of air in the second cup. These vibrations are then discerned by the ear of the listener.

Improving the phone always involves trying to make the message clearer and carrying it a longer distance. Here are some other ideas to experiment with.

- Try pinching the line while someone is talking. What happens? What happens if the line touches a chair, a wall, or another person?
- Will the phone work if the line gets a tangled knot in it?
- Will it work if the line is allowed to get loose? Why do you think the line must be tight?

The Best Bubble Maker

Learn about the properties of soap.

Materials

- string or thin twine
- insulated wire
- straws
- liquid handwashing dish detergent
- vegetable oil

Procedure

Use this formula to make a strong bubble solution:

- 20 ounces (600 mL) of liquid handwashing dish detergent (Dawn, Joy, etc.)
- 6 ounces (180 mL) of vegetable oil
- 2 gallons (7.6 L) of water

Stir the solution thoroughly in a tray or tub.

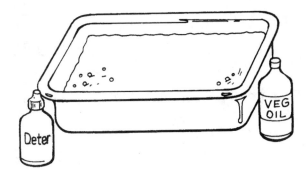

The Two-Handle Frame

Cut a piece of string or thin twine about 30 inches (76 cm) long. Thread the string through the two straws and tie the ends of the string together.

Using the two straws as handles, dip the frame into the bubble solution and see how large a bubble you can lift out of the solution.

Twist the frame to create two triangles. Can you lift two bubbles out of the solution with this frame?

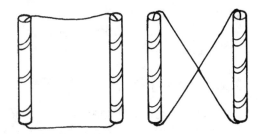

Wire Frames

Twist thin, insulated wire into several of the shapes illustrated here.

Try these shapes in your bubble formula. Observe how the bubbles form. Can you get any long bubbles using some of these frames? Thread wire through short pieces of cut straws to create the plane geometric figures illustrated here.

Facts About Chemical Reactions

Refer to the information below as you complete the activities on pages 195 and 196.

Chemicals react in many ways. They react and undergo chemical change to form new substances with new properties. Chemical changes are indicated when one of the following situations occurs:

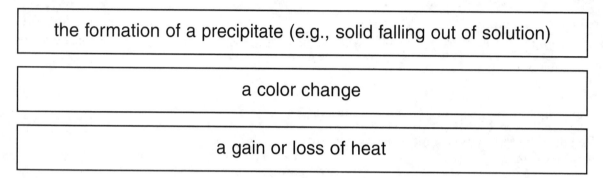

the formation of a precipitate (e.g., solid falling out of solution)

a color change

a gain or loss of heat

Some of the ways that chemicals react are as follows:

- **Oxidation**

  In general, this is a reaction in which the element oxygen combines chemically with another substance.

- **Synthesis or Combination**

  In this chemical reaction, different substances (chemicals) are added together to form new substances (chemicals).

- **Decomposition**

  This is a chemical reaction in which a substance breaks down into its component parts.

- **Replacement**

  In this chemical reaction, at least one part of a chemical switches places with a corresponding part of another chemical.

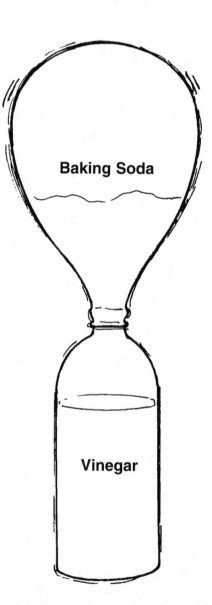

Baking Soda

Vinegar

Add Oxygen

Learn about how chemicals react with oxygen.

Materials

- crayon
- apple
- piece of white paper
- water
- data-capture sheet (page 196)
- potato
- steel wool pad
- plastic knife
- paper cup

Procedure

1. Using the plastic knife, cut the potato in half. Note its appearance, and set it aside for later use.

2. Using the plastic knife, cut the apple in half. Note its appearance, and set it aside for later use.

3. Fill the paper cup two-thirds full of water.

4. Note the appearance of the piece of steel wool pad. Place a piece of it in the cup of water. Set it aside for about 20 minutes and again note its appearance.

5. Place the piece of wet steel wool on a sheet of white paper, and let it dry overnight.

6. Again note the appearance of the cut potato and the cut apple.

7. Let the cut potato and the cut apple sit overnight.

8. The next day, note the appearance of the cut potato, the cut apple, and the piece of steel wool.

9. Compare the information on your data-capture sheet. What do you think happened to each item when it was exposed to the oxygen in the air?

The Big Why

This activity reminds us that oxygen is present in the air. It demonstrates what happens when oxygen combines with various substances and what the resulting chemical reaction produces.

Add Oxygen (cont.)

Data-Capture Sheet

Item	Initial Appearance	Appearance at Second Observation	Appearance After Sitting Overnight
Cut Potato			
Cut Apple			
Steel Wool			

Grow a Crystal Garden

Learn about crystal formation.

Materials

- small bowl or plastic cup
- 3 tablespoon (45 mL) each of laundry bluing (usually found in grocery stores or drugstores), water, and ammonia
- 2 tablespoons (30 g) of salt (Regular table salt will work well.)
- dropper bottles of food coloring or colored ink
- sponge or charcoal (You may also want to try Styrofoam, a tennis ball, or a rough rock.)

Procedure

You can grow a lovely crystal garden at home. The crystals are delicate and look like white snowflakes. You can add food coloring before the crystals form, and they will be colored red, blue, green, yellow, or a combination of those colors where the drops overlap. This is a good activity to do outside since the ingredients include bluing and ammonia, which have a strong odor.

1. Mix the ingredients together in a bowl or measuring cup and stir to dissolve the salt.
2. Put the dry sponge or charcoal into a separate bowl. (This recipe is enough for three or four containers.)
3. Pour the liquid mixture over the sponge, charcoal, or other object.
4. Scatter several drops of food coloring over the solution.
5. Leave the dish in a well-ventilated room or outside.
6. The crystals take about 24 hours to form, less if it is a dry day. They will continue to grow until all the liquid has evaporated. They are delicate crystals which will break if bumped or touched.

Grow a Crystal Garden (cont.)

In the boxes below, make drawings of the crystals you see in your crystal garden.

Picture inside container just after pouring solution.

Time: _____

Date: _____

Picture inside container 15 minutes after pouring solution.

Time: _____

Date: _____

Grow a Crystal Garden (cont.)

In the boxes below, make drawings of the crystals you see in your crystal garden.

Picture inside container just after pouring solution.

Time: _____

Date: _____

Picture inside container after 24 hours of crystallizing.

Time: _____

Date: _____

Testing Towels

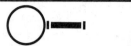

Learn to test variables and make observations.

Materials

- four different brands of paper towels
- facial tissue
- water
- clear plastic cups
- food coloring

Racing Water

1. Fill a clear plastic cup almost full of water. Place a few drops of food coloring in the water and stir.
2. Carefully tear four paper towels from four different brands of paper towel along the perforated line.
3. Roll each towel into a long, thin tube about equal in length to each other.
4. Mark the name of each towel on one end of the tube.
5. Write down the exact time. Place all four tubes in the cup at the same time.
6. Observe how the water climbs the paper towel tubes.
7. Keep track of which towel the water climbs fastest and which is second, third, and fourth.
8. Keep track of the elapsed time.

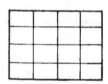 

9. Do two more trials to confirm your results.
10. Make a chart illustrating the results of your trials.
11. Compare your results with other classmates.

The Squeeze Test

1. Arrange the four paper towel tubes as you did in the first activity. Make sure that only one piece of toweling is used from each brand and that they are about the same size, torn along the perforation as you would do in taking a paper towel for use. Make sure you have marked the brand name for each towel.

2. Wait until all four towels have absorbed water and are dripping onto the table.
3. Carefully remove one towel. Record the brand name.
4. Gently squeeze every drop from the toweling into the empty clear plastic cup.

Testing Towels (cont.)

The Squeeze Test *(cont.)*

5. Pour the squeezed water into a measuring cup to determine exactly how many milliliters (or cubic centimeters) of water it holds. (If your measurement cup doesn't indicate milliliters or cubic centimeters, you can use fractions of a fluid ounce on the cup or the millimeters measurement on a ruler to measure the height of the water.)

6. Squeeze the water out of each towel in turn and record the amount of water the paper towel held.

7. Make a chart indicating the amount of water absorbed by each towel.

Paper Towel Siphons

1. Choose any two of your paper towel brands.

2. Position two empty clear plastic cups near the cup of water.

3. Roll one towel from each brand into a long, thin tube. Bend the tubes slightly and put both of them into the cup of colored water. Write down the exact time.

4. As the water climbs up the paper towel, bend each tube so that it is leaning over one of the empty plastic cups.

5. Record the name of the towel leaning over each empty cup.

6. Leave the cups and paper towels undisturbed.

Observe what happens to the water which has climbed up the paper towel.

• Did the paper towels fill each cup as high as the water remaining in the first cup?

• Which paper towel carried water faster than the other?

• Do this activity again but place the full cup of water on a book or some elevated position with the empty cups at a lower level.

• How much water is carried out of the first cup?

Did either of the two empty cups fill more than the other?

• Do the same activity again with the empty cups situated on a raised area and the full cup at a lower level.

• Describe what happens to the water.

• Determine which paper towel holds the most water.

• Why might that indicate it is the best paper towel?

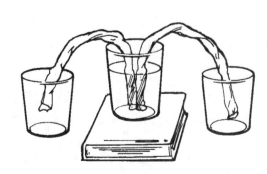

Testing Towels (cont.)

The Dry Test

This is one way to test the strength of a dry paper towel.

1. Use four pieces of masking tape to attach the four corners of one dry paper towel to an area between two desks.

2. Allow about two inches (5 cm) of each side of the towel to lie on the desk. The rest of the towel will be between the desks.

3. Keep count as you place pennies on the stretched-out paper towel.

4. Place as many pennies on the dry towel as you can until it breaks or tears apart. Retest only if the tape gives way.

5. Test each of the four paper towel brands in the same way.

6. Make a chart illustrating how many pennies each of the dry paper towels held.

   • Can you put more than 100 pennies on any towel?

7. Design another way of testing the strength of dry paper towels.

   • How much can you lift using each towel?

   • Do you get the same results using your test?

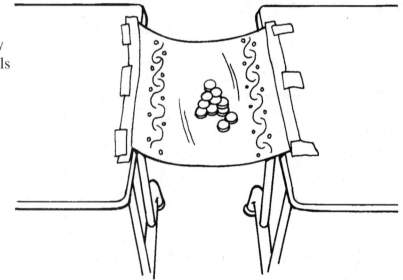

The Wet Test

Test the strength of a wet paper towel.

1. Dip one paper towel in water and gently squeeze out any dripping excess water.

2. Use four pieces of masking tape to attach the four corners of one wet paper towel to an area between two desks as you did in the dry test.

3. Place as many pennies on the wet towel as you can until it breaks or tears apart. Keep an accurate count.

4. Test each of your four paper towel brands in the same way.

5. Make a chart illustrating how many pennies each of your wet paper towels held.

6. Did you get more than 50 pennies on any wet towel? Did any of the paper towels do as well or better wet than dry?

7. Record the results of your wet paper towel test on a chart. Compare results with your classmates.

Testing Towels (cont.)

Double Layer Towels

Do two layers of towels actually work much better than one layer? Repeat the dry paper towel test that you used on the last page using two layers of each paper towel for the test.

Tape the first layer of towel and then the second layer. Record how many pennies the double layer holds for each brand. Do you get more than 150 pennies on any double towel layer? Which results surprise you? Why?

Test the strength of double layers of wet paper towels in the same way. Tape each layer separately and gradually place pennies on the stretched-out layers.

- Are any of the double layers particularly strong?

- Can you get more than 75 pennies on any wet double layer?

- Do any of the results surprise you?

The Stretch Test

How far will each paper towel stretch before it tears? Test one layer of each brand of dry paper towel in this manner:

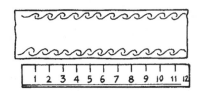

1. Fold one paper towel the lengthwise into four layers.

2. Hold one end of the paper towel near the beginning of a ruler and pull gently on the other end until the paper towel tears apart.

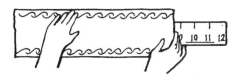

3. Record how many centimeters each brand of paper towel stretched beyond its original length before breaking.

Test the stretching capacity of the four brands of paper towels when they are wet.

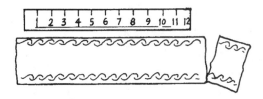

1. Soak each paper towel. Wring out the dripping, excess water.

2. Lay the wet towel along the length of the ruler and record how far it will stretch before tearing.

Design Your Own Tests

Paper towels are used for many different purposes, not just soaking up clean water.

Design some tests of your own to determine the best brand of towel.

Some of the tests might include the following:

- strength tests with soapy water
- ability to absorb cooking oil

- strength tests in holding different objects
- how many towels it takes to clean up a specific spill

The Earth

Learn about the earth's mantle.

Materials

- cornstarch
- water
- two plates

Procedure

1. Mix cornstarch and water until it is like a thick syrup.

2. Pour "magma" into one of your hands. Push the cornstarch together between your hands. Roll it quickly as if you were making a mudball. (This is like magma under pressure.)

3. Release the pressure and try to pass the cornstarch ball to your other hand. Keep it over your plate! (This is like magma without pressure.)

4. Draw the "magma" here.

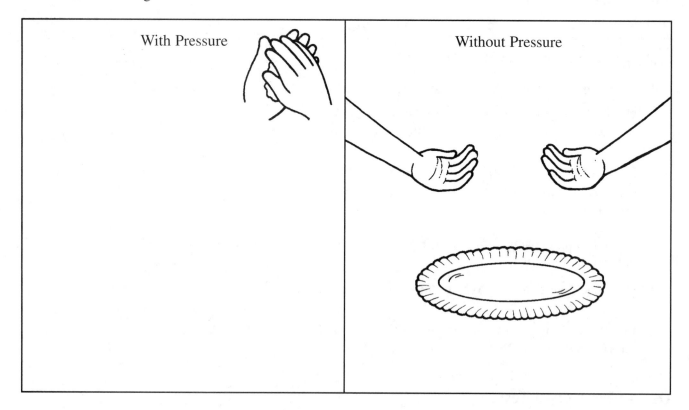

5. On the back of this paper, describe what happened when the cornstarch was under pressure and when it was not. What did you learn?

The Big Why

The earth's mantle is made of melted rock, or magma. When magma is under pressure below the earth's crust, it has one kind of property. When the magma (lava) escapes through a volcano and is no longer under pressure, it has a different property.

Shifting Crust

Learn about earthquakes.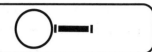

Materials

- three pieces of fresh whole wheat bread

- strawberry jam

- smooth peanut butter

- 2 tablespoons (30 g) of melted plain chocolate bar

- plastic spreading knife

- waxed paper and napkin or paper towel

- copy of The Movement of the Earth's Crust (page 207)

- data-capture sheet (page 208).

Procedure

1. Be sure to wash your hands before doing this activity.

2. Melt the chocolate bars in a microwave or over boiling water on a hot plate.

3. Divide students into groups and distribute the materials needed.

4. Spread the waxed paper in the middle of your work area and put the three slices of bread on the paper.

5. Have students work together to make a sandwich as follows:

   Spread a thin layer of chocolate on a slice of bread and spread peanut butter over it.

   Spread a thin layer of chocolate on a second slice of bread and spread jam over it.

6. Each of the materials represents:

   - *Chocolate*—igneous rock which was melted and forced between layers of rock

   - *Peanut butter*—metamorphic rock, made by rock changed through the pressure of grinding

   - *Jam*—sedimentary layer, with seeds being sedimentary rocks deposited in the ocean

   - *Bread*—more sedimentary layers

7. Put your bread together into a sandwich. (See diagram on page 206.)

Shifting Crust (cont.)

8. Draw on the data-capture sheets the three types of faults using your peanut butter and jelly sandwiches as a model.

9. Move your sandwich slices to represent the faults and to watch the results.

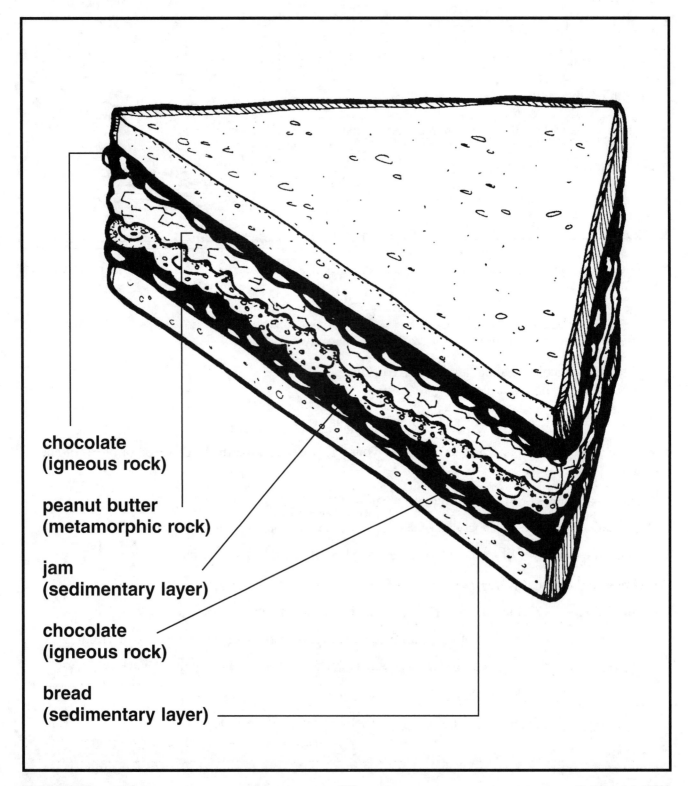

**chocolate
(igneous rock)**

**peanut butter
(metamorphic rock)**

**jam
(sedimentary layer)**

**chocolate
(igneous rock)**

**bread
(sedimentary layer)**

Shifting Crust (cont.)

The Movement of the Earth's Crust

The movement of the earth's crust is called *faulting*. This movement of the crust causes earthquakes. The three main types of faults are normal faulting, reverse faulting, and strike-slip faulting. All three are shown below.

Normal Faulting: Two blocks of the earth's crust move apart from each other. One block may also drop below the other.

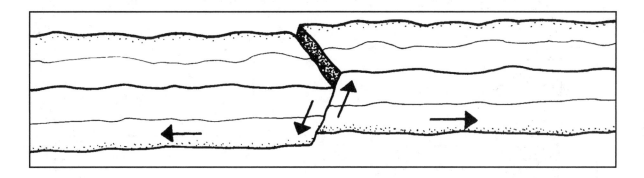

Reverse Faulting: Two blocks push together, and one is pushed under the other. This is called *subduction.*

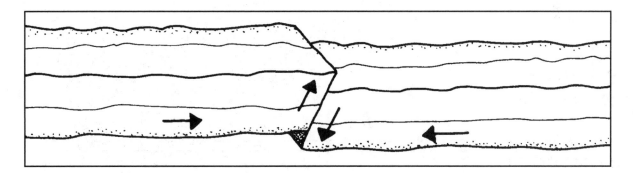

Strike-slip Faulting: The two blocks slide past each other, but neither moves up or down.

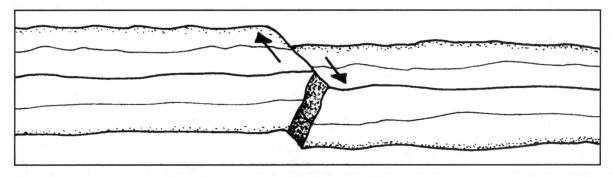

Shifting Crust (cont.)

Data-Capture Sheet

Draw and label each of the three types of faults using your peanut butter and jelly sandwich as a model.

Cold Tracks

Learn about glaciers.

Materials

- pint milk carton
- rocks
- water
- freezer
- sand
- dirt mound

Procedure

1. Fill a pint milk carton one-fourth full with sand and rocks. Fill the rest with water. Shake it, tape it closed, and freeze it.

2. Outside, make a dirt mound.

3. Peel off the carton and place the ice block on top of the dirt mount. Draw a BEFORE picture.

4. Watch what happens. Draw an AFTER picture.

BEFORE

AFTER

5. On the back of this paper, describe what happened. Did your glacier dig a valley? Is that what you thought would happen? What did you learn?

The Big Why

A force that changes the earth's surface is moving ice, called a glacier. A glacier moves slowly, but it is so strong that it can dig out the ground as it moves. Glaciers can even dig out valleys and make lakes. A glacier carries large rocks, depositing them as it melts.

Invasion of the Mold

Learn about growing a simple plant.

Materials

- two pieces of white bread

- cup of sand

- paper plates

- magnifying glass

- large needle

- jelly or jam (any flavor)

- sealable plastic bag

- data-capture sheet (page 211)

Procedure

1. Day 1

   Place one slice of bread on a paper plate, sprinkle it with water. Place it in a plastic bag and seal it tightly. Set it in a warm place and observe it for a few days.

2. Day 4

   Step 1: Remove the bread from the plastic bag. Using a needle, carefully remove some spores from the mold. On a clean paper plate, sprinkle some sand and carefully put some spores on it. Seal the bag and put it in a warm place for 3-4 days. Watch what happens.

   Step 2: Put some spores on another piece of bread. Do not moisten the bread. Put the bread in a sealed plastic bag and set it aside for 3-4 days.

3. Add some jelly to the plate with the sand and spores on it. Reseal and set it in a warm place for 3-4 more days.

4. Record your findings on your data-capture sheet when all steps have been completed.

The Big Why

A simple plant mold is one that does not produce a seed. They must live off another plant or animal to get their food.

Invasion of the Mold (cont.)

Data-Capture Sheet

Draw a picture of what grew on each medium.

Moistened Bread	**Dry Bread**
Sand	**Sand with Jelly**

In your own words explain what your findings are. _____

_____

_____

_____

_____

Moldy Old Cheese

Learn more about growing simple plants.

Materials

- small piece of Muenster cheese
- small piece of Brie or Camembert cheese
- small piece of Roquefort or blue cheese
- 1 oz. (90 g) of cream cheese
- knife
- large-eyed needle
- straight pin
- waxed paper
- measuring spoons
- shallow dish
- pencil with an eraser
- magnifying glass
- data-capture sheets (pages 213 and 214)

Procedure

1. Cut three pieces of Muenster cheese.

2. Using a knife, scrape some mold off the Brie or the Camembert cheese.

3. Slide the mold onto a piece of Muenster cheese.

4. Wrap the cheese in waxed paper for some protection against airborne organisms.

5. Mix $\frac{1}{2}$ teaspoon (2.5 g) of Brie cheese mold with $\frac{1}{2}$ teaspoon (2.5 mL) of water.

6. Spread mixture over the second Muenster cube and a piece of cream cheese.

7. Let the water from the mixture evaporate, and wrap with waxed paper.

8. Construct an inoculation needle by sticking the large-eyed needle into the eraser of your pencil.

9. Punch some holes in the third cube of Muenster cheese and in some cream cheese.

10. Scrape some blue cheese from the Roquefort and put it into the holes you made.

11. Wrap the Muenster and cream cheese in waxed paper.

12. Using your straight pin, punch holes into the paper on all sides of the remaining pieces of cheese.

13. It will need to be set in a safe place for 17 days. Keep at room temperature! Be sure to place the cheese/materials where no one will eat them.

14. Observe and record information on your data-capture sheet.

The Big Why

A cheese manufacturer moved his/her factory. The cheese did not ripen properly in the new location. A worker took some cheese that was made in the old location and rubbed it on the walls. The new cheese ripened properly after that. How did this happen?

Mold cultures must be transferred from one kind of cheese to another. Mold is a type of fungus that forms a fuzzy coating on the surface of damp, or decaying substances.

Moldy Old Cheese (cont.)

Data-Capture Sheet

Draw and describe what your cheese looks like.

	Cube 1	Cube 2	Cube 3
Day 3			
Day 6			
Day 9			

Moldy Old Cheese (cont.)

Data-Capture Sheet *(cont.)*

Draw and describe what your cheese looks like.

	Cube 1	Cube 2	Cube 3
Day 12			
Day 14			
Day 17			

The Sun's Energy

Learn about how plants grow.

Materials

- two plants (Use the same kind and size of plants.)
- water

Procedure

1. Label one plant "More Light." Keep it in a sunny window.

2. Label one plant "Less Light." Keep it in an enclosed area except for putting it in a sunny window two hours each day.

3. Water both plants the same.

4. Check the plants every day for two weeks.

5. Use the chart below to record your observations. Complete a section at the end of each week.

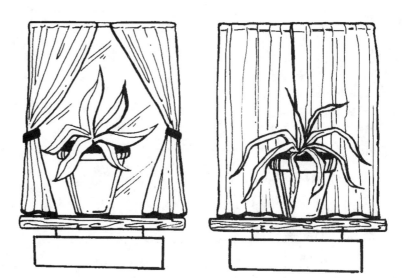

More Light	Less Light
End of Week 1	**End of Week 1**
End of Week 2	**End of Week 2**

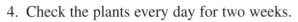
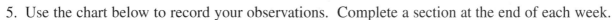

6. Do the results reflect what you thought would happen?

7. What did you learn?

The Big Why

The sun gives the leaves of a plant the energy they need to make food.

Get To the Root of It!

Learn about the function of plant roots.

Materials

- paper towel
- plastic sandwich bag
- several kinds of seeds

Procedure

1. Fold a paper towel into four parts.

2. Place the folded towel flat inside a sandwich bag.

3. Put the seeds on top of the paper towel inside the bag.

4. Wet the towel.

5. Close the bag.

6. Put your bag on a countertop and wait for results.

7. Observe what happens to the seeds. In the box, draw a picture of what you see at the end of the experiment.

8. Do the results reflect what you thought would happen? _____

9. What did you learn? _____

_____

The Big Why

Roots are formed from the growing seedling. The roots find and take in the water and minerals that a plant needs to live and grow. They also hold the plant in place.

Growing, Growing, Grown

Learn about plant growth.

Materials

- seeds (Bean or radish seeds grow quickly.)
- potting soil
- paper cups (or a planter)
- ruler

Procedure

1. Put potting soil in the paper cups.

2. Plant two or three seeds. If you are using packaged seeds, follow the directions on the package. Otherwise, place the seeds about an inch (2.5 cm) below the top of the soil.

3. Water the seeds, making sure not to overwater them. Put them in a place where they can get some sunlight for at least part of the day.

4. Continue to water the seeds as needed.

5. Observe the plants as they grow. Use the space below to keep a record of the observations you make every two or three days. Begin by recording the date and writing down exactly what you see. Then use your ruler to take measurements as your plants grow. Draw a sketch to show what your plants look like.

Record of Observations Date:	**Record of Observations** Date:
Record of Observations Date:	**Record of Observations** Date:

Flowers

Learn about the parts of a flower.

Materials

- a flower
- craft knife
- magnifying glass
- transparent tape
- plastic wrap
- copy of the Flower Identification Sheet (page 219)
- data-capture sheet (page 220)

Procedure

1. Put your flower on your data-capture sheet and examine it.

2. Compare your flower to the diagram on your Flower Identification Sheet (page 219). Can you find similar parts? You may need your magnifying glass to help you.

3. Carefully take your flower apart. Extra care is needed when using a craft knife.

4. Use transparent tape to attach your flower parts to your data-capture sheet (page 220).

5. Label the parts of your flower and cover your data-capture sheet with plastic wrap.

6. Research why each part of a flower is important to a plant.

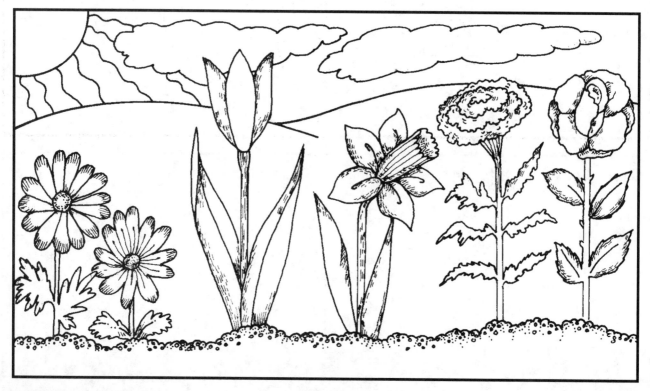

Flowers (cont.)

Flower Identification Sheet

Parts of a Flower

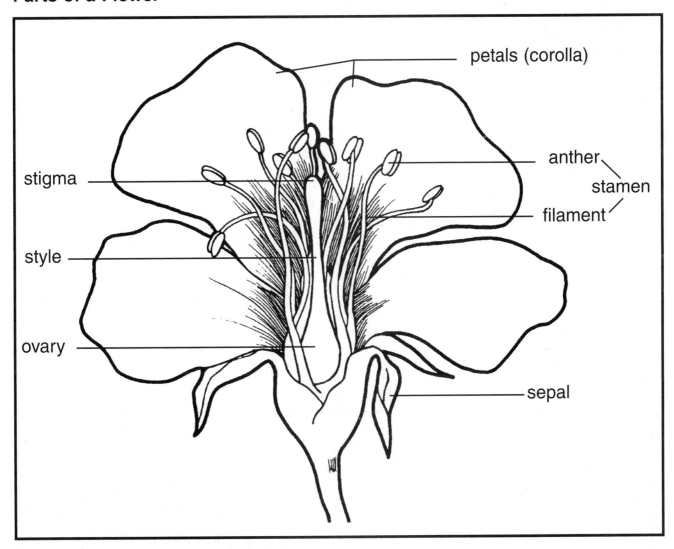

Flowers (cont.)

Data Capture Sheet

Use transparent tape to attach your flower inside this frame.

Stems

Learn about the function of stems.

Materials

- celery stalk
- glass
- dark food coloring

Procedure

1. Put a stalk of celery in a glass of colored water. Leave it in the glass for one day.

2. Observe what happens. Draw pictures in the BEFORE and AFTER boxes to show the results.

BEFORE

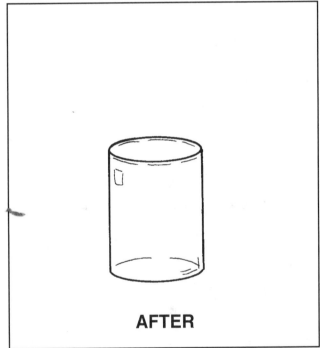

AFTER

3. Write why you think this happened. _____

_____

_____

_____

_____

_____

The Big Why

Stems carry water and minerals from the roots to the leaves. They carry the materials in the leaves to all parts of the plant. Stems also hold the leaves and flowers up in the air so they can get light.

How Does Your Garden Grow?

Learn about the growth of seeds.

Materials

- jar with top
- paper towels
- data-capture sheet (page 223)
- seeds (e.g., bean, pea, lentil, flower, vegetable)
- water

Procedure

1. Choose ten different kinds of seeds. Record the seeds you chose on your data-capture sheet.

2. Soak your seeds in water overnight.

3. Prepare the jar. Cut two paper towels to the height of the jar. Cut the length so that the top of the paper fits just to the rim of the jar top.

4. Wet the inside of the jar. Line the jar with the paper towels. The dampness inside the jar should help the paper towels to stick to the jar.

5. Put 1" (2.5 cm) of water into the jar.

6. Carefully tuck each seed between the toweling near the top of the jar and screw on the lid.

7. Watch the seeds daily. Add a little water if necessary. Be sure to keep the toweling moist.

8. Draw a picture of your seedlings every 2-3 days on your data-capture sheet.

9. Do some research about angiosperms and gymnosperms. Examine your seeds to determine if they are angiosperms or gymnosperms.

10. Record the differences on your data-capture sheet.

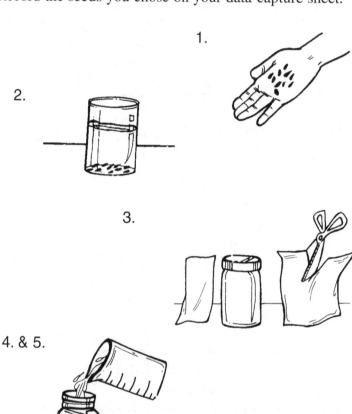

How Does Your Garden Grow? (cont.)

Data-Capture Sheet

Draw and label your seeds.

Measure and record the length of the seed tails.

Record the progress of your seeds.

Which seeds sprouted first? _____

Which sprouted next? _____

Which sprouted last? _____

What does this experiment tell you about angiosperms and gymnosperms?

_____

It's Not Easy Being Green

Materials

- two green plants
- petroleum jelly
- data-capture sheet (page 225)

Procedure

1. Place the two plants next to each other in the sun.

2. Carefully rub the petroleum jelly on all the leaves of one of the green plants. Be sure to coat both the tops and bottoms of the leaves.

3. Observe your plants every other day for two weeks.

4. Record the results of your plants' progress on your data-capture sheet.

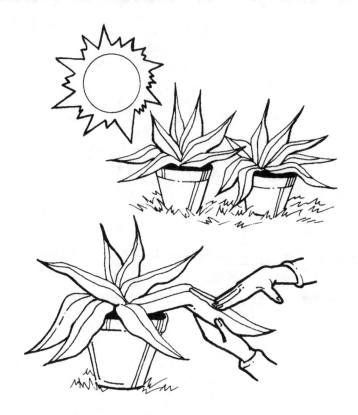

The Big Why

Why are some plants green? Chloroplasts are responsible for the green color in plants, but not all plants contain chloroplasts. Plants which are not green do not have chloroplasts. Only green plants produce their own food. Chloroplasts contain the substance chlorophyll, which is green. Chlorophyll plays an important part in the food-making process (photosynthesis) of a plant. *Photo* means light, and *synthesis* means to combine simple elements into a more complex one. Simply said, photosynthesis is the plant using light to make its own food. During photosynthesis, light from the sun is captured by the chloroplasts as light energy. The light energy combines with the water and carbon dioxide found in the cell and reacts to make glucose and oxygen.

$$\text{water} + \text{carbon dioxide} \xrightarrow{\text{light energy}} \text{glucose (sugar)} + \text{oxygen}$$

It's Not Easy Being Green (cont.)

Data-Capture Sheet

Draw a picture every other day of your plants and comment about what happened to your plants at the end of your experience.

Day 1

Day 3

Day 5

Day 7

Day 9

Day 11

What happened? _____

_____

_____

_____

_____

_____

Cardinal Points

There are four directions that are of prime importance when we learn our way around the world in which we live. These directions are north, south, east, and west, and they are sometimes referred to as the four cardinal points. Cardinal points are shown on maps by the use of a compass rose.

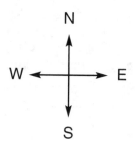

There are several ways to make a compass rose.

North and south indicators are often longer than east and west indicators.

Fill in the direction words that are missing.

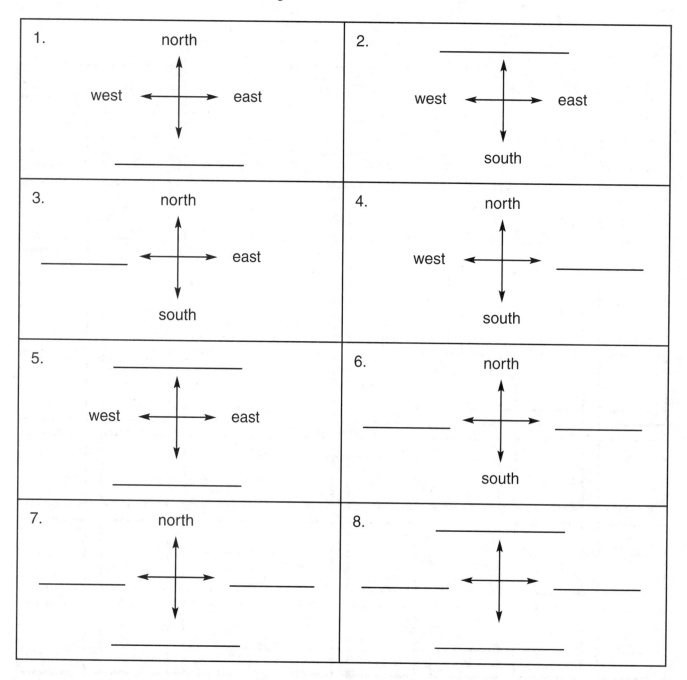

Through the Squares

Can you find your way through the squares by following the directions? Color your path as you go.
Write your name in the square where you finish.

1. Start above the square marked start here.

2. Go south 5 squares.

3. Go east 2 squares.

4. Go north 3 squares.

5. Go east 4 squares.

6. Go south 2 squares.

7. Go west 3 squares.

8. Go south 3 squares.

9. Go west 4 squares.

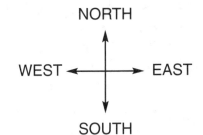

Start here.

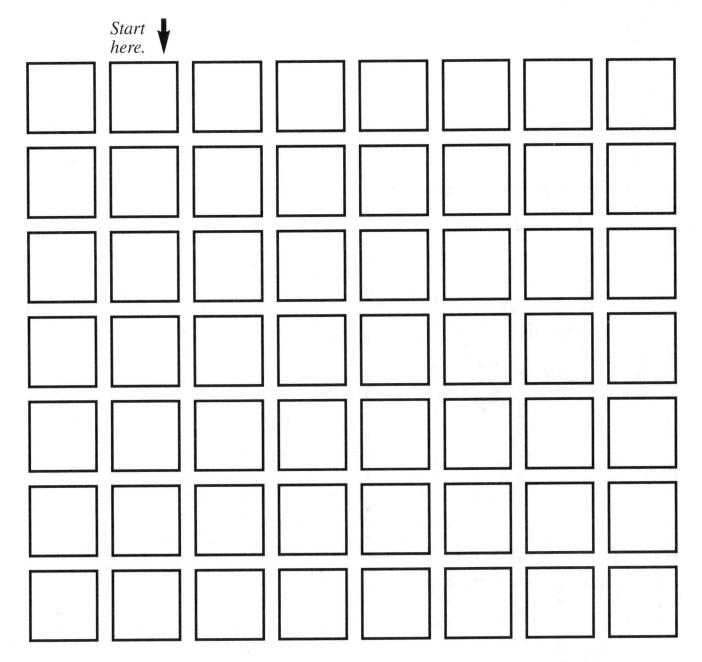

Intermediate Points

You are familiar with the four cardinal points used to indicate the primary directions. There are times when directions cannot be given using simply north, south, east, or west. You need to be able to show points that come between the four primary directions.

Intermediate points give a map maker just such a tool. Study the compass rose on the right. As you can see, the new direction words are made by combining the names of the cardinal points.

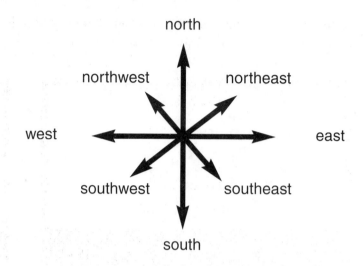

Directions

Using cardinal and intermediate points, write the locations represented by the numbers in the box on the left.

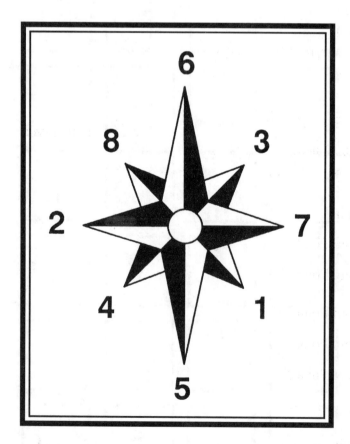

1. _____

2. _____

3. _____

4. _____

5. _____

6. north _____

7. _____

8. _____

Scale

Map makers can make things on a map larger or smaller than they really are. They can do this by using a map scale. A map scale shows us a way to measure distance. We are told by the scale what kind of measurement equals what kind of distance.

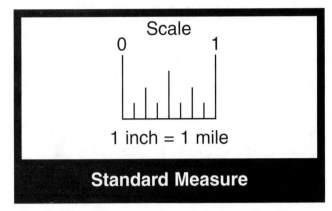

Standard Measure

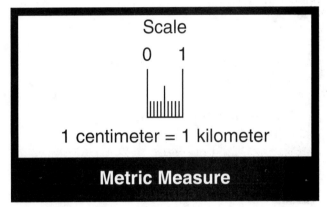

Metric Measure

Look at this scale. One inch represents one mile. A road five miles long can be shown on the map as five inches. A road 10 miles long can be shown as 10 inches.

Look at this scale. One centimeter stands for 1 kilometer. A road five kilometers long can be shown on the map as five centimeters. A road 10 kilometers long can be shown as 10 centimeters.

Directions

Use the scales on this page to complete the activities below.

1. Point A is   _____ miles from Point F.

   _____ kilometers from Point E.

   _____ kilometers from Point C.

2. Point B is   _____ kilometers from Point A.

   _____ kilometers from Point G.

   _____ kilometers from Point E.

3. Point H is   _____ miles from Point D.

   _____ miles from Point A.

   _____ miles from Point F.

How Far?

Directions

Use this map scale and metric ruler to answer the distance questions on this page.

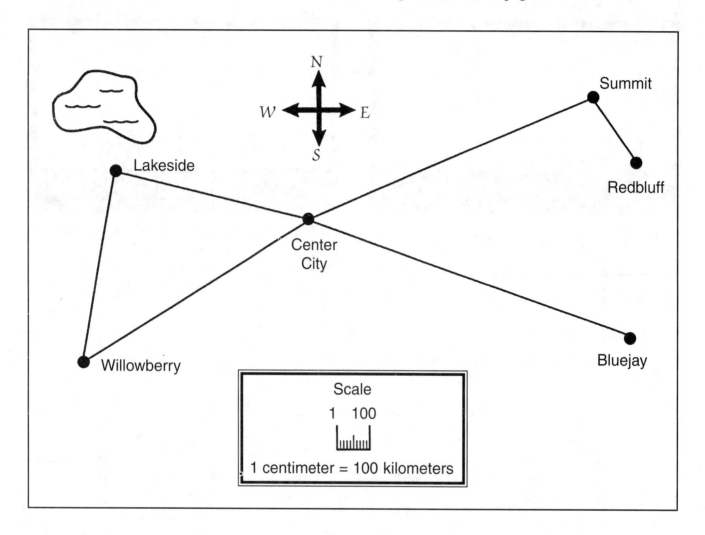

1. Center City is _____ kilometers from Bluejay.

2. Summit is _____ kilometers from Redbluff.

3. Willowberry is _____ kilometers from Lakeside.

4. Bluejay is _____ kilometers from Lakeside.

5. Summit is _____ kilometers from Center City.

6. Center City is _____ kilometers from Lakeside.

7. Willowberry is _____ kilometers from Summit.

8. Center City is _____ kilometers from Willowberry.

How to Measure

When you measure distances using a map scale, you can measure several different ways. The easiest and most accurate way is to use a standard-measure or metric-measure ruler.

You can also use a piece of string, paper, the joints of your fingers, a pencil or pen, or other things that could help you mark size.

Once you have chosen your measurement, place it along the imaginary or real line between the distances you want to measure.

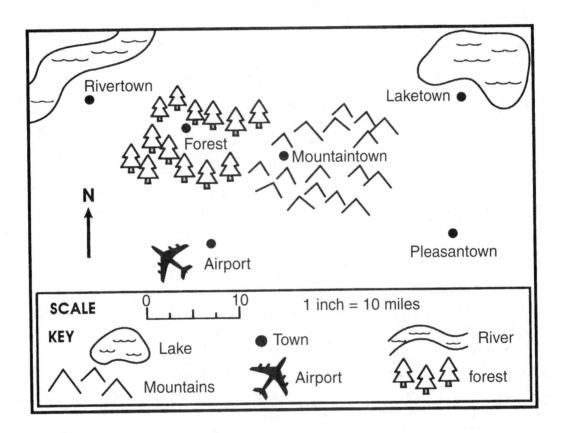

Directions

Find the distance in miles between the following places:

1. Rivertown and the airport _____

2. Mountaintown and the forest_____

3. Rivertown and Laketown_____

4. Mountaintown and Pleasantown _____

5. Laketown and Mountaintown _____

6. Rivertown and the forest _____

I've Got the Key!

Map makers draw the symbols that are in a map key. The map key explains what each symbol represents.

Directions

Look at this map and the map key. Use them to answer **true** or **false** for the statements below. If a statement is false, write the correct answer on the back of this paper.

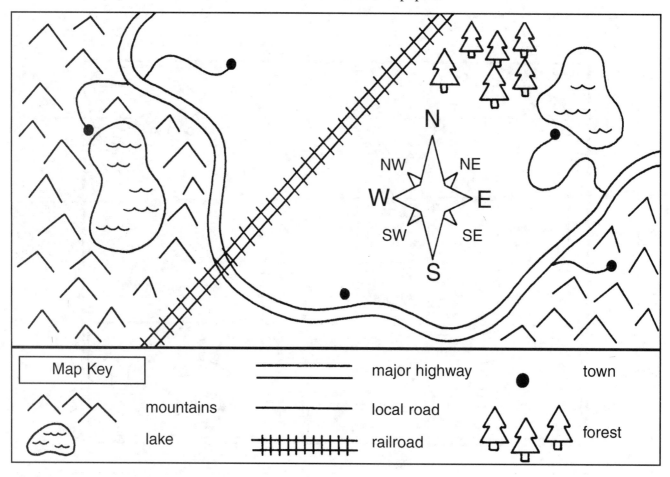

1. _____ A railroad track runs southwest to northeast.

2. _____ Mountains cover the northern section of the map.

3. _____ A lake and a forest are in the southeast.

4. _____ All towns can be reached by the major highway.

5. _____ There are towns along the railroad track.

6. _____ There is a large forest east of the lake and west of the railroad.

7. _____ The southernmost town is next to the major highway.

Using Grids

A grid is an arrangement of blocks that are made by vertical and horizontal lines intersecting on a page. Numbers and letters are used on the grid to help you name the blocks. You can find something on a grid by putting a finger of your right hand on a number and a finger of your left hand on a letter. Then, slide your fingers together until they meet. When grid points are identified, the letter is written before the number.

Grid A

	1	2	3	4
A	white	yellow	orange	gold
B	pink	green	tan	red
C	blue	purple	brown	silver
D	black	ivory	gray	lavender

Grid B

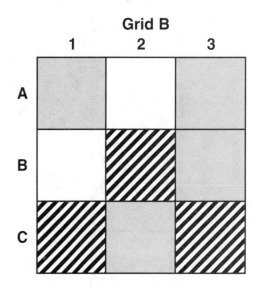

Directions

1. Use grid A to name each of the following colors:

   A1 _____   D3 _____   B4 _____   D2 _____

   C4 _____   A2 _____   D1 _____   C2 _____

   B3 _____   A4 _____   C3 _____   B1 _____

   D4 _____   B2 _____   A3 _____   C1 _____

2. Use grid B to answer these questions.

   Which blocks are shaded?   _____

   Which blocks are striped?   _____

   Which blocks are unmarked?   _____

Where in This City?

Directions

Use the grid on the city map to find the places listed at the bottom of the page. Write the letter before the number for each place you find.

1. Medical Center _____

2. Machinery Warehouse _____

3. The Mall Shops _____, _____, and _____

4. Elementary School _____

5. Sammy's Diner _____

6. Green Park _____, _____, _____, and _____

7. Wilson's Factory _____, _____

8. City Zoo _____ and _____

9. City Bank _____

10. Town Hall _____

11. Ball Field _____

12. Arcade _____

13. Fire Station _____

14. Post Office _____

15. Grocery Store _____

16. High School _____

Your Map, Your Key

Directions

Create your own map on this page. Add map key symbols. Draw a compass rose on your map, too.

Map Key

The Equator and Hemispheres

The earth is divided into two parts by an imaginary line called the equator. The part of the earth that is north of the equator is called the Northern Hemisphere. The part of the earth that is south of the equator is called the Southern Hemisphere.

The equator is like an imaginary line that divides the sphere of the earth into two half spheres, or hemispheres.

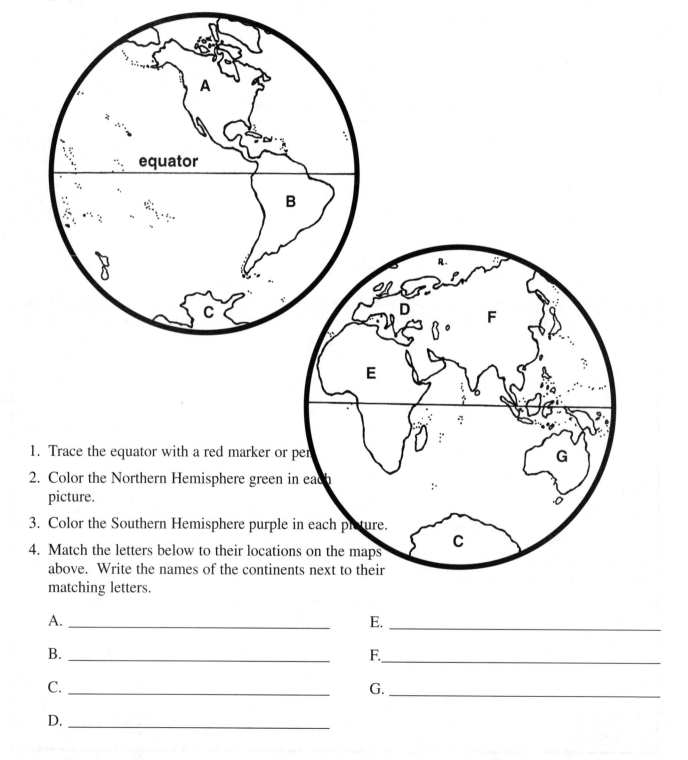

1. Trace the equator with a red marker or pen.

2. Color the Northern Hemisphere green in each picture.

3. Color the Southern Hemisphere purple in each picture.

4. Match the letters below to their locations on the maps above. Write the names of the continents next to their matching letters.

A. _____   E. _____

B. _____   F._____

C. _____   G. _____

D. _____

Where Is It?

Use the hemisphere maps on this page to help you locate the correct hemispheres for the places listed below.

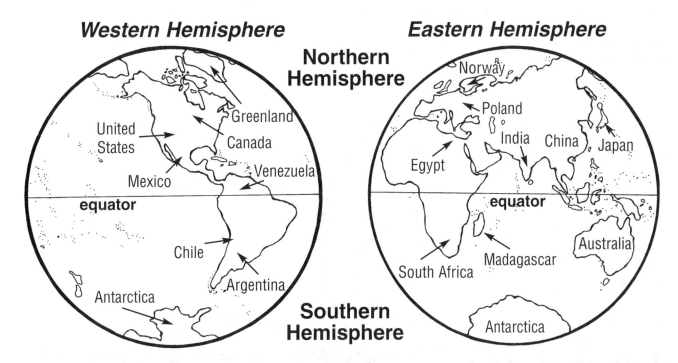

Hemisphere Location Chart		
Place	*Hemisphere (Northern or Southern)*	*Hemisphere (Eastern or Western)*
1. South Africa		
2. Norway		
3. Venezuela		
4. Canada		
5. Japan		
6. Mexico		
7. China		
8. Egypt		
9. United States		
10. Argentina		
11. Poland		
12. Greenland		
13. India		
14. Chile		
15. Madagascar		
16. Australia		

Latitude and Longitude

You can find places in the world by knowing how to read latitude and longitude lines. **Latitude** and **longitude** lines (also called **meridian** lines) are imaginary lines that divide the earth. You have already learned one of these lines—the equator. The equator is the main line of latitude. The **prime meridian** is the main line of longitude.

Latitude

Latitude lines run from west to east. They measure distances north and south of the equator.

The equator cuts the world into north and south latitude. The equator is marked 0 degrees. The latitude lines north of the equator are marked N (degrees north) and the latitude lines south of the equator are marked S (degrees south).

Longitude

Longitude lines run from north to south, pole to pole. They measure distances west and east of the prime meridian.

The prime meridian cuts the world into west and east longitudes. The longitude lines west of the prime meridian are marked W (degrees west) and the longitude lines east of the prime meridian are marked E (degrees east).

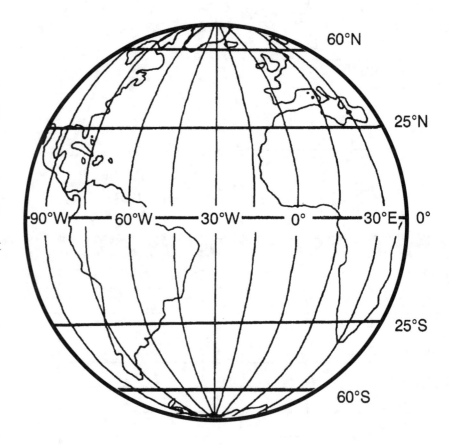

1. Which lines run from west to east? _____

2. Which lines run from north to south? _____

3. The equator is a line of (latitude or longitude)_____.

4. The prime meridian is a line of (latitude or longitude) _____.

Latitude and Longitude (cont.)

The intersection of the Earth's latitude and longitude lines form a grid. All of these lines have degree markings. If you know the degrees of latitude and longitude of a certain place, you can easily find it on a map.

The map of Colorado below shows the latitude and longitude lines that divide the state. Use the map to complete the activity at the bottom of the page.

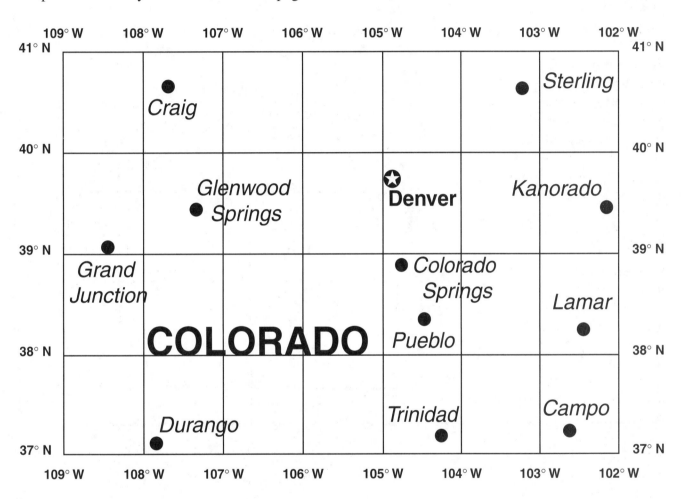

Which city is near each of these latitude/longitude lines?

1. 39°N, 108°W?_____

2. 41°N, 103°W?_____

3. 40°N, 105°W?_____

4. 38°N, 102°W?_____

5. 37°N, 108°W?_____

6. 39°N, 105°W?_____

7. 39°N, 107°W?_____

8. 37°N, 103°W?_____

9. 41°N, 108°W?_____

10. 39°N, 102°W?_____

Continents and Oceans

Use the following map to answer the questions on this page.

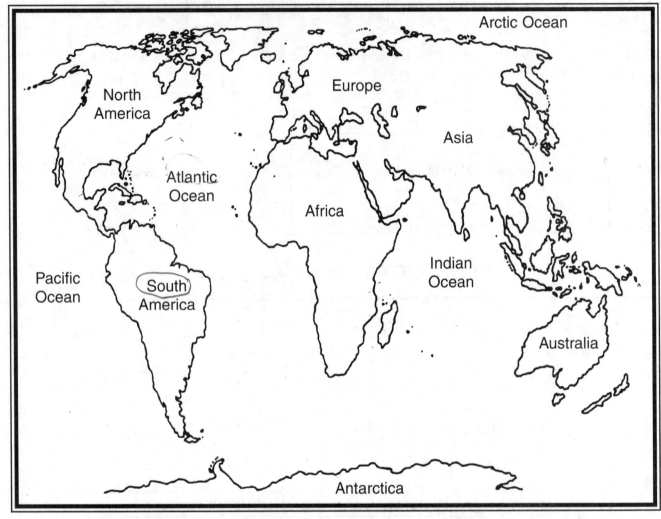

North
America

Europe

Asia

Arctic Ocean

Atlantic
Ocean

Africa

Pacific
Ocean

South
America

Indian
Ocean

Australia

Antarctica

1. The largest areas of land in the world are called continents. There are seven continents. Which continent do you live on?

   _____

2. The largest areas of water in the world are called oceans. There are four main oceans. Which ocean is closest to you?

   _____

3. What are the names of the seven continents?

   _____   _____

   _____   _____

   _____   _____

4. What are the names of the four major oceans?

   _____   _____

   _____   _____

Test Your Map Skills

I LOVE My Grandma

Use the map on this page for the activity on pages 242 and 243.

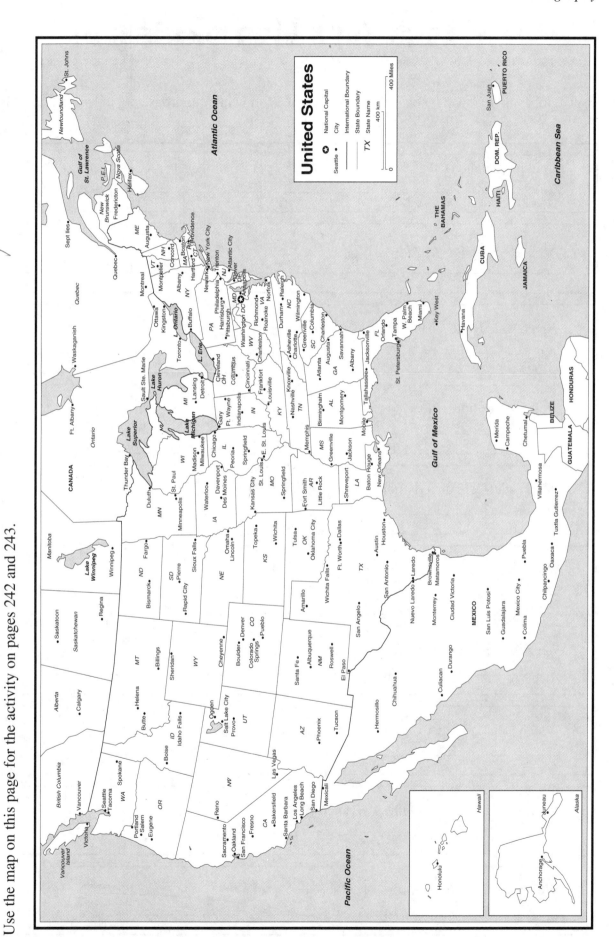

Test Your Map Skills (cont.)

Use a globe and the map on page 241 to answer the following questions.

1. Which mainland state is the farthest south?

   _____

2. Which state is the largest?

   _____

3. Which state is the smallest?

   _____

4. Which states border Iowa?

   _____

5. Which states are directly north of the Oklahoma border?

   _____

6. Which states have shorelines on the Gulf of Mexico?

   _____

7. Which state is made up of eight islands?

   _____

8. Which state is farther west—Colorado or Idaho?

   _____

9. What state is directly south of Wisconsin?

   _____

10. Which state is farther north—New York or Virginia?

   _____

Test Your Map Skills (cont.)

11. Which states border California?
_____

12. Which states begin with the letter M?
_____

13. Which states have shorelines on the Atlantic Ocean?
_____

14. Which states have shorelines on the Pacific Ocean?
_____

15. Which states have shorelines on the Great Lakes?
_____

16. Which state reaches farthest west?
_____

17. Which state is the farthest north?
_____

18. Which states border on Mexico?
_____

19. Which states border on Canada?
_____

20. Which island has the largest United States city on it?
_____

Geography Genius

How well do you know your world geography? As you play Geography Genius you will learn more about land formations, bodies of water, and places around the world.

Preparation

Cut out the rules below and the individual cards (pages 245–258).

(**Note:** For durability, you may wish to copy the game cards, rules, and answer key onto card stock, laminate all pieces, and store them in a box. If several groups are to play at the same time, make enough copies of the rules and the answer key so that each group has its own rule box and answer key.)

Rules for Geography Genius

This game is for three or four players and one judge.

1. The judge shuffles the cards and spreads them face down on the table.

2. The player to the judge's left goes first.

3. The first player takes a card, reads aloud the card number and question, and answers the question.

4. The judge checks the answer with the answer key.

5. Players earn points by keeping cards for questions they have answered correctly. When a player answers a question incorrectly, the card is shuffled back into the card pile to be used again.

6. When the game time is over or when all cards have been used, players count their cards. The player with the most cards is the winner.

1.

A man-made channel filled with water and used for boat transportation or for irrigation is called a _____.

2.

A deep, narrow gorge with high, steep sides that has been cut by running water is called a _____.

3.

A word meaning elevation or height above sea level is _____.

4.

The entire area that is drained by a large river is called a _____ _____.

5.

What word refers to a bay, cove, or other recess along the coast?

6.

What do we call the part of a river where it empties into a large body of water?

7.

An area of land that gets very little rainfall and has little plant life is called a _____.

8.

When a river empties into a larger body of water, it forms a triangle-shaped area of mud, sand, and silt known as a _____.

9.

When we measure the degree of hotness or coldness of an environment, we are measuring the _____.

10.

Moisture that falls from the clouds as sleet, rain, snow, or hail is known as _____.

11.

A small river that flows into a larger one is called a _____.

12.

A stream or other body of water where a river begins is called the river's _____.

13.

What landform is completely surrounded by water?

14.

What landform is surrounded by water on three sides?

15.

The periodic rise and fall of the water level of the ocean is called the _____.

16.

The rise and fall of the tide is caused by the gravitational pull of the _____.

17.

The point on a mountain above which there is snow all year round is called the _____ _____.

18.

What word is defined as a narrow passageway of water that connects two large bodies of water?

19.

What do we call the highest point of a hill or a mountain?

20.

A _____ is a large stream of water of natural origin which drains an area of land and empties into another body of water.

21.

Low, spongy ground that is too wet for farming but has abundant plant and animal life is called a _____.

22.

The point on a mountain above which no trees will grow because of the cold temperature is called the _____ _____.

23.

The average level of the ocean's surface as measured along the shoreline is known as _____ _____.

24.

A flat, elevated region of land is known as tableland or a _____.

25.

Useful materials that are found in nature such as water, minerals, and trees are called _____ _____.

26.

A small, still body of water that is smaller than a lake is called a _____.

27.

The vast area of natural grassland in the middle part of the United States is called the _____.

28.

The part of a river or stream where the water flows swiftly over rocks is called the _____.

29.

A cone-shaped mountain formed by eruption of molten rock, cinders and steam is called a _____.

30.

What is the general term for all growing plants?

31.

A _____ is a bank beside a stream or river created to prevent flooding.

32.

Imaginary lines that are used to help locate places and objects are called lines of _____ and _____.

33.

What is the imaginary line that divides the Northern Hemisphere from the Southern Hemisphere?

34.

A very large ocean inlet such as the one that separates Florida from Mexico is called a _____.

35.

The wearing away of soil and rock by wind and water is called _____.

36.

When someone recycles newspapers, cans, and plastic containers, he or she is helping to save natural resources by practicing _____.

37.

A book of maps is called an _____.

38.

The portion of a continent that is submerged beneath the ocean is called the _____ _____.

39.

The bowl-shaped depression at the top of a volcano is called a _____.

40.

The line where the earth and sky seem to meet is called the _____.

41.

A hill or a ridge of sand that is piled up by the wind is called a _____.

42.

A narrow piece of land that joins two larger areas of land is called an _____.

43.

The largest bodies of land on the earth are called _____.

44.

Name the largest continent.

45.

Name the smallest continent.

46.

On which continent is Canada located?

47.

What do we mean when we say the "contiguous" 48 states? Name the two U.S. states that are not "contiguous."

48.

What do we call a person who follows a career of mapmaking?

49.

Name the "grand" natural site in the western U.S. where the Colorado River flows.

50.

This large lake in the western U.S. has no outlet, loses water only through evaporation, and is called the _____ _____ _____.

51.

On which of the Hawaiian Islands is the capital city of Honolulu located?

52.

Name the largest island in the Hawaiian Islands group.

53.

Name the longest river in the U.S.

54.

Name the Great Lakes.

55.

The lowest place in the U.S. is in California. Name this valley.

56.

What American desert is located in Southern California?

57.

The deepest lake in the U.S. is almost 2,000 feet deep. It is in Oregon. Name this lake.

58.

The place in the world which receives the most rain is in the U.S. state of _____.

59.

On the east the U.S. is bordered by an ocean. On the west the U.S. is bordered by an ocean. Name these oceans.

60.

New York City, the largest city in the U.S., is located at the mouth of what river?

554

61.

The world's second largest country is located in North America. Name this country.

62.

The world's second largest lake is in North America. Name this lake.

63.

The second largest lake in the world is Lake Superior. What two countries border on this lake?

64.

What famous waterfall is located on the river that connects Lake Erie and Lake Ontario?

65.

If one travels across the Great Lakes from west to east, on which lake will one begin the trip?

66.

All of the 48 contiguous states border at least two other states except for one. Name this state that borders only one other U.S. state.

67.

The U.S. is divided into 50 states. Canada is divided into two territories and ten _____.

68.

What large U.S. river flows east and empties into the Mississippi River at St. Louis, Missouri?

69.

Name the seaway that connects the Great Lakes with the Atlantic Ocean.

70.

The city of Chicago is located on the shore of what body of water?

71.

What major U.S. river flows west and empties into the Mississippi River at Cairo, Illinois?

72.

The Rocky Mountain ridge that separates rivers that flow west to the Pacific and rivers that flow east to the Atlantic is called the _____ _____.

73.

Which Great Lake is the smallest in length and width?

74.

The best-known swamp in the U.S. is a national park in Florida. Name this swamp.

75.

Which U.S. state has a coastline on both the Atlantic Ocean and the Gulf of Mexico?

76.

Which mountain chain in the United States has the highest mountains— the Rocky Mountains or the Appalachian Mountains?

77.

Name the river that separates Texas from Mexico.

78.

What large body of water is bordered by Texas, Louisiana, Mississippi, Alabama, and Florida?

79.

What large island is located approximately 200 miles from Miami, Florida?

80.

Which of these California cities is closest to the Mexican border: Los Angeles, San Francisco, or San Diego?

556

81.

The Yucatan is a land area of Mexico. Is the Yucatan a mountain, a desert, or a peninsula?

82.

Baja California is a long, narrow peninsula that is part of Mexico. What U.S. state borders this peninsula on its north?

83.

If you were visiting the states of Sonora and Chihuahua, you would be in what country?

84.

The people of Mexico and other countries of Central America speak what language?

85.

What is the capital of Mexico?

86.

If you fly due south from New York City and you land in Brazil, on what continent will you be standing?

87.

The second longest river of the world is in South America. Name this river.

88.

Which country of South America has the largest area?

89.

Which country of South America is the second largest in area?

90.

Name the very high mountain range that runs 4,000 miles down the west coast of South America.

91.

What animal found in South America's Andes Mountains has been tamed to carry both people and materials?

92.

The world's largest waterfall is Angel Falls. Name the country and continent where you would go to see this famous waterfall.

93.

The world's highest city is 9,343 feet above sea level and is the capital of Ecuador in South America. Name this capital city.

94.

The driest place in the world is the Atacama Desert in a long, narrow South American country that borders Argentina. Name this country.

95.

If you left South America and sailed east along the equator, you would come to what continent?

96.

The longest river in the world is the _____ River on the continent of _____.

97.

The highest mountain in Africa is in Tanzania. Name this mountain.

98.

The largest city in Africa is the capital of Egypt. Name this capital city.

99.

Name the large body of water that borders Africa on the north.

100.

Egypt has coastline on what two seas?

101.

Africa is bordered by the _____ Ocean on the west and by the _____ Ocean on the east.

102.

The world's largest desert covers much of Northern Africa. Name this desert.

103.

Name the southernmost country of Africa.

104.

The country of South Africa is well-known for mining what valuable gems?

105.

If you were visiting the African savannah, would you be in a jungle or grassland?

106.

Name the largest country of Africa.

107.

Liberia, a country on the west coast of Africa has a capital city that is named for a U.S. President. Name this city.

108.

Name the long, narrow sea that separates Africa from the Middle East country of Saudi Arabia.

109.

Name the canal that is a passageway between the Mediterranean Sea and the Red Sea.

110.

Name the waterway through which ships pass from the Mediterranean Sea into the Atlantic Ocean.

111.

The Strait of Gibraltar separates the African country of _____ and the European country of _____.

112.

You are traveling by boat from Greece westward to Turkey. What small sea are you crossing?

113.

Which two countries of Europe are separated by the English Channel?

114.

What boot-shaped country of Europe is a peninsula that sticks out into the Mediterranean Sea?

115.

The Iberian Peninsula is surrounded by ocean on three sides. What two European countries make up this peninsula?

116.

In the Norwegian Sea, about halfway between Norway and Greenland, is the island nation of _____.

117.

The two most well-known cities of Europe are _____, the capital of England, and _____, the capital of France.

118.

Iceland, a large island in the North Atlantic Ocean is a part of what continent?

119.

Name the four countries that make up the area known as Scandinavia.

120.

Name the four countries that make up the area known as Great Britain.

121.

What mountains separate Europe from Asia?

122.

What ocean lies to the south of Asia?

123.

The largest country in Asia is also the largest country in the world. Name this country.

124.

Name the second largest country of Asia.

125.

What large desert lies in northern China and southern Mongolia?

126.

Name the large sea that borders Turkey on its north.

127.

The world's highest mountain is in Asia. Name this mountain.

128.

The world's largest city in terms of population is _____, located in the small island nation of _____.

129.

What large gulf separates Saudi Arabia from Iran?

130.

Name the large country of southern Asia that is bordered on the east by the Bay of Bengal and on the west by the Arabian Sea.

131.

Mount Everest, the world's highest mountain, is in what Asian mountain chain?

132.

Name the capital of India.

133.

Name the capital of Russia.

134.

Name the capital of China.

135.

Name the capital of Japan.

136.

What is Japan's largest island?

137.

The Asian country of _____ has more people than any other country in the world.

138.

What name is often used to refer to Europe and Asia together?

139.

The Caspian Sea is bordered on three sides by Russia. What Asian country borders the Caspian Sea on the south?

140.

The Philippines is a country made up of a group of islands lying southeast of China. Name the capital of this island country.

Answer Key for "Geography Genius"

1. canal
2. canyon
3. altitude
4. river system
5. inlet
6. mouth
7. desert
8. delta
9. temperature
10. precipitation
11. tributary
12. source
13. island
14. peninsula
15. tide
16. moon
17. snow line
18. strait
19. summit or peak
20. river
21. swamp
22. tree line
23. sea level
24. mesa or plateau
25. natural resources
26. pond
27. prairie
28. rapids
29. volcano
30. flora or vegetation
31. levee or dike
32. latitude; longitude
33. equator
34. gulf
35. erosion

36. conservation
37. atlas
38. continental shelf
39. crater
40. horizon
41. dune
42. isthmus
43. continents
44. Asia
45. Australia
46. North America
47. states that touch each other; Alaska, Hawaii
48. cartographer
49. Grand Canyon
50. Great Salt Lake
51. Oahu
52. Hawaii
53. Mississippi River
54. Huron; Ontario; Michigan; Erie; Superior
55. Death Valley
56. Mojave Desert
57. Crater Lake
58. Hawaii
59. Atlantic; Pacific
60. Hudson River
61. Canada
62. Lake Superior
63. Canada; United States
64. Niagara Falls
65. Lake Superior
66. Maine
67. provinces
68. Missouri River
69. St. Lawrence Seaway
70. Lake Michigan

Answer Key for
"Geography Genius" (cont.)

71. Ohio River
72. Continental Divide
73. Lake Ontario
74. Everglades
75. Florida
76. Rocky Mountains
77. Rio Grande
78. Gulf of Mexico
79. Cuba
80. San Diego
81. peninsula
82. California
83. Mexico
84. Spanish
85. Mexico City
86. South America
87. Amazon River
88. Brazil
89. Argentina
90. Andes Mountains
91. llama
92. Venezuela, South America
93. Quito
94. Chile
95. Africa
96. Nile; Africa
97. Mount Kilimanjaro
98. Cairo
99. Mediterranean Sea
100. Mediterranean Sea; Red Sea
101. Atlantic; Indian
102. Sahara Desert
103. South Africa
104. diamonds
105. grassland

106. Sudan
107. Monrovia (named for James Monroe)
108. Red Sea
109. Suez Canal
110. Strait of Gibraltar
111. Morocco; Spain
112. Aegean Sea
113. France; England
114. Italy
115. Portugal and Spain
116. Iceland
117. London; Paris
118. Europe
119. Norway; Sweden; Finland; Denmark
120. England; Scotland; Northern Ireland; Wales
121. Ural Mountains
122. Indian Ocean
123. Russia
124. China
125. Gobi Desert
126. Black Sea
127. Mount Everest
128. Tokyo; Japan
129. Persian Gulf
130. India
131. Himalayan Mountains
132. New Delhi
133. Moscow
134. Beijing (formerly Peking)
135. Tokyo
136. Honshu
137. China
138. Eurasia
139. Iran
140. Manila

Impact

The first meetings between the Europeans and the natives of the "new world" resulted in change that profoundly affected both peoples. Some changes benefited the Europeans, but many changes had a negative impact on the Native Americans. Find out more about these changes by reading the paragraph below. Unscramble the groups of letters to make words that will complete each sentence. If you need help, use the Word Bank at the bottom of the page.

Some Europeans became (*eltwayh*) _____from all the gold,

silver, and fur that they obtained from the (*aitvNe*)_____Americans.

The European diet changed as new foods such as corn, (*ocaoc*) _____,

and (*mosetato*) _____were introduced.

The Native Americans, however, did not fare well. Contagious (*seidases*) _____

were passed on to them by the explorers. (*plamSlxo*) _____killed

close to (*enysvet-vfie*) _____percent of the Native Americans who

once inhabited both North and South (*rAicmea*) _____. Many

others died when they were forced to (*bolar*) _____in mines and on farms.

Their lives were changed forever as they acquired European (*solot*) _____,

weapons, and cooking (*slenutis*) _____; began to breed horses,

cows, and (*heicksnc*) _____; and grew wheat and rice.

Word Bank

diseases	Smallpox	utensils	tomatoes
tools	chickens	wealthy	America
Native	labor	cocoa	seventy-five

A Colonial Word Search

Test your knowledge of daily life in the 13 colonies. Use these clues to find the 20 words in the word search.

1. the only sport in which women could participate
2. metal from which some plates and cups were made
3. the only utensil used for eating
4. common method of punishment for criminals
5. type of home built by early Dutch settlers
6. plant used in making candles
7. girls embroidered these
8. they sold wares and spread news
9. cloth spun from the flax plant
10. dish made from wood or stale bread
11. children ages six to eight attended these
12. plant grown for its blue dye
13. windows were made by soaking cloth in this oil
14. a basic ingredient of soap
15. game in which metal rings were tossed at an iron stake
16. one page of letters fastened to a wooden frame
17. waist-length jacket worn by men
18. fried cornmeal bread
19. type of house with sloping roof
20. day of worship

o	a	l	p	p	l	i	n	s	e	e	d	m	n	i
s	t	o	s	e	y	c	u	t	a	p	i	h	d	n
f	x	h	r	w	e	e	s	i	m	p	e	u	u	d
o	o	t	e	t	v	s	t	o	c	k	s	o	g	i
e	m	a	l	e	a	k	e	u	b	o	c	f	o	g
y	a	b	d	r	e	a	d	q	h	o	g	e	u	o
r	t	b	d	b	a	t	d	o	u	b	l	e	t	w
r	r	a	e	x	u	i	h	e	u	n	e	n	i	l
e	e	s	p	o	o	n	v	l	c	r	b	b	n	j
b	n	d	e	b	e	g	d	c	m	o	o	d	a	a
y	c	z	r	t	p	f	m	y	j	h	q	z	x	o
a	h	e	f	l	j	o	h	n	n	y	c	a	k	e
b	e	g	d	a	m	e	s	c	h	o	o	l	u	k
r	r	h	t	s	a	m	p	l	e	r	s	n	r	l

Where Did It Happen?

For this activity you will need a United States and a European map with clearly marked latitude and longitude lines.

Draw a line to match each place with its grid point. Then write the matching points and answers to the questions at the bottom of the page.

London	47°N 71°W
West Point	36°N 80°W
Yorktown	41°N 74°W
Paris	37°N 76°W
Boston	35°N 82°W
Savannah	49°N 2°E
Cowpens	43°N 74°W
Guilford Courthouse	42°N 71°W
Quebec	32°N 81°W
Saratoga	51°N 0°(Prime Meridian)

1. Treaty that officially ended the Revolutionary War was signed here.

   Place _____   Grid Point_____

2. Cornwallis surrendered to Washington here.

   Place _____   Grid Point_____

3. In this place, Richard Montgomery and Benedict Arnold lost to the British.

   Place _____   Grid Point_____

4. This major Southern port was held by the British.

   Place _____   Grid Point_____

5. Victory here convinced France that the Americans could win in a war against the British.

   Place _____   Grid Point_____

6. Soon after this battle, Cornwallis decided to leave North Carolina.

   Place _____   Grid Point_____

7. This is where the taxes for the North American colonists were decided.

   Place _____   Grid Point_____

8. Patriots dressed as Indians and dumped tea into this city's harbor.

   Place _____   Grid Point_____

9. Benedict Arnold asked George Washington to give him command of this defensive post.

   Place _____   Grid Point_____

10. The riflemen of the Southern Army won a battle in this cattle-grazing area.

    Place _____   Grid Point_____

Frontier Words

Frontier living generated many new words that were commonly used by the pioneers. Figure out these words by reading the clues first. Then find the coordinates on the grid below.

Write the letter that is in that space on the proper lines. (To find the coordinates, go across the first number of spaces. From there, count up the second number of spaces.)

4	l	d	s	i	g	e	m	c	p	s	u	g	l	a	t
3	f	e	a	n	r	o	i	u	i	h	e	u	o	n	d
2	p	o	h	e	m	a	s	f	c	y	m	t	p	r	s
1	c	a	e	y	l	t	g	r	o	n	d	o	a	f	s
0	1	2	3	4	5	6	7	8	9	10	11	12	13	14	15

1. ___ ___ ___ ___ ___   a prairie sod house
   3,4 13,3 2,4 11,1 10,2

2. ___ ___ ___ ___ ___ ___ ___ ___ ___ ___ ___   also known as johnnycake
   8,4 9,1 5,3 4,3 15,3 2,2 2,4 5,4 6,4 14,2 7,2

3. ___ ___ ___ ___ ___ - ___ ___ ___ ___ ___ ___   they rushed to California to find gold
   8,2 12,1 8,1 15,4 4,1   4,3 7,3 10,1 3,1 5,3 10,4

4. ___ ___ ___ ___ ___   dried buffalo manure used for fires
   8,4 3,2 9,3 13,2 3,4

5. ___ ___ ___ ___ ___ ___ ___ ___ ___   settlers of the western frontier
   4,2 7,4 4,4 7,1 5,3 2,1 14,3 6,1 7,2

6. ___ ___ ___ ___   disease now known as malaria
   6,2 12,4 8,3 11,3

7. ___ ___ ___ ___ ___ ___ ___ ___   thieves who stole cattle
   5,3 11,4 15,2 6,1 13,4 2,3 8,1 15,1

8. prairie ___ ___ ___ ___ ___ ___ ___ ___   nickname for covered wagon
   7,2 1,1 10,3 2,2 9,1 14,3 3,1 5,3

Identify the Locations

For this activity you will need a United States map with clearly marked latitude and longitude lines.

In the two columns below, you will find places and grid points that will identify the locations of those places on a map. Draw a line to match each place with its grid point. Then write the pairs as answers to the questions at the bottom of the page.

Place	Latitude	Longitude
Ohio River	39°N	78°W
Chattanooga	39°N	83°W
Vicksburg	40°N	77°W
Kansas	37°N	77°W
Andersonville	38°N	100°W
Harpers Ferry	32°N	84°W
Richmond	32°N	81°W
Savannah	33°N	80°W
Gettysburg	32°N	91°W
Fort Sumter	35°N	85°W

1. Once crossed, slaves knew they were nearly free.

   Place _____   Grid Point_____

2. The Civil War began here.

   Place _____   Grid Point_____

3. This city served as the capital of the Confederacy.

   Place _____   Grid Point_____

4. John Brown tried to start a slave rebellion in this place.

   Place _____   Grid Point_____

5. This was the key city that guarded the Mississippi River.

   Place _____   Grid Point_____

6. An overcrowded prison was located in this Confederate camp.

   Place _____   Grid Point_____

7. This was an important battle in the Tennessee campaign.

   Place _____   Grid Point_____

8. This July battle was the turning point of the war.

   Place _____   Grid Point_____

9. The first case of popular sovereignty was tested in this place.

   Place _____   Grid Point_____

10. Sherman's march through Georgia ended in this place.

    Place _____   Grid Point_____

Time Zones and Daylight Savings

Use the information below to complete the activity on page 267.

Why is it that at the time many New Yorkers are enjoying a lunchtime meal, most Californians are eating their breakfast? Why is the United States, as well as the entire globe, divided up into various sections of time?

The divisions of time that surround the earth, known as time zones, clarified some of the problems that once plagued the modernizing world. For hundreds of years each town in the United States decided what the time would be. When the sun was directly overhead, casting no shadows, it was noon. Radios and televisions had not been invented, and telephones were not available yet. Travel was slow by horse and buggy, so it really was not much of a problem that each town was in charge of its own time. In fact, it worked quite well until the railroad was built. Can you imagine how hard it was to print train schedules of arrivals and departures when each town had a different time? This confusing problem was finally resolved in 1883 when the railroad helped devise the system of standard time. Standard time means that everyone in a certain region shares the same established time. Since time zones span great distances, it is no longer necessarily true that the sun will be directly above you at noon. Today, people set their clocks and watches according to the standard time instead of by the sun.

With the new "standard time," the United States was divided into four zones going from east to west—eastern standard time, central standard time, mountain time, and Pacific standard time. Later, when Alaska and Hawaii became part of our country, we added Yukon standard time, Alaska standard time, Bering standard time and Hawaii-Aleutian standard time to the group of time zones in the United States.

In 1884 a conference with countries from all over the globe joined together to develop a system of 24 time zones around the earth. Each segment or zone is 15 longitude degrees apart from the next. It takes the earth one hour to rotate these 15 degrees. Some time zone lines are not perfectly straight because it is often more convenient to follow state or town boundaries. There is an imaginary line in the Pacific Ocean at 180 degrees longitude where all the time zones begin and end. This international dateline is where each new day first begins.

When World War I broke out, a new custom was started in keeping time. During war time resources were scarce. In order to save the coal supplies (which were burned to make electricity), it was decided to move the clocks ahead one hour. This way, there would be more light at the end of the day, and people would not need to turn on their lights as early in the evening. Even after the war ended, daylight savings time continued because people enjoyed having more daylight during the summer months. For a while it was confusing since all the states did not practice daylight savings time. Today, almost every state in our country turns its clocks ahead one hour the first Sunday in April. On the first Sunday in November the clocks are turned back one hour. "Spring ahead—fall back" may be an easier way to remember which way to move the hands on your clocks.

So the next time you sit down to eat your lunch, think about what other meals students may be eating in time zones other than your own. Now that's food for thought!

Time Zone Riddle

Directions: Circle the correct answers to each of the statements. Enter that letter in the "Your Choice" box. Once you have all 14 answers, rearrange the letters to discover the answer to the riddle at the end of the puzzle. See the example below. Do not use the answer in the example to solve the puzzle!

	True	False	Your Choice
Example: The automobile industry invented our system of time.	K	S	*S*

	True	False	Your Choice
1. Each state must vote to determine whether they are to follow daylight savings time.	M	E	
2. Some of the irregular divisions exist on the map to avoid towns being split into two time zones.	N	P	
3. The continental U.S. has 4 time zones.	D	M	
4. Turn your clock back one hour in the fall when daylight savings is finished for the year.	A	C	
5. Daylight savings time was started during World War II to save fuel.	B	C	
6. There are 20 time zones in the world.	N	U	
7. After World War I ended, daylight savings time continued because people liked having the extra daylight.	I	T	
8. In 1884, representatives gathered to develop a standard system of time.	L	W	
9. It takes the earth one hour to rotate 15 degrees of longitude.	N	S	
10. If you never adjust your clocks to daylight savings time, you will be on time for about eight months of the year.	F	R	
11. When the sun is directly overhead, it must be 12:00 noon in all areas of the time zone.	L	D	
12. We turn our clocks ahead one hour in the spring.	H	D	
13. The U.S. government devised the first standardized system of time.	S	N	
14. The grand international dateline is where each new day begins.	E	N	

Unscramble all of the letters that you have collected in the "Your Choice" column and solve the following riddle. Do not include the example letter in the riddle answer.

What are two things a cowboy cannot eat for breakfast?

___ ___ ___ ___ ___   ___ ___ ___   ___ ___ ___ ___ ___ ___

Famous Faces of WWI

Match the names of the following people with their involvement in World War I. You may use a variety of resource materials to help you.

A. He wrote the words to a famous World War I song.

_____ Archduke Francis Ferdinand

B. His assassination initiated the beginning of World War I.

_____ Woodrow Wilson

C. He wore a black moustache, stood straight and rigid, and had been the bold leader of Germany since 1890.

_____ General Ferdinand Foch

D. He urged the passing of the League of Nations and wrote the famous Fourteen Points.

_____ Captain Eddie Rickenbacker

_____ Lt. Colonel Wise

E. He was chosen to be the commander in chief of the American Expeditionary Force.

F. He was the commander in chief of the French Army.

_____ George M. Cohan

G. He was named the Supreme Allied Commander.

_____ Hans Otto Bischoff

H. He was the commander of the British Fifth Army.

_____ Kaiser Wilhelm

I. He directed the German defense at Belleau Wood.

_____ General John "Black Jack" Pershing

J. His battalion had stopped the Germans at their closest point to Paris.

_____ General Sir Hubert Gough

K. He was America's leading ace of World War I.

_____ General Henri Pétain

Events of the Great War

Listed below are events that occurred during World War I. Create a time line and place each event on the line.

- President Wilson revealed his "Fourteen Points."
- First Armistice Day
- Belgium was invaded by Germany.

- United States declared war on Germany.
- Germans first used chlorine gas.
- British first used army tanks.

June 28, 1914   Archduke Francis Ferdinand was assassinated.

August 3, 1914   _____ .

October 30, 1914   Turkey joined the Central Powers.

April 22, 1915   _____ .

May 7, 1915   German submarine sank the *Lusitania*.

September 15, 1916   _____ .

December 5, 1916   The Allies finally stopped the Germans in the Battle of Verdun.

April 6, 1917   _____ .

November 7, 1917   The Bolsheviks took over Russia.

January 8, 1918   _____ .

September 26, 1918   Allies began their last attack on the Western Front.

November 11, 1918   _____ .

Extension:

On Armistice Day, the German army surrendered to the Allies. Armistice today is now called Veterans Day, and it is a time set aside to honor war veterans. Research this day and contact your local veterans groups for more information.

Time Line of World Events, 1933-1945

Use your knowledge of World War II and research skills to match the event with the correct date.

Event　　　　　　　　　　　　　　　　　　　　　　　　　**Date**

_____ 1. General Montgomery leads the Allies to a victory over the Axis troops in North Africa.

A. 1940

_____ 2. The Germans take over Austria.

B. 1933

_____ 3. Adolf Hitler becomes the leader of Germany.

C. 1945

_____ 4. Japanese planes bomb the United States naval base at Pearl Harbor.

D. 1941

E. 1944

_____ 5. The Japanese attack China.

F. 1937

_____ 6. Germany surrenders (V-E Day) and Japan surrenders (V-J Day).

G. 1938

_____ 7. Japan takes over the Philippines.

H. 1939

_____ 8. Poland is invaded by German and Soviet troops.

I. 1942

_____ 9. The Allies send invasion forces to Normandy, France.

J. 1943

_____10. Franklin D. Roosevelt is re-elected as president of the United States for a third term.

Now, use the dates and events that you matched above to construct a time line for World War II.

Time Line of World Events, 1933–1945

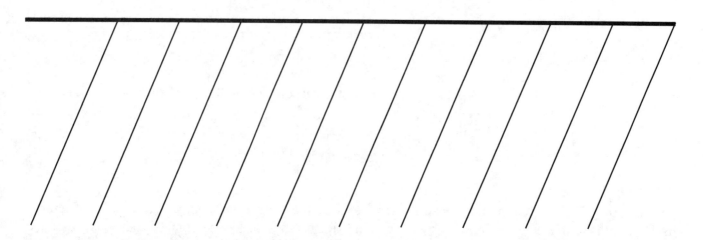

In the Know

This brief study guide lists, defines, and explains six documents that played an important role in the history of the Constitution. After you have studied, test your knowledge with a partner. One partner reads the name of each document aloud, while the other partner describes the term in as much detail as possible. Then trade roles. You can also play a matching or concentration game after cutting the cards apart.

Document	Explanation
Declaration of Independence	One of the most famous documents in the world, it officially declared the American colonies free and independent from British rule. It was signed into effect on July 4, 1776.
Articles of Confederation	During the Revolution, the thirteen states wrote a set of governing rules. This document unified them in their fight against the British. Each state had only one vote and the rules could not be changed unless every state agreed.
Virginia Plan	This document did away with the "one state—one vote" rule and suggested two houses of Congress. Edmund Randolph's plan further called for three branches of government—the Executive, the Legislative, and the Judicial.
Great Compromise	An alternate plan of electing officials was designed by a specially appointed committee. In this plan, Congress would have two houses. One house (Representatives) would be based on population and in the other house (Senate) each state was considered equal with two votes each.
Constitution	This is the basic set of laws for our nation. It contains rules for writing and passing the laws which affect every citizen. A group of 55 delegates wrote these provisions during a four-month period in 1787.
Bill of Rights	These first 10 amendments to the Constitution list those things the government cannot take away from its citizens. They protect the individual from the power of the government.

Which Came First?

Work with a partner. Read the following pairs and determine which came first. Circle the appropriate answer for each set of choices.

1. the Continental Congress | or | the Constitutional Convention

2. the War of 1813 | or | the Revolutionary War

3. James Madison | or | Ben Franklin

4. ratification by Rhode Island | or | ratification by New Hampshire

5. Constitution | or | Articles of Confederation

6. Whisky Rebellion | or | Shay's Rebellion

7. Federalists | or | Republican Party

8. Louisiana Purchase | or | Treaty of Ghent

9. Great Compromise | or | Virginia Plan

10. Capitol in Washington, D.C. | or | Capitol in Philadelphia

11. Bill of Rights | or | Constitution

12. ratification by New York | or | ratification by North Carolina

13. Preamble | or | Virginia Plan

14. U.S. freedom from England | or | U.S. becomes a nation

15. the Federalist Papers | or | Bill of Rights

16. Declaration of Independence | or | Constitutional Convention

17. "Star-Spangled Banner" | or | "Yankee Doodle"

18. Sedition Act | or | Embargo Act

Citizenship Test

People who apply to become United States citizens must answer 10 or 15 randomly selected questions about American history and government. Below are a few from the list of 100 possible questions. Could you pass the test?

1. What do the stripes on the American flag represent? _____

_____

_____

2. What country did we fight during the Revolutionary War? _____

3. What are the three branches of our government? _____

_____

4. Who becomes president should the president and vice president die?_____

5. What did the Emancipation Proclamation do? _____

_____

6. Who has the power to declare war? _____

7. What kind of government does the United States have? _____

8. What are the first 10 amendments to the Constitution called?_____

9. Name one right guaranteed by the first amendment. _____

10. Who was the first president of the United States? _____

11. How many U.S. Supreme Court justices are there? _____

12. Who helped the Pilgrims in the New World? _____

13. Which countries were our enemies during World War II? _____

14. Who is the Chief Justice of the U.S. Supreme Court? _____

15. How many amendments are there to the Constitution? _____

16. How many states are there today?_____

17. What are the colors of the American flag and what does each symbolize? _____

_____

_____

18. What are the duties of Congress? _____

_____

_____

What Do You Know?

Fill in the answers to the clues by using the word parts in the box. The number of groups of letters from the box to be used in each answer is shown in parentheses. The first answer has been done for you. (**Note:** The letter groups in the box are listed so that each group must be used once.)

A	A	AD	AR	BRU	CAR	COLN	CON
DE	DY	FE	GIN	VER	HO	DAMS	WASH
ING	I	IA	KA	LAN	LAS	LIN	LU
LU	MAD	NO	NON	NIX	O	Y	ON
ROO	SE	SON	TED	TER	GRESS	VELT	VIR
MOUNT	TON						

1. Theodore Roosevelt's nickname (2) __Teddy_____

2. The face on the quarter (3) _____

3. Franklin Roosevelt's middle name (3) _____

4. The father of the Constitution (3) _____

5. A month for celebrating presidents (4) _____

6. President whose father was also a president (2) _____

7. The capital of Hawaii (4) _____

8. A president and a peanut farmer (2) _____

9. The sixteenth president (2) _____

10. The first president to resign from office (2) _____

11. An original colony (3) _____

12. The home of George Washington (2 words) (3) _____

13. The state closest to Russia (3) _____

14. A face on Mount Rushmore (3) _____

15. The Senate and House of Representatives (2) _____

American Social Studies Trivia

1. What does *"e pluribus unum"* mean? _____

2. How long is a senator's term of office?_____

3. Which president is shown on the five-dollar bill? _____

4. Where is the Alamo?_____

5. During what years was the Civil War fought? _____

6. Who wrote "The Pledge of Allegiance"? _____

7. The president is chief of which branch of government? _____

8. Which president's former occupation was acting? _____

9. On the flag, what does red signify? _____

10. Who became president after Dwight D. Eisenhower?_____

11. Who invented the cotton gin? _____

12. Which was the last state to join the Union? _____

13. On the Statue of Liberty, is Miss Liberty carrying the torch in her left or her right hand? _____

14. Which English explorer sailed along the West Coast in 1579? _____

    _____

15. What is the official song of the president of the United States?_____

    _____

Famous Women

Match these women to their major accomplishments. Put the letter of the accomplishment before the corresponding name.

_____ 1. Harriet Tubman

_____ 2. Harriet Beecher Stowe

_____ 3. Grandma Moses

_____ 4. Juliette Gordon Low

_____ 5. Shirley Chisholm

_____ 6. Pearl S. Buck

_____ 7. Mary McLeod Bethune

_____ 8. Clara Barton

_____ 9. Louisa May Alcott

_____ 10. Susan B. Anthony

_____ 11. Jane Addams

_____ 12. Amelia Earhart

_____ 13. Helen Hayes

_____ 14. Helen Keller

_____ 15. Victoria C. Woodhull

A. social worker and humanitarian

B. primitive painter

C. novelist and reformer

D. stage and screen actress

E. author of _The Good Earth_

F. aviator

G. author of _Little Women_

H. educator who worked to improve educational opportunities for blacks

I. significant "conductor" of the Underground Railroad

J. first woman to run for president of the U.S.

K. first African American woman in the U.S. Congress

L. founded the Girl Scouts of America

M. founded the American Red Cross

N. overcame physical handicaps; helped thousands of handicapped people lead fuller lives

O. reformer and leader in the American women's suffrage movement

Presidents' First Names

Listed below are some last names of former presidents. Write each president's first name on the blank.

1. _____ Adams

2. _____ Eisenhower

3. _____ Reagan

4. _____ Jefferson

5. _____ Nixon

6. _____ Lincoln

7. _____ Carter

8. _____ Hoover

9. _____ Roosevelt

10. _____ Washington

11. _____ Coolidge

12. _____ Cleveland

13. _____ Grant

14. _____ Taylor

15. _____ Harrison

16. _____ Truman

17. _____ Buchanan

18. _____ Polk

19. _____ Garfield

20. _____ Johnson

Which President?

1. Which president was nicknamed "Honest Abe"? _____

2. Which president was called the "Father of the Constitution"?

   _____

3. Which president and his wife were the first to occupy the White House in Washington, D.C.? _____

4. Which future president was the author of the *Declaration of Independence*?

   _____

5. Which president was the only one to serve two nonconsecutive terms of office? _____

6. Which president was nicknamed "Old Rough and Ready"?

   _____

7. Which president was assassinated in Ford's Theater? _____

8. Which two presidents are buried in Arlington National Cemetery?

   _____

9. Which president served more than two terms? _____

10. Which president was in office when the White House was set on fire?

    _____

11. Which president was the grandson of another president?

    _____

12. Which president was the shortest? _____

13. Which president never married? _____

14. Which president was the first to talk to a man on the moon?

    _____

15. Which seven presidents were/are left-handed? _____

    _____

    _____

Answer Key

Page 313

photography, Mo-Qu

dinosaurs, Cu-Ex

Hawaii, Gy-Ju

chocolate, A-Cu

rattlesnakes, Qu-Ty

lightning, Ju-Mo

wildflowers, We-Z

computers, A-Cu

Beatles, The, A-Cu

volcanoes, Ty-We

space shuttle, Qu-Ty

gorillas, Ex-Gy

Page 314

1. fact
2. opinion
3. opinion
4. fact
5. fact
6. opinion
7. opinion
8. fact
9. fact
10. opinion

Page 321

Nouns:

1. summer time year
2. weather children swimming
3. schools people time vacation
4. days hours sunlight
5. pool beach lake
6. teacher Mr. Dawson Metropolitan Museum of Art New York City July
7. care concern visitors
8. friends Tim Carol Statue of Liberty Ellis Island
9. scent flowers Central Park lunch
10. hamburgers grill backyard

Person:

Ms. Lizt

Dr. Forest

Place:

France

city

building

Texas

Thing:

clouds

shoelaces

bicycles

sounds

glasses

table

Idea:

happiness

science

loyalty

fairness

love

pain

Page 322

1. action
2. action
3. linking
4. linking
5. linking
6. action
7. linking
8. action
9. action
10. action
11. action
12. linking
13. linking
14. linking

Page 324

A.1. beautiful
2. slowly
3. thinly
4. very

B.1. pretty
2. big
3. green
4. happy
5. thin

6. round
7. wet
8. excellent
9. broken
10. smelly

C.1. slowly
2. quickly
3. quickly
4. down
5. joyfully
6. sloppily
7. closely
8. loudly
9. badly
10. wildly

Page 327

1. All birds have feathers, wings, and beaks.
2. My sister is sleepy, grumpy, and clueless.
3. I would have done my homework, but I was abducted by aliens, was left in Siberia, and had to wait for the Marines to rescue me.
4. I ordered a pizza with cheese, pickles, and sliced cherries.
5. Please go to the store and get flypaper, chopsticks, and kumquats.
6. I went to the door with rollers in my hair, a mud mask on my face, and wearing my bathrobe.
7. My dog has brown spots, a short tail, and fuzzy feet.
8. My little brother can't go anywhere without his blanket, his stuffed duck, and his rabbit's foot key chain.
9. When I go to college, I am taking a stereo, a microwave, and a treadmill.
10. For her birthday, Mindy wants some edible flowers, sparkly socks, and a pony.

Answer Key (cont.)

1. My rabbit has long, floppy ears.
2. A large, heavy sparrow could weigh 200 pounds.
3. My teacher has a green, pointy nose.
4. My dad used to have curly, frizzy hair.
5. A friendly, playful giraffe ate all my spaghetti.

Page 328

A.
1. My parents bought their first home on January 13, 1976.
2. My mon was born on March 31, 1948.
3. We went to Disneyland on Tuesday, August 18, and it was really crowded!
4. My brother's birthday is November 17, 1973.
5. On Saturday, April 19, we are flying to my grandma's house.
6. I get my tonsils out on Monday, September 16, and then I can eat lots of ice cream.
7. Our puppies were born on February 14, 1997.
8. It rained cats and dogs on January 18, 1995.

C.
1. Yesterday, I met a girl from Canberra, Australia.
2. A hurricane went on shore at Acapulco, Mexico.
3. I've never been to Seattle, Washington.
4. It can get very cold in Buffalo, New York.
5. Yesterday I received e-mail from Bordeaux, France.
6. Many movie stars live in La Canada-Flintridge, California.
7. Alexandria, Virginia, is an interesting historic town.

8. You can take a great train ride in Durango, Colorado.
9. Have you been on the roller coasters in St. Louis, Missouri?
10. The mountains are really high in Vail, Colorado.

Page 329

1. H
2. Halloween, Hanukkah
3. Saturday and Sunday, Tuesday and Thursday
4. January, June, and July; March and May; April and August

Page 330

1. Amanda Panda
2. Jeffrey R. Hardy
3. Carlos Custard Appleseed
4. Gilbert McGillicutty
5. Leslie Q. Presley

Page 331

1. I love my purple bicycle!
2. I saved enough money to buy it last year.
3. Would you like to try it?
4. My brother has a blue bicycle.
5. One time he crashed into me, and I fell off my bike.
6. Have you ever fallen off your bike?
7. Did you skin your knee?
8. I was so mad at my brother!
9. He told me he was sorry.
10. I'm so glad that my bike did not break. Or: I'm so glad that my bike did not break!
11. Watch out for the glass in the road!
12. Don't ride your bike in the street! Or Don't ride your bike in the street.
13. Can you park a bike right here?
14. I have to go inside now.
15. Will I see you tomorrow?

Page 332

1. The first day of school is exciting.
2. Freddy Wilson's frog Peepers hopped into Mrs. Woolsey's purse.
3. As I walked outside, I smelled smoke.
4. In the play, Robin Hood was played by Lieutenant Bronksy.
5. The fourth Thursday in November is Thanksgiving.
6. I like Halloween best when it is on a Saturday.
7. Aunt Susan went to Yellowstone National Park.
8. Connie lives on Maple Street in Bismark, North Dakota.
9. Brazil, Argentina, and Peru are in South America.
10. The Mediterranean Sea and the Atlantic Ocean touch Spain.
11. The letter was signed, "Love always, Esther."
12. Davis Medical Center opened in January last year.
13. One of the religions practiced by many African people is Islam.
14. Italians and Germans belong to the Caucasian race.
15. Last Tuesday Ruben walked his dog Spotty down Tulip Street to Central Park.

Page 336

B.

1 bait a hook

3 clean a fish

5 eat a fish

2 catch a fish

4 cook a fish

C.

4 mail the letter

2 put the letter in an envelope

1 write a letter

5 wait for an answer

3 seal the letter

Answer Key (cont.)

D.

3 write a book report

2 click on word processing

4 turn on the printer

1 turn on the computer

5 print book the report

E.

4 slap your arm

2 see a mosquito

3 feel a bite

1 hear a buzz

5 scratch a bump

F.

3 buy popcorn

5 leave the theater

1 stand in line

2 buy a ticket

4 watch a movie

G.

2 find an old Halloween mask

1 clean up your room

4 sneak up on your brother

3 put it on

5 jump out at him

H.

3 snap on the leash

5 guide your dog back home

1 get the leash

2 whistle for your dog

4 walk your dog

Page 341

A.

1. c	4. b
2. d	5. a
3. e	

B.

1. His accomplishments were as follows: He was a painter, a publisher, a writer, an inventor, a scientist, a diplomat, a statesman, and an inspiration to others.

2. He decided to devote himself to the study of science.

3. He proved that lightning was electricity and that things could be positively or negatively charged with electricity.

4. He did not patent his inventions. He wanted to share them freely with the world.

5. Answers will vary.

Page 342

A.

1. c	4. a
2. d	5. b
3. e	

B.

1. The name of the poem was "The Defense of Fort McHenry."

2. The bombardment of Fort McHenry was taking place.

3. It became the official national anthem on March 3, 1931.

4. President Herbert Hoover signed the bill.

5. Answers will vary.

Page 343

A.

1. b	4. e
2. c	5. a
3. d	

B.

1. A system of dashes and dots is used.

2. Samuel Morse developed this code.

3. No, is not used a telephone to send messages with Morse code.

4. Morse code is most commonly used in emergency situations.

5. Answers will vary.

Page 344

A.

1. b	4. d
2. c	5. a
3. e	

B.

1. You can find them at Stanley Park in Vancouver, B.C., and at Thunderbird Park in Victoria, British Columbia.

2. Totem poles have been used by Native Americans as a way to record history.

3. Animals, birds, fish, plants, or other natural objects that would represent a Native American tribe are carved on totem poles.

4. The family's symbol is at the top of the pole.

5. Answers will vary.

Page 345

A.

1. c	4. a
2. d	5. b
3. e	

B.

1. The Frisbie company began in the late 1800s.

2. They threw them to each other.

3. It was marketed as the Pluto Platter.

4. The sales of the Frisbee took off in the 1960s.

5. Answers will vary.

Page 346

A.

1. d	4. c
2. e	5. a
3. b	

B.

1. They were looking for a product to eliminate moisture from electrical circuitry and to prevent corrosion on airplanes.

Answer Key (cont.)

2. Norman Larsen, president and head chemist at the Rocket Chemical Company, invented it.
3. It was a water displacement (WD) formula developed on his fortieth try.
4. The Friendship VII was covered with it.
5. Answers will vary.

Page 347
A.
1. c   4. e
2. b   5. a
3. d

B.
1. John Lennon started the group.
2. The name of the first group was "the Quarrymen."
3. Ringo Starr replaced Pete Best.
4. The Ed Sullivan show made them famous in America.
5. Answers will vary.

Page 348
A.
1. c   4. a
2. d   5. b
3. e

B.
1. Butchart Gardens is located in Victoria, British Columbia.
2. You can find Japanese gardens, a rose garden and a sunken garden.
3. People go and count how many flowers and buds they see.
4. Children are given an hour off of school to help count.
5. Answers will vary.

Page 349
A.
1. c   4. b
2. d   5. a
3. e

B.
1. Spider-Man is Peter Parker, the freelance photographer.
2. He got his special powers by being bitten by a spider that had been exposed to huge amounts of radiation.
3. He made a red and blue uniform for himself to wear when he was Spider-Man.
4. His uncle was killed by a burglar and as a result Spider-Man decided to devote his life to fighting crime.
5. Answers will vary.

Page 350
A.
1. b   4. c
2. e   5. a
3. d

B.
1. The first Olympics were in 776 B.C.
2. They have changed over the years.
3. The first Olympic Games were held in Greece.
4. No, the winter and summer games are held 2 years apart.
5. Answers will vary.

Page 351
A.
1. e   4. b
2. d   5. a
3. c

B.
1. Barbie made her debut in 1959.
2. Ruth Handler invented Barbie.
3. She invented Barbie for her daughter who preferred to play with dolls designed for teens.
4. Ruth Handler went on to be president of Mattel, Inc.
5. Answers will vary.

Page 352
A.
1. d   4. c
2. a   5. b
3. e

B.
1. It was the fastest selling toy for 6 months.
2. The craze did not last very long.
3. The Hula-Hoop was based on wooden hoop used by Australian youths.
4. Richard Knerr, a partner in the Wham-O toy manufacturing company, invented it.
5. Answers will vary.

Page 353
A.
1. d   4. b
2. e   5. c
3. a   6. f

B.
1. In the mid 1980s fur trade was thriving.
2. The sea otter was prized for its pelt and demand was high.
3. It is illegal to hunt sea otters today.
4. The sea otters off the coast of California are increasing.
5. Answers will vary.

Page 354
A.
1. b   4. f
2. e   5. d
3. c   6. a

B.
1. No one knows the identity of the real Spider Woman.
2. No one knows if she was born with special powers or acquired them later.
3. She concentrates intensely to create a web and does not need any separate devices.

Answer Key (cont.)

4. She can sense danger as well as an ordinary person and no better than one.
5. A criminal can only break loose from a web that is weaker and far away from Spider-Woman.
6. Answers will vary.

Page 355

A.
1. b
2. d
3. e
4. a
5. c

B.
1. Walter Elias Disney was born on December 5, 1901.
2. Walt's wife, Lillian, thought his original name, Mortimer the Mouse was too stuffy. She made it up.
3. Walt went into business with his brother, Roy.
4. Mickey Mouse's first movie was *Steamboat Willie*.
5. Answers will vary.

Page 356

A.
1. c
2. d
3. f
4. e
5. a
6. b

B.
1. Construction began for a major trans-Amazon highway.
2. Huge areas of the Amazon rain forest were cut down and burned.
3. Each family would be given a 240-acre piece of land, housing, and a small salary for a few months.
4. Schools, health facilities and other services would be available for these families.
5. The plan was a failure. Life in the rain forest was too difficult.
6. Answers will vary.

Page 357

A.
1. f
2. b
3. e
4. d
5. c
6. a

B.
1. Robin Hood was a legendary English hero.
2. A group of outlaws rescues him.
3. His faithful followers were Maid Marian, Friar Tuck, and Little John.
4. He treats them with contempt.
5. He treats them with respect.
6. Answers will vary.

Page 358

A.
1. a
2. e
3. c
4. d
5. b

B.
1. Kristi was born in Hayward, California, in 1971.
2. She was 6 years old.
3. She decided to concentrate on her singles career.
4. She won the gold medal.
5. Answers will vary.

Page 359

A.
1. c
2. d
3. a
4. e
5. b

B.
1. The zeppelins were 40 times bigger than blimps.
2. The largest and most luxurious zeppelin ever built was the Hindenburg.
3. The Hindenburg was going to America in 1937.
4. When it landed there was a loud thump, and the tail section burst into flames.
5. Answers will vary.

Page 360

A.
1. a
2. e
3. d
4. b
5. c

B.
1. The first book was *Are You there God? It's Me, Margaret*.
2. She was an A student and did as she was told.
3. She liked to read Nancy Drew mysteries, biographies, and horse stories.
4. She met and married John W. Blume and took his last name.
5. Answers will vary.

Page 361

A.
1. b
2. d
3. e
4. c
5. a

B.
1. She helped to hunt for food.
2. She met him in a shooting match.
3. She could shoot a dime that was in her husband's hand or a cigarette that was in his mouth. She also could shoot a playing card thrown in the air 90 feet away from her.
4. Her nickname was "Little Sure Shot."
5. Answers will vary.

Page 362

A.
1. b
2. d
3. e
4. a
5. c

B.
1. The statue symbolizes welcome and a promise of freedom for immigrants to the Untied States.

Answer Key (cont.)

2. The statue was given to the United States by the people of France in 1884.
3. Frédéric Bartholdi designed and sculpted it.
4. Bartholdi named the statue Liberty Enlightening the World.
5. The seven spikes stand for the seven seas, the seven continents, and the seven liberties.

Page 363
A.
1. c   4. e
2. d   5. a
3. b

B.
1. He became a writer when his brother bet that he couldn't compose a verse.
2. During WWI he wrote his first children's book and a play to entertain the troops.
3. He wrote *Winnie-the-Pooh* in 1926.
4. Walt Disney Company made it into a movie.
5. Answers will vary.

Page 364
A.
1. b   5. a
2. d   6. f
3. e
4. c

B.
1. Ancient people used the stars to guide their way and lives.
2. We call them constellations.
3. The constellations written about were the Big Dipper, the Bear, the Wagon, the Plow, Seven Rishis, and Cassiopeia.

4. Many of the stars names were based on ancient stories and myths.
5. She claimed that she was more beautiful than the lovely sea nymphs.

Page 365
A.
1. e   4. a
2. c   5. b
3. d

B.
1. Hercules' father was Zeus.
2. When he was a baby he killed two serpents who were about to attack him.
3. Hercules learned wrestling, archery and fencing. (you only need two)
4. He was banished from Thebe because of his bad temper.
5. He had to serve King Eurystheus for 12 years and accomplish many difficult tasks.
6. Individual answers.

Page 366
A.
1. c   4. b
2. e   5. a
3. d

B.
1. He was a pilot for the US Navy.
2. The name of the space flight was Gemini 8.
3. After docking, the two spacecrafts went into a violent roll. They were able to deal with it and save the mission.
4. He retired in 1971 and became an aerospace engineering professor.
5. Answers will vary.

Page 367
A.
1. b   4. f
2. d   5. a
3. e   6. c

B.
1. He was born in Baltimore.
2. As a child he got into trouble and went to a Catholic boy's school where he played baseball.
3. He played as a pitcher, an outfielder, and a left-handed pitcher.
4. In 1920 he broke the 1884 record of 24 home runs in one season by hitting 54.
5. Yankee Stadium was also called "the house that Ruth built."
6. Answers will vary.

Page 368
A.
1. e   4. d
2. b   5. c
3. f   6. a

B.
1. When Elvis was eight, he won his first talent contest.
2. He recorded his first song as a present for his mother.
3. He was drafted into the army.
4. He started doing live tours.
5. He made over 40 albums in his lifetime.
6. Answers will vary.

Page 369
A.
1. c   4. a
2. b   5. e
3. d

B.
1. Baseball was his favorite sport.
2. He could not play in college at first because his grades and his playing were not good enough.

Answer Key (cont.)

3. He started as a pitcher for the Los Angeles Dodgers minor-league team.

4. He was not a great player, however, his coach felt that he had potential and convinced him to keep working on his pitch.

5. Answers will vary.

Page 371

A.

1. b	4. f
2. d	5. c
3. e	6. a

B.

1. Merlin, the magician, raised Arthur.

2. He easily pulled it from the stone and became king of Britain.

3. He was a fair and wise ruler.

4. This table was round and could seat 1,600 knights without anyone knight having a better seat than another. Arthur felt that this would keep his knights from arguing.

5. When Arthur returned home from conquering most of western Europe, he had to fight and kill his nephew, Mordred. He was injured badly and later died.

6. Answers will vary.

Page 373

1. Beethoven was born in Bonn, Germany, in 1770.

2. He began to study music when he was four years old.

3. His father wanted him to be a musician.

4. Beethoven went on his first concert tour when he was 11 years old.

5. Beethoven was 17 years old when Mozart heard him play.

6. He went to Vienna, Austria.

7. Beethoven studied with Haydn, another great musician and composer.

8. Beethoven wrote about 300 pieces of music.

9. His compositions included sonatas, symphonies, concertos, and operas.

10. Beethoven gradually lost his hearing after an illness.

Page 374

1. Austria
2. Bonn
3. composer
4. composition
5. concerto
6. Germany
7. harmony
8. Haydn
9. melody
10. Mozart
11. musician
12. notation
13. opera
14. orchestra
15. piano
16. sonata
17. symphony
18. tempo
19. Vienna
20. violin

Page 375

```
S D F G H J K P Q W E A U S T R I A X C
A C O M P O S I T I O N Z X C S T V O P
M O O N B V C A E X Z O V I O L I N I
L M K N J H G N G F M D S T A N Q E E R
U P Y T C T R O S E R P F G A A H N H U
B O N N M E L O D Y A S O D F T H N A Y
G S T O P E R A R G M E D C V A I A Y T
A E S D F G H T K L E P M N B V C O D A
Q R W E R T Y O O I O R H P L K J H N C
A M U S I C I A N Q U I M O Z A R T S D
A S D F G H J K L P O I U A N Y T R E W
O R C H E S T R A H A R M O N Y A S D F
Q A Z X S W E D C V F R T G B Y J U I L
```

Page 377

Chapters 1-4

1. Sara has low self-esteem, and she feels like nothing in her life is right.

2. Charlie is Sara's retarded 10-year-old brother.

3. Their mother died and their father works in a different state, so their aunt moved in to look after them.

4. Sara compares her life to a kaleidoscope because it seems that it has been turned around. Now the pieces are no longer the same; everything has changed and continues to change from moment to moment.

5. She feels she has no time to herself or space of her own because she has Charlie to entertain all day and Wanda sharing her room all night.

Page 378

Chapters 5-9

1. Charlie loves to look at and listen to the watch because the ticking sound and rhythm make him feel secure.

2. Charlie squeezes Sara's hand, and he stares at the swans.

3. Most of the time the swans live on a lake at the university.

4. Sara says she does not like Frank because he ignores Charlie and because he calls Wanda by a pet name. She may be jealous of the affection Frank and Wanda have for each other.

Chapters 10–14

1. Sara goes back to the lake because she thinks that Charlie will go there to see the swans.

589

Answer Key (cont.)

2. She does not know what to do. She does know that something is really wrong because she has the same feeling in her neck that she always gets when something bad happens.

3. Aunt Willie promised the children's mother that she would take good care of Charlie and not let anything happen to him.

4. Aunt Willie feels that if she had sewn on Charlie's button as he wanted instead of watching television, Charlie would not have run away.

5. Sara begins to doubt herself and her feelings of revenge toward Joe Melby when he explains that he did not steal Charlie's watch and offers to help her find Charlie.

Page 379
Chapters 15-18

1. Mary tells Sara that Aunt Willie confronted Joe about stealing the watch and learned the truth—that he had found it and returned it to Charlie.

2. Sara is embarrassed to face Joe after accusing him of stealing and finding out she was wrong.

3. Joe tells of a guru who had the same problem of trying to find the right words to say.

4. Charlie becomes very stressed when he realizes his wristwatch has stopped. He gets upset.

5. Joe makes it easy for Sara to apologize. He does not make her feel bad for falsely accusing him, he helps Sara find Charlie, and he encourages her to keep trying when she is about to give up.

Chapters 19-20

1. Sara twists Charlie's bedroom slipper as she listens and looks for Charlie.

2. Charlie feels secure when his same routine is followed regularly and there are not surprises.

3. Joe lets Charlie wear his own wristwatch so that Charlie will feel secure.

4. Once Sara understands that she was wrong about Joe, she also realizes that perhaps she could be wrong about others, including her father.

5. Sara realizes there are more important things in life than looks. She begins to feel better about herself and her life. She feels she understands people better. She knows that a boy finds her attractive enough and likes her enough to ask her to a party.

Page 380
Matching

1. d
2. b
3. e
4. a
5. c

True or False

1. false
2. true
3. true
4. false
5. true

Short Answer

1. Sara constantly complains about how she looks.

2. Aunt Willie cares for the children because their mother died and their father works in a different state.

3. Charlie suffered two high fevers in a row that left him retarded and unable to speak.

4. Sara thinks Wanda is prettier, is jealous that Wanda has a boyfriend, and resents sharing a room with Wanda. Sara feels

conflicted over her love for her brother and her feelings of being responsible for him. Sara thinks that Aunt Willie keeps her from having any fun, even though she is glad her aunt is there to take care of them. Sara loves her father and misses him. He is withdrawn, and she does not know how to reach him. Consequently, she thinks the worst of him.

5. Sara was so convinced she was right that she went out of her way to make Joe feel bad. Then she found out she was wrong about Joe.

Page 381
Chapters 1-3

1. On one of his late afternoon strolls, Marty spotted the dog by the Shiloh schoolhouse. Shiloh followed shyly along until Marty whistled. That is when Shiloh exploded with affection. He followed Marty all the way home.

2. The three children are Marty, 11; Dara Lynn, 7; Becky, 3.

3. The story takes place in Friendly, West Virginia. It is summertime.

4. Judd kicks Shiloh. Later, he doesn't feed him dinner. Marty is upset by Judd's actions.

5. Marty wants to save money by collecting aluminum cans.

Page 382
Chapters 4-7

1. Marty promises Shiloh that Judd Travers will never kick him again.

2. Marty keeps Dara Lynn off the hill by telling her it is snake-infested.

3. We learn that Judd was beaten

Answer Key (cont.)

by his father. Marty feels sorry for him.

4. At Mr. Wallace's store, Marty spends the 53 cents he earns collecting cans. He asks Mr. Wallace for old food so that he may feed Shiloh.

5. Some of the lies Marty tells include telling Dara Lynn the hill has snakes, telling his dad he is looking for ground hogs on the hill, telling his mom he wants to save food for after dinner, telling Judd he has not see his dog, and telling Mrs. Howard that his mom has had a headache.

Chapters 8–11

1. Marty plans to save Shiloh by holding up a sign by the side of the road. The sign would say something like "Free World's Best Dog."

2. Shiloh gets hurt when Baker's German shepherd leaps into his pen and attacks.

3. At Doc Murphy's, Shiloh is stitched up. The doctor finds out Shiloh is Judd's dog. Marty and his dad go home, unsure of Shiloh's survival.

4. Marty feels relieved after he tells David Howard about Shiloh. David is mesmerized and has a hard time letting Marty tell the story!

5. The Prestons and Judd agree that Shiloh will be returned once his wounds are healed.

Page 383

Chapters 12–15

1. Marty knows that the authorities will not have time for an animal abuse case. He also knows that he has no proof that Judd is mistreating his dogs.

2. Some of Marty's chores include cutting weeds, mowing grass, hoeing corn, picking beans, cutting wood, and digging holes. (Accept supported statements.)

3. Judd leaves out the name Shiloh. Marty insists Judd include the name in case he tries to give him another dog.

4. Judd says the contract is no good because they had no witness.

5. When Marty completes his work, Judd gives him a dog collar. It is a sign of their camaraderie, their newly found understanding of one another.

Page 384

Matching

1. e
2. a
3. j
4. h
5. c
6. g
7. b
8. d
9. f
10. i

True or False

1. false
2. true
3. false
4. true
5. false

Sequence

3, 5, 2, 4, 1

Short Answer

1. Some towns in Tyler County include Friendly, Parkersburg, and Middlebourne.

2. Marty will not go to heaven if Shiloh is not allowed in.

3. Shiloh responds to a whistle.

Page 385

1. 15
2. 9
3. 17
4. 13
5. 5
6. 8
7. 14
8. 7
9. 16
10. 10
11. 13
12. 6
13. 6
14. 5
15. 8
16. 4
17. 11
18. 10
19. 7
20. 12
21. 7
22. 18
23. 6
24. 8
25. 12
26. 13
27. 14
28. 11
29. 7
30. 10
31. 15
32. 4
33. 9
34. 14
35. 1
36. 14
37. 9
38. 17
39. 10
40. 13
41. 10
42. 9
43. 12
44. 9

Answer Key (cont.)

45. 3
46. 6
47. 8
48. 13
49. 16
50. 11

Page 386

51. 8
52. 11
53. 14
54. 7
55. 4
56. 2
57. 15
58. 6
59. 2
60. 8
61. 12
62. 9
63. 3
64. 12
65. 16
66. 5
67. 9
68. 11
69. 5
70. 9
71. 7
72. 10
73. 4
74. 14
75. 11
76. 5
77. 12
78. 9
79. 10
80. 5
81. 0
82. 7
83. 15
84. 10
85. 3
86. 2
87. 9

88. 8
89. 6
90. 11
91. 13
92. 8
93. 3
94. 10
95. 7
96. 8
97. 6
98. 10
99. 2
100. 12

Page 387

1. 6
2. 12
3. 5
4. 13
5. 10
6. 11
7. 17
8. 19
9. 15
10. 16
11. 14
12. 19
13. 10
14. 12
15. 20
16. 16

Page 388

1. 26
2. 6
3. 18
4. 15
5. 9
6. 17
7. 15
8. 22
9. 18
10. 23
11. 20
12. 20

Page 389

1. 52
2. 49
3. 52
4. 38
5. 33
6. 35
7. 42
8. 46
9. 50
10. 38
11. 46
12. 31
13. 37
14. 40
15. 22
16. 27

Page 390

1. 19
2. 20
3. 17
4. 49
5. 60
6. 53
7. 30
8. 75
9. 78
10. 87
11. 45
12. 61
13. 58
14. 22
15. 63
16. 19
17. 35
18. 87
19. 87
20. 50
21. 57
22. 42
23. 97
24. 56
25. 98

Answer Key (cont.)

Page 391
1. 121
2. 154
3. 131
4. 94
5. 81
6. 89
7. 44
8. 120
9. 91
10. 39
11. 124
12. 47
13. 125
14. 138
15. 107
16. 196
17. 111
18. 67
19. 54
20. 127
21. 120
22. 119
23. 160
24. 135
25. 73

Page 392
1. 169
2. 217
3. 191
4. 157
5. 132
6. 179
7. 111
8. 148
9. 188
10. 195
11. 181
12. 81
13. 218
14. 192
15. 187
16. 176

Page 393
1. 266
2. 300
3. 182
4. 265
5. 182
6. 246
7. 212
8. 148
9. 358
10. 303
11. 248
12. 91

Page 394
1. 898
2. 825
3. 1,072
4. 873
5. 988
6. 1,019
7. 1,336
8. 861
9. 389
10. 1,117
11. 1,090
12. 621
13. 843
14. 1,402
15. 1,012
16. 1,670
17. 823
18. 1,822
19. 967
20. 938
21. 1,248
22. 925
23. 623
24. 947
25. 1,314

Page 395
1. 2,035
2. 1,879
3. 2,160
4. 1963
5. 1,431
6. 1,762
7. 1,260
8. 2,275
9. 1,661
10. 1,744
11. 1,994
12. 1,622
13. 1,700
14. 1,832
15. 2,013
16. 1,023

Page 396
1. 1,404
2. 2,675
3. 1,096
4. 1,824
5. 3,184
6. 1,825
7. 1,671
8. 2,210
9. 3,056
10. 2,359
11. 2,678
12. 2,361

Page 397
1. 17,339
2. 14,490
3. 15,499
4. 5,737
5. 13,216
6. 10,335
7. 6,869
8. 16,045
9. 4,685
10. 14,358
11. 10,519
12. 7,336
13. 8,610
14. 8,323
15. 12,244
16. 7,787

Answer Key (cont.)

17. 7,753
18. 8,040
19. 9,097
20. 12,031
21. 8,415
22. 10,786
23. 16,877
24. 7,129
25. 5,166

Page 398

1. 19,555
2. 14,017
3. 9,155
4. 15,563
5. 16,152
6. 17,552
7. 17,169
8. 15,388
9. 15,817
10. 12,793
11. 14,186
12. 24,204
13. 24,649
14. 17,700
15. 25,076
16. 13,821

Page 399

1. 27,788
2. 27,827
3. 24,036
4. 25,815
5. 12,814
6. 29,265
7. 25,490
8. 23,657
9. 28,244
10. 12,801
11. 25,132
12. 18,138

Page 400

1. 76
2. 11
3. 120

4. 9
5. 15
6. 4,670
7. 39
8. 17
9. 181
10. 1,778
11. 140
12. 19
13. 180
14. 1,843
15. 18
16. 16
17. 158
18. 101
19. 3,449
20. 110

Page 401

1. 9
2. 8
3. 8
4. 6
5. 5
6. 8
7. 5
8. 6
9. 8
10. 5
11. 7
12. 5
13. 0
14. 4
15. 4
16. 3
17. 6
18. 6
19. 7
20. 9
21. 5
22. 9
23. 4
24. 3
25. 6
26. 6

27. 6
28. 5
29. 7
30. 4
31. 9
32. 2
33. 9
34. 9
35. 1
36. 7
37. 3
38. 9
39. 7
40. 4
41. 9
42. 0
43. 3
44. 7
45. 3
46. 6
47. 5
48. 8
49. 9
50. 4

Page 402

51. 7
52. 8
53. 4
54. 4
55. 1
56. 2
57. 7
58. 3
59. 1
60. 6
61. 5
62. 2
63. 1
64. 8
65. 7
66. 0
67. 4
68. 7
69. 3

Answer Key (cont.)

70. 1
71. 1
72. 1
73. 0
74. 8
75. 2
76. 2
77. 4
78. 5
79. 8
80. 1
81. 0
82. 3
83. 8
84. 3
85. 2
86. 9
87. 6
88. 1
89. 2
90. 3
91. 5
92. 2
93. 0
94. 1
95. 2
96. 0
97. 1
98. 2
99. 0
100. 7

Page 403

1. 35
2. 14
3. 34
4. 44
5. 41
6. 75
7. 13
8. 81
9. 91
10. 85
11. 88
12. 46

13. 94
14. 50
15. 53
16. 70
17. 41
18. 21
19. 67
20. 53
21. 32
22. 79
23. 8
24. 90
25. 25

Page 404

1. 360
2. 625
3. 219
4. 349
5. 581
6. 823
7. 533
8. 247
9. 534
10. 340
11. 118
12. 381
13. 457
14. 262
15. 930
16. 764
17. 339
18. 879
19. 533
20. 595
21. 678
22. 357
23. 657
24. 826
25. 553

Page 405

1. 845
2. 159
3. 257

4. 821
5. 888
6. 201
7. 233
8. 759
9. 406
10. 461
11. 532
12. 555
13. 167
14. 223
15. 708
16. 585
17. 887
18. 233
19. 840
20. 816
21. 146
22. 748
23. 250
24. 708
25. 443

Page 406

1. 4,213
2. 3,311
3. 2,322
4. 4,227
5. 4,173
6. 2,860
7. 4,251
8. 9,332
9. 1,612
10. 1,831
11. 5,162
12. 2,131
13. 6,305
14. 9,050
15. 7,130
16. 9,233
17. 7,634
18. 3,630
19. 7,246
20. 8,242
21. 2,234

Answer Key (cont.)

22. 8,112
23. 7,570
24. 9,640
25. 1,171

Page 407

1. 9,331
2. 1,243
3. 9,117
4. 5,651
5. 8,312
6. 4,125
7. 2,451
8. 7,123
9. 9,841
10. 6,153
11. 4,041
12. 3,246
13. 1,533
14. 4,510
15. 5,330
16. 8,015
17. 6,311
18. 3,271
19. 7,174
20. 6,404
21. 4,153
22. 759
23. 1,647
24. 4,266
25. 6,633

Page 408

1. 62
2. 24
3. 330
4. 785
5. 7,146
6. 8,448
7. 75
8. 2,788
9. 9,605
10. 8,922
11. 125
12. 7,767

13. 8
14. 6,594
15. 1,148
16. 815
17. 40
18. 854
19. 29
20. 68

Page 409

1. 0
2. 169
3. 2
4. 532
5. 2
6. 1,833
7. 8,557
8. 5,783
9. 115
10. 5
11. 209
12. 5
13. 189
14. 3,204
15. 4,452
16. 524
17. 118
18. 3
19. 3,916
20. 6,758

Page 410

1. 36
2. 0
3. 21
4. 28
5. 72
6. 48
7. 35
8. 12
9. 0
10. 30
11. 8
12. 36
13. 14

14. 6
15. 8
16. 12
17. 0
18. 15
19. 5
20. 54
21. 7
22. 16
23. 21
24. 7
25. 30
26. 20
27. 42
28. 42
29. 54
30. 2
31. 25
32. 56
33. 14
34. 0
35. 3
36. 81
37. 9
38. 18
39. 24
40. 36
41. 0
42. 8
43. 27
44. 0
45. 9
46. 15
47. 6
48. 10
49. 63
50. 8

Page 411

51. 1
52. 56
53. 64
54. 48
55. 18
56. 0

Answer Key (cont.)

57. 6
58. 4
59. 4
60. 0
61. 0
62. 12
63. 28
64. 12
65. 40
66. 45
67. 63
68. 0
69. 0
70. 27
71. 3
72. 9
73. 18
74. 24
75. 24
76. 32
77. 24
78. 49
79. 45
80. 40
81. 0
82. 6
83. 0
84. 72
85. 0
86. 0
87. 4
88. 16
89. 20
90. 32
91. 0
92. 0
93. 18
94. 1
95. 35
96. 0
97. 16
98. 5
99. 0
100. 10

Page 412

1. 378
2. 792
3. 288
4. 90
5. 584
6. 405
7. 45
8. 616
9. 176
10. 231
11. 375
12. 552
13. 36
14. 304
15. 567
16. 225
17. 108
18. 36
19. 144
20. 70
21. 90
22. 490
23. 864
24. 150
25. 272

Page 413

1. 44
2. 273
3. 276
4. 295
5. 104
6. 51
7. 252
8. 291
9. 44
10. 284
11. 84
12. 78
13. 175
14. 255
15. 290
16. 388
17. 162

18. 33
19. 258
20. 96
21. 455
22. 266
23. 344
24. 192
25. 285

Page 414

1. 770
2. 1,771
3. 484
4. 3,074
5. 5,170
6. 3,216
7. 2,590
8. 8,008
9. 561
10. 3,869
11. 3,162
12. 8,118
13. 2,914
14. 1,116
15. 1,260
16. 7,722
17. 2,523
18. 2,432
19. 4,686
20. 1,092
21. 522
22. 3,416
23 713
24. 1,298
25. 7,275

Page 415

1. 1,568
2. 3,872
3. 2,664
4. 3,038
5. 576
6. 3,626
7. 4,158
8. 1,421

Answer Key (cont.)

9. 3,854
10. 1,748
11. 3,752
12. 2,964
13. 2,788
14. 2,596
15. 2,304
16. 6,461
17. 5,621
18. 1,914
19. 2,233
20. 4,704
21. 2,945
22. 2,700
23. 4,118
24. 6,935
25. 4,264

Page 416

1. 3,080
2. 3,875
3. 1,260
4. 5,553
5. 5,391
6. 2,802
7. 1,284
8. 1,982
9. 930
10. 1,010
11. 3,846
12. 1,738
13. 1,816
14. 4,270
15. 864
16. 3,528
17. 602
18. 6,147
19. 2,648
20. 3,664
21. 4,788
22. 1,089
23. 6,699
24. 1,718
25. 2,370

Page 417

1. 1,981
2. 2,076
3. 7,384
4. 1,592
5. 2,384
6. 4,055
7. 1,848
8. 1,236
9. 1,074
10. 2,559
11. 5,456
12. 1,053
13. 1,272
14. 7,956
15. 3,716
16. 393
17. 2,422
18. 4,010
19. 597
20. 7,640
21. 1,728
22. 3,328
23. 2,184
24. 1,125
25. 3,405

Page 418

1. 2,547
2. 4,476
3. 985
4. 738
5. 896
6. 5,481
7. 4,374
8. 2,205
9. 6,376
10. 1,812
11. 1,028
12. 4,398
13. 4,254
14. 5,988
15. 261
16. 2,680
17. 228

18. 3255
19. 576
20. 4590
21. 498
22. 4004
23. 109
24. 5769
25. 4522

Page 419

1. 37,351
2. 47,124
3. 5,248
4. 24,012
5. 32,034
6. 11,856
7. 10,934
8. 29,634
9. 34,056
10. 38,184
11. 23,304
12. 58,044
13. 83,979
14. 52,785
15. 31,140
16. 25,704
17. 9,177
18. 4,995
19. 13,498
20. 15,950
21. 20,925
22. 13,545
23. 34,892
24. 25,428
25. 7,696

Page 420

1. 18,531
2. 4,131
3. 29,481
4. 51,810
5. 21,600
6. 4,408
7. 16,215
8. 80,132